JIM BAKKER

JIM BAKKER:

MISCARRIAGE
OF JUSTICE ?

James A. Albert, J.D.
Legal Expert

OPEN COURT
Chicago and La Salle, Illinois

The author and Carus Publishing Company gratefully acknowledge the use of PTL photographs on the cover and interior photograph section of this book.

First printing 1998

Printed and bound in the United States of America.

Library of Congress Cataloging-in-Publication Data
Albert, James A.
    Jim Bakker : miscarriage of justice / James A. Albert.
      p.   cm.
    includes bibliographical references and index.
    ISBN 0-8126-9369-8 (cloth : alk. paper). — ISBN 0-8126-9370-1
(pbk. : alk. paper)
    1. Bakker, Jim, 1940-   —Trials, litigation, etc. 2. Trials (Fraud)—
North Carolina—Charlotte. 3. PTL (Organization)—Corrupt
practices.   I. Title.
KF224.B25A43   1998
345.73′0263—dc21   97-22581
                                                       CIP

Contents

Preface

Many paths led me to Jim Bakker's prison cell to interview him about his tumultuous dethroning as the country's most famous televangelist.

My curiosity was stirred by several things about his trial that simply did not add up. For starters, he was given a forty-five-year prison sentence that far eclipsed what many killers and rapists receive. A federal appeals court later found some of the comments made by Bakker's trial judge so objectionable and out of line that they took the unusual step of sending the case back for resentencing before a different judge. And in a dispatch from the Charlotte courthouse, one reporter sounded an alarm that no one seemed to hear at the time—that prosecutors had belittled the religious beliefs of one of Bakker's star witnesses during a key cross-examination.

None of that seemed right, of course, and as a law professor and trial lawyer I decided to probe further into Bakker's spectacular trial, which had been called the trial of the century in the South. I had graduated from the Notre Dame Law School in 1976 and then served as an attorney for the Federal Communications Commission in Washington, D.C., where I earned my stripes as a broadcast lawyer. At the time, Jim Bakker and PTL were becoming very well known to the FCC. It was then that I developed an interest in the PTL whirlwind that was drawing millions of television viewers. Since leaving the FCC nineteen years ago, I have taught broadcast law at two universities and for the last fourteen years have litigated major cases as a member of counsel of Galligan, Tully, Doyle & Reid, a Des Moines trial firm. I have written a dozen nationally published law journal articles, two other books, was named the law professor of the year nationwide in 1989 by the Delta Theta Phi International Law Fraternity, and was twice named Leland Stanford Forrest Outstanding Law Professor at Drake University. I place my academic and law practice credentials on the line in researching and writing this book on Jim Bakker. (I have retained some conventions of legal writing. A group of asterisks, ***, signifies the omission of one or more complete sentences from a quotation, while "at 29" means "p. 29.")

This was exciting for me. Researching whether there was more to Bakker's trial and more to the question of his guilt or innocence than the Letterman and Leno monologues at the time reflected, was like solving a puzzle. The courtroom drama in that Dixie courthouse during Bakker's five-week trial was the type of thing that Perry Mason or F. Lee Bailey dreams about. The trial had everything—a nationally known television celebrity on trial for fraud, top gun lawyers battling it out, surprise witness testimony, and a hurricane that roared through Charlotte postponing the trial and prompting Tammy Faye Bakker to claim that it was a warning from God. If it was, the jurors didn't heed it.

My purpose in writing this book is to answer several questions: Did Jim Bakker get a fair trial? No cameras were allowed in the courtroom and the only reports filtering out that cast any doubt about Bakker's guilt or the trial itself were not widely publicized, but what was going on inside those guarded doors that the rest of us didn't hear about? That there might be another take on all of it seemed at least possible to me given the fact that a federal appellate court certainly did later overturn Bakker's forty-five-year sentence. While most of the country was laughing, had a significant federal trial left the tracks?

I spoke in depth with many witnesses who testified, and with the biggest witness of all—Bakker himself. Bakker allowed me to question him in a series of intense, lengthy interviews in prison that spanned the last two years of his incarceration. I then put every word of the 4,000-page trial transcript under a microscope and I examined key government exhibits. In three years of research, I scrutinized thousands of pages of documents, countless videotapes, and uncovered several new revelations. (In fact, because I became so familiar with the case in researching this book, Bakker requested my help during his parole appeal. See chapter 27.)

My research assistant, Suzan Brooks, and I interviewed many of the Bakker jurors. They told us things about the trial that were never reported, like the tart note one alternate juror sent the judge complaining that the judge was always biting Bakker's head off in court and beating up on Bakker's attorneys. She didn't think it was a fair fight. The other jurors didn't agree with her and were satisfied that Bakker was guilty beyond a reasonable doubt. I write of the jury's deliberations in a chapter that captures the drama that unfolded in that jury room.

My goal in this book is to present hard hitting and lucid analysis of the gauntlet which must be run by national celebrities on trial for major crimes. I have attempted here to transport the reader to the front row in that Charlotte courthouse during the five sweltering weeks of Bakker's trial. They will see some very interesting characters in action, including presiding Judge Robert "Maximum Bob" Potter, the nation's harshest sentencing judge, who refused to sequester the jury and once harshly threatened to have Bakker's attorney thrown out of the courtroom. There were the celebrity lawyers for both the defense and the government, and an array of FBI agents who investigated Bakker and testified against him. Several well-known witnesses were there, including Bakker's friend, Efrem Zimbalist, Jr., who played Inspector Lewis Erskine on television's *FBI*. That's as close as Bakker came to helpful testimony from the Bureau. With Tammy Faye Bakker in the gallery from time to time and offering running commentary on the trial on television, the cast of characters was complete. It was a volatile mix, which when shaken during those five weeks produced an explosive and thrilling trial.

This book is no whitewash. I am not one of Bakker's

followers and I do not share his religious views. This is an honest, straight-down-the-middle account of the downfall of a national television celebrity who was seen in 13 million homes a day, before he ended up watching CNN by himself in a ten by ten foot cell in the middle of Minnesota.

Well into the research for this book and after having learned so much about his trial, I came to believe much of what Bakker had been telling me and had attempted to say in his defense during the trial. Frankly, I found Jim Bakker to be far different in person than I had been led to believe by press accounts I had read about him over the years. He is not the person his public caricature suggests and I write about that at some length in this book as I recount the things he told me in prison and the evidence I later found which confirmed much of what he told me. As a result, while certainly being far from any apology for Jim Bakker, this book is more positive about him than his detractors might expect. Of course, my personal judgments about Jim Bakker's motives that are expressed in the book are conclusions that I have drawn based on my study of the facts and on my two years of interviews with Bakker. In the book, I do not delve into a moral evaluation of Jim Bakker or attempt to arrive at a conclusion about the morality of activities at PTL. Instead, my focus is on the legal and other related issues that drove his downfall and his trial. I do not say here that Jim Bakker is blameless; nor, of course, does he claim that today, freely admitting that he believes he was wrong in different respects.

I have sought true balance in this book. The scholarship that undergirds it, all the research I did over three years' time, alone determined every inch of the course of the book, its tone and my conclusions.

I must also confess that my sense of humor couldn't be extinguished and that I had some fun writing about some of the crazy things that happened here during the trial and the years before and after it. So, I suspect that some readers will be surprised at some of the perspectives they read here, but my commitment was to be honest in writing the book and the chips will just have to fall where they may.

I am an Episcopalian, as were generations in my family before me. I grew up with very little exposure to Pentecostals and Pentecostalism. Writing this book, I did have an opportunity to learn more about the Pentecostal world view and, relevant to the Bakker saga, why Pentecostals in this country believed so strongly in Bakker's dream of building Heritage USA, the small-town-sized Pentecostal Mecca that he cleaved out of the pine forests of North Carolina and which became the third most popular theme park in the United States. It was Heritage USA, and the enormous costs of keeping it afloat and buying television time for their *PTL Club* program, that contributed mightily to Bakker's downfall. So, to understand not only Bakker's phenomenal success as a television star but also to explain why it all unraveled so quickly, I asked many hard questions of Pentecostals who supported him. What they told me is revealing and casts Pentecostalism in a new light for me.

Bakker himself was a broadcasting visionary. Even his detractors admit that he predicted the power of beaming television signals off satellites 22,000 miles in space while most people in broadcasting were still rustproofing their transmitter antennas at the end of town. And his program, *The PTL Club,* was seen in its heyday in more homes than Johnny Carson. Bakker was a natural on television and millions of people loved watching him. In interviewing him and getting to know him, I found him absolutely fascinating. In this book, I write about a side of Jim Bakker that most of us have never seen before.

I am proud to be a lawyer. I think the law can be exciting and its stories rich with meaning and emotion. I now know that this is one of those stories.

Acknowledgments

It took five years of work to complete this book—three years of researching, investigating and analyzing, and two years of writing and rewriting. When I spent three months going over the 4,000-page Bakker trial transcript, for instance, my dictated highlights, summary and analysis itself exceeded 500 pages when typed.

Neither this book nor the five-year quest for answers that it represents would have been possible without the help and encouragement of some exceptional people.

This book is dedicated to each of them.

To Karla Westberg, faculty legal secretary at the Drake University Law School, who meticulously typed literally thousands of pages of four draft manuscripts of the book, countless interviews and hundreds of pages of evidence and trial transcript summaries; and who added perspective and analysis, and helped make the long process enjoyable day after day.

To Suzan Kelsey Brooks, who as my Research Assistant was primarily responsible for interviewing the Bakker jurors and scrutinizing the evidence in Bakker's trial—tasks which took two solid years and in which she showed great intellect, enthusiasm and a passion for justice.

To Lisa Hermann, Sherry VonBehren, and Carol Smith, of the Drake University Law Library, for always so cheerfully saying "yes, glad to help!" to hundreds of my requests for Nexis research queries, books, and faxes as we ground out the research on the Bakker case.

To Ben MacDougall, my Research Assistant, who painstakingly proofread the 1,600 footnotes in this book, double-checked the accuracy of outside sources against hard copies, and researched several trial leads.

To my dedicated colleagues and the magnanimous staff at the Drake University Law School.

To Charles Randall, David Herd, and Jennifer Benning, my Research Assistants who tenaciously dug deep into every aspect of the Bakker trial.

To Michael Mock, David Miller, Michael Dolich, Dennis Mitchell, Sabra Craig, Edward J. Cord, and Robert Lantz, the law clerks whose outstanding legal work I relied on during these key years.

To my friends, for their zest and humor reflected in several chapters: Steve and René Ridge, Mike Hupfer, Stever Durick, Shannon Holz, Sherri Soich, Jim Beatty, Hector and Elizabeth Lareau, Jeanne Vaudt, Justin Tade, Ann Troge, Jim Frankenfeld, Mike Gellerman, Mike Clarizio, Chris Bruns, Joe Barrows, John McGehee, Bob Miller, Dennis and Louise Barr, Pat Kelley, and Gerry Thies.

To Michael J. Galligan, consummate and spectacular trial lawyer, whose brilliant mind and unflagging commitment to justice for others distinguish him as a master of his calling and as a person, with whom I have had the privilege of practicing law and fighting for others for 13 wonderful and fulfilling years.

To the memory of Dr. John J. Broderick, "the Chief," who, as my professor at the Notre Dame Law School, inspired me and changed my life with his boundless passion for life and his embodiment of the palpable spirit of Notre Dame.

To Tom Riley, courtroom lion, author and legislator, whose steel and intellect forged a relentless and successful fighter for the rights of others, and my first mentor who for 35 years has been an inspiration to me.

To Shirley Fulbright, one of those amazingly resourceful and efficient people who can get virtually anything done, who pried loose the 4,000-page Bakker trial transcript and unlimited sources for me and who was always such a joy to speak with.

To Kerri Mommer, Jeanne Kerl, and David Ramsay Steele of Open Court, who had faith in this book and were willing to publish a chronicle of the PTL saga that casts Bakker in a far better light than previously afforded him by others in the media.

To my loving family: Jack and Betty Albert, Deborah Albert, Sue and Steve Strautz, John and Julie Albert, Eileen Munger, Roy Munger, Kay Warren, and Tom Munger.

To the memories of my wonderful dad, Richard M. Albert; my dear aunt, Grace Munger; and great friend, Tim Carlucci; who did not live to see this book completed but without whose faith I never would have even begun it.

To my amazing mother, Neva E. Albert, who has seen so much in her life but still is so youthful, for her unwavering and constant encouragement and strength.

To my fantastic twin sons, Brian J. Albert and Bradley J. Albert, who of course are the beacons in my life.

To the local Coca Cola bottler. It's amazing how much work you can get done on something like this after two or three Cokes at 10:00 P.M.

To Butterscotch, our nocturnal and affectionate cat, who sat in my den at home every single one of the hundreds of nights I would pull out the pocketsized Dictaphone and start working on this, who is so near-sighted she never saw the hand-held machine, and who every night thought I was talking to her for the entire three or four hours. Did she ever love the attention; and I'll never tell her that every word of it was about this book.

Part One

BEFORE THE TRIAL

Chapter 1

Hallelujah Hollywood

The PTL Club

The most exciting attraction at Heritage USA, Jim and Tammy Bakker's 2,200-acre Christian Disney World, was the Bakkers' daily television program which was broadcast live from the grounds. While the sprawling resort cost Jim Bakker $3 million a week to operate and eventually landed him in prison, it resonated with down home fun and Hollywood glamour as millions of viewers each year eagerly drove through its gates for the chance to sit in the audience of a major national TV show. Everyone knew this was one of the greatest sanctuaries of all in the Electric Church.

A television pioneer who recognized the potential of the medium to reach millions of homes with the gospel, it was Bakker who adapted the TV talk show format to Christian broadcasting. He invented the genre and was its most consummate practitioner. The innovation drew millions of viewers who found the addition of entertainment to religious nurturing a welcome change. He considered himself a missionary using television seeking out souls for Jesus.

> **Jim Bakker:** My spiritual gift, my specific calling from God, is to be a television talk-show host. That's what I'm here on earth to do. I love TV. I eat it, I sleep it.[1]

Bakker was not the first to effectively use national TV for the propagation of religion—that place in broadcast history belongs to Catholic Bishop Fulton J. Sheen. But Bakker's entertainment-intensive show differed dramatically from that of Bishop Sheen, whose groundbreaking *Life is Worth Living* program was carried by ABC on 170 stations across the country from 1952 to 1957. The first truly national media clergyman, Bishop Sheen attracted millions of viewers and his program was so well regarded that it actually won an Emmy for broadcast excellence. In fact, his TV show made Bishop Sheen such a popular television celebrity that the Catholic Church, uncomfortable with one of its bishops as a media celeb, axed the show. The irony, of course, is that the Catholics and other main line denominations thereafter defaulted and simply left television to the religious evangelicals, and it was only then that the word "televangelist" was added to the nation's lexicon.[2]

But Bishop Sheen was all business, like a school principal, and his programs consisted essentially of fireside chats on such subjects as war, the Communist threat, Stalin, and placid topics like psychiatry and even the importance of a sense of humor in one's life. The show was all staid preaching and counseling, comparable to the Mother Angelica format today, and tame by Pentecostal standards.

Bakker's talk show was also a far cry from the broadcast norm set by modern televangelists, including the somber Billy Graham sternly warning a stadium of people that the devil was going to have their souls, or the snarling and pacing Jimmy Swaggart who threatens people that if they don't toe the line in their lives they'll go straight to hell. Local ministers appearing on their hometown television stations sometimes offer similar threatening messages. I vividly remember being jolted by one such sermonette several years ago on a station in the Midwest while traveling as a young attorney for the FCC. The stern-looking pastor, dressed all in black and looking like Clint Eastwood in *Pale Rider,* looked straight into the camera and said: "Remember, if you mess up God is going to strike you down." That was how many ministers used TV before Jim and Tammy rode into town.

The Bakkers' program debuted in 1974 and became the

most popular religious show on television. Within four years, it was carried on 1,300 cable systems in the country to 13 million homes. Its ratings soared, and by PTL's own count, more people watched it each day than tuned in to Johnny Carson's *Tonight Show*. The *Saturday Evening Post* proclaimed PTL "America's most viewed daily television program."[3] While there was undeniably plenty of religious content to each of the PTL broadcasts, the program was encased in music, laughter, and light talk show–type interviews with different guests. Even magicians and comedians would occasionally appear on the show. It was fun to watch, millions of people loved it, and Jim and Tammy quickly blew past all the other televangelists to achieve national superstar status.

Bakker simply had the touch for broadcasting and he knew what he was doing. For starters, he didn't produce his show cheaply. With equipment and facilities as elaborate as the best of any major commercial network, and with technicians and crews that knew their business, the production values of Bakker's programs were first rate and the shows were network caliber. And, just as CBS would do years later in renovating the beautiful 461-seat Ed Sullivan Theater on Broadway for David Letterman's arrival at Black Rock, Bakker built a huge TV studio at the eastern edge of Heritage with a sumptuous set and seating for 1,800 in the studio audience. From it, the early *Jim and Tammy TV Ministry Hour* was broadcast each day.

People watching at home would see on their TV screens a richly appointed set that featured a concert stage for the large PTL orchestra and the interior of a newer, beautifully decorated home. There were sofas for the Bakkers and their guests, a book-lined library, and even a brightly hued kitchen. In many respects, several of the rooms looked like the set of *Good Morning America* with fresh flowers, a fireplace in the background, and comfortable furnishings.

The stage was warm and eye-pleasing, and came alive with a daily parade of the top gospel singers from around the country who were backed up by the big band sound of PTL's own musicians. Joining them were well known born-again singers, including Pat Boone, Norma Zimmer, Anita Bryant, Pearl

Bailey, and Della Reese. Jim also broke new ground for a Pentecostal by employing women ministers at PTL who would join him on the air to preach.[4]

Celebrities with religious messages were always great guests, and Jim and Tammy interviewed them all—Mickey Rooney, Roy Rogers and Dale Evans, Gavin MacLeod, Efrem Zimbalist, Jr., and even Donna Douglas from the *Beverly Hillbillies* who cuddled a goat on the air. Guests would be politely questioned in some depth about their careers, personal lives, and religious beliefs. The religious experiences and messages of each guest were the focal points, and viewers loved hearing them.

For any religious leader, this was the venue of choice, the Cadillac of all religious programs and simply the best show to guest on. Billy Graham was there, as were Robert Schuller, Oral Roberts, Rex Humbard, and Mother Angelica.

As guests spoke of the power of God in their lives, the phone number of PTL's prayer line was superimposed on the screen and viewers were urged to call in with any personal prayer request. A bank of sixty phones to Bakker's right on the set was staffed by volunteers from the studio audience to take the calls that came in. Tens of thousands of viewers responded and gave their lives to Jesus. In one two-year period alone, 50,000 people called those telephones to become "born-again" in the Christian faith.[5]

In addition to the guest interviews, there was more traditional religious content to the program in the form of prayer, scripture study, and sermons from Jim. But it went down well for two hours, and later one hour, each day in millions of homes because it wasn't boring or leaden. It was alive. What David Letterman does to capture the excitement of New York City by putting live cameras on the streets, Jim Bakker was doing years before with cameras positioned all around the Heritage grounds to capture its colorful atmosphere. Millions watched at home as guests stood around the grand piano in the atrium of the Heritage Grand singing Christmas carols, and as squealing children careened down Heritage Mountain into the convivial lagoon.

The PTL singers would set the mood for each day's show with upbeat gospel music to the strains of the PTL orchestra. And Uncle Henry Harrison, the round and jovial co-host of the show, added well-timed "amens" and "praise the Lords" when his boss was speaking. But the stars of the show were Jim and Tammy, and they were as welcome in their viewers' homes during the day as Johnny Carson was in the homes of his loyal viewers at night.

Jim wore business suits only occasionally, and would more often dress in sweaters, casual slacks, and sometimes even shorts. Viewers saw his wide smile and in his face a certain sincerity, openness, and unpretentiousness. Like many charismatics, he wept openly if moved by the emotion of the moment. He exuded genuineness as he looked into the camera each day and, with virtually no scripting, let the Spirit move him. He would speak about some event that he had observed, like a street person in downtown Charlotte whom he saw sleeping on a steam vent without a blanket, or about something that his daughter had done that day in school. He spoke from the heart.

Bakker's Theology

One of the keys to the phenomenal success of his program was that Bakker's religious message was inclusive enough to reach far beyond the Assemblies of God Church or the precincts where other evangelists had long labored. He was never rigid or political, like Swaggart and Falwell.

> **Jim Bakker in prison:** I think the greatest mistake of the church this century was getting involved in politics. I tried not to be political. I don't think the church should be a political machine.
>
> I watched the [1992] Republican National Convention on television in the wing where I live. Other inmates watch the stock ticker and business channels all day [laughing]. But I watched that convention and I was struck by how mean-spirited many of the speakers sounded. I was born and raised a Republican, but I was very saddened by what I saw.[6]

There were three basic tenets to Bakker's theology, and they perfectly explained his appeal. First, rather than glower into the camera that all people are terrible sinners and that God is going to make them burn for their sins unless they get cracking, Bakker told viewers: "If you have a mental picture of the Lord being some cantankerous old man with a long, white beard sitting around . . . dreaming up ways to make your life miserable, get that idea out of your head. That's a complete and total lie of the devil. God loves you!"[7] He emphasized on several programs that "God is interested in you. He's concerned with you as a person. *** He cares for you."[8] He continually encouraged people, saying, "Whatever your problem might be—I want you to trust God for the answer to your problem. God won't fail you. [He] . . . isn't going to pull the rug out from under you."[9] He would say continually that "God is love" and he ended each one of his programs with the words, "God loves you, he really, really does."[10] It was a message to which millions warmed.

The second pillar of Bakker's faith was what was known in the vernacular as the "prosperity gospel."[11] His programs were laced with repeated examples of this health and wealth theology at work in peoples' lives. The story of the laborer who was broke, jobless, and destitute who prayed for divine intervention, and whom God heard and helped with a new job. Or the worshiper who gave all the money he could for God's work, and who was then blessed with a financial miracle which left him wealthy. People found hope in those messages, too.

The third pillar of Bakker's faith was the basic Pentecostal charismatic doctrine that God doesn't wait for you to come and see Him in church on Sundays. Pentecostals don't confine Jesus Christ to Sunday School history lessons. Instead, He is personally involved in their lives every day and orchestrates everything that happens to them. In that way, the Holy Spirit moves in everybody's life, and things that occur at home, on the job, or while they're at the grocery store are the result of God's personal intervention.[12] And an enormous charismatic revival swept across America in the 1970s and 1980s fueled by those beliefs. It would be a powerful tailwind propelling Bakker.

To deny that Bakker's tripartite theology caught a wave in

our nation ignores the reality that his beliefs connected with millions of people who found religious nurturing and comfort in the substance of his message. What he preached touched them and moved them. He became the most popular televangelist in the country because people liked what they saw and heard.

Giving Jim Bakker His Due

Tens of thousands of viewers would write Bakker, confirming what he steadfastly believed was the mission God sent him to accomplish. One woman wrote, "I first started watching PTL after the death of my daughter. I wanted to die too. The phone calls that used to fill the house became still, she wasn't calling Mom anymore. I needed help. Your show fed the Word to me like a healing oil everyday. Day after day, week after week your show fed me. I belonged to a church but my clergyman came by to see me only once. Your show came into my living room everyday."[13]

It is an incorrect thesis to presume that Bakker was a fake and that somehow the powerful medium of television permitted him to shove his slickly packaged, yet worthless, program down the throats of his viewers. Or, that somehow those who watched his show were gullible, unsophisticated rubes whose religious tastes were not wellborn enough to merit any respect.

Of course, lost on those professing that condemnation is the point that this country was founded by colonists who left Europe for one reason—to avoid being persecuted or belittled because their religious beliefs were different from others. Bakker's viewers were watching him voluntarily and exercising their right to worship as they chose. That is certainly a primary reason our Constitution safeguards religious freedom and the right to hold religious beliefs not shared by other people, or by reporters for the *Charlotte Observer* or others in today's dominant media culture. It is a right to stand on straw under a tent and clap your hands and worship in your own way. It is a right to watch a Pentecostal preacher on TV. And the point our country's founders understood and fought for was that worshipping or believing differently doesn't justify others looking down on you. In America, there is no State church. Everybody is on equal ground—whether it's marble or sawdust.

Bakker's Detractors

That is not to say Bakker didn't have his critics within the church. Fellow Assembly of God fire breather Jimmy Swaggart snarled that the prosperity gospel was New Age BS, and that Heritage USA was a silly amusement park. In one salvo, Swaggart complained that shows like Bakker's featured "get rich quick schemes, psychological philosophies, rock and roll entertainment, and all the way down to the exhibition of homosexual guests."[14] He even accused Bakker of "preaching a false religion."[15]

The *Charlotte Observer* vilified Bakker, its lead reporter and Bakker watcher, Charles Shepard, calling him an "ossified, self-centered man child sheltered by success and self deception."[16] Pat Robertson privately told Bakker that he was wasting the money of God's people to gratify his own ego and competitive spirit.[17]

What they found offensive were Bakker's frequent appeals for money and the unabashed materialism that characterized his lifestyle. He traveled like royalty, owned a sun-washed vacation villa in Palm Springs, and lived in luxury. The prosperity gospel didn't look too bad from his thongs when he was relaxing in Hawaii or picking out a new $48,000 Mercedes 300 SL convertible at VIP Motors in Palm Springs. His detractors just gagged at the unseemliness of it.

Columnist Dave Barry found humor in it, writing, "I think the Bakkers were successful because they personalized a . . . philosophy that . . . You can't do good unto others unless you feel good about yourself, and you can't feel good about yourself unless you have a lot of neat stuff. And the Bakkers did."[18]

Full Speed Ahead at PTL

Jim's supporters were unfazed by the criticism and actually seemed to delight as much as Bakker himself in God's largess. Jim was so excited with his first Palm Springs home that he took his television audience on a complete tour, as a camera crew went through every room and even into the closets to show viewers how much space there was. When he happened upon an antique Rolls Royce for sale in California and bought it, the first people he took on a ride were his viewers by mounting a camera in the back seat and driving the Rolls flat out through barrel cacti along a dusty road in the desert.[19]

Bakker's followers wanted him to live well. Not that it was necessarily payback time for all of the decades that Pentecostal evangelists were mainstream religion's poor relation, but because God wanted all His people to live well. In defending the opulence of some of the buildings at Heritage USA, Bakker himself asked, "Why should I apologize because God throws in crystal chandeliers, mahogany floors, and the best construction in the world?"[20] His viewers felt the same—no apologies needed.

His show roared on, hot as a pistol in the early and mid-eighties, far eclipsing Pat Robertson's *700 Club,* Robert Schuller's *Hour of Power,* Jerry Falwell's *Old Time Gospel Hour,* and Jimmy Swaggart's *Jimmy Swaggart Hour.* As PTL hit stride, Tammy Faye's role expanded and there was more to her than the doubting reporters for the *Charlotte Observer* were willing to admit. Music was a major part of the program each day and viewers felt few could sing gospel better than she.

As co-host of the show, helping interview guests or simply talking with Jim, she added to the chemistry that made them fun to watch. Tammy was such a hit, in fact, that she also starred in a spinoff, *Tammy's House Party,* where she would sing to Heritage vacationers or join born-again chefs in a Julia Child–like segment broadcast from a studio kitchen. She would also do remotes and interview well known guests, like her classic chat up of Mr. T who was clad in a bright red bathrobe while on location of his latest film. As odd a combination as they made, her questions brought out the religious beliefs the two of them shared. But Tammy was every bit as much a Pentecostal as Jim. After all, that's how they started twenty years before as two nineteen-year-old itinerant evangelists traveling from fundamentalist church to church in West Virginia and North Carolina in a beat-up station wagon.

The contrary view of Tammy Faye, to which millions were exposed in comedians' monologues for years, was that she was a joke and about as stable as nitroglycerin. Often, it looked like she applied her thick make-up with a trowel. Dressed to the nines, she obviously enjoyed cruising boutiques and beauty salons, rather than scrubbing out the church basement. She would say on the air that she had a "shopping demon" and her image in many circles was that of a Pentecostal Imelda Marcos, living for the mall with an insatiable appetite for mascara, clothes, and jewelry.

A television critic for *New Yorker* magazine described Tammy as "scatter brained" on the TV show,[21] slathering nonsensical comments punctuated by inappropriate giggling and chattering. She did say the darndest things:

- I wear wigs all the time and Jim never knows who I'm going to be.[22]

- [God told me] Tammy, let Me be your psychiatrist.[23]

- [Answering a question from host Phil Donahue on his TV program during her husband's trial] **Q:** Were you a virgin when you got married? **A:** That's none of your business whether I am or not.[24]

- We were raising money [when traveling evangelists in their early twenties] to be missionaries in the Amazon.[25]

- [When I first tried on false eyelashes and make-up] I knew that it had to be wrong and of the Devil. It scared me when I first saw make-up on me. *** Then I thought, "Why can't I do this?"[26]

- I think God wants us to protect our sexual urges from Satan.[27]

Chicago Tribune columnist Mike Royko howled, "They're telling the bumpkins that the Lord wants them to send money so the work of the PTL can go on. What work? The last time they sent money, Tammy used some of it to have her breasts inflated with silicone. . . . Is that what the Lord wanted—for both of Tammy's cups to runneth over?"[28] But Tammy Faye Bakker was not the first television personality who struck people as odd, and life for the Bakkers just kept getting better.

Jim's broadcasting genius could be seen in some high grass along the eastern edge of the Heritage grounds, which he dubbed "Satellite Valley." There, with satellite technology as advanced as NASA could boast, he bounced the broadcast signal of his daily television program from sea level to a satellite hovering 22,000 miles above the earth (*Galaxy One* in continuous geosynchronous orbit tuned to Transponder 17), where it was in turn reflected instantly back to earth receive dishes located at more than 1,300 cable television systems all across America. Those cable systems, in turn, retransmitted the signal to the homes of their subscribers.[29]

Bakker called it the "PTL Satellite Network" and vowed when dedicating it on April 3, 1978: "We have begun a broadcast that will not stop until Jesus returns."[30] It was truly a blowtorch that he fired up as his technicians adjusted the feeding dishes skyward each morning, and he kept adding other programs to the schedule until eventually he was providing twenty-four hours a day of religious programming to America's cable television systems. He didn't stop there.

In the early 1980s, PTL donated several earth receive dishes to high security prisons so that inmates could receive Christian television programming. Bakker himself helped install the dish at the Huttonsville Correctional Center in Huttonsville, West Virginia, where he later delivered a sermon to inmates. He received letters from hundreds of prisoners across the country who told him they came to know the Lord, not by reading the Bible since many of them couldn't read, but by watching the television programs that he beamed to their facilities.[31]

Ironically, of course, by the time he got to prison a few years later, his network had gone dark. But before it did, PTL left an indelible mark. Televangelism in America would never again be the same.

NOTES

1. Yancey, "The Ironies and Impact of PTL," *Christianity Today,* September 21, 1979 at 29.

2. Brinton, "Forgiven: The Rise and Fall of Jim Bakker and the PTL Ministry," *Washington Monthly,* April 1990 at 49.

3. "The Gospel Boom," *Saturday Evening Post,* April 1979 at 34.

4. FitzGerald, "Reflections," *New Yorker,* April 23, 1990 at 76.

5. "PTL: Please Toss a Lifesaver," *Christianity Today,* December 5, 1978 at 41.

6. Jim Bakker, interview by author, in Rochester, Minnesota, September 25, 1992.

7. Bakker, *The Big Three Mountain-Movers* (Logos International, Plainfield, N.J., 1977) at 3.

8. *Id.* at 3, 9.

9. *Id.* at 9, 13.

10. FitzGerald, *supra,* n. 4 at 77.

11. Bakker, *supra,* n. 7 at 14–15. See also Bakker, *Move That Mountain* (Logos International, Plainfield, N.J., 1976) at 37–49.

12. Bakker, *Move That Mountain* (Logos International, Plainfield, N.J., 1976) at 101–12.

13. Jim Bakker, letter to New Covenant Partners (July 1989).

14. FitzGerald, *supra,* n. 4 at 86.

15. *Id.* at 67.

16. *Id.* at 82.

17. Trial transcript, *United States of America v. James O. Bakker,* Docket C-CR-88-205-1, U.S.D.C. (W.D., N.C.), October 2–5, 1989, vol. 10 at 1833–34.

18. Barry, "Jim and Tammy Faye Bakker," *People,* October 4, 1989 at 70.

19. Jim Bakker, interview by author, in Rochester, Minnesota, April 4, 1993.

20. FitzGerald, *supra,* n. 4 at 74.

21. *Id.* at 73.

22. "The World According to Jim and Tammy: Quotations from the Books of Jim and Tammy Faye Bakker," *Playboy,* July 1987 at 48.

23. Bakker, *Move That Mountain, supra,* n. 12 at 86.

24. Leland and Shepard, "Pardon The Yawns," *Charlotte Observer,* September 15, 1989 at 12-A (Westlaw printout).

25. "The World According to Jim and Tammy: Quotations from the Books of Jim and Tammy Faye Bakker," *supra,* n. 22 at 41.

26. *Id.* at 48.

27. *Id.*

28. "Mike Royko" [syndicated column], *Des Moines Register,* May 19, 1987 at 9-A, col. 6.

29. Mariani, "Television Evangelism, Milking the Flock," *Saturday Review,* February 3, 1979 at 22, 24; Gillespie, "The Coaxial Congregation," *Cable Marketing,* November 1981 at 41.

30. PTL, *Jim and Tammy Bakker Present the Ministries of Heritage Village Church* (Boulton Publishing Services, Toronto, Canada, 1986) at 154.

31. *Id.* at 69.

Chapter 2

Heritage USA: Jim Bakker's Christian Paradise

It All Began in Tents

Before television replaced the automobile as the single most important American appliance, a Rantoul, Illinois, teenager named Dorothy bounced along in the back seat of her father's 1940 Ford as they drove out to the edge of town for tent revivals. Dorothy's family, like other members of the fledgling Assemblies of God Church scattered primarily throughout the Midwest and South, didn't flock to picture perfect, steepled churches in town on Sundays. They didn't have many churches. So when traveling evangelists would visit the area and erect tents for two week stints, thirsty believers crowded in for sermons that rocked them with strong doses of Puritanical preaching.

"If we were lucky, we had straw on the floor—otherwise, it was dirt,"[1] Dorothy remembers. With dust blowing and hot canvas snapping in the wind, those early fundamentalists didn't have an easy time of it. But they found the religious nurturing they sought. They saw the sick healed by the laying on of the evangelist's hands. They joined in spontaneous hallelujahs and amens, their arms reaching out to God as they closed their eyes tightly. And those truly filled with the Spirit started speaking incomprehensibly in tongues, the quintessential Pentecostal trademark.[2]

During the summers, the faithful did not have to wait for evengelists to travel to their hometowns. They could go to the evangelists, by packing up their families and spending a week or two at "camp meetings." There, in existing campgrounds around the country with small, primitive cabins, they congregated with other fundamentalists to rejoice in the Lord, and have fun with their families. Many of those early travel motels were located in desolate wooded areas near parks and lakes, making them ideal retreats for the vacationing pilgrims seeking isolation.[3]

But when they got back to town, the Pentecostals were often belittled and denigrated.

Jim Bakker in prison: The people, particularly in Charlotte, felt that Pentecostals were on the fringe and not as good as they were. And I was just one more of them.[4]

Dorothy applied the values she learned in those tents as a girl to her entire adult life. She married a fellow believer, Arnold Santjer, and while raising a family they built a construction business in Illinois working eighteen-hour days and breaking their backs. Their faith remained rock solid through the years. They lived conservatively. And as the years passed, like so many millions of other Pentecostals, they prospered.[5]

After thirty years, Arnold and Dorothy moved to Florida and branched out into the ship-loading and bridge-building businesses, and did well. It was while living in Bradenton that they first saw a young Pentecostal minister on television who inspired them like the tent evangelists forty years before. His name was Jim Bakker.

Moving On Up

The Santjers became not only members and ushers in his church, but close personal friends of both Jim and Tammy Faye. Arnold and Dorothy generously donated their time to PTL for five solid years. Arnold used his construction savvy to help build and maintain the expansive PTL resort grounds, and Dorothy worked from 9:00 A.M. until the wee small hours of the next morning answering PTL phones during frequent telethons. The Santjers worked their hearts out to help Jim and

Tammy because they saw the good that PTL was doing and the large number of people who were being saved by the PTL ministry.

They also opened up their wallets to the Bakkers. In fact, Arnold and Dorothy gave more money than anyone in the country to help Bakker build his phenomenal dream for modern Pentecostals—the Heritage USA Christian family resort.[6]

Carved out of 2,200 acres of pine forest straddling the border of North and South Carolina ten miles south of Charlotte, Heritage USA was a marvel that excited born-again Christians all over the country. Hundreds of thousands of the *PTL Club*'s loyal television viewers joined in and donated millions of dollars in the early 1980s to cleave twenty-five miles of roads through the timber and then erect the first buildings.

> **Jim Bakker on the witness stand:** My greatest religious experience as a young man was at the camp meeting in Fahola Park in Jackson, Michigan, and that is where I really met God and had my first real religious experience, is at the camp meeting. *** I remember when I was there, there would be broken screens and there would be mosquitoes in the room and there was no air conditioning. *** And the mattresses were stained, and it was a very rough place, and I think society began to pass by the old-fashioned camp grounds, and yet I felt there was such a need for people to come together. I know what it had meant to me in my first experience with God, and so I felt that I was almost born with this vision in my heart, and God just kept speaking to me about building . . . and to bring camp meeting into the twenty-first century, and that was my vision and dream from God.[7]

Within three years, the once barren pasture and pine land was transformed into a thriving small town. On any day in 1985, 1986, or 1987—PTL's Golden Years when most of Heritage was built and booming—thousands of Pentecostals like the Santjers would turn off Interstate 77 near Charlotte. Often behind the wheels of new Cadillacs and otherwise outwardly manifesting wealth, PTL vacationers would then turn south on Highway 21 for the three-mile jog to the fundamentalist Mecca which they had so generously helped underwrite. As they turned into the Heritage USA grounds and onto Mulberry Lane, it would take their breath away.[8]

What they saw was a gleaming small hamlet, lush in nature's own landscaping and topped in Tiffany. It was a dream come true. They had arrived at Heritage, and with its magnificence all Pentecostals had arrived. Sure, over the years fundamentalists had constructed local churches as membership in those denominations swelled, but these grounds were a more stunning national statement.

> **W. Ryan Hovis, attorney:** When I was growing up in the South, the Pentecostals were kind of second-class citizens, white trash. Their summer campgrounds had tar-paper shacks and yellow mattresses. PTL was a sign that they were as good as everybody else.[9]
>
> **Pastor Robert Cilke, Jim's Bible College roommate:** If you were in one of the traditional denominations you were accepted. We were not accepted. Then, we were from the wrong side of the tracks.[10]

Just inside the gate, PTL members would turn onto the wide Avenue of Flags. Construction crews could be seen everywhere. To their left was the hillside being cleared for Billy Graham's boyhood home, which Bakker saved from the wrecking ball in downtown Charlotte and transported to Heritage. Next in sight was the work on the new Mulberry Village condominiums silhouetted against dense woods. To their right was construction on a dozen new single-family homes, three apartment buildings, and more condominiums in the rolling Dogwood Hills development on Manor Lake. In all, there would be 442 homes in Heritage's residential section. The whole place looked like Colonial Willliamsburg.[11]

They would turn onto Farm Road and drive by a petting zoo with several barns painted bright red. A bustling general store and the large Heritage Inn Motel would follow. They could count seven smaller man-made lakes and two large swimming pools. Several busy restaurants would soon ring the perimeter—McMoose's the Crystal Palace Cafeteria, the Little

Horse Restaurant, and the Youth Center Pizza Parlor. In fact, by PTL's count, the cafeteria broke the *Guinness Book of World Records* mark for serving the most meals in a single day.[12]

The drive took them by tennis courts and several upscale campgrounds on Heritage Boulevard en route to one of the biggest television studios outside Hollywood—the PTL Broadcast Center with 1,800 seats and state-of-the-art technology. They could see the shimmering satellite dishes which beamed *PTL Club* broadcasts around the world. Also prominent would be impressive facilities throughout the grounds for religious services, including a 5,000-seat church, a lakeside theater for live Bible plays, and a castle-like building called the "Upper Room" for twenty-four-hour-a-day prayer.[13]

> **Jim Bakker on the witness stand:** [I] . . . laid out [Heritage USA] by hand and by the feel of the land. Not to destroy the hills. Too many times bulldozers cut in and they take all the quality and terrain and take all the stones that are naturally there, and we tried to save everything that was there naturally. . . . We went through this place and began to place the buildings, put parking lots where fields were already cleared so we wouldn't have to take down the trees for parking lots. . . . *** [There was a small lake on the aerial charts that we could not find] and one day I was so determined to find the lake because we were charting it by hand, and we had to crawl on our hands and knees through the thickets. So we made our way through and found this beautiful oasis back in the woods and we decided that one of the camp loops would be on that lake so people could enjoy it.[14]

The blue waters of a five-acre lake glistened at the center of the village. To its side, a small mountain would be built and one of the world's largest water slides constructed. The sound of hundreds of happy children shrieking as they slid into the lake was one memory of Heritage that most visitors never forgot. The religious significance of the elaborate water park was not lost on them, either, as people to whom immersion was doctrinal. Nor did Bakker miss a beat in staffing all lifeguard positions with Bible college students who were there to minister to the happy little eels as well as make sure they didn't drown.[15]

On the other side of the lake, as visitors would turn back

eastward on Heritage Boulevard, they could see the resort's sparkling *pièce de résistance*—the PTL Partner Center with its huge, opulent 500-room Heritage Grand Hotel. From the outside, it could pass for any leading Hilton or Hyatt. The Grand and its attached mall were the length of three football fields.[16] As guests drove under the canopy, elegantly uniformed doormen met them and opened the doors to their cars, extending the salutation given all visitors, "God loves you." And as every fundamentalist, born-again Christian disembarked, it wasn't on straw or dirt that they were walking. This was no tent.

On euphoric moments like their arrivals at Heritage for vacations, the Santjers would never have believed that the same road they had taken to the Heritage Grand Hotel would be the one that would take Jim Bakker to prison four years later. Or that Arnold Santjer would be called as one of the key witnesses in Bakker's trial.

That hotel is the key to understanding the entire sordid Bakker saga. Like the board game and movie *Clue,* every clue to Bakker's crime is in that hotel. Not that the answer is, "Tammy Faye in the kitchen with the lead pipe," but within the walls of the Grand Hotel lies the true Bakker story.

For starters, Bakker spent 1989 through 1994 in a prison cell because the government proved to a jury's satisfaction that he defrauded followers who contributed money for the construction of the Grand and its companion hotel, the Towers.

The naked truth is that Heritage USA quickly became a monster. Like Frankenstein, it was made by people whose motives were good but who couldn't contain it. The place absolutely caught fire among fundamentalists in the country. It became so popular that the additional 500-room Towers had to be built just to accommodate all the visitors who wanted to stay overnight on the grounds. In fact, Heritage USA attracted six million visitors a year by 1986, making it the third most popular theme park in the country, just behind Disney World and Disneyland.[17] Nobody believed it, even those who already respected the power of television. Bakker, as surprised as anyone, had to hire 3,000 employees at a cost of $30 million a year to run the place.[18] It worked for the first few years. They kept the monster in its cage and sang the nights away.

The Religious Right Emerges

What brought the millions to Heritage each year was the belief in religious fundamentalism which they shared. By the mid-1980s, a sea change in religion had occurred in America exploding the ranks of those small Pentecostal circles of the Santjers' youth. Fifty million Americans, many middle class and college educated, professed to be "born-again," believing they had a personal relationship with Jesus and had been forgiven for their sins.[19] Not only did millions of these evangelicals watch national TV programs like the *PTL Club,* at the local level a new Christian radio station went on the air every single week in 1987.[20]

"Evangelicals" are Protestant Christians who hold conservative views about the teachings of the Bible. Personal morality is a linchpin of their faith and salvation is earned by leading a cleansed, Godly life. Personal conversion to Christ and a zest for Christian living set evangelicals apart. "Evangel" means "good news" and evangelicals believe and propagate the good news of Christ—personal salvation and a personal relationship with Jesus. The major evangelical churches include the Southern Baptist Convention, which has grown from 14 million adherents in 1987 to 16 million in 1995, and the Church of the Nazarene. Former President Jimmy Carter and the Reverend Billy Graham are among the best-known evangelicals in the U.S.[21]

"Fundamentalists" are a sober brand of evangelical who believe in the very literal word of the Bible, which they regard as infallible. They stress the "fundamental" tenets of Christianity, such as the doctrines of the virgin birth, and crucifixion and resurrection of Jesus Christ. Often, their lifestyle is quite strict as many fundamentalists abstain from alcohol, tobacco, and dancing. Reverend Jerry Falwell, an independent Baptist, is the paradigm fundamentalist.[22]

"Pentecostals" are evangelicals who believe strongly in personal, daily communication with God. They believe that each day is a walk with God, rather than limiting the experience to Sunday morning church services. Once they are born-again, Pentecostals receive the baptism of the Holy Spirit, when they may "speak in tongues" (known as *glossolalia*) and experience intense joy during deep prayer. As Pentecostals read the Bible, God can reveal certain passages for them to obey, which is known as the gift of prophecy. And, they can be healed by faith if they are sick and one of God's chosen places his hands on them. The Pentecostal movement propelled its flagship church, the Assemblies of God, to 2 million members in 1988 and a rank as one of the ten largest Protestant denominations in the country. Reverend Jimmy Swaggart is the classic Pentecostal.[23]

"Charismatics" are emotional and enthusiastic in their worship, but the term is a broad one and embraces the charismatic renewal movements in both the Roman Catholic Church and several non-Pentecostal Protestant churches. The thread uniting them is a belief in "spirit-filled" living. The "prosperity gospel," the belief that God will financially reward those who contribute generously to their church, was once popular among leading charismatics but is waning today. (Even Jim Bakker disavows it now; see chapter 25.) Rather than await rewards in the afterlife, charismatics live for today and are ebullient about living. The Reverends Jim Bakker, Pat Robertson, and Oral Roberts are unabashed charismatics.[24]

The differences are real between evangelicals, fundamentalists, Pentecostals, and charismatics on the one hand and the so-called main-line churches on the other. Traditionalists in the main-line churches typically do not profess to ever having actual dialogues with God. They don't speak in tongues.

In terms of doctrine, the main-line churches do not necessarily believe that every word in the Bible is the word of God. A few waiver on the virgin birth, for instance, and others do not believe in all of the Bible's enumerated miracles such as faith healing. Some main-line churches tolerate social conduct that evangelicals abhor, such as abortion and homosexuality. The emphasis in other main-line churches on good works as a route to salvation is also heresy to evangelicals who are devout in their belief that only a personal belief and obedience to Jesus can save a soul. For many, the schism can never be bridged, which explains why evangelicals seeking religious retreat search out places where they can be with others who believe as they do.[25]

Heritage USA Becomes the Hottest Christian Venue in the Country

To those Christians who vacationed at Heritage, the perfect trip was spending several days worshipping and living with fellow believers. Heritage was self-contained and had everything from an indoor mall to endless recreation and cruise-ship caliber food. What it didn't have was nonbelievers who did not share their strict values. They were by themselves there, thousands at a time and away from the vices of the outside world. They didn't have to listen to anybody's profanity as they might back home; they didn't have to watch junior high school kids in tattered jeans making out or smoking at the mall; and they didn't have to try to eat a nice meal out with a loud drunk in the next booth. They were isolated from secular conduct that offended them, and they prayed and played in the kind of Christian environment that they were never going to find at Busch Gardens.

Bill Sacco, Heritage USA (a permanent resident) on the witness stand: I saw the place grow. I saw a pile of dirt turn into a water park. It cost, oh, 10 million dollars. I saw the foundation to the Grand hotel being poured, and a beautiful hotel built and a Main Street . . . and I thought . . . this is wonderful. *** Betty said, "Gee, Dad, you're retired, why don't you come down. . . ." *** We moved down in December of '85. I live there today.[26]

Lochie Schuessler, Monterey, California on the witness stand: I'm a minister's daughter. *** To have a Christian atmosphere to go for vacation time without having to worry about safety, alcohol, smoking and the various things that Heritage did not allow, it seemed like a paradise to us. . . . *** [In 1985 I became very ill with rheumatoid arthritis and] there were those times when we came to Heritage when I was prayed for in the restaurants, in the lobby of the hotel and various places, where Christians saw that I was in pain and in need of help, they would stop and pray for me. It was a marvelous experience to be there around Christian people.[27]

Margie Green, Newark, Ohio on the witness stand: Maybe some people can't understand that, but when we walked in, there were Christians, I mean Christians all over the place and there was love, there was fellowship, there was all denominations that walked together and worshipped the Lord. *** I brought my mother down. *** At 10:30 at night, we'd go down and have prayer in the Upper Room. I took my mother there. She loved it. We would have prayer with people from all over the United States. *** We became brothers and sisters in Christ. *** So it was just the power of the Holy Spirit there. That's what we went for.[28]

Eighty-six separate religious services were conducted each week at Heritage. Every night, all night long, ministers prayed with, healed, and gave communion to visitors in the Upper Room, a fortress-like chapel duplicating the shrine in Jerusalem where Jesus met with His disciples for the Last Supper. Up to twelve hundred communicants an hour prayed in the Upper Room. Prayer meetings were held in the hotel lobby each day, and every wake-up call to guests was a recorded prayer. Converts were baptized in ceremonies in the hotel pool. The Bakkers' TV show was piped directly into each room. When the *PTL Club* was off the air, nonstop gospel music was played. There were camp meetings every night. Church services began each day at 6:00 A.M. There was Sunday School for children, from newborn through high school, staffed by Christian teachers. Adults could attend advanced Bible school classes. Sunday church services were elaborate and packed to the rafters, with Tammy Faye leading the congregation in song and Jim delivering the weekly sermon.[29]

For the tens of thousands who were interested in studying the Bible and learning more about their faith, Bakker offered a variety of intensive workshops and seminars each week. Subjects included putting faith into daily practice and winning souls for Jesus. There were occupation-specific seminars as well, such as the one for Christian nurses on healing the whole person, and seminars for church leaders. Workshops for married couples, essentially Christian marriage counseling, were also popular.[30]

Recreation was also a priority at Heritage and opportunities abounded for visitors to enjoy their favorite sports and activities. There were eight lighted tennis courts, a miniature golf course, two baseball fields, and a regulation basketball court. Guests could also play volleyball, racquetball, horseshoes, or shuffleboard. Many had fun rollerskating. There was fishing, canoeing, and paddle boating on the several lakes throughout the grounds; and the picturesque property was ideal for horseback riding and bicycling. Walking trails throughout the park invited many, and the rest were welcome to use the Heritage tram or even a liveried horse and buggy in navigating the hamlet. For the same experience in a more circular motion, one could pick a steed on the park's full-sized carousel.[31]

The biggest recreational attraction was the huge Heritage Island Water Park. In designing Heritage, one of Bakker's premises was that there had to be abundant activities for every member of the family. He didn't want children having to go into town for fun. The water park was what Bakker saw keeping families together, and it was extravagant. "The summers are so hot in Charlotte that people coming from their vacations were sweltering in the heat, so we brought the ocean to Charlotte,"[32] Bakker gleamed.

In all, it took three years and $13 million to complete, and it remains a phenomenon of engineering and construction. Its basic design broadly resembles Disney's Pirates of the Caribbean—a huge, man-made mountain surrounded by lagoons. It looks like an island right down to the thousands of tons of sand that were brought in to make beaches all around it. Bakker even installed a gigantic wave machine so that water would realistically lap up on the shore, making it the world's largest wave-making pool.[33]

Jim Bakker: Why is it we can almost enshrine a mouse—a Mickey Mouse? Why can't we have something where young people will be connected to Jesus Christ?[34]

There were forty different activities in the water park including the Raging Canyon Rapids where kids floated down one side of the mountain on inner tubes and the Typhoon, a sixty-foot water slide. For a break, they could relax in the underwater observation room. If they got hungry, there was the Sea Cave Cafe located under the giant waterfall.[35] Without a doubt, it was the recreational centerpiece of the entire place. At the same time, the one hundred Bible school student lifeguards stayed alert to any opportunity to talk about Jesus.

But Heritage was not without its critics. In news articles, the *Charlotte Observer* blasted Bakker for what it calculated to be staggering cost overruns on the water park alone and a construction delay of two full years to build the lake.[36] Jimmy Swaggart sniped, "the Gospel is not entertainment. It is very sober. It has no place for amusement parks."[37]

The retreat was also the butt of many jokes, and often derided as "Six Flags over Jesus."[38]

Humorist P.J. O'Rourke, in his book *Holidays in Hell,* laughed at the plastic, new-money facades. To his eye, the Grand Hotel looked like "Monticello mated with a Ramada Inn" and the rest of the park was overdone, with "bogus Victorian house fronts" and paint "in colors unfit for baboon posteriors."[39]

Bakker was undaunted, and claimed victory on his show. "We won again, Hallelujah!" he rejoiced when the lake filled up. "If the Bible says we are to be fishers of men, then a water park is just the bait. And I don't see anything wrong in using some pretty fancy bait," he told viewers.[40]

Still, not everyone in the area was a fan. "I used to play tennis with the wife of one of his financial people," a Ft. Mill woman told UPI. "Every time she served she yelled 'Praise the Lord.' It got on my nerves."[41]

Of course, a favorite form of recreation for many adults is shopping. Nobody knew that better than Tammy Faye and she made sure her guests weren't deprived during their stay at Heritage. Attached to the Heritage Grand Hotel was an enclosed, thirty-five-store mile-long shopping mall which they called "Main Street Heritage USA." Specialty shops like Perry's Jewelry Emporium, Goosebumps Collectibles, and Noah's Toy

Shoppe lined the promenade and did fantastic, brisk business. Crowds were elbow-to-elbow.[42]

Evenings were magic at Heritage. Guests could attend a nighttime concert or relax and listen to strings in the lobby of the Grand. They could watch fireworks or join in an all-night gospel sing. Programs were offered at the Christian Dinner Theater. On Tuesday evenings, a musical featuring gospel and folk music performed by the PTL singers was always presented in the 3,500-seat outdoor amphitheater. "Sing, America, Sing" with Broadway favorites and gospel music performed by the PTL orchestra was a favorite, too. And at 8:00 P.M. three nights a week in the summer, a spectacular Passion Play depicting the spiritual warfare between Jesus and Satan was performed. With a set that cost over $1 million, a cast of one hundred players, three camels, and several other live animals, it was elaborate and moving. Sent by his newspaper to investigate, a reporter for the *London Observer* wrote back that the play was said to be so dramatic the audience was moved to tears.[43]

Heritage USA was an inviting place for Christians of many denominations who yearned for a religion-oriented vacation. The retreat's appeal was so broad-based that as time went by more Catholics and Baptists walked through the gates than any other denominations. Millions of visitors each year felt welcome there.

Lodging at Heritage

Central to the Heritage concept was that there be enough lodging on the grounds so that every visitor could remain there the length of their vacation. It would simply spoil the trip for most evangelicals if, after a full day of Bible study and fellowship with like believers, they had to drive into Charlotte at night to stay at the Holiday Inn where the lounge would shake them until 2:00 A.M. So, from the beginning, Heritage was designed as a destination resort and priority was given to overnight accommodations.

Primarily designed for people like the Santjers traveling with RVs, the modern Fort Heritage Campground opened in 1978 and was ultimately expanded to over 400 campsites on 350 acres of prime Heritage countryside. Each campsite had water, lights, sewer hook-up, a grill, and a picnic table. The campsites also were completely wired for cable television, allowing vacationers to watch twenty-four-hour religious programming on the PTL Network. Telephones at each campsite were connected directly to the PTL pastoral counseling center. And sixty miles of state-of-the-art fiber optic cable connected every corner of Heritage so that reception of the *PTL Club* would be crystal clear no matter where anybody was on the grounds. Driving through the campgrounds, you would see American flags flying over RVs and trailers, but you'd never find a beer can by the side of the road. These folks did not drink. Smile to another camper, though, and they would often respond "Praise the Lord."[44]

The Heritage Inn Motel, with ninety-six rooms, was opened in 1983 and resembles most Ramada Inns or Holiday Inns, although the extensive use of slate rock on the exterior and generous landscaping give it a richer touch.[45]

The 500-room Heritage Grand was opened in December, 1984 as the crown jewel of all lodging at Heritage.[46] Two sixteen-room bunkhouse hotels, featuring Western architecture and large rooms which would accommodate up to six family members a night, were completed in 1986.[47] On the shores of Lake Heritage, lakeside lodges and A-frame chalets that look like the set from *The Sound of Music,* were also opened in 1986.[48] But the phenomenal popularity of Heritage quickly stretched existing lodging to the limit, and Bakker scrambled to build more to meet demand.

Of the millions who vacationed at Heritage each year, some decided to make it their permanent homes. Bakker anticipated that and kept building homes as fast as he could for them, too. For those permanent residents, Heritage even had its own real estate office which helped home buyers choose from among several townhouse, condominium, single family dwelling, and duplex designs. Prices for two bedroom homes at Heritage ranged from $66,500 to $75,000. Dogwood Hills was the first condominium tract, with one-story adjoining units in a densely wooded area. They look more like expensive lakeshore cabins in an exclusive resort.[49]

Nice homes with expansive decks and outdoor whirlpools can be found at Mulberry Village, a mile or two away. Painted in bold colonial blues, grays, and yellows, they look like homes on any Eastern seaboard street from Cape Cod to Kitty Hawk. Hundreds of people, mostly retirees, still live there. Jim Bakker's eighty-six-year-old parents and the widow of his longtime on-air sidekick, Uncle Henry Harrison, are among the residents. Of course, they own the deeds to their homes which protected them from the bankruptcy and later sale of Heritage itself. When Bakker ran the place, neighborhood prayer meetings and Bible study groups were organized by a traveling minister who actually spent five hours a day on horseback visiting each neighborhood in the sprawling grounds.[50]

Parades, Fireworks, and Christmas Lights

With so many permanent and transient residents, the need for a variety of services burgeoned at Heritage.

The educational needs of children had to be met. The Heritage Village Church Day Care Center offered recreation, Bible study, and supervision of toddlers under the watchful eyes of certified teachers. For grade school age children, the Heritage Village Church Academy was operated on a level comparable with other Christian schools in the country. There was even the Heritage School of Evangelism and Communication for college students wishing to go into televangelism and wanting to learn from the master. Offering courses in television production, video and audio technology, evangelism, graphic arts, and radio production, the college graduated hundreds of students who became full-time ministers in the Assemblies of God and other Pentecostal churches.[51]

The village had its own newspaper, the *Heritage Herald,* and a branch of the Home Federal Bank. There was a street maintenance department, security force, and complete water and sewer system capped with an eighty-foot-tall water tower emblazoned with "Heritage USA." Street signs cautioned motorists, "Speed Checked by God!"[52]

Like any small town, Heritage USA loved parades and celebrations. One of the most memorable was a televised ticker tape parade on April 1, 1986 when Jim and Tammy celebrated their twenty-fifth wedding anniversary. And every year without fail, the Fourth of July was wildly celebrated in conjunction with the annual Victory Celebration marking the anniversary of the founding of Bakker's ministry. That pageant included all-day outdoor worship services, parades, and one of the largest fireworks displays in the South. A festival was held each Labor Day with an arts and crafts fair, Christian entertainers, and an all-night sing. Gala black tie dinners were held in the Heritage Grand to mark special achievements, like the completion of major buildings and the anniversary of PTL.[53]

But the biggest celebration of all was the yearly "Christmas City" extravaganza. Like its less ambitious counterparts in cities and towns across America, Heritage offered a living nativity scene, with live animals and choir members dressed in detailed costumes. There were colorful Christmas pageants and children's shows for weeks during the celebration. So spectacular was Bakker's use of the million and a half lights and budget of $1,000,000 each year to light up the streets of Heritage, that the Association of American Travel Agents named it one of the top one hundred must-see sights in the country.[54]

Hundreds of thousands of area residents from throughout North and South Carolina, as well as visitors from far beyond, jammed the highways leading to Heritage each year for the chance to drive down the magnificently decorated streets of Bakker's theme park at Christmas. Among them were James McAllister and Barbara Dalley. Mrs. Dalley told us that "You've never seen anything like what they did with lights."[55] Good reviews like that didn't help Jim Bakker. Three years later Dalley became one of the jurors who convicted him of fraud in a Charlotte courtroom and sent him to prison for forty-five Christmases.

NOTES

1. Arnold and Dorothy Santjer, interview by author, in Bradenton, Florida, January 14, 1993.

2. Packard, *Evangelism in America* (Paragon House, New York, 1988) at

69; Reinhold, "Pentecostals' Split Exposed by Bakker Affair," *New York Times,* March 28, 1987 at 7-A, col. 1–3.

3. PTL, *Jim and Tammy Bakker Present the Ministries of Heritage Village Church* [photographs] (Boulton Publishing Services, Toronto, Canada, 1986) at 88–91.

4. Jim Bakker, interview by author, in Rochester, Minnesota, October 31, 1992.

5. Arnold and Dorothy Santjer, interview, *supra,* n. 1.

6. *Id.* See also trial transcript, *United States of America v. James O. Bakker,* Docket No. C-CR-88-205-1, U.S.D.C. (W.D., N.C.), September 26–27, 1989, vol. 8 at 1359.

7. Trial transcript, *United States of America v. James O. Bakker,* Docket No. C-CR-88-205-1, U.S.D.C. (W.D., N.C.), September 29–29, 1989, vol. 9 at 1612–13.

8. Arnold and Dorothy Santjer, interview, *supra,* n. 1.

9. Stille, "The Legal Fight for an Evangelical Empire," *National Law Journal,* September 28, 1987 at 41.

10. Kopkind, "Jim Bakker's Lost America," *Esquire,* December 1987 at 176.

11. PTL, *Jim and Tammy Bakker Present the Ministries of Heritage Village Church supra,* n. 3 at 14, 30, 61–62, 94–96, 105–7, 116–17, 120–24; PTL, *Together,* January/February 1984 at 7–9.

12. Trial transcript, *supra,* n. 7 at 1660.

13. PTL, *Jim and Tammy Bakker Present the Ministries of Heritage Village Church, supra,* n. 3 at 6–7, 22, 31, 33, 45, 58, 66–67, 154, 173, 175, 194.

14. Trial transcript, *supra,* n. 7 at 1620–22.

15. Trial transcript, *supra,* n. 7 at 1691–92; trial transcript, *United States of America v. James O. Bakker,* Docket No. C-CR-88-205-1, U.S.D.C. (W.D., N.C.), October 2–5, 1989, vol. 10 at 1912–13.

16. "Better Bait for Evangelism," UPI [wire story], December 23, 1984, AM cycle (Nexis printout).

17. Trial transcript, *supra,* n. 7 at 1651; "Fun and Games for Bible-thumpers," *Economist,* October 19, 1985, p. 29 (Nexis printout).

18. Jim Bakker, interview by author, in Rochester, Minnesota, September 25, 1992.

19. Range, "A Language Spoken Only by Believers," *U.S. News & World Report,* April 6, 1987 at 66.

20. Rosenfeld, "Putting out the Word and Bringing in the Bucks—Incomes and Audience Figures in the Eyes of the Beholder," *Washington Post,* May 3, 1987 at 1-F.

21. Buursma, "TV Preachers Prove They're Not All Alike," *Chicago Tribune,* April 5, 1987 at 1-P (Nexis printout); Reinhold, "Pentecostals' Split Exposed by Bakker Affair," *New York Times,* March 3, 1987 at 1-A, col. 2 and p. 7, col. 1.

22. *Id.*

23. *Id.*

24. *Id.*

25. Roberts, *Religion in Sociological Perspective* (Wadsworth Publishing

Co., Belmont, Calif.) at 232–38; Schmidt, "TV Minister Calls His Resort 'Bait' for Christianity," *New York Times*, December 24, 1985 at 8-A, col. 2; trial transcript, *infra*, n. 26.

26. Trial transcript, *United States of America v. James O. Bakker*, Docket No. C-CR-88-205-1, U.S.D.C. (W.D., N.C.), September 19–25, 1989, vol. 7 at 677–78.

27. *Id.* at 970–71.

28. Trial transcript, *supra*, n. 6 at 1028–30.

29. PTL, *Jim and Tammy Bakker Present the Ministries of Heritage Village Church, supra*, n. 3 at 6–7, 17–18, 20–21, 42–44, 52, 66, 155.

30. *Id.* at 82–83. See also PTL, *Heritage Herald*, April 1986, at 3.

31. *Id.* at 56–58, 120, 124–27, 129, 131.

32. Trial transcript, *supra*, n. 7 at 1691.

33. Bakker, *Appeal to the U.S. Parole Commission*, Exhibit 15, June 1, 1993 at 3; *Id.*, vol. I [photographs and Lifetime Partner newsletters] at 36, 48.

34. "Better Bait for Evangelism," *supra*, n. 16.

35. "Heritage Island Water Park Attractions," *Together Update* [PTL Lifetime Partner newsletter], September/October 1986 at 2, col. 1.

36. Shepard, *Forgiven* (Atlantic Monthly Press, New York, 1989) at 245–46, 318–20.

37. Reinhold, "Pentecostals' Split Exposed by Bakker Affair," *New York Times*, March 28, 1987 at 1-A, col. 4.

38. Lohmann, "PTL scandal taking its toll," UPI [wire story], May 3, 1987, BC Cycle.

39. O'Rourke, *Holidays in Hell* (Random House, New York, 1989) at 93.

40. Schmidt, "TV Minister Calls His Resort 'Bait' For Christianity," *New York Times*, December 24, 1985 at 8-A, col. 2.

41. Daniel, "Video Evangelism—Bakker Defends 'Praise the Lord' Club; His Critics Say PTL Means 'Pass the Loot'," United Press International [wire story], May 25, 1983, BC cycle (Nexis printout).

42. PTL, *Jim and Tammy Bakker Present the Ministries of Heritage Village Church, supra*, n. 3, at 106–7, 114–18.

43. "Fun and Games for Bible-thumpers," *Economist*, October 19, 1985 p. 29 (Nexis printout); PTL, *Jim and Tammy Bakker Present the Ministries of Heritage Village Church, supra*, n. 3 at 33, 170–75.

44. Trial transcript, *supra*, n. 7 at 1686; PTL, *Jim and Tammy Bakker Present the Ministries of Heritage Village Church, supra*, n. 3 at 45, 94–95; "PTL Launches Disney-Type Campground," *Washington Post*, July 15, 1978, at 8-B, col. 1; Daniel, *supra*, n. 41.

45. PTL, *Jim and Tammy Bakker Present the Ministries of Heritage Village Church, supra*, n. 3 at 120.

46. *Id.* at 14, 105.

47. Bakker, *Appeal to U.S. Parole Commission*, vol. II [photographs and Lifetime Partner newsletters], June 1, 1993 at 73.

48. PTL, *Jim and Tammy Bakker Present the Ministries of Heritage Village Church, supra*, n. 3, at 121.

49. *Id.* at 122–23.

50. *Id.* at 45, 61–62, 122–23; PTL, *Together,* January/February 1984 at 7–9.

51. *Id.* at 52–55, 100–101; Trial transcript, *supra,* n. 7 at 1636; PTL, *Together,* January/February 1984 at 22.

52. *Id.* at 133; PTL, *Heritage Herald,* April 1986; AP, "PTL Launches Disney-Type Campground," *Washington Post,* July 15, 1978 at 8-B, col. 1.

53. *Id.* at 175, 179, 181–82, 188, 192–95.

54. *Id.* at 182, 186–87, 191; Bakker, *supra,* n. 47 at 85; "Enjoy Christmas City," *Together Update,* September/October 1986 at 1.

55. Barbara Dalley, telephone interview by Suzan Brooks, June 21, 1993.

Chapter 3

Good Works at PTL

Even though the hundreds of guests packing the studio each day for the broadcast of the *PTL Club* sang their hearts out when the orchestra cued up familiar gospel refrains, it wasn't all preaching to the choir at Heritage. While coveting his village as an island for evangelicals to be with their own, Bakker made it a priority to reach out and undertake good works to benefit a variety of needy people. Bakker did a lot of good with PTL which, in fairness, history should acknowledge. Instead of operating Heritage merely as a country club for charismatics, for instance, Jim brought street people and unwed mothers to live there, and attempted to do the same for handicapped children. And he and the PTL faithful spent hours every day on major charitable projects for others.

Venerable movie and television star Dale Evans arrived at Heritage on July 4, 1986 to cut the ribbon dedicating Fort Hope, a thirty-acre complex on the southwest corner of the grounds for street people with nowhere else to turn. Ben Kinchlow, co-host of Pat Robertson's *The 700 Club,* offered a prayer asking God to change the lives of those who would now call Fort Hope their home. The ceremony was broadcast live to Bakker's national television audience with outdoor cameras zooming in on three newly constructed buildings resembling one-story Red Roof Inns. It looked like a small community college campus with a quadrangle between the buildings and wide walkways connecting the different structures. Stately trees surrounded the property.

There was a large main lodge and dining room, and two dormitories. Cameras showed a few men in their rooms, each furnished with bunk beds and desks. Another group was seated around a PTL counselor in the recreation center with Bibles opened on their laps. Viewers also saw residents eating home-cooked food in the fellowship hall, one man being taught automotive repair under the hood of a blue Chevy truck, and two men learning landscaping and lawn care in the Fort Hope greenhouse.[1]

Bakker preached that it was through the love of Jesus Christ that these men's lives would be restored, and he built Fort Hope to be much more than a homeless shelter. It was a one-year program of schooling, vocational training, counseling, and Christian discipline. Volunteers from Heritage joined the professional staff of counselors and instructors to work with those in the program. Drug and alcohol abuse were tackled head-on, and the program was limited to street people between the ages of seventeen and forty who were serious about trying to learn a trade and the living skills necessary to lead productive lives. Success stories would be written in those buildings, and they would be among Bakker's greatest triumphs.[2]

Across the road from a large fenced pasture where horses were corralled on the western edge of Heritage, Bakker built a home for unwed mothers which he called Heritage House. The L-shaped stone and cedar home was opened in 1984 and offered accommodations and support for expectant young mothers who chose birth over abortion. For those who planned to keep their children, there were cooking classes and instruction in proper nutrition in addition to professional counseling on child care. Part-time employment was also offered. For those who decided to place their children for adoption, Heritage operated the Tender Loving Care Adoption Agency.[3]

As with every other activity at Heritage, underpinning the girls' home was a religious component which took the form of spiritual guidance for the residents from staff ministers. In addition, expectant mothers were given the opportunity to be "adopted" themselves by church families who offered additional support and companionship. Heritage House itself was first class, with furnishings that looked like they came straight from an Ethan Allen showroom. There was a large kitchen where residents shared the cooking responsibilities, private rooms overlooking the countryside, and a huge landscaped courtyard and patio to tap the Carolina sun.[4] Bakker was proud of Heritage House and would occasionally well over with emotion on the air when showing photographs of newborn babies and when reading letters from young mothers thanking him for standing behind them.[5]

On the other side of Highway 21 at the westernmost edge of Heritage, Bakker operated a People That Love Center which provided food, clothing, and furniture without cost to people in need. The building itself was a yellow one-story, nine-room, wood-frame home, with black shutters on the windows and an orange and black sign near the road identifying it as the PTL People That Love Center. Inside, some rooms were lined with shelves stocked with groceries, and others had racks of clothes or furniture and household necessities.[6] It filled a need and within a few years, PTL had organized a network of churches and civic groups to operate satellite People That Love Centers in nearly 1,000 communities across the country. The impact was so visible that President Reagan publicly commended Bakker for the deed.[7]

The last of the major outreach projects at Heritage proved to be a clinker and it came back to haunt Bakker years later. In the summer of 1986, Bakker erected a 3-story Victorian mansion with 13,000 square feet of living space right in the middle of the Heritage grounds and named it Kevin's House for Disabled Children. Its namesake, Kevin Whittum, was a seventeen-year-old who suffered from brittle bone disease and weighed only twenty pounds. Bakker was moved to build the home when young Kevin, vacationing at Heritage with his family, fell in love with the place and cried when he had to return home to Michigan. Standing with Bakker in front of the Heritage Grand

Hotel, Kevin told Jim sorrowfully that he did not want to leave, but wished he could live at PTL. Bakker didn't hesitate, and blurted out, "Kevin, I'll build you a house [here] in thirty days."[8]

But as an example of good works at Heritage, Kevin's House is the subject of some debate. On one hand, it was built, it was beautiful, and Kevin and his family surely lived there. Indeed, Bakker granted Kevin's wish. He made the tiny teenager's dream come true and Kevin lived until his death in 1992 in the center of what to him was his Disney World.[9]

On the other hand, Bakker insisted on a frenetic pace to have the home constructed within just two months. Corners had to be cut and there was no time to build in the design components necessary to obtain state approval as a group home—fire resistant bedroom walls, a system of fire extinguishers and sprinklers, and flooring which met commercial standards. As a result, Kevin's House never received government approval to operate as a group home and only Kevin and his family, including a handicapped sister, ever lived there.[10]

Newspapers hit Bakker hard over Kevin's House, reporting that it only cost $1.5 million to build but that Bakker milked $3 million from contributors whose hearts went out to the pitiful child. It was reported that Bakker had never leveled with his television audience about the fact that only Kevin lived in the home, and instead continually implied that it was being operated as a home for several other disabled children.[11]

Kevin's House, like a glass, can be viewed as either half full or half empty. As the *Observer* contended, it was half empty in that it didn't meet code specifications and was not permitted to operate as a group home. But from the perspective of Kevin, his sister, and his parents who were ebulliently thankful every day of their lives that they could live in such a fantastic setting, the glass was overflowing. The problem, of course, was that there were clear indications here of loose, effervescent fundraising representations that overstated the matter, diminishing what otherwise would have been a noble undertaking.

PTL's outreach, however, extended far beyond the confines

of the Heritage grounds and literally encircled the globe. Fifty-two countries on seven continents received PTL telecasts. In many of them, including China, Japan, France, and Italy, local television personalities hosted their own versions of Jim and Tammy's show. Bakker's international programming, then, was more than simply blasting his own programs by satellite to every country under which the big bird passed in orbit. He financially underwrote and produced local companion programs, and his diplomatic savviness in respecting differences in culture earned PTL permission from at least two governments, Zimbabwe and Thailand, as the only television program permitted in those countries to openly proselytize for Christianity.[12]

In addition to the television ministry, PTL helped build local schools and hospitals in emerging nations. An Assemblies of God Bible College in India was built with PTL funds, and starving children were fed in several trouble spots. There were PTL offices in many countries, including ones fully staffed in Panama and Japan. Bakker himself frequently visited foreign countries to preach in different churches and visit local hospitals and orphanages.[13]

Another component of PTL's outreach took the form of books and records which could be found in the homes of millions of people. Bakker was a prodigious author and committed to making a mark on the Christian world with his writing. In fact, Bakker wrote so many books and the demand for them from his viewers was so great that a large warehouse and distribution center had to be constructed on the Heritage grounds to accommodate the orders that would pour in each day. The most popular of Bakker's books were the *PTL One Year Bible,* which rearranged the entire Living Bible in 365 daily readings, the *PTL Parallel Bible,* which contrasted on the same pages all the verses from both the King James version and Living Bible versions, and the *PTL Club Devotional Guide,* which contained daily thoughts and words to live by.[14]

For Christians who believed in the daily presence of God in their lives, books like these which could be turned to each day for a different message were ideal. Other books he authored included *Survival—Unite to Live* about overcoming adversity, *The Lord Is on Your Side,* another collection of daily devotionals, and *You Can Make It* about achieving success and fulfillment in life. He also wrote two autobiographies, *Move That Mountain* and *The Big Two Mountain Movers,* which chronicled his walk through life. Toward the end of his reign at PTL, Bakker branched out into audiocassettes and offered a series of tapes of his sermons from the Heritage pulpit.[15]

Tammy had a real presence in this area as well, and her credits included two books and a string of top-selling records. She wrote *Run to the Roar* offering her insights on how to overcome fear which included a foreword by Efrem Zimbalist, Jr., and *I Got to Be Me,* her own autobiography. She was better known for more than twenty rip-roaring gospel albums, including *Old Hymns,* with songs like "Rock of Ages," "What A Friend We Have in Jesus," and "Amazing Grace." She also recorded three different top-selling Christmas albums with carols and classics. And her *In the Upper Room* album, recorded on the Heritage grounds, became a favorite of Christian radio stations throughout the country. With all her albums, she earned widespread recognition in gospel music and was named Best Female Vocalist in 1985 by Religion in Media.[16]

Recording and publishing became a family affair for the Bakkers when daughter Tammy Sue's first album was released when she was only sixteen, and with the publication in 1985 of a book entitled *Mother's Favorite Devotional* which was a collection of daily devotions and messages from Jim's mother, Furnia.[17]

Prophetically, as the grounds of Heritage USA shook underneath them and Bakker's days as head of PTL became numbered, a hint of impending doom was reflected in Tammy's music. Her last two albums, *Tammy Faye—Peace in the Midst of the Storm* and *Tammy—Don't Give Up!* said it all. A bit less prophetic were two of Jim Bakker's own cassette sermons offered toward the end—*Forgive and Be Forgiven* and *The Church Must Forgive,* which were described in PTL's advertising as Bakker's "most powerful, moving messages."[18] They turned out to be not powerful enough.

NOTES

1. Bakker, Appeal to U.S. Parole Commission, vol. II [photographs and Lifetime Partner newsletters], June 1, 1993 at 88–89.

2. *Id.;* trial transcript, *United States of America v. James O. Bakker,* Docket No. C-CR-88-205-1, U.S.D.C. (W.D., N.C.), September 26–27, 1989, vol. 8 at 1306.

3. Bakker, *supra,* n. 1 at 78–79; PTL, *Jim and Tammy Bakker Present the Ministries of Heritage Village Church* [photographs] (Boulton Publishing Services, Inc., Toronto, Canada, 1986) at 76–79; trial transcript, *United States of America v. James O. Bakker,* Docket No. C-CR-88-205-1, U.S.D.C. (W.D., N.C.), Sept. 19–25, 1989, vol. 7 at 629–36.

4. *Id.*

5. *Id.*

6. Bakker, *supra,* n. 1 at 79.

7. PTL, *supra,* n. 3 at 70–71; trial transcript, *supra,* n. 3 at 1030–31.

8. Dortch, *Integrity* (New Leaf Press, Green Forest, Ark., 1992) at 62.

9. *PTL, supra,* n. 3 at 202.

10. Wright, "Kevin's House Is New Focus of PTL Probe," *Charlotte Observer,* February 19, 1988 at 1-C (Westlaw printout); Shepard, *Forgiven* (Atlantic Monthly Press, New York, 1989) at 416–17, 419–21.

11. *Id.*

12. *PTL, supra,* n. 3 at 84–87.

13. *PTL, supra,* n. 3 at 86–87.

14. Bakker, Appeal to U.S. Parole Commission, vol. III [photographs], June 1, 1993 at 97, 100, 109.

15. *Id.* at 97, 101, 104, 112; Bakker, *Move That Mountain* (Logos International, Plainfield, N.J., 1976); Bakker, *The Big Three Mountain Movers* (Logos International, Plainfield, N.J., 1977).

16. Bakker, *supra,* n. 14 at 98–99, 102, 104–5, 107–8, 110–11.

17. *Id.* at 98, 103.

18. *Id.* at 99, 104, 107.

Chapter 4

The Price Tag

About one thing in this case everyone agrees—it cost more than $100 million to build and operate Heritage USA and Bakker's television ministry.[1] PTL's costs were staggering, wildly driven by forces which demanded the expenditure of tens of more millions of dollars each year. And it was his unending pleas for contributions to keep things going that particularly nettled Bakker's detractors.

This was a broadcast ministry fed to millions of homes by increasingly expensive technologies. To bounce his signal from the $5 million studio on the Heritage grounds to the 1,300 cable systems in the country waiting for it each day cost Bakker dearly. He had to buy a field full of satellite equipment for transmitting. He had to lease time and space on a communications satellite circling the globe 22,000 feet above the earth's surface. That R-2-D-2 look-alike hurtling through space received the live signal of the PTL program and flashed it back with the speed of a laser to participating cable systems. The traveling time for that signal from the sound stage at Heritage to the cable system in Seattle was two seconds. Transportation like that doesn't come cheap. PTL's 1987 satellite tab was nearly $2.5 million.[2] Local cable systems charged fees on top of that totaling $837,000.[3]

Additionally, in order to reach the millions of homes not subscribing to cable, PTL purchased air time on from 180 to

200 local TV stations blanketing the country. Those stations did not donate time for the *PTL Club* program—they charged through the nose for it. This wasn't a two-minute test pattern sermonette to end the day, or a low-key Sunday morning service from a local church carried by the friendly hometown television station.

This was a glossy, hour-long daytime show from the national PTL Television Network which was never intended to be shunted to the peripheral hours. It was live, and millions watched it in their living rooms at 11:00 A.M. every day. Stations naturally expected to be compensated for their time and the cost depended on the size of the cities served by those stations and the audiences they delivered. By 1987, PTL was being charged $15.5 million each year by local stations,[4] but Bakker was in a corner. Air time is the lifeblood of a television ministry and the cost for it is as essential to a televangelist as is a church in town to a local congregation of Presbyterians.

Former PTL Finance Director Peter Bailey, testifying for the government at Bakker's 1989 trial, calculated that it cost $1 million a week to operate PTL, with $50,000 a day spent buying television time alone.[5]

> **Tammy Faye:** Television, to Jim and me, has nothing to do with ego. It is what God has called us to do! We have a calling to reach people through television that is so heavy we can hardly bear it.[6]

The other stressor that required the expenditure of millions was the theme park itself. Transforming 2,200 acres of Carolina bottomland into the nation's third most popular destination theme park cost real money. And Bakker didn't build it cheaply, either. He insisted that his followers have nothing but the best at Heritage. To the smallest detail, everything was exquisite. The buildings, the landscaping, the recreational facilities, the stores, the lodging, and the service were five-star caliber across the board.

The place was in a constant building frenzy, too, with Bakker beginning construction for new buildings even before old ones were finished. He seemed absolutely driven to put his vision into bricks and mortar, and he wanted it all done yesterday. To build for a perfectionist like Bakker who wanted everything done both quickly and first class was a contractor's dream. Roe Messner, Jim's builder, made millions and his laborers spent thousands of hours at Heritage.[7]

On top of construction costs, the place was a money pit once it opened. Jim had to hire, at different points, between two thousand and three thousand employees to run it and accommodate the millions of guests who flocked to it. Six million guests a year would challenge any vacation site. That's 12 million aching feet, after all. And even though those evangelicals who sought The Word at Heritage were probably not as destructive as some fraternity boys renting a few hotel rooms for their yearly formal, there were still enormous inescapable costs in maintaining the grounds and accommodating each day's onslaught.

Another force that drove costs was Bakker's success itself. Business leaders profess, in explaining such things, that success breeds success. Here, the equation was a simple one. If so many millions of people hadn't wanted to watch Jim Bakker on television each day, there would have been no need for him to purchase time on so many television stations. And, if so many millions of fundamentalists hadn't wanted to spend some vacation time at a Christian retreat, Heritage USA would never have been built. If Bakker had been wrong about the need for such a unique facility, it would have folded within a week. But he wasn't wrong and the place struck a cord with millions who overran its gates. If the response Heritage USA ignited within the evangelical community hadn't been as phenomenal as it was, there would have been no need for the construction of so many hotels and recreational activities on its grounds. The bottom line is that, in this case, success also bred astronomical costs.

By 1986, Bakker was under the strain of having to raise nearly $3 million a week to meet budget and keep everything going.[8] At the time, he never uttered a word letting others know what a burden that truly was for him, nor did he complain that the gargantuan task rested on his shoulders alone. Later, he was forced to reflect on it:

> **Jim Bakker on the witness stand:** [W]e began to grow in such a rapid fashion that it was overwhelming. I liken it to stepping into a roller coaster and not being able to get off. *** [The outside computer analysts] . . . told me that we grew 7,000 percent in one and-a-half years.[9]

From 1977 until Jim Bakker left PTL in 1987, his books were audited thoroughly by two of the largest accounting firms in the country. Until the fiscal year that ended May 31, 1984, Deloitte Haskins & Sells prepared annual audits of all of PTL's books using the tough auditing standards and accounting principles required by the profession. For the two fiscal years beyond that, the firm of Laventhol and Horwath, another huge national CPA firm with a stellar reputation, audited the books and prepared similar tabulations. The key to the reliability of CPA firm audits lies in the fact that they are done by outside, independent examiners.

> **Jim Bakker in prison:** I had auditors on top of auditors. I submitted myself personally, annually to auditing and income tax preparation by a Big Eight accounting firm. We paid a million dollars a year for those audits. I hired lawyers, fifteen CPAs, one hundred people in the financial office.
>
> I took no tax deductions and paid 60 percent of everything I made in taxes. In 1986, out of $1,100,000 in income, I took a half million dollars and paid $600,000 in taxes. Melvin Belli told me that if I was a criminal, I was the dumbest criminal he'd ever seen.
>
> I didn't write a check for years—assistants did. With so much money coming in, I wanted to maintain distance from it. I don't know what I could have done differently. My attorneys were advising me every inch of the way about money.[10]

Professionally and ethically, those CPAs were duty bound to ferret out any financial wrongdoing, misspending of funds, or fraud. With an operation the size of Bakker's, such an undertaking typically consumed months; and staff auditors for those firms actually were on the premises of Heritage continuously pouring over the books. During the last two years alone, auditors for Laventhol and Horwath spent more than four thousand hours counting every penny of PTL's income and every dime it spent.[11] Credibility of that kind comes with a price tag of its own, of course, and PTL spent millions over the years on auditors' fees.[12] The ministry ended up with yearly audits of its financial condition prepared by the best independent auditors in the business.

Unfortunately for Bakker, he told me that his trial attorneys never called those auditors as witnesses on his behalf.[13] What their audits show, not surprisingly, is millions of dollars being spent by PTL for the television ministry and expenses at Heritage. In many respects, they vindicate the evangelist.

In its audit for the year ending May 31, 1984, Deloitte Haskins & Sells reported the following expenditures. The column on the left reflects money spent in FY (fiscal year) 1984, and the column on the right that spent in FY 1983. Reproduced on page 46 is the actual page from the Deloitte audit.[14]

The comparable page from the audit for the fiscal year ending May 31, 1986 prepared by Laventhol and Horwath is reproduced on page 47. Again, the columns represent what these auditors confirmed as the money actually spent for various purposes in both FY 1986 and FY 1985.[15]

Several line item costs are particularly noteworthy. Television and satellite time cost Bakker in the $12 million range for both 1983 and 1984, but raced to $20 million in 1985 and $21 million in 1986. General operating expenses at Heritage were under $3 million in 1983, climbed to over $4 million the next year and jumped to $11 million by 1986. Printing and postage remained relatively constant through the years, under $4 million, but were still significant expenses. The money paid for total salaries exploded from $12 million in 1983 to over $31 million in 1986. Heritage USA was no Kool Aid stand, and these audits trace the money that Bakker was raising and spending each year to keep going.

Yet audits of this kind are not technically capable of monitoring management's financial stewardship of a company, and they cannot be read here as certifying that none of PTL's money was misspent. To the contrary, facts that later surfaced point to

HERITAGE VILLAGE CHURCH AND MISSIONARY FELLOWSHIP, INC. (NOTE 1)

COMBINED STATEMENTS OF REVENUES, EXPENSES AND
ACCUMULATED EXCESS OF REVENUES OVER EXPENSES
FOR THE FISCAL YEARS ENDED MAY 31, 1984 AND 1983

	NOTES	1984	1983
REVENUES:			
Contributions	1	$52,932,581	$48,236,282
Store sales and production revenues		3,518,703	1,675,073
Real estate sales	5	5,172,236	3,057,177
Lodging		1,780,879	531,311
Food service		1,532,420	1,301,246
Tuition, room, board, etc.		209,289	30,284
Other		1,149,885	657,643
Total revenues		66,295,993	55,489,016
COSTS AND EXPENSES:			
Cost of television and satellite time		12,957,641	12,256,713
Other television broadcast expenses		2,972,762	1,835,279
Cost of store sales and production revenues		1,885,949	1,365,875
Cost of real estate sales		4,089,395	2,495,222
Cost of food service sales		780,008	506,365
Salaries, wages, other payroll costs and contract labor		18,039,008	12,048,607
Bibles, books and other partner gifts		3,566,696	2,420,183
Missions and contributions		3,887,235	5,511,262
Periodic publications, printing and postage		3,537,201	3,364,271
Depreciation and amortization		4,184,802	2,609,957
Rental expense		865,734	590,985
Maintenance and repairs		1,005,366	817,069
Interest		2,366,667	1,366,321
Travel for guests and staff		1,187,379	680,665
Legal and professional fees		898,380	577,743
Telephone		740,036	288,298
Other operating expenses (no category in excess of $500,000)		4,110,196	2,763,498
Total expenses		67,074,455	51,496,313
EXCESS (DEFICIENCY) OF REVENUES OVER EXPENSES		(778,462)	3,990,703
ACCUMULATED EXCESS OF REVENUES OVER EXPENSES AT BEGINNING OF YEAR		25,534,756	21,544,053
ACCUMULATED EXCESS OF REVENUES OVER EXPENSES AT END OF YEAR		$24,756,294	$25,534,756

See notes to combined financial statements.

Auditors' statement of PTL/Heritage finances, year ending May 31, 1984

HERITAGE VILLAGE CHURCH AND MISSIONARY FELLOWSHIP, INC.
AND RELATED ORGANIZATIONS

COMBINED STATEMENTS OF REVENUES AND EXPENSES AND
ACCUMULATED EXCESS OF REVENUES OVER EXPENSES

YEARS ENDED MAY 31, 1986 AND 1985

	1986	1985
Revenues:		
Contributions (Note 5)	$ 43,691,001	$42,056,222
Amortization of deferred revenue (Note 5)	50,781,495	3,585,246
Food service, lodging and retail sales	17,598,781	10,290,061
Real estate sales	6,430,558	8,362,584
Satellite network time charges	4,787,347	4,136,597
Other	5,481,013	3,746,586
	128,770,195	72,177,296
Expenses:		
Cost of sales excluding salaries, wages and other labor costs:		
Food service, lodging and retail sales	7,904,921	3,961,154
Real estate sales	5,035,201	7,378,482
Satellite network time charges	3,527,509	2,096,233
Salaries, wages and other labor costs	31,639,440	27,218,163
Television time, missions and contributions	21,036,123	20,618,379
Bibles, books and other partner gifts	4,996,846	4,430,841
Depreciation and amortization	7,690,116	4,259,918
Interest (Note 6)	4,406,504	2,102,237
Professional and legal	1,395,359	812,600
Publications, printing and postage	3,976,482	3,478,113
Repairs and maintenance	1,865,209	2,154,961
Travel and hospitality for guests and staff	1,432,749	1,334,492
Utilities and telephone	2,728,542	2,053,079
Other operating expenses	11,287,205	7,808,818
	108,922,206	89,707,470
Excess (deficiency) of revenues over expenses	19,847,989	(17,530,174)
Accumulated excess of revenues over expenses, beginning of year (Note 12)	7,342,118	24,872,292
Accumulated excess of revenues over expenses, end of year	$ 27,190,107	$ 7,342,118

See notes to combined financial statements.

Auditors' statement of PTL/Heritage finances, year ending May 31, 1986 financial mismanagement at PTL and a discernible lack of spending discipline. That Jim and Tammy were overly carefree spenders should come as news to no one.

At the peak of PTL's building frenzy in 1986, Roe Messner's company was running a $300,000 a week payroll for its Heritage operation and had hundreds of workers on site. Because construction was proceeding so fast, Messner was running ahead of PTL's cash on hand to pay for it. His bills to Bakker at times showed arrearages in the millions. At one point, PTL owed him $10 million in outstanding bills. Charging 12 percent and, later, 10 percent interest on unpaid balances, Messner billed Bakker for $2 million just in interest and finance charges during the boom years on PTL's immense outstanding balances. Roe sometimes had to wait a few weeks or months for Jim to raise the money from his TV viewers, but he always did. As the builder frequently explained, Bakker always paid slow, but he always paid.[16]

Other facets of the ministry's costs of doing business unreflected on audit summary sheets include the thousands of dollars PTL had to pay for checks that it bounced. It eventually honored every one of them, but the banks charged $15.00 for every insufficient funds check and it mounted up.[17] This was just one more example of PTL spending money before the cash was in hand, of living by faith that the money would be there tomorrow.

And in terms of PTL expenditures not reflected on the spreadsheets the auditors saw, the $265,000 settlement promised Jessica Hahn belongs on the list. It is that money and the incident behind it that years later would trigger Bakker's humiliating resignation from PTL. The date that Hahn, a twenty-one-year-old church secretary from Long Island, came into Bakker's life was Saturday, December 6, 1980. That afternoon, at the Sheraton Sand Key Resort in Clearwater Beach, Florida, she and Bakker had sex. And from that moment until Bakker's astonishing public admission and resignation from the ministry in 1987, the incident ticked like a time bomb and cost PTL cash.[18]

While the total salaries of all PTL employees were reflected in the audits, the money paid Jim and Tammy in the form of salaries and bonuses was not broken out. Only later would it be revealed that Jim's salary alone went from $52,000 a year in 1978 to $313,000 in salary, $790,000 in bonuses and $132,000 in pension contributions in 1986.[19] Tammy received $99,900 in salary and $265,000 in bonuses in that same year.[20]

Jim Bakker in prison: I didn't keep my own checkbook. I was broke all the time.[21]

Many of their ardent supporters maintain to this day that the Bakkers were worth every penny of it, and that heads of corporations far smaller than PTL were paid more. Arnold Santjer told me that "nobody else could have put Heritage USA together. I don't know how he did it. You can't say enough good about Jim. He's a great man."[22]

Bakker had a national television ministry. He traveled in jets and rode in Mercedes. Billy Graham takes the bus from Minneapolis to his latest crusade? The PTL Board justified Bakker's hearty salary by the fact that he was killing himself with eighteen-hour days to build Heritage while shouldering the immense stress of producing and starring in one of the nation's most watched daily TV shows.

Tammy Faye Bakker: We don't get what Johnny Carson makes, and we work a lot harder than him.[23]

Still, it is tough to argue that some dollars from PTL's collection plate weren't spent on worldly possessions that most hometown ministers would never feel right about—like the $900,000 five-story, split-level parsonage on Charlotte's Lake Wylie with a fish-shaped swimming pool, three kitchens, and a 600-square-foot closet for Tammy's baubles.[24] It cost more to run PTL than it should have, but considering the millions that were pouring in each week in contributions it was more like the U.S. Air Force spending $500 for a wrench. Sure, there were examples of wasteful spending but the planes still flew. Bakker pulled it off. And the huge behemoth that was Heritage was flying high, too, with more contributions rolling in each day.

NOTES

1. Bakker, Appeal to U.S. Parole Commission, Exhibits 10–12 [certified audits of PTL], June 1, 1993.

2. *Id.*, Exhibit 12, sheet 2 [Laventhol & Horwath audit].

3. *Id.*

4. *Id.*

5. Trial transcript, *United States of America v. James O. Bakker,* Docket No. C-CR-88-205-1, U.S.D.C. (W.D., N.C.), September 13–14, 1989, vol. 5 at 1627, 1744.

6. Tammy Faye Bakker, letter to New Covenant Church Partners, August 1990, p. 4.

7. Trial transcript, *United States of America v. James O. Bakker,* Docket No. C-CR-88-205-1, U.S.D.C. (W.D., N.C.), September 19–25, 1989, vol. 7 at 865, 869.

8. Trial transcript, *United States of America v. James O. Bakker,* Docket No. C-CR-88-205-1, U.S.D.C. (W.D., N.C.), September 28–29, 1989, vol. 9 at 1649.

9. *Id.* at 1609.

10. Jim Bakker, interview by author, in Rochester, Minnesota, October 31, 1992.

11. Tidwell, *Anatomy of a Fraud* (John Wiley & Sons, Inc., New York, 1993) at 221.

12. Jim Bakker, interview by author, in Rochester, Minnesota, *supra,* n. 10.

13. Jim Bakker, interview by author, in Rochester, Minnesota, September 25, 1992.

14. Bakker, *supra,* n. 1 [Exhibit 10].

15. *Id.* at Exhibit 11.

16. Trial transcript, *supra,* n. 7 at 867, 878, 881–82, 908.

17. Trial transcript, *supra,* n. 5 at 1658, 1701.

18. Trial transcript, *United States of America v. James O. Bakker,* Docket No. C-CR-88-205-1, U.S.D.C. (W.D., N.C.), September 14–18, 1989, vol. 6 at 72–81; Rosenfeld, "Swaggart Tells of Deposition by Hahn; Falwell Calls for Cease-Fire in Preacher's Battle," *Washington Post,* March 27, 1987 at 1-D (Nexis printout); Wadler, "Breaking Faith, Two TV Idols Fall," *People,* May 18, 1987 at 81, 86.

19. *Id.,* trial transcript at 428.

20. *Id.* at 429.

21. Jim Bakker, interview by author, in Rochester, Minnesota, October 31, 1992.

22. Arnold and Dorothy Santjer, interview by author, in Bradenton, Florida, January 14, 1993.

23. Schmidt, "For Jim and Tammy Bakker, Excess Wiped Out a Rapid Climb to Success," *New York Times,* May 16, 1987 at 8-A, col. 2.

24. "Bakker's Parsonage Could Fetch $1 Million," UPI [wire story], March 12, 1988, AM Cycle.

Chapter 5

How Bakker Raised the Money

Jim Bakker had the Midas touch. He was surely not born to money—his father was a machinist at the Sealed Power Corporation piston ring factory in Muskegon, Michigan. Nor did the young Bakker ever pursue any formal education in business or finance. In fact, after graduating from high school in 1959, he attended Bible College in Minneapolis, where he met and fell in love with fellow student Tammy Faye LaValley. They soon married, and left school in 1961 to become traveling evangelists. Jim would preach and Tammy would sing and play the accordion. What they did know about money, their Pentecostal faith taught them: God provides it when you need it.

After more than two years criss-crossing North Carolina, West Virginia, and Tennessee preaching at week-long revivals and living with local pastors, Jim and Tammy began to yearn for a travel trailer of their own to haul behind their 1959 Cadillac. Their dream was to be able to park it in a campground and stay in it at night rather than in somebody else's guest bedroom. They began praying for a travel trailer at a 1963 revival meeting in the North Carolina mountains, and, sure enough, people in the small congregation were spontaneously moved to donate $1,500 to the young evangelists. With it they bought a twenty-eight-foot Holiday Rambler, complete with a bedroom, bathroom, and kitchen. They were ecstatic. It was God's first financial intervention in Jim and Tammy's lives.[1]

Then, a few days later, the trailer became unhitched from the car while driving along a Virginia highway and it careened into a utility pole. It was a total loss. At their revival meeting the next night, Tammy was so distraught over their misfortune that she couldn't sing. Instead, Jim recalls, she "laid her head on her accordion and began sobbing."[2] Then, all the people in the church started crying and praying over the trailer, and a short time later the dealer who sold it to them replaced it free with an even better model. The young evangelists saw that as another miracle, which they'd been taught to expect. It was one more rapid-fire example of God personally meeting any financial need or emergency that arose in their lives. Those, then, were their courses in finance and the subject couldn't have been clearer to them. As Jim later explained, "If you pray for a camper, tell God what color because if you don't you are asking God to do your shopping for you."[3]

Another time, Jim and Tammy were attending Sunday morning services on the road with only $25 to their names. But Jim felt God urging him "to empty my wallet into the collection plate" even though it was their only money for groceries. Jim remembers, "I put the whole $25 in . . . [and] began praying, 'Lord, have somebody ask us out to dinner today. And Lord, please remember, You'll have to take care of our groceries for a week, too.'"[4] Sure enough, on their way out of church, three different parishioners handed them cash, and another invited them to dinner and gave them enough money for two weeks worth of groceries. "We had trusted God," said Jim, "it was a lesson I would need to remember many times."[5]

In September, 1965, Jim and Tammy felt the call to leave the traveling ministry and move on to something new. They accepted positions at the Christian Broadcasting Network's Portsmouth, Virginia, TV station—WYAH, Channel 27, to host a one-half-hour children's puppet program. Jim was twenty-five years old; Tammy was twenty-three. Tammy was crouched behind the counter working the puppets and using different voices for the members of the puppet family. Jim was out in front playing straight man to the puppets. They agreed to take the kids' show because station owner Pat Robertson promised that Jim would be given the chance to develop a nighttime Christian TV talk show later.

Disgusted by the unwholesomeness of late night talk shows like Johnny Carson's *Tonight Show* and others, which Jim slammed for featuring "movie stars talking about their latest love affairs," an idea came to him. "Why can't Christians have a talk show, too?" he muttered to Tammy one night in their kitchen.[6]

On November 28, 1966, Bakker got his chance, when Robertson introduced Jim and his new show to Channel 27's viewers. Jim called it *The 700 Club,* for the seven hundred area stalwarts who each contributed ten dollars to keep the station afloat. Jim and Tammy didn't let them down, either, their program an enjoyable combination of interviews, music, and religion. Bakker hosted the show until November 8, 1972 when, Jim remembers, God told him to move on.[7]

The Bakkers relocated to Los Angeles in 1973, where Jim began producing and hosting a new talk show on station KBSA, Channel 46, in Santa Ana. He named it *The PTL Club.* But after six months on the air in Southern California, Jim and Tammy felt called to return to the East Coast. Jim remembers God telling him, "[h]ow much clearer do I have to make it [that God wanted Jim to move to Charlotte, North Carolina]?"[8]

Jim's specific mission in Charlotte was to evangelize the area through the medium of television. Like the cavalry, the Bakkers arrived in early 1974 with their PTL show and telegenic personalities, and turned the local religious TV station, WRET, Channel 36, into a phenomenal success. Nobody could draw viewers like Jim and Tammy, and PTL quickly became the hottest show on the station.

The PTL Club was so fantastically popular in Charlotte that Jim decided later in 1974 to see if it had national appeal. He converted an old downtown furniture store into a studio larger than WRET's and moved the show there. He bought time on nearly fifty different local stations across the country from New York to California. And then he turned on the one-hundred-pound RCA television cameras.[9]

Overnight, *The PTL Club* was a national hit. The show was

so fantastically popular that Bakker needed to move to an even larger studio two years later. In 1976, his viewers committed $200,000 to purchase twenty-five acres of prime real estate in Charlotte where Jim would erect a church with a 102-foot steeple. All the cameras and broadcast equipment were inside the church, and the steeple was actually a mammoth TV transmitting antenna.[10]

With the rest of the property, they constructed a miniature version of Colonial Williamsburg and called it Heritage Village. It soon resembled the campus of a small college, with traditional brick buildings and tree-lined walkways.

PTL was unstoppable. It repeatedly set broadcasting milestones and Jim and Tammy became national celebrities. In 1976, the show was carried by seventy local TV stations and twenty cable television systems. Donations from viewers soared to $5 million and then to $20 million in one year. By 1978, Bakker would pioneer satellite technology and beam his show to 1,300 cable systems covering the continent.[11]

PTL was growing so rapidly that it again needed more studio and broadcasting space, and on January 2, 1978, Jim broke ground at Heritage USA.

Bakker believed that God wanted to use his life for a special purpose—to raise money from the brethren for God's work. Early in his television ministry, Bakker explained: "From the moment that I stepped before a television camera at CBN, God began to anoint me to raise money for Christian television. I realized it the night I wept during the first *700 Club* telethon. Many times since then, God similarly anointed me."[12] Many would eventually share in the largess.

As Bakker's own view of religion developed over the years, the more he subscribed to the so-called "prosperity gospel" according to which believers not only count on God to provide the money for their basic human needs but also to enable them to live well. One of its corollaries is that the more a contributor gives, the more the Lord will bless them. PTL's pledge envelopes quoted Corinthians: "[the person who] soweth bountifully shall reap also bountifully."[13]

Oral Roberts, the dean of tent revivalists, became the best

known modern-day prophet of the doctrine in the 1950s when he started preaching that God wanted His people to prosper. That revelation was a lightning bolt to rank-and-file Pentecostals who for a hundred years had been told that God wanted them to live in poverty and deny themselves the pleasures of life while on earth.[14] Bakker enthusiastically embraced the new thinking.

> **Jim Bakker:** I've been criticized because of the quality of the [Grand] hotel. They say it's too nice. There are still people who believe in junk for Jesus, but I'm not one of them.[15]
>
> [On his newly remodeled dressing room with gold-plated plumbing fixtures and an $11,678 sauna that simulates ocean breezes and sunshine] I think Christians ought to have beautiful surroundings. I think my guests would be disappointed if I were dressing in some back room in a pile of junk.[16]
>
> [On the recent PTL purchase of a $375,000 Florida vacation condo for Jim and Tammy] I work all day, I fall into bed at night exhausted from my daily work. . . . He [God] wants to bless me. . . .[17]

Another important facet of the Pentecostal litany that provides further insight into Bakker's fund-raising at Heritage is the belief that God speaks to believers and personally directs their daily lives. Jim admits to numerous in-depth conversations with God. While on vacation in Arizona during his CBN days, for instance, Bakker remembers the Lord ended a lengthy discussion by telling Jim, "You must come away to talk with Me more often."[18]

Jim recalls that on November 8, 1972, as he was dressing for work, the Lord spoke to him. He later reported the exchange in his autobiography.

> **The Lord:** I want you to resign your job at CBN today.
>
> **Jim Bakker:** [resisting] I have an expensive house to continue paying for, and without a regular paycheck, I will quickly lose it as well as my automobile. God, I'll make a deal with You. You sell my house, and then I'll resign my job.
>
> **The Lord:** No. You must resign first, and then I will sell your house.[19]

Jim obeyed. He quit his job and put his home up for sale. There were no early buyers interested in it, however, and Jim and Tammy were getting desperate. Suddenly, one morning as Jim was shaving, God spoke again.

The Lord: Get your house ready. I have someone coming to buy it today.[20]

Sure enough, the house was sold that day to a couple from New Jersey who were out house hunting, got lost, and happened down Bakker's street "accidentally."[21]

All through the years, Jim listened for God to tell him what to do. And God did. That is the Pentecostal way. Examples abound of God directing Jim's major life decisions, and plenty of minor ones too. It is an ongoing dialogue. God tells Jim to take a vacation [to the Florida Keys after leaving CBN because Jim would be working so hard later that it would be his last vacation until Jesus returned to Earth];[22] to dispose of his trailer [God said, "I don't want you to sell that trailer, I want you to give it away." And then He told Jim who to give it to];[23] and to let Him decide how to raise money at PTL. [Jim, dejected during a break in a telethon that was not bringing in enough contributions, heard God speak: "Believe me for 300 partners at $10 a month." Jim: "We just made it by the skin of our teeth last time." The Lord: "Do you trust Me?" Jim: "Yes." The Lord: "Get on my shoulders, then, and I'll ride you across. I don't want you to ask for any more money. You let me do it."[24] And within thirty minutes, five hundred viewers phoned in their contributions.][25]

At times, God would tell Jim to write checks on ministry accounts when there was not enough money in the bank to cover them. One $20,000 check which God ordered Jim to write on a Friday on an empty account was fully covered by Monday after an unexpected surge of donations over the weekend. The next Friday, the same thing happened. Then again, again, and again over the months and years ahead. As Bakker explained, "with God's mighty help, we faced every bill individually and paid it as the Holy Spirit directed, no matter what the amount. God never failed us."[26]

Of all the times God spoke to Jim, none turned out to be more pivotal than the time in 1983 He gave Jim the idea for the ultimate PTL money raising plan. "God gave me the concept of . . . the Lifetime Partners,"[27] Bakker acknowledged.

So, as Bakker went about financing his theme park and TV ministry and raising the money to operate both, he was locked in to what by that time were articles of faith for him—the beliefs that God would surely meet any financial need or request, that if necessary God would intervene with a miracle to accomplish the financially impossible, and that everyone along the chain of believers who were part of it should prosper themselves.

Bakker raised the money for PTL in a variety of ways. Like at most churches, collection plates would be passed at the conclusion of services at Heritage on Sundays among the 3,000 people who would typically attend. Thousands more jammed the Heritage broadcast studios each day during the week for his television program and they had an opportunity to make offerings as well. In fact, all of the millions of people who visited Heritage each year and those who remained at home and watched on TV could make whatever contributions they wished to support the ministry. According to *Charlotte Observer* reporter Charles Shepard, 405,000 people around the country contributed $50 million to PTL in 1981 alone, mostly in faithful monthly donations of fifteen or twenty dollars.[28]

Jean Albuquerque, a former PTL greeter who by 1987 had become disenchanted with Bakker, told the *Los Angeles Times* that while older women would often appear at the studio with gifts in hand for Bakker, "he didn't have time for them."[29] She remembered specifically "two spinsters in gingham dresses, hicks. No one would see them, so they asked me, 'Will you come out to our car? We want to give something to the ministry.' So I walked out, they lifted the trunk and there were eleven bars of silver! People gave us Hummels, furs, diamonds. . . ."[30]

Beyond that, specific purpose contributions were aggressively solicited on the television program. Many people who caught glimpses of Jim and Tammy on the air found their fundraising appeals to be incessant and unseemly. Others responded to them with relish. And hard cash. So much money poured in from hundreds of thousands of television viewers across the country that the U.S. Postal Service gave Bakker his own zip code in North Carolina (28279).[31]

PTL pulled in $416,000 a month in income in the late 1970s. By 1986, that figure was $10 million a month.[32]

Tight security guarded a small counting room inside the pyramid-shaped building on the Heritage grounds that housed Bakker's executive offices. Heavy, bulging canvas sacks of mail would be delivered daily and five trusted employees would cut open each envelope and remove the offering. By the time the television show hit its stride in the mid 1980s, more than $200,000 a day was being removed from those envelopes.[33] At Bakker's zenith just before his resignation, he told me that he was bringing in more than $3 million a week.[34] The routine never varied and at 3:00 P.M. sharp every day, an armored car pulled up to the side of the counting building and hauled that day's take to the bank.

To accelerate fund-raising, Bakker kept a live television camera on the grounds at Heritage so viewers could see the progress that was being made on the construction of different buildings. He would sometimes ask for help with specific buildings or projects, like Kevin's House. Little Kevin himself would appear with Bakker on the TV program, his crippled body a very emotional sight. It opened up the hearts of more than 40,000 viewers who responded with contributions in excess of $3 million to build the home for Kevin.[35]

But by far the most successful fund-raising appeals Bakker ever launched were his lifetime partnership programs which he offered on television and through the mails from 1984 through 1987. In total, there were eleven different partnership packages that could be obtained, most of them including several nights of free lodging each year at Heritage. The response from people

all over the country was phenomenal. Bakker offered partnerships in the Grand Hotel for $1,000 which entitled purchasers
to stay at the park's flagship hotel three nights and four days
every year for the rest of their lives. He issued 66,683 of those
partnerships for $66.9 million.[36]

After that, he announced a similar lifetime partnership
program in the new high-rise Towers Hotel which would also
entitle takers to three nights and four days' free lodging each
year for the rest of their lives in return for a $1,000 donation.
Bakker issued 68,755 of those and raised $74.2 million in the
process.[37] And toward the end, the Victory Warrior lifetime
partnership plan was offered which included three nights and
four days' lodging at the partner's choice of the Towers Hotel,
the Grand, the Heritage Inn, the Bunkhouse, or a PTL campground. Free admission to activities and events at Heritage was
thrown in for the $1,000 price, and Bakker raised $36,238,315
through 35,984 Victory Warrior partnerships.[38]

When discussing the Victory Warrior program with his TV
viewers, Bakker explained: "The Lord said to me . . . Jim, I'm
just as tired of these bills as you are."[39] Bakker was referring to
the enormous costs of operating Heritage USA and the debt
that was rapidly accumulating. In fact, it was later revealed that
PTL was in acute financial distress at the time the partnerships
were sold.

Even as Heritage was sinking into a debt in the tens of
millions of dollars and it owed millions to creditors for
outstanding unpaid bills, the Bakkers never doubted God
would take care of it just as he did when Tammy was pumping
her accordion in West Virginia. Jim and Tammy would sit there
and pray on television that the financial needs of PTL be met.
There was often urgency to it and they would tell viewers that
they needed $500,000 or $750,000 by the end of the month to
pay for television time or they'd go off the air, or for money to
avert some other crisis. And the envelopes would roll in from
around the country and they'd always make it. It worked.

It was also controversial. The *Charlotte Observer,* which
spent more than ten years printing stories that Bakker was a

phony, ran a series of articles as early as January, 1979, reporting that out of all the $281,000 that was contributed by viewers for the Korean PTL Mission, not one dollar of it was ever sent to Korea. And beyond that, of the $56,000 that was donated for a transmitter in Cyprus, the paper claimed that the transmitter was never constructed and all of the money was spent for other purposes. The newspaper charged that the donations earmarked by viewers for those specific purposes were used by Bakker to pay rapidly accumulating PTL bills in America. In that early series of articles, the paper described PTL as debt-ridden and mired in financial and management crises.[40]

In response to those published reports, the Federal Communications Commission in 1978 launched a three-year investigation into PTL's fund-raising. The agency sought to determine if Bakker had committed fraud by wire or violated any other FCC rules, including those prohibiting misleading or deceptive fund-raising, or whether he in any way posed a threat to the public. The FCC investigation was exhaustive and it subpoenaed PTL's fund-raising records and videotapes of programs on which Bakker had asked for donations. The agency conducted hearings in Washington and even subjected Bakker himself to nine days on the witness stand being questioned by four tough FCC attorneys.[41]

In a memo to their agency bosses, the staff attorneys who had been dogging Bakker summarized the evangelist's testimony on the witness stand. They calculated that his testimony under oath had been contradicted by PTL documents eighteen times, by the sworn testimony of former PTL officers twenty-seven times, and by his own testimony and videotaped statements on the air thirty-six times.[42]

The Commission's investigation ended in December 1982, however, when a bare 4–3 majority on the FCC voted not to proceed further against Bakker. The beleaguered evangelist was allowed to transfer his ownership of a Canton, Ohio, TV station and in that way move outside the FCC's criminal jurisdiction. The FCC only has authority over the owners of TV stations—not stars who perform on them.

The three commissioners who dissented felt that Bakker's PTL fund-raising remained "under a cloud of serious misconduct"[43] and that the FCC should have dug deeper to see if he should be prosecuted.

The majority disagreed, however, and instead forwarded a report of the Commission's lengthy Bakker investigation to the Justice Department for any action it wished to take. Soon after, Justice declined to prosecute Bakker, concluding that there was insufficient evidence that PTL misused solicited funds.[44]

Ben Armstrong, the executive director of the National Religious Broadcasters Association, saw the decision as a complete vindication of Bakker. "If there were a serious problem, then the FCC would have taken it up," he told the press.[45]

But only four years later, the same Justice Department turned around and went after Bakker with a meat cleaver for the same kind of fund-raising it had signed off on earlier. One difference, of course, was that by 1987 Bakker was wounded by the Hahn scandal and didn't have his TV show with which to fight back.

NOTES

1. Bakker, *Move That Mountain* (Logos International, Plainfield, N.J., 1976) at 43–46.

2. *Id.* at 45.

3. FitzGerald, "Reflections," *New Yorker*, April 23, 1990 at 73.

4. Bakker, *supra*, n. 1 at 28.

5. *Id.* at 29.

6. *Id.* at 51.

7. *Id.* at 106.

8. *Id.* at 138–47; trial transcript, *United States of America v. James O. Bakker,* Docket C-CR-88-205-1; U.S.D.C. (W.D., N.C.), September 28–29, 1989, vol. 9 at 1606.

9. Trial transcript, *supra*, n. 8 at 1607–8; Bakker, *supra*, n. 1 at 141–42, 147–48, 157, 161–62.

10. Trial transcript, *supra*, n. 8 at 1607–9; Yancey, "The Ironies and Impact of PTL," *Christianity Today*, September 21, 1979 at 30; Bakker, *supra*, n. 1 at 169–72.

11. Bakker, *supra*, n. 1 at 182; Tidwell, *Anatomy of a Fraud* (John Wiley & Sons, Inc., New York, 1993) at 25.

12. Bakker, *supra*, n. 1 at 63.

13. Daniel, "Video Evangelism; Bakker Defends 'Praise the Lord' TV Club; His Critics Say PTL means "Pass the Loot'," UPI [wire service dispatch], May 25, 1983, BC Cycle.

14. Reinhold, "Pentecostals' Split Exposed by Bakker Affair," *New York Times,* March 28, 1987 at 7-A, cols. 1–2.

15. Preston, "Prosecutors Wrap Up Case Against Bakker," UPI [wire story], September 20, 1989, BC Cycle.

16. "Regional News," UPI [wire story], February 11, 1983, AM Cycle.

17. *Id.*

18. Bakker, *supra,* n. 1 at 103.

19. *Id.* at 106.

20. *Id.* at 109.

21. *Id.* at 110.

22. *Id.* at 112.

23. *Id.* at 159.

24. *Id.* at 146–47.

25. *Id.* at 147.

26. *Id.* at 154–55.

27. Trial transcript, *supra,* n. 8 at 1625.

28. Shepard, *Forgiven* (Atlantic Monthly Press, New York, 1989) at 220.

29. Isikoff and Harris, "PTL Fund Raising—A Tangled Saga," *Washington Post,* May 23, 1987 at 1-A (Nexis printout).

30. *Id.*

31. Trial transcript, *United States of America v. James O. Bakker,* Docket C-CR-88-205-1, U.S.D.C. (W.D., N.C.), August 28, 1989, vol. 4 at 1317.

32. Bakker, *Appeal to U.S. Parole Commission,* Exhibit 11 [Laventhol & Horwath audit], June 1, 1993 at 3; Bakker, *Move That Mountain, supra,* n. 1 at 182.

33. Isikoff and Harris, *supra,* n. 29.

34. Trial transcript, *United States of America v. James O. Bakker,* Docket No. C-CR-88-205-1, U.S.D.C. (W.D., N.C.), September 28–29, 1989, vol. 9 at 1649.

35. Dortch, *Integrity* (New Leaf Press, Green Forest, Ark., 1991) at 62–63; Tidwell, *Anatomy of a Fraud* (John Wiley & Sons, Inc., New York, 1993) at 202; Bakker, *Appeal to U.S. Parole Commission,* vol. II [photographs and Lifetime Partner newsletters], June 1, 1993 at 73.

36. Trial transcript, *United States of America v. James O. Bakker,* Docket No. C-CR-88-205-1, U.S.D.C. (W.D., N.C.), September 19–25, 1989, vol. 7 at 568.

37. *Id.* at 566, 569.

38. *Id.* at 573–574.

39. Shepard and Wright, "Jury Sees Bakker on Video, Prosecution Argues He Lied on TV," *Charlotte Observer,* September 20, 1989 at 1-A (Westlaw printout).

40. Cowan and Gaillard, "PTL Donations for Foreign Missions Used at Home," *Charlotte Observer,* January 18, 1979, at 1-A, col. 4.

41. *In Re PTL of Heritage Village Church & Missionary Fellowship, Inc., Licensee of Station WJAN-TV, Canton, Ohio,* 71 F.C.C. 2d 324 (1979);

Albert, "Federal Investigation of Video Evangelism: The FCC Probes the PTL Club," *Oklahoma Law Review* 33 at 782, 783–86 (Fall 1980).

42. Malone, "Bush and the Bakker Connection; On His Way to the White House, the Vice President Wooed the Preacher," *Washington Post,* December 18, 1988, p. 1-C (Nexis printout).

43. "FCC Ends Its Investigation of the PTL Organization," *Christianity Today,* January 21, 1983 at 24.

44. Malone, *supra,* n. 42.

45. "FCC Ends Its Investigation of the PTL Organization," *supra,* n. 43.

Chapter 6

Bakker's World Collapses and *The PTL Club* Becomes a Soap Opera

The slide Jim Bakker took from the pinnacle of televangelism to the defense table in federal court was painful and tortured. Ironically, the medium that made him—television—chronicled every inch of it for the nation to see.

January 2, 1987 to March 19, 1987

1987 began as a banner year at Heritage with Bakker pushing his ministry to dizzying new heights and more millions of people around the country supporting him than ever before. Bakker marked his forty-seventh birthday on January 2, 1987 with a gala ground-breaking ceremony at Heritage. There, with hundreds of partners and employees cheering him on, he dug a spade into the ground to symbolically begin construction on what the blueprints showed would be the spectacular crown jewel of his life and ministry—the Crystal Palace Ministry Center, the largest church in the United States.

In remarks to the crowd, Bakker explained that the new superstructure would seat up to 30,000 people and be the "world's largest church." It would span more than 1.25 million square feet; its length would exceed three football fields. Once built, it would eclipse by 300 feet the Basilica of St. Peter in Rome, listed in the *Guinness Book of World Records* as the world's largest church.[1] The gigantic iron and glass structure was modeled after London's historic Crystal Palace, an architectural wonder built in 1851. It was Bakker's latest obsession, and he was confident enough that millions of additional visitors would be attracted to it that he drew up plans for a new six-lane road through the Heritage grounds to handle the traffic.[2] It would cost $100 million and take three years to build, and his plan was to sell time share condominiums in the edifice to raise the money. It would be the most ambitious project of his lifetime and, characteristically, he was driven to begin it before some other structures, including the Towers Hotel, were finished.

But almost as soon as Bakker's birthday candles went cold, the rest of the year turned to unrelenting agony. That same month, Tammy was admitted to the Eisenhower Medical Center in Palm Springs, California, where she was diagnosed with not only pneumonia but drug dependency. Doctors confirmed she was addicted to Atavan and nasal spray.[3] "I saw demons coming at me. I saw hell. It was like Satan was trying to kill me,"[4] she said. From what twelve-year-old son Jamie revealed, the demons took the form of large cats flying along on the wings of her airplane.[5] Her doctors ordered detoxification.

On January 26, she entered the Betty Ford Center, where so many other celebrities have beaten drugs and alcohol in the past. But for Tammy the place was too confining. After one night, she checked out but did agree to continue treatment on an out-patient basis. She would return to Betty Ford from her home in Palm Springs each night for four hours of counseling and treatment. Jim, David Taggart, and Vi Azvedo participated with her—standard procedure in drug programs of that kind.[6]

By the end of January, then, Jim was anchored in Palm Springs and left the day-to-day operation of Heritage to his second in command, PTL Vice President Richard Dortch. Pastor Dortch took over hosting the daily television program in Jim's absence and Bakker was essentially incommunicado during the six weeks he was in Palm Springs with his wife. He would call Heritage several times a week to monitor developments, but he made a commitment to put his family first and his work second for the first time in his life.

True to form, though, in the free time that he had each day, he scoured Southern California for vacant land on which to build a Heritage USA West. He actually took architects and contractors with him as he conceptualized for them his plans for a sprawling new Christian retreat center to accommodate people on the West Coast who couldn't travel all the way to North Carolina.

Back at headquarters, the PTL money pump was sputtering. A check for $1 million dated January 8, 1987, and given to Roe Messner toward the $10 million Bakker owed him for past construction, bounced like a beach ball. PTL was able to cover it within the month, yet there were definitely signs of stress on the ministry's accounts. But in February, with Tammy nearing the end of her Betty Ford program, the Bakkers decided to move up in Palm Springs and bought the $600,000 Spanish-style Florsheim estate on fashionable Palm Canyon Drive.[7] Government prosecutors would later criticize Bakker for accepting $250,000 in bonuses from PTL in order to swing the deal on the home at a time when the ministry was in increasing financial trouble, but the flap over his desert digs was nothing compared to the undertow that was about to seize him.

Against the backdrop of Tammy's drug dependency being front page national news in early 1987, and with Jim Bakker sitting in the middle of the desert 3,000 miles from his broadcast studio with its access to his millions of supporters, a series of events unfolded in rapid-fire order that toppled him within a month.

On February 23, the *Charlotte Observer* telephoned Richard Dortch requesting an interview. Reporters told him they knew about the Jessica Hahn episode and wanted to give him a chance to respond. No interview was granted.[8]

On the March 6 *PTL Club* broadcast, with Pastor Dortch as host, fellow charismatic Pentecostal Oral Roberts told viewers that God had assured him that "never again will Satan be able to harm PTL."[9]

On the March 11 broadcast, Jim appeared on tape from California and sounded a warning that people who attacked him would fail. Said Bakker: "[b]ecause when you touch God's anointed . . . you're not touching that individual. The Bible says you are touching God."[10] That would be his last broadcast as head of PTL.

On March 12, Jimmy Swaggart dramatically intensified his campaign within the Assemblies of God to have Bakker investigated and defrocked for his tryst with Jessica Hahn. Swaggart just didn't keep it in-house, either, and put on a full-court press against Bakker by getting the word to newspaper reporters and other Pentecostal leaders. Jerry Falwell, who at the time was more or less minding his own business running the *Old Time Gospel Hour* in Lynchburg, Virginia and heading up the Moral Majority, learned of the Hahn episode. Whether Falwell's true motive was to confront and in that way begin the process of rehabilitating his brother Bakker or whether he saw it as a golden opportunity to steal PTL by befriending Bakker and offering to protect PTL from a hostile takeover by Swaggart, Falwell had his jet fueled and ordered his pilot to make preparations for a flight to Palm Springs.[11] Falwell instigated and arranged an urgent meeting between himself and Bakker, telling Dortch that Falwell's help was desperately needed to control the damage to PTL that news of the Hahn episode would surely soon cause. Dortch agreed to make the trip as a guest on Falwell's plane.

On March 17, Jerry Falwell, attorney Norman Grutman, *Old Time Gospel Hour* CEO and later Moral Majority head Jerry Nims, and Falwell aide Mark DeMoss arrived at Maxim's Hotel in Palm Springs to meet Bakker and Dortch. In a private suite, Bakker and Falwell first met alone for an hour.[12]

Jim Bakker in prison: Norman Roy Grutman, Falwell's attorney, deceived me. And it was Falwell, through Jerry Nims, who prompted the grand jury investigation.

Dortch will tell you what Falwell did. Falwell told me to step aside for thirty days to weather the storm, then he and Billy Graham would go to Swaggart to get him off my back. There was never any doubt about it—it was always meant to be temporary.

Falwell assured me that he would never go to PTL. I turned the ministry over to Pastor Dortch.

But within twenty-four hours, Falwell returned to Heritage. I saw him say on television: "I don't know anything about a hostile takeover of Bakker's ministry." That was on the nightly news or on *Nightline*. When I saw it, I knew I had been betrayed. [That was because the hostile takeover in the works was Swaggart taking over PTL, the whole reason Bakker asked Falwell to step in.]

One day I had 3,000 employees, the next day I didn't even have a typewriter.[13]

On March 18, the full PTL board of directors met on the grounds at Heritage, with Richard Dortch presiding and Jim Bakker on the speakerphone from Palm Springs. According to the minutes of the meeting, Pastor Dortch reported to the speechless board members that the *Charlotte Observer* was preparing to publish an article on Bakker's liaison with Hahn. He told them that the revelation would cause "irreparable harm" to the ministry unless the problem were somehow confronted, and he explained to them that Bakker had decided to immediately resign and appoint Jerry Falwell as president of PTL. Only in that way could they diminish the impact of the *Observer*'s story and at the same time make sure that Jimmy Swaggart didn't somehow seize PTL for himself in its moment of weakness. Bakker's board approved the plan. Then, going around the table, each of them resigned as well.[14]

Jerry Falwell joined the meeting by phone from Lynchburg and exercised his right to hand-pick a new board. Named were former Reagan cabinet member and Secretary of the Interior James Watt, evangelist Rex Humbard, the Reverend Bailey Smith, the former president of the Southern Baptist Convention, and Jerry Nims. Pastor Dortch was also asked to serve on the new board.[15]

On March 19, Bakker announced to the public that he was resigning. In a statement which he read to reporters from his home in Palm Springs, he said, "Tammy Faye and I and our ministries have been subjected to constant harassment and pressures by various groups and forces whose objective has been to undermine and to destroy us."[16] He stated that the stress lately had been overwhelming and "more than we can bear."[17] He resigned not only the presidency of PTL, but turned in his credentials from the Assemblies of God which punishes any of its ministers found to have engaged in the kind of moral misconduct alleged against Bakker. He said, "I am not able to muster the resources needed to combat a new wave of attack that I have learned is about to be launched against us by the *Charlotte Observer,* which has attacked us incessantly for the past 12 years."[18]

He maintained absolutely that he never sexually assaulted anyone, and that the Hahn story was being trumped up to defame and vilify him. He added, "I sorrowfully acknowledge that seven years ago, in an isolated incident, I was wickedly manipulated by treacherous former friends and then-colleagues who victimized me with the aid of a female confederate. They conspired to betray me into a sexual encounter at a time of great stress in my marital life."[19]

[Hahn remembered it otherwise in a signed statement sent to church elders: the encounter lasted for "what seemed like an hour and a half"[20] with Bakker forcing her to engage in oral sex and intercourse. She claimed "I tried to get him off of me. He couldn't get enough. He had to find new things to do."[21] Bakker's admission of marital stress apparently confirmed the rumors that Tammy for a time had some affection for shaggy-bearded country singer Gary Paxton who produced the Oldies classic, "Monster Mash." Nobody knew for sure.[22]]

Tammy Faye Bakker: In America and all over, we are constantly bombarded with Satan's sexual traps.[23]

Bakker told the reporters, however, "I have sought and gratefully received the loving forgiveness of our Savior who forgives us of our sins. I have told Tammy everything and Tammy, of course, has forgiven me, and our love for each other is greater and stronger than it has ever been."[24]

Bakker acknowledged that the episode had degenerated to blackmail and that in order to spare PTL and his family "money was paid . . . to appease these persons who were determined to destroy this ministry. I now, in hindsight, realize payment should have been resisted, and we ought to have exposed the blackmailers to the penalties of the law. I'm truly sorry for all this. . . ."[25]

At the end of his remarks, he flabbergasted reporters by revealing, "I've asked my friend, Jerry Falwell, to help me in my crisis [by assuming the Presidency of PTL]."[26] In parting, Bakker expressed optimism that "God has a redemptive plan for PTL and for Jim and Tammy."[27]

The news rocked the nation, and was a blockbuster story. The *Charlotte Observer* sold more papers that day featuring its extensive reporting of the Bakker resignation than any other issue in its history, save the one that reported the death of Elvis Presley.[28] Ted Koppel interviewed Jim and Tammy on *Nightline* twice in the next two months and drew more viewers to his program than at any time in its history, including its first year on the air during the Iran hostage crisis.[29]

March 19, 1987 to August 17, 1987

Jim's resignation was a savvy move, really. With it, he checkmated Swaggart, put the best possible face on the Hahn story by breaking it himself, and protected PTL by appointing a national religious figure of considerable stature to oversee it in his absence. But the kindly, mellifluous-toned peacekeeper from Lynchburg metamorphosed into the biggest nightmare in Bakker's life. The two soon began warring, using the weapon they knew best—television.

Within a few weeks, Bakker contacted Falwell and told him that he was ready to return to PTL. Falwell balked. Bakker turned to Ted Koppel. In an hour-long live interview, in May 1987, Bakker told the *Nightline* audience that Falwell had tricked him out of his ministry. "I made a terrible mistake,"[30] Bakker reflected. He explained that Falwell and Grutman had promised him that whenever he wanted to return to PTL as its president, he simply had to ask.

Jim Bakker in prison: Having Jerry Falwell help you is like having someone throw you a life preserver and hitting you on the head with it.[31]

Falwell was livid. He immediately scheduled a press conference and railed at Bakker for ninety minutes live on CNN. Falwell said that Bakker "either has a terrible memory, or is very dishonest, or he is emotionally ill."[32] He chortled that, "to say that Jerry Falwell . . . stole PTL . . . is like accusing someone of stealing the Titanic just after it hit the iceberg."[33] He said regardless of any earlier agreement, all bets were off because he had uncovered wrongdoing on Bakker's part "that made my blood boil."[34]

What Falwell had learned sitting in Bakker's chair, he told reporters, was that PTL funds had been used to silence Jessica Hahn, that the Hahn encounter was grislier than Bakker had let on, and that "men . . . have told me of . . . [Bakker's] homosexual advances."[35] Falwell explained that his own accountants had gone through PTL's books, uncovering steep salaries and bonuses that Jim and Tammy had been receiving as well as the money spent on their regal lifestyles. "I see the greed. I see the self-centeredness. I see the avarice that brought them down,"[36] bellowed the Baptist.

What Falwell's bean counters discovered was that Jim and Tammy, who had told television viewers that they earned only "a living salary" at PTL, were paid $1.6 million in 1986. The deeper that auditors dug, the more they would learn, too, but the tip of the iceberg was exposed. The nation recoiled. Enterprising artists captured the prevailing mood with nearly a dozen songs, like Ray Stevens' country chart topper, "Would Jesus Wear a Rolex on His Television Show?" Another country and western hit was titled "The PTL Has Gone to Hell, So Where Do I Send the Money?" by a new group calling itself Reverend Needmore and the Almighty Bucks. Falwell was bitter. "I don't remember a time when people were having such a heyday ridiculing all that is Christian,"[37] he told followers.

To make his point, Falwell escorted reporters on tours of Jim and Tammy's private penthouse in the Grand Hotel, walking them through Tammy's fifty-foot closet and showing them gold-plated bathroom fixtures. He noted that it wasn't only the Bakkers who were living well during their tenure at PTL, their dogs had it pretty good, too, living in an air-conditioned doghouse. "It is my personal opinion, and I say this with great pain, but I do not believe that Jim Bakker is fit for the ministry of the Gospel,"[38] he decreed.

A *New York Times* reporter found the Bakkers on Melvin Belli's yacht in San Francisco harbor and sought their reaction to all the disclosures.

> **Tammy Fay Bakker:** Jim stayed on the couch for weeks and curled up in a ball listening to Bible tapes.[39]
>
> **Jim Bakker:** I hurt every day. I pray almost daily to die. I would really like to die. I wish I were dead. I would have committed suicide had it not been for God.[40]

Albeit briefly and uncharacteristically, Bakker was so infuriated by Falwell's attack that he began to fight back. He told Belli to do everything necessary to recapture PTL. Jim himself devoted the next five months of his life to regaining the PTL helm and the ministry he built from twigs. But Falwell and Bakker's other adversaries met fire with fire and fought him for control of PTL. Their public sniping became known as the 1987 "Holy Wars," and the press reveled for months in reporting each skirmish.

One can get a taste from an October 1987 edition of *Nightline* alone.

> **Ted Koppel:** I mean, what kind of a role model do you think you are?
>
> **Jim Bakker:** Well, I hope I haven't inflicted myself on the American people, and the only role model I hope I could be is a sinner saved by grace, and that there's hope for me and there's hope for everyone else. That's—
>
> **Ted Koppel:** That's fine, but why should you be preaching anything? *** I'm saying, here is a man who certainly mismanaged funds—
>
> **Jim Bakker:** There is no money missing at PTL. This was a hoax perpetrated by Jerry Falwell, the $92 million missing and all these other things. It's just simply not so.[41]

On May 6, 1987, the elders in the Assemblies of God accepted Swaggart's version of Bakker's moral missteps over the years and defrocked him. Swaggart was breathing fire, referring to Bakker's conduct as "the most filthy, the most rotten, the most diabolical, the most hellish of sin."[42] "God deliver us from these pompadour boys, hair done, nails done, fresh from the beauty shop, preaching the gospel,"[43] thundered the Louisiana evangelist.

In June, Belli arrived in Charlotte and vowed to oust Falwell from PTL, saying, "It's good to be on the side of the Lord."[44]

That same day, a hearty group of PTL partners opened a "Bring Bakker Back" headquarters in the Fort Mill Holiday Inn, two miles from Heritage. Headed by Vicky Goodman Meadows and endorsed by Jim Bakker himself, the group set to work at once to mobilize hundreds of thousands of partners and PTL contributors to demand Bakker's reinstatement. Bakker's daughter, teen-age Tammy Sue, would work out of the office each week.[45]

On June 10, Jim and Tammy returned to their PTL parsonage in Charlotte after several weeks of seclusion in Palm Springs. They were mobbed by supporters when they visited the Heritage grounds, and Jim promised the faithful that he had returned to reclaim it.[46]

On June 12, fearing that Bakker was dead serious about retaking the ministry and that a majority of PTL's contributors might back him up on it, Falwell's PTL board thrust the ministry and Heritage USA into bankruptcy. Undeniably, PTL owed creditors over $70 million, providing legal justification for the move, but the practical effect and real purpose was to place PTL out of Bakker's reach. From that point on, the ministry and Heritage were essentially wards of the court and nothing could be done at PTL without the approval of the bankruptcy judge in Charlotte who, by the way, proved to be quite adverse to Jim Bakker. The legal significance of the bankruptcy was that it absolutely forestalled any storming of the gates by Jim Bakker or the partners whose $1,000 contributions had built the place.[47]

On June 22, Falwell defended his move, arguing that letting Jim Bakker back would be "like handing the asylum over to the inmates."[48] He emphasized, "I don't think for one minute he thinks we're going to let the fox back in the hen house."[49]

Jim Bakker in prison: Jimmy Carter called Falwell a liar at page five of his memoirs.[50]

Also on that day, Melvin Belli returned to California from strategy sessions with Bakker in North Carolina, and said that singer Pat Boone should be put in charge of PTL rather than some bankruptcy judge. Falwell rejected the idea out of hand. Boone, a born-again Christian and frequent guest on the *PTL Club,* had criticized the television programs coming out of Heritage since Falwell took over the organization, saying that the shows were boring and had driven viewers away. Falwell retorted that the old TV show was gone forever and, beyond that, he wasn't going to permit any more Hollywood sideshows or monkey business.[51]

On June 23, Jim and Tammy bowed to Falwell's ultimatum that they vacate the million dollar PTL parsonage because they were no longer a part of PTL. The Bakkers told supporters that they would move to a mountain chalet formerly owned by Roe Messner in Gatlinburg, Tennessee, five hours from Charlotte by car. At the same time, Jim and Tammy said they hoped that their controversy with Falwell could be mediated and that their return to PTL would be expedited.[52]

On June 25, and continuing for three days, Jessica Hahn made the rounds of all the major television talk shows. On Phil Donahue, she cried, "I want this over with. It's caused me enough pain."[53]

On June 27, the Bakkers arrived in Tennessee and the townspeople welcomed them with open arms.

On June 30, Jim and Tammy appeared before the Gatlinburg Chamber of Commerce and were asked to sign a replica of the U.S. Constitution. The Happy Goodmans and ten other Bakker supporters met with them that day in Tennessee to chart activities for the Bring Bakker Back Club. Melvin Belli told reporters the Bakkers had gone to the mountaintop and would give up all worldly possessions when they returned to their ministry.[54]

Also on June 30, Pat Boone cautioned reporters that they shouldn't count Jim Bakker out. Boone told them Bakker could in fact get up off the canvas, and that Jim was still a viable Christian leader.[55]

On July 2, Jim Bakker appeared on *Good Morning America* and defended his lifestyle. With the clearest possible reference to the prosperity gospel that had been a foundation of his ministry, he asked Charles Gibson, "What do we do with the scripture that says Christ wanted us to prosper?"[56] When asked about his efforts to wrest control of PTL from Jerry Falwell, he said, "We will vigorously defend ourselves. And this is what Mr. Belli is going to be doing."[57] Tellingly, Bakker shrugged off questions about the IRS and Justice Department probes that were under way regarding his tenure at PTL. "History will prove the Bakkers are honest people,"[58] he said, shaking his head.

On July 7, Melvin Belli excoriated Jerry Falwell, claiming he had not only stolen PTL, but was now milking it for all it was worth. Falwell responded from the other end of the continent by characterizing Belli's remarks as senseless babble. The Baptist claimed that Belli was blind to the facts of the PTL case and that his eighty-year-old mind was fading.[59]

On July 12, Jim and Tammy were in San Francisco for Belli's rowdy, wine-flowing eightieth birthday bash. In recognition of the lawyer's clout, city officials actually closed off an entire city block for the loud and raucous party, which featured a scantily clad young woman diving out of a huge birthday cake to greet the hundreds of partiers. The Bakkers were there with a ten-person entourage and gave Belli an autographed Bible as a birthday present. Back in Charlotte, new PTL pastor Sam Johnson lambasted the Bakkers for attending such a steamy booze-fest with the warning that "the Bible says don't throw your pearls before swine."[60] The Bakkers responded that Belli wasn't swine, that instead "This man is a living legend. We are happy to be here."[61]

On July 24, Jerry Falwell complained that while he was on the PTL show trying to raise money to keep Heritage afloat, 1,800 Jim Bakker supporters jammed PTL's pledge lines with prank, obscene, and threatening phone calls demanding that Falwell resign.[62]

On August 6, saying that they were out of money and didn't even have enough to pay professional movers, Jim and Tammy loaded up a yellow and black Ryder rental truck with their remaining possessions from the PTL parsonage and moved what was left to Tennessee. Vicki Goodman, holding back tears, said that Tammy wanted to fight back hard and sue everybody possible over what had happened.[63]

On August 7, Falwell formally broke with the doctrine of the charismatic Pentecostals, publicly deploring the prosperity gospel. He said it was "God's slot machine"[64] for religious fund-raising. Belli took up the mantle from California and lashed out at Falwell, pronouncing his name at the news conference as "foul-well."[65] Falwell shot back that Belli, who had been married five times to much younger women, needed marriage counseling.[66]

On Monday, August 17, 1987, Judge Robert Potter of the U.S. District Court for the Western District of North Carolina swore in a twenty-three-member federal grand jury of fourteen men and nine women to investigate PTL's fund-raising and spending during Jim Bakker's reign to see if any federal laws were broken. Judge Potter announced that the grand jury would meet during the third week of each month for at least one year and would review thousands of documents which had been subpoenaed from 1980 on, including everything on Jessica Hahn and all of Jim and Tammy's tax returns during those years.[67]

NOTES

1. Dart, "Park That PTL Built Rides Roller-Coaster of Success, Scandal," *Los Angeles Times,* March 30, 1987 at 3-A, col. 4; "S.C. Church May Be Largest," *Engineering News-Record,* January 22, 1987 at 33 (Nexis printout).

2. "Roadway Progress Is Made," *Heritage Herald,* January 1987 at 24, col. 2.

3. "Tammy Faye Still Angry at Jessica Hahn," UPI [wire story], July 20, 1987, PM Cycle.

4. "Paying the Wages of Sin," *Newsweek,* March 30, 1987 at 28.

5. Perkinson, "Tammy Bakker Admits to Drug Addiction," UPI [wire story], March 7, 1987, PM Cycle.

6. Trial transcript, *United States of America v. James O. Bakker,* Docket C-CR-88-205-1, U.S.D.C. (W.D., N.C.), August 28, 1989, vol. 1 at 185–87.

7. Trial transcript, *United States of America v. James O. Bakker,* Docket C-CR-88-205-1, U.S.D.C. (W.D., N.C.), September 14–18, 1989, vol. 6 at 422.

8. Shepard, *Forgiven* (Atlantic Monthly Press, New York, 1989) at 475–76.

9. *Id.* at 487.

10. *Id.* at 493.

11. Stille, "The Legal Fight for an Evangelical Empire," *National Law Journal,* September 28, 1987 at 40, col. 1.

12. Dortch, *Integrity* (New Leaf Press, Green Forest, Ark., 1992) at 158–59.

13. Jim Bakker, interviews by author, in Rochester, Minnesota, September 25, 1992; October 31, 1992; and June 26, 1993.

14. Dortch, *supra,* n. 12 at 163–65.

15. *Id.*

16. "Regional News," UPI [wire story], March 20, 1987, BC Cycle.

17. *Id.*

18. *Id.*

19. *Id.*

20. "New Bakker Charge," *Newsweek,* April 13, 1987, at 6.

21. *Id.*

22. Wadler, "Breaking Faith, Two TV Idols Fall," *People,* May 18, 1987 at 86; "Tammy Faye Still Angry at Jessica Hahn," *supra,* n. 3.

23. "The World According to Jim and Tammy," *Playboy,* July 1987 at 48.

24. "Regional News," *supra,* n. 16.

25. *Id.*

26. *Id.*

27. *Id.*

28. Shepard, *supra,* n. 8 at 515.

29. "The Best of Nightline with Ted Koppel 1980–1990" [transcript of ABC News special], April 24, 1990.

30. "Heaven Can Wait," *Newsweek,* June 8, 1987 at 60.

31. Jim Bakker, interview by author, in Rochester, Minnesota, October 31, 1992.

32. "Heaven Can Wait," *supra,* n. 30 at 58.

33. *Id.* at 60.

34. *Id.* at 61.

35. *Id.*

36. "Falwell Denies Trying to Steal PTL, Assails 'Greed' of Bakkers," *Des Moines Register,* May 28, 1987, at 3-A, col. 5.

37. Wadler, *supra,* n. 22 at 81.

38. "Heaven Can Wait," *supra,* n. 30 at 60.

39. Klott, "Rested Bakkers Plot Moves from Yacht," *New York Times,* July 17, 1987, at 10-A, col. 1.

40. *Id.* at cols. 1–2.

41. "The Best of Nightline with Ted Koppel 1980–1990," *supra,* n. 29.

42. Associated Press, "Church Leaders to Meet with New PTL Chief," *Cedar Rapids [Iowa] Gazette,* March 29, 1987 at 14-A, col. 1.

43. *Id.*

44. Van Dyke, "Domestic News," UPI [wire story], June 20, 1987, AM Cycle.

45. *Id.*

46. Lohmann, "Domestic News," UPI [wire story], June 11, 1987, AM Cycle.

47. *See* Examiner's Report (filed October 6, 1987), *In Re Heritage Village Church and Missionary Fellowship, Inc., et al.,* In Proceedings For A Reorganization Under Chapter 11, BK No. 87-01956, U.S. Bankruptcy Court (D., S.C.), at 2.

48. Perkinson, "Domestic News," UPI [wire story], June 22, 1987, AM Cycle.

49. *Id.*

50. Jim Bakker, interview by author, in Rochester, Minnesota, October 31, 1992.

51. Perkinson, *supra,* n. 48.

52. Perkinson, "Regional News," UPI [wire story], June 23, 1987, AM Cycle.

53. Perkinson, "Regional News," UPI [wire story], June 25, 1987, AM Cycle.

54. McLaughlin, "Bakker Cronies May Leave PTL-Owned Homes," UPI [wire story], June 29, 1987, AM Cycle.

55. Boshart, "Boone Steers Clear of PTL Fight," UPI [wire story], June 30, 1987, PM Cycle.

56. "Regional News," UPI [wire story], July 2, 1987, AM Cycle.

57. *Id.*

58. "Jim and Tammy Bakker Welcome Federal Probe," Reuters [wire story], July 2, 1987, AM Cycle.

59. Van Dyke, "Belli, Falwell Trade Verbal Jabs," UPI [wire story], July 8, 1987, PM Cycle.

60. Mould, "Regional News," UPI [wire story], July 12, 1987, AM Cycle.

61. Papalus, "Regional News," UPI [wire story], July 12, 1987, AM Cycle.

62. Perkinson, "Regional News," UPI [wire story], July 24, 1987, AM Cycle.

63. Mould, "Evicted Tammy Packs Up Personal Items," UPI [wire story], August 6, 1987, AM Cycle.

64. Papalus, "Falwell: PTL Will Heal Itself," UPI [wire story], August 7, 1987, AM Cycle.

65. "Falwell, Belli Trade Charges in PTL Battle," Reuters [wire story], August 7, 1987, AM Cycle.

66. *Id.*

67. Van Dyke, "Regional News," UPI [wire story], August 17, 1987, AM Cycle.

Chapter 7

Trying to Reassemble the Fiddle Section of the PTL Orchestra while Heritage Burns

During the sixteen months that the grand jury listened to witnesses, watched *PTL Club* videotapes, and weighed the evidence against Jim Bakker, the evangelist spent all of his time and energy trying to retake control of PTL. A tidal wave was forming but rather than head for high ground, Bakker kept looking for his surfboard to get back in the water.

By the summer of 1987, federal agents from the Department of Justice, the IRS, and the U.S. Postal Service had established permanent working offices on the grounds of Heritage to facilitate their painstaking scrutiny of all records and videotapes that the ministry possessed. It could not have been more ominous.

But Bakker told me, "I never dreamed that I would be indicted."[1] At the time, he simply brushed it off. *People* magazine reported the position Bakker was taking in public:

> **Jim Bakker:** The grand jury hasn't got a thing. And, of course, Tammy and I know there's nothing. Friends of ours who have gone to the grand jury, they say—
> **Tammy (interrupting):** They say, it's little old ladies' gossip![2]

Amazingly, the government blindsided him while he was chasing around all over the country to get back on television. The calendar tells the tale.

August 17, 1987 to December 5, 1988

On August 28, 1987 attorney Belli announced that Bakker would sue to remove both Falwell and attorney Grutman from their positions at PTL because they had used "trickery and deceit"[3] in wresting control from its founder.

On August 29, Jim Bakker emerged from his Tennessee chalet to tell fifty supporters who drove 200 miles from Fort Mill for a love rally that the devil hated Heritage USA and was trying to destroy it from within. One of those who made the trek expressed confidence that Bakker would be reinstated: "We have God on our side and we have Melvin Belli. God's never been known to lose a case and neither has Melvin Belli."[4]

On September 20, the day before Jessica Hahn was to appear before the grand jury, Belli blasted Grutman as a "prodigious son of a bitch."[5] And Falwell? Said Belli, "I think he's a no good hypocrite."[6] And for the grand jury, they were a bunch of "voyeurs."[7]

After two days of testimony before the grand jury, Jessica Hahn said she felt closer to God after telling them everything they wanted to know. A day later, on *A Current Affair,* she admitted that she would have kept silent if Bakker had apologized to her and sent her a flower. "If the man had come back to my room ten minutes later with one lousy flower and said, 'Jessica, I'm sorry,' I probably could have looked the other way. He probably still would have PTL."[8]

Of all the witnesses to appear before the grand jury, Hahn caused the most excitement in Charlotte. During a break in the proceedings, which was also the week that *Playboy* hit the stands with her semi-nude photos, she walked over to Giorgio's Restaurant on Trade Street. Local diners were speechless at the sight of such a celebrity, and watched as she quietly ate a deluxe cheeseburger, drank a large glass of milk, and strolled back to the courthouse. The regulars went wild. Proprietor Giorgios Koutsoupias told visitors, "For a long, long time, the men always said, 'We want to sit in Jessica's booth!'"[9]

On September 23, Hahn told *Playboy,* "I am not a bimbo." She went on to prove it by pocketing close to a million dollars for her story and several topless poses in their November, 1987 issue.[10]

On September 24, Tammy Faye told reporters that she was going to tell her side of the PTL scandal in a new record she would release the following week entitled "The Ballad of Jim and Tammy," which she would sing to the melody of Tom T. Hall's "Harper Valley PTA."[11]

In October, movie star Mickey Rooney made a television commercial in support of the Bakkers asking that people call Jim and Tammy's 900 number: "Won't you call Jim and Tammy now? They need your friendship."[12] The two minute recorded message, for which the Bakkers netted thirty-five cents from each caller, consisted of Tammy interviewing Jim:

> **Tammy:** Do you really want PTL back?
> **Jim:** I really don't want to go back. The *Charlotte Observer* has attacked us for 15 years straight. To go back there is going to be hell. We know that.
> **Tammy:** Yes, we do know.
> **Jim:** [But . . . we would return] to fulfill our commitment [to Heritage USA, the] 21st century Christian retreat center. If the people want that.[13]

On October 7, federal bankruptcy judge Rufus Reynolds decided that PTL's creditors and partners could file a reorganizational plan for the court's consideration which conflicted with one filed earlier by Jerry Falwell. The partners' proposal would have created a much larger role for them, including adding six of Bakker's former partners to the PTL board of directors.[14]

On October 8, enraged by Judge Reynolds's decision, Falwell and his entire board resigned, six months after taking over the ministry. Bakker reacted gleefully to the news, telling reporters that Falwell and company simply didn't want to face Melvin Belli and have their conspiracy exposed to take over PTL. Bakker, with Falwell out of the picture, was exuberant, enthusing that he and Tammy were ready to return to "our baby."[15]

On October 9, it was Falwell who returned to baby Heritage and at a news conference called Bakker "the greatest scab and cancer of Christianity in the past 2000 years of church history."[16] He said that Bakker's scandals had become the "Watergate of Christianity"[17] and that Bakker was wrong if he thought that Falwell's resignation would pave the way for his return. Instead, Judge Reynolds would now have the right to appoint a trustee to oversee and manage PTL. The judge indeed did that, appointing David Clark, a former marketing executive with CBN. Bakker's response was that he was willing to leave his return to PTL in God's hands. For now, he and Tammy were going back to Palm Springs. It was winter.

On January 18, 1988, Bakker announced that he would build a new Heritage USA on the West Coast which would dwarf the Carolina retreat. It would cost $2 billion to build and would feature a 1,000-room hotel and duplications of several towns described in the Bible. It would be built one hundred miles east of Los Angeles and include a state of the art broadcast center from which would be beamed a new Jim and Tammy television show five times a week. Bakker promised the new show would be on the air by March.[18]

On February 1, new PTL trustee Clark proved he was no ally of Jim Bakker when he sued Jim and Tammy for $53 million in misspent PTL funds, alleging mismanagement, inappropriate cash advances, and unjustified compensation.[19]

On February 18, Clark announced plans to sell twelve PTL homes and other properties, including Bakker's $900,000 Tega Cay parsonage and Dortch's $575,000 Lake Wylie home, in order to put a dent in the $72 million that PTL owed creditors. Interestingly, Clark reported at the time that PTL was still receiving $110,000 a day in contributions, but was spending $127,000 a day to stay in business.[20]

On March 14, Bakker filed suit against Grutman in York County, South Carolina for "months of personal anguish and torment."[21] Said Belli, "We'll just go after that son of a bitch."[22]

By March 19, Jessica Hahn was feeling better, living in the Playboy mansion in Los Angeles and driving a new Mercedes.

She told reporters that she wanted to do *Saturday Night Live* and tell Jim and Tammy jokes.[23]

On March 28, former PTL employees complained that they were having trouble in job interviews. They said that having PTL on their résumé was a death knell and that what most interviewers were interested in was asking why Tammy wore so much make-up.[24]

On March 31, the *Charlotte Observer* won the Pulitzer Prize for its PTL exposés about the Jessica Hahn payoff and the misuse of ministry funds that toppled Jim Bakker.[25]

On April 19, Bakker sent a letter to Judge Reynolds asking for a chance to return to PTL and save Heritage USA.

> **Jim Bakker's letter to the Bankruptcy Court:** Tammy and I for over a year have sought God and completed an inventory of our lives. We have asked God to forgive us all of our sins and know that He has. *** We have waited as many leaders have had a chance to do their best to run PTL. *** [But it has been] . . . brought down to death's door. *** Please let Tammy and me, along with the partners who worked so hard to birth PTL and Heritage USA, fight for its right to continue.[26]

On April 22, the IRS retroactively revoked PTL's tax exempt status, subjecting the Bakkers and their ministry to millions of dollars in back taxes and penalties. The reason given by the agency was that the Bakkers had received excessive compensation and had channeled ministry money to their own personal inurement.[27] [This was a turn-around for the windblown IRS bureaucrats who a few years earlier had found no cause for legal action against PTL. At that time, they quizzed Bakker about $13 million in loosely accounted for PTL funds. One of his explanations had been that "the devil got into the computer."][28]

On May 14, the owner of the Charlotte Hornets professional basketball team expressed an interest in buying Heritage and turning it into a sports complex. When word spread that beer would be served in the stadium, the stalwarts who revered those alcohol-free grounds erupted angrily and opposed George Shinn's plan. Understanding, however, that beggars cannot be choosers, Shinn shot back that his stadium on Heritage property would "certainly [be] more compatible than a nudist colony . . . that could . . . end out there."[29]

In June, Tammy learned that the new regime at PTL had bulldozed thousands of her record albums into an open pit on the Heritage grounds and covered them over with eight feet of Carolina topsoil. Embittered, she ripped into Falwell:

> I would like to say I hope that Jerry Falwell and his family never have to suffer the way they have made our family suffer. I wake up every morning wishing they had killed me, and Jim does, too. It would have been much kinder for them to have put a bullet in us but they didn't and so we're still here.[30]

On July 7, Jim himself submitted a formal proposal to buy PTL, claiming to have a $100 million line of credit and hard money backing from a Greek magnate.[31]

On September 1, every indication from the bankruptcy court was that Bakker indeed was the leading candidate to buy PTL's assets with a $165 million bid and that he would be back in control soon. The trustee said it was the best offer he had received.[32]

On September 9, Bakker met personally with trustee Benton but was unable to prove that he had the money from the Greeks after all.[33]

On September 25, Bakker began conducting church services at a roller rink in North Carolina, joking that "now we really are holy rollers."[34] Tammy told the congregation that she knew they'd be back at PTL soon because God had told her so while she was putting on her makeup that morning.[35]

And on December 5, 1988, the grand jury itself spoke to Jim Bakker indicting him on twenty-four counts of fraud and conspiracy.[36]

The Grand Jury

The accused is never represented by counsel in grand jury proceedings and jurors never hear arguments or explanations from attorneys for the defendant. Because these unique panels are so frequently controlled by prosecutors, lawyers joke that a grand jury will indict a ham sandwich if the prosecutor tells it to.

Jim Bakker was the Justice Department's lunch meat this time and he got the kiss of death from the grand jury.

The indictment itself stretched twenty-eight pages and included several harrowing allegations. The grand jury found that Bakker and co-pastor Richard Dortch had defrauded contributors of $158 million by making false representations about the lifetime partnership lodging plans which they promoted on television and through the mails. The jury charged that Bakker knowingly made false promises on television about those lodging plans which resulted in the acquisition of 152,903 of them by unsuspecting and innocent viewers.

> **Jim Bakker in prison:** I really believed everything I said. It was all done live on TV each day. Sometimes, I literally dreamed out loud. * * * I'm telling you before God, I didn't know about any fraud.[37]

One of the videotapes the jurors watched showed Bakker unveiling the Grand Hotel partnerships on TV February 20, 1984, saying that it was "the most exciting project probably ever undertaken in the history, I think, of Christianity."[38] The grand jury didn't fault that bit of exaggeration, but it did take offense at his initial representations on the air that he was only going to offer 25,000 Grand partnerships. They found, instead, that by May 31, 1987 he had sold 66,683 of them. The fraud that they saw in that was that with 500 rooms, the Grand could accommodate 25,000 partners spending three nights and four days there each year. But it could never hold 66,683, meaning that at least half of those who were promised free lodging each year would never be able to stay there.[39]

Another thing that rankled the grand jury was evidence that out of the $66,938,820 Bakker raised with the sale of Grand partnerships, only $35,365,201 was actually spent on the hotel. The rest of it went to pay daily operating expenses at PTL and

to support his media star lifestyle—all of which were supposedly concealed from those who were buying the Grand
partnerships.[40]

The jurors also took offense at the April 11, 1985 announcement by Jim and Tammy on the air that because 900 bad checks
had been received in payment for Grand partnerships, they were
going to open up the sale of the Grand for a limited time to
make up the difference and bring the total up to where it was
supposed to be. But the grand jury saw PTL records which
showed that on that day 34,983 Grand partnerships had already
been purchased. There was evidence that what Bakker did was
to use the bad check and dishonored commitment ruse to run
up the total in the next few months and sell 20,000 more.[41]

The grand jury was shown a videotape of the September 17,
1984 PTL program in which Jim announced the Towers Hotel
partnership program and represented that there would be a
limit of 30,000 sold. The statement was also made on that
program that the $30 million raised would be spent in a certain
way: $15 million to pay for construction of the Towers; $10
million to pay for the completion of construction of the Grand;
and $5 million to pay local television time. But the jurors found
that Bakker raced past the 30,000 limit and eventually sold
68,755 Towers partnerships which, in their view, would make it
impossible for at least half of them to ever find a room at the
inn. Beyond that, of the $74,292,751 raised through the sale of
those partnerships, only $11,422,684 was ever spent on the
Towers. The hotel was never completely finished.[42]

The grand jury found that the Bunkhouse partnership
program which Bakker announced on August 4, 1986 was a
fraud because he sold 9,682 Bunkhouse partnerships and raised
$6.6 million, but spent less than $1 million on Bunkhouses and
ended up with only one. And that lone bunkhouse had a scant
eight rooms available for those several thousand partners to use
each year. The rest of the money was spent on PTL's other
expenses as well as bonuses for Jim, Tammy, and Pastor Dortch.
The jurors believed that the motive behind the fraud was to
continue "lavish and extravagant lifestyles" for the Bakkers.[43]

It was the grand jury's view that Bakker and Dortch had misled both PTL's own board of directors and the millions of people who watched the TV show by concealing PTL's day-to-day financial bind. Never disclosed was the fact that they really needed to sell lifetime lodging partnerships in order to raise the millions each month that it took to keep the theme park open and the television program on the air around the country. Hotels and bunkhouses were built with what was left.[44]

In all, Bakker and Dortch were indicted on twenty-four different counts of broadcast fraud, mail fraud, and conspiracy. They were ordered to stand trial on the charges before a jury of their peers in federal court in Charlotte.

Jim Bakker in prison: I wasn't stealing from these people—I was giving them everything. Several newspapers reported that I stole $3.7 million, which was the total income for Tammy and me for five years. The *Star* reported that I stole $150 million. The truth is that I was neither indicted nor convicted for stealing anything.

How can they say I stole money when I put all the money in Heritage? My largest take home pay was one-half million dollars in 1986, my last year. I paid sixty percent in taxes. I owe taxes today. I was never charged with stealing any money. Nobody ever testified at the trial that I had stolen any money.

We donated $8 million in royalties from twenty-five records back to the ministry. My Bible made $50 million which I gave back to the ministry. My daughter's album made when she was sixteen years old made $1.6 million. All my books made millions. Tammy's record made $2 million. How could I have stolen $3.7 million if I donated $8 million in royalties?

I put the money into that place. The elaborate TV studio sat 1,500 people comfortably and 2,000 people to the rafters with an overflow in the barn. The money was all right there, including $13 million in the water park.

If this was a ripoff, why would I give them all this. [Showing me pictures of the hotel that he built and all the large, poshly appointed rooms. His point was if he was ripping off people and overselling those rooms with the thought in mind that they would never see them, why would he appoint them so elegantly and build this five-star hotel.][45]

December 5, 1988 to August 21, 1989

The Charlotte grand jury boldly raised the stakes in the Monopoly game that had been played with real hotels for several years at Heritage. If convicted on all twenty-four counts, Bakker's punishment would be 120 years in prison and $6 million in fines. He was looking down the end of a very long rifle.

A federal criminal indictment is nothing less than a call to arms. The person charged is in immense immediate danger of losing their freedom and being sent to jail. It is the opening salvo in the legal war that the trial will become.

When you are indicted, the immediate and natural response is to defend yourself. You fight back. You sense the danger, your adrenaline is moving, and you fight like a dog to avoid going to prison. You get the best attorney possible, you make sure he or she is up to the task of winning the case for you, and you bear down on that attorney every day of the week to make sure they are doing the job for you.

On your own, you spend every waking minute and every ounce of energy working on your case. You go over and over in your mind every event that the grand jury found unlawful and you try to come up with anything that will prove them wrong. You look for evidence of any kind—every document and every piece of paper that you can put your hands on that could possibly help you. You beat the bushes for witnesses who will stand with you and verify your version of the facts. You pour your whole life into responding to the biggest threat in your life. Those are both the intuitive and intellectual manifestations of anyone's instinct for survival.

But amazingly, his indictment wasn't even a wake up call for Jim Bakker. He had ten months to trial. But he spent eighteen hours a day for most of those months putting a brand new national TV show on the air. First he returned to television on a small number of stations from his home in North Carolina and later out of a strip mall in Orlando, Florida. Then, he began planning a whole new Heritage USA on a tract of land near Interstate Highway 4 ten miles from Disney World. There is something wrong in this picture: an army of federal prosecutors, IRS investigators, and FBI agents have dedicated themselves to spending the next ten months to build a case against you and send you to prison. You are standing outside Disney World with an armful of blueprints talking with contractors about building a new retreat for fellow Christians who want to get away from wordly stresses for the weekend.

My interviews with Jim Bakker convinced me that two things explain his odd reaction to the indictment. First, he didn't hear the tires squealing. He didn't see the truck. He simply did not think he was in any danger. It must be remembered that Bakker is a charismatic Pentecostal, one who believes that God directs his life through daily intervention and miracles. If that doesn't seem too realistic to others, it was his reality and his world view. It's how he lived his life. Christian Scientists don't seek the help of physicians, either, and they sometimes pay the price. But that, too, is their own way of going through life and responding to symptoms of illness. Who is to say they are right or wrong, any more than anyone can say Jim Bakker was right or wrong in having the faith that God would see him through?

> **Jim Bakker in prison:** I did not even want a lawyer. I trusted God. *** I knew I was innocent. I thought it would be an open and shut case. God had kept me in His hands since I was eighteen years old and I trusted Him to bring me through this, too.[46]

Secondly, I am convinced that Jim Bakker is not now and has never been a fighter. His executioner, Jerry Falwell, looks like a force to be reckoned with—big, stern, and imposing. He just looks tough. The same with Jimmy Swaggart—he looks like someone you would want on your side in a street fight. Tenacious and combative.

But Jim Bakker isn't cut from that cloth. He is a kinder and gentler evangelist, one who wouldn't commit you to hell in a handcar for some transgression. His ministry over the course of fifteen years on television was an accurate reflection of his own personality and psyche. He didn't call his organization "People

Who Will Hunt You Down Like a Dog if You Disobey God's Will." For Bakker, it was "People That Love."

I saw in him in prison the same traits that millions saw on television for years: he is very emotional and compassionate. He doesn't get mad. You can't make him mad. On several occasions, his attorneys disappointed him. But he didn't get mad. He didn't confront them. He didn't fight. He just took it. That's his make-up—he's no fighter. It is not in his psychological repertoire to confront people. When he is attacked, he turns the other cheek.

And the surest proof of the accuracy of that characterization was his reaction to the impending indictment before his fledgling new congregation on December 4, 1988 at the Charlotte roller rink. Bakker, tears running down his cheeks, said: "What can I do? You've got the IRS against you, the FBI, the KGB—no, the CIA—all these government agencies. If I thought it would help Christianity, I would get a gun and blow my head off. Then I'd be gone and you'd have no one to blame your problems on."[47] To which Jessica Hahn responded at a news conference in Phoenix the next day, if Bakker "wants to blow his head off, let him."[48] But the point is that blowing your head off is the same as putting your head in the sand. It's refusing to engage the enemy. It's giving up rather than putting up your fists. It's not fighting back.

This was exactly the pattern that he followed from the end at Heritage to the day they slammed the prison gate behind him. Bakker had ten months before his trial to fight his adversaries. And even though he twice toyed with a confrontation at Melvin Belli's suggestion, Bakker dismissed Belli after a few months and refused to fight. Belli wanted to go straight for the throats of Falwell and attorney Norman Roy Grutman for allegedly deceiving Jim and stealing PTL from him in broad daylight. Argued Belli to United Press International:

> Grutman wrote out Bakker's resignation in his own handwriting. He said he was Bakker's lawyer but didn't tell Bakker he was also Falwell's lawyer and had adverse interests. It's despicable. Jim Bakker would never have resigned if he had known this was a

Falwell trick. . . . We are asking that both Falwell and this miserable bastard Grutman be kicked out.[49]

Belli had both Falwell and Grutman in his sights. He always
thought it was "fitting that Falwell would get a porno lawyer to
represent him," referring to *Penthouse* attorney Grutman. Belli
would also tweak Grutman when they spoke privately by calling
him "Herr Grutman," a salutation that really infuriated Grutman.

But Bakker didn't have the stomach for it and instead spent
his time trying to build a new theme park. Of course, the only
accommodations at the end of the road was an 8-foot by 10-foot
cell in a federal penitentiary. Some would say that Bakker's
refusal to get involved in his own defense is sure evidence of his
innocence and clear conscience, and that may well be. Some
would scoff that he had been caught dead to rights with his
hands in the Heritage cookie jar and it would have been futile
for him to try to prove his innocence. Others would see his
refusal to engage as a strategic misstep from which he could
never recover.

The enormity of the error can be appreciated if one considers what Bakker didn't do before trial, in comparison to what
other high profile celebrity defendants have done who have
been indicted and acquitted in the last few years. Does anyone
really think William Kennedy Smith, when indicted by a West
Palm Beach grand jury on rape charges in 1991, didn't drop
everything else in his life and work his heart out to do
everything he could for his case? He even postponed his
medical school residency to devote every day he could to the
fight. Not Jim Bakker.

It wasn't that the evangelist spent the months leading up to
his trial languishing all day on the sofa in his underwear eating
Froot Loops and watching MTV. He is not lazy. He is a type-A
dynamo, a workaholic. And he was very busy during those
months.

It is no secret that preparing a new TV program takes
months or years of hard work. New series simply cannot be
thrown together. To attain a level of broadcast quality, months
of back-breaking preparation on the part of technicians, camera
people, directors, writers, set designers, stage hands, and stars is

required. Television personalities who are also perfectionists, like Jim Bakker, demand even more in terms of technical preparation for flawless performances. Even broadcasting bombs like the 1993 Chevy Chase late night talk show, which lasted only a month amid merciless reviews and surprisingly uncomfortable performances by Chase, was more than eighteen months in full-time preparation. And that was for a bad show. On top of that, once a new show is under way, the burden of daily preparation remains. Ask any star, series television will drain you and it demands every waking minute of your life.

So while Justice Department attorneys prepared the case of their lives against the nation's best known televangelist, their target was polishing the lenses of two new television cameras. On Bakker's birthday, January 2, 1989, he and Tammy returned to TV in a one hour daily program broadcast on several stations. Short on funds, they used the home of a friend in Charlotte as their new set. Their program was a lot like their old one at PTL, and included pleas for donations to buy television time to keep the show on the air. They were back.

The only problem was that city officials in Charlotte claimed the Bakkers were violating local zoning ordinances by broadcasting their new program from that residence. It was time to move on, and Jim and Tammy found an out-of-the-way strip mall in Orlando, Florida that they thought would be perfect for a television studio. It was in the middle of the city's factory outlet district and only minutes from Disney World. But first, since he was under federal indictment, Bakker had to obtain permission from the U.S. magistrate to move to Florida while awaiting trial later that year. The magistrate approved and the Bakkers were on their way.[50]

Jim and Tammy refurbished the empty storefront and painted their new set red and blue. They decorated it with a few flowers and plants. A bank of nine telephones was installed for pledges and prayers.

And in May of 1989, their new show debuted from Orlando. It was three months before his trial was to begin, but his monthly letters to followers that year revealed his priorities:

- Being able to do our program seems like such a miracle to us. There were so many times in the last two years that we thought we would never be back on television with you again. (January 1989 letter)[51]

- I believe that, one day, we will all be together again at Heritage USA, praising the Lord! (January 1989 letter)[52]

- . . . it was God telling us it was time to leave Charlotte. . . . We desperately need a miracle! The expense of relocating our television crew, our office staff, our television studios, our living quarters, and the expense of paying our television air time is more than we can even handle. . . . Please. . . . send your best offering this month along with your monthly pledge. . . . (May 1989 letter)[53]

- We have several sites [for a new Heritage] in mind and need your help to let us know exactly what you would like to see us purchase for you and your family. Would you like to be on the ocean or a large lake? Are you a camper or do you prefer a hotel room? Would you like to be near shopping or out in the country more? (May 1989 letter)[54]

- Tammy and I are excited about what God is doing for us as we are beginning our new television ministry in Orlando. . . . At this location, near Disney World, we are believing God to recreate Heritage USA and will be calling it Heritage Springs International. *** As you know, without your financial support, none of this would be possible. (June 1989 letter)[55]

- My trial begins in less than four weeks. . . . Meantime, our ministry here is facing crisis. Already some of our affiliates have canceled our program and many others are threatening to take us off the air if we cannot pay nearly $400,000 immediately! *** Please give generously. (August 1989 letter)[56]

In terms of trial preparation, the move to Florida was definitely unwise. The evidence that would either acquit or convict Bakker, including thousands of hours of videotapes of old *PTL Club* broadcasts and fund-raising, remained in Charlotte. Hundreds of witnesses loyal to Bakker who could have been readied for trial were also in the Carolinas, many of them still working or living at Heritage. Importantly, Bakker's trial attorney, Harold Bender, practiced in Charlotte. Exactly what kind of trial preparation are you going to have with your client 500 miles away doing a daily television show?

The fact of the matter was that, in my opinion, Bakker himself was one of the keys to his own defense. No witness knew more about the Jim and Tammy television program or Heritage USA. Based on the indictment that had been handed down by the grand jury, the direction the government's case against him would take was crystal clear. The way to have mounted a strategy to counter it would have been to exhaust Bakker's own recollection about everything that had gone on at Heritage relevant to the grand jury's findings. Beyond that, he should have been active in identifying and recruiting witnesses who would help him and actual evidence that would save him. Whether that meant him personally reviewing thousands of hours of *PTL Club* videotapes or digging through hundreds of pages of financial documents, it should have been done and his energies should have been directed toward the looming trial. They were not and it showed in the shellacking that he took at trial.

Bakker alone should not be faulted on this point. He devoutly believed that he had been literally called by God to the television ministry. It was God's plan for his life. That was the role God had chosen for him. And so, it was not at all surprising that Bakker would have remained intransigently focused on returning to television, and as he saw it saving lives for Jesus through that medium, rather than ensconcing himself in some bunker in Charlotte for a year and a half preparing for trial. After all, the Lord had never told him to prepare for his trial but had, years before, spoken to him and told him to get on television. That he didn't have the litigation instincts to be pouring himself into trial preparation was not really his fault. It is trial lawyers who have litigation instincts and his trial lawyers should have exercised a little client control and refused to let him return to daily television.

Two years after the dust from the trial had settled, Harold Bender candidly acknowledged as much when asked what he would have done differently, if he, rather than George Davis, had been lead counsel. "The first thing I would have done is I would have associated a young, bright lawyer to assist. I would have insisted that the client become more involved in the investigative stage. [Bakker] was, during that period of time, trying to re-establish his television ministry."[57]

Before long, it was August 21, 1989, and time to select a jury to sit in judgment of the case. The federal clerk of court in Charlotte sent 300 subpoenas to randomly chosen residents of the thirty-two-county federal district comprising the jurisdiction in which Bakker would face his accusers, demanding that they appear on August 21 at the federal courthouse where they would be considered for the Bakker jury.

NOTES

1. Jim Bakker, interview by author, in Rochester, Minnesota, October 31, 1992.

2. Levin, "It's Jim and Tammy Time Again!" *People,* July 4, 1988, at 35.

3. "Bakker Asking Court to Oust PTL Lawyer and Falwell," UPI [wire story], August 28, 1987, AM Cycle.

4. Perkinson, "Domestic News," UPI [wire story], August 29, 1987, AM Cycle.

5. VanDyke, "Jessica Hahn to Be Leadoff Witness at PTL Hearing," UPI [wire story], September 20, 1987, AM Cycle.

6. *Id.*

7. *Id.*

8. Mandulo, "Bakker's Apology Might Have Brought Her Silence, Hahn Says," UPI [wire story], September 23, 1987, BC Cycle.

9. Leland and Wright, "Smile, Say Cheese," *Charlotte Observer,* September 8, 1989 at 6-A (Westlaw printout).

10. VanDyke, "Hush Money Negotiators Talk to Grand Jury," UPI [wire story], September 23, 1987, AM Cycle.

11. VanDyke, "Tammy Faye on Tour," UPI [wire story], September 24, 1987, PM Cycle.

12. Rosenberg, "Reagan Media Mavens Know Their Networks," *Los Angeles Times,* October 16, 1987 at 1–6, col. 2.

13. *Id.*

14. "Domestic News," UPI [wire story], October 7, 1987, AM Cycle.

15. Lillard, "Subdued Bakkers Happy with Falwell's Departure," UPI [wire story], October 8, 1987, AM Cycle.

16. Craig, "Domestic News," UPI [wire story], October 9, 1987, PM Cycle.

17. *Id.*

18. Preston, "Bakker Plans New Retreat, Television Ministry," UPI [wire story], January 18, 1988, AM Cycle.

19. "PTL's Clark Sues Bakkers, Top Aide for $53 Million," UPI [wire story], February 1, 1988, BC Cycle.

20. Bower, "PTL to Auction Off Bakker's 'parsonage'," UPI [wire story], February 18, 1988, BC Cycle.

21. VanDyke, "Regional News," UPI [wire story], March 16, 1988, AM Cycle.

22. *Id.*

23. "A year after PTL: How the Mighty Have Fallen," UPI [wire story], March 19, 1988, AM Cycle.

24. "PTL Scandal Dogs Former Employees," UPI [wire story], March 28, 1988, BC Cycle.

25. Jacobson, "Pulitzer Prize for Sinking Jim Bakker," UPI [wire story], March 31, 1988, PM Cycle.

26. "Regional News," UPI [wire story], April 19, 1988, BC Cycle.

27. "PTL Sues Jessica Hahn over Hush Money," UPI [wire story], April 22, 1988, BC Cycle.

28. "Paying the Wages of Sin," *Newsweek,* March 30, 1987 at 28.

29. "Domestic News," UPI [wire service dispatch], May 13, 1988, BC Cycle.

30. "Tammy Faye Says Family Will Fight to Keep PTL Parsonage," *Des Moines Register,* June 18, 1987 at 3-A, col. 2.

31. Preston, "Bakker Makes a Bid for PTL," UPI [wire story], July 7, 1988, AM Cycle.

32. "Bakker Top Choice to Buy PTL's Assets," Knight-Ridder Newspapers, *Chicago Tribune,* September 1, 1988 at 2-C (Nexis printout).

33. Preston, "Bakker Fails to Prove He Has Funds for PTL," UPI [wire story], September 10, 1988, PM Cycle.

34. "Bakker Preaches from Roller Rink," UPI [wire story], September 25, 1988, AM Cycle.

35. *Id.*

36. Bill of Indictment, *United States of America v. James O. Bakker,* Docket No. C-CR-88-205-1, U.S.D.C. (W.D., N.C.), December 5, 1988.

37. Jim Bakker, interviews by author, in Rochester, Minnesota, October 31, 1992 and April 4, 1993.

38. *PTL Club* television program, February 20, 1984 [videotape of program preserved as Trial Composite Tape No. 1, Document 3628, *United States of America v. James O. Bakker,* Docket No. C-CR-88-205-1].

39. Bill of Indictment, *supra,* n. 36 at 4–6, 27.

40. *Id.* at 13–16.

41. *Id.* at 6.

42. *Id.* at 7, 10, 27.

43. *Id.* at 11–12, 21.

44. *Id.* at 10–12, 21–22.

45. Jim Bakker, interview by author, in Rochester, Minnesota, September 25, 1992.

46. Jim Bakker, written answers to questions from the author, September 1992; Jim Bakker, interview by author, in Rochester, Minnesota, October 31, 1992.

47. Preston, "Regional News," UPI [wire story], December 5, 1988, BC Cycle.

48. *Id.*

49. "Bakker Asking Court to Oust PTL Lawyer and Falwell," *supra,* n. 3.

50. "Bakker Gets Permission to Move to Florida," *St. Petersburg Times,* April 2, 1989 at 7-A (Nexis printout); Jim Bakker, letters to New Covenant Partners (May and June 1989).

51. Jim Bakker, letter to PTL Partners, January 1989.

52. *Id.*

53. Jim Bakker, letter to New Covenant Partners, May 1989.

54. *Id.*

55. Jim Bakker, letter to New Covenant Partners, June 1989.

56. Jim Bakker, letter to New Covenant Partners, August 1989.

57. Boudrow, "Bender for the Defense," *[Charlotte] Business Journal,* November 11, 1991 at 12–1 (Nexis printout).

Chapter 8

I'll Get By with a Little Help from My Friends

Jim Bakker, in a 1988 sermon: I've always said if I could give you a gift, the most important gift would be a good friend.[1]

There is a line from Frank Sinatra's hit song, "That's Life," which perfectly fits the Bakker saga: "Riding high in April, shot down in May." The only difference is that in Bakker's case it was multiple gunshot wounds with virtually every other nationally known evangelist publicly opening fire on him. Those virulent attacks on Bakker raged continuously for months before his trial.

Charlotte area citizens who would eventually become jurors in the case were being feted in their daily newspapers to the reactions of prominent evangelists to the same evidence those jurors would later see in the courtroom. For a year and a half before Bakker's trial finally convened, thousands of newspaper articles, television programs, and talk show monologues treated the allegations as proof of guilt. Few cases have ever generated as much pretrial publicity over more months.

But, it wasn't only the media piling on.

Jimmy Swaggart

It was the sound of Swaggart's footsteps that spooked Bakker into resigning as president of PTL. Bakker believed that Swaggart knew everything about the Hahn affair and was going to go straight to the *Charlotte Observer* with the story in order to topple Bakker and seize control of PTL.[2] The scenario was not completely far-fetched because Swaggart and Bakker were the only two nationally known Assemblies of God televangelists, and the PTL by-laws provided that if anything ever happened to Bakker the entire PTL ministry would revert to the Assemblies of God Church.[3] As well, there had been bad blood between the two since Bakker axed Swaggart from the PTL satellite network. The religious philosophies of the two men contrasted sharply, with Swaggart's criticism of Catholicism as a "non-Christian superstition" and his intolerance of the Jewish faith at odds with Bakker's open-mindedness.[4]

To see why PTL might be the subject of a hostile takeover attempt, it must be understood that the most important asset of the empire Bakker built was surely not the 600-foot water slide or even the entire theme park itself. It was PTL's satellite network, billed at the time as the country's only twenty-four-hour, all-religion network. Received in more than twelve million homes fed by hundreds of cable television systems, it was a lifeline to a bounty of viewer contributions for any televangelist who appeared on it.

But it could also well have been that Swaggart simply disliked Bakker enough that he wanted to see him deposed, without having any interest at all in PTL for himself.

Swaggart certainly sounded hostile. On *Larry King Live,* Swaggart unloaded on Bakker, calling him "a cancer that needs to be excised from the body of Christ."[5] He angrily dismissed Heritage USA, which Bakker had claimed was a vision from God, saying, "I don't think the church ought to be involved in making hamburgers, or building waterslides, or having pony rides. Man needs salvation. He doesn't need a ride down the waterslide."[6] Swaggart scoffed at Jim and Tammy's television program as more sitcom than religious revival, and objected to Bakker's openness to all religious denominations.[7] He also fed the rumors he was hearing about Bakker's affair with Jessica Hahn directly to officials in the Assemblies of God church in Springfield, Missouri, demanding that they repudiate Bakker.[8]

Jim Bakker in prison: Swaggart wrote these letters [about Jessica Hahn] in which he stated the Assemblies of God was going to do this and this, and that the *Charlotte Observer* was going to do this and this as far as making it [the Hahn story] public.

The irony is that despite Swaggart and the *Observer* knowing about Jessica Hahn [before I resigned] neither of them was going to go public. Neither of them was going to do anything about it.

Grutman convinced me it was going to be made public and that I needed to voluntarily step aside while it did.

Grutman played a key role in all of the negotiations that led up to my resignation from PTL. He told me to play dead for thirty to ninety days and that during that time the Jessica Hahn scandal would dissipate and I could return to my position. I did this to submit to the brethren in order to weather the Hahn scandal which the *Observer* was about to break.

I probably should have stayed put, and my partners would have stood with me. That way Falwell would not have had the chance to take over the ministry.[9]

Swaggart's dislike of Bakker went deep. On *Face the Nation*, he dropped the bombshell that he had seen proof that Bakker had consorted with homosexuals and prostitutes.[10] To 14,000 evangelicals crowded into L.A.'s Sports Arena, Swaggart called for a cleansing of church leadership. He tore into Bakker as one of the "charlatan" preachers who "don't know what's right and what's wrong . . . and are duping" millions of TV viewers with their "slick productions."[11] Calling Bakker's prosperity gospel a "fraud," Swaggart concluded, "You can stay more holy watching 'Miami Vice' than by watching Christian Television."[12]

Bakker was stung by the harshness of the Louisianan's rhetoric. He responded quickly: "I have never been to a prostitute. I am not and have never been a homosexual. Those who say such things should have . . . [to] prove their accusations."[13]

Swaggart, unwilling to let it die, shot back during a *700 Club* appearance, "I don't appreciate a preacher who commits adultery and then goes out and blames me."[14] And, as for Bakker's charge that Swaggart's attempted hostile takeover of

PTL caused Bakker's fall, Swaggart snorted, "He brought himself down."[15] "I'm as innocent as a baby,"[16] Swaggart told Larry King.

Swaggart's cousin, rock 'n' roll bad boy Jerry Lee Lewis, leaped to Swaggart's defense from a gig at a Tennessee nightclub and backed his cuz's version, "Jimmy . . . don't have to lie about nothing."[17]

When Chattanooga evangelist John Ankerberg suggested that he and Swaggart help Bakker through his crisis by letting him confess his sins and repent, Swaggart would have nothing of it. He wrote Ankerberg: "Please believe me. There is absolutely no chance of Bakker and Dortch stepping down for any type of rehabilitation. First they will try to lie their way out of it, but the documentation should be irrefutable."[18]

Bakker wasn't the only televangelist to feel Swaggart's wrath. Swaggart took public pot shots at the dean of all tent preachers, Oral Roberts, lambasting him for his "shenanigans"[19] after Oral told his own television viewers in March of 1987 that if he didn't receive $8 million in contributions for his medical school, God would call him home. Nor did Swaggart ever buy Oral's representations that he could heal the sick, ridiculing that as crazy. He seethed at Roberts, too, for speaking kindly about Catholics and Jews, which to Swaggart was "blasphemy."[20]

Swaggart trained some of his fiercest fire on New Orleans televangelist Marvin Gorman, who lost his ministry after Swaggart publicly accused him of adultery. Gorman fought back, slapping Swaggart with a $90 million lawsuit for trying to steal his ministry.[21]

Swaggart was brazenly unafraid of controversy, and he was dangerous.

Jerry Falwell

Many of Bakker's Pentecostal followers were astonished by his choice of Baptist fundamentalist Jerry Falwell to succeed him. After all, PTL was a charismatic amalgam, with Heritage as its Mecca. Yet Falwell had long rejected Pentecostal doctrine. He had publicly belittled Christians who speak in tongues as "people who ate too much pizza last night."[22] And after taking over PTL, he rejected the charismatic's prosperity gospel theology as "pure, religious baloney" and "damnable heresy."[23]

But to Bakker, the choice made sense. First, Falwell alone among religious broadcasters had sufficient clout to prevent a Swaggart takeover of PTL. The founder of the Moral Majority, the leader of the Religious Right, and prominent supporter of Ronald Reagan and George Bush, the Virginian had the muscle to protect PTL from predators. At the same time, Falwell was an ideal caretaker from Bakker's perspective because the Baptist's strict fundamentalism was never going to be accepted by PTL's rank and file Pentecostals, presenting no risk to Bakker that Falwell would be a long-termer.

Falwell's public explanation for agreeing to take control of PTL was that unless things were quieted down there, "a backlash that would hurt every gospel ministry in America, if not the world"[24] would result. That's a reasonable explanation, too. He was earning elder statesman stripes among all televangelists, his merit badge in scandal cleanup, by moving into the fray and calming the waters at PTL. It was a step up, as well, from his Thomas Road Baptist Church, where he preached each week, and his relatively obscure *Old Time Gospel Hour* which was broadcast to only 438,000 households in the country. Jim Bakker had that many people watching his test pattern at PTL. So, from the perspectives of both men, it was a good business decision at the time. But how incredibly sour it turned.

Within a month, Falwell had seen enough in the PTL books that he blasted Bakker for having the gall to accept $2.6 million in salary the previous two years while PTL was on the financial ropes.[25] To Falwell, that was the basest greed. Falwell also acquired new information about the Hahn episode and heard other accusations which shook his Baptist riggings to the core. Within weeks, he proclaimed that he would never allow Bakker to return to PTL because he was "morally unfit"[26] to be a preacher.

In press conferences, television news interviews, and appearances on such programs as *Nightline,* Falwell took the gloves off and pummeled Bakker with a running diatribe that ravaged Bakker's reputation. He accused Bakker of paying blackmail to Jessica Hahn, and having "homosexual problems dating back to 1956."[27] Beyond that, Falwell crowned Bakker "the greatest scab and cancer of Christianity in the past 2,000 years of church history."[28]

Of lethal significance, Falwell's people gave the Justice Department the startling financial records they found at PTL. Those documents ended up in the hands of the grand jury, of course, and later in the Charlotte courtroom where they would prove so embarrassing to Bakker.[29]

Many Bakker supporters steadfastly believed Falwell wanted Jim out of the way to seize control of the PTL satellite network for his own ministry.

> **Jim Bakker in prison:** There really was a Holy War. Jerry Falwell . . . wanted the PTL Network for his *Old Time Gospel Hour.* I can prove that.
>
> I built PTL from nothing. It was worth half a billion dollars, I think. Why in the world would I give it to anyone? That would have been like a father walking away from a child. I surely didn't give it to Falwell. The pact with him was that I would return.
>
> Once he betrayed the agreement we had, though, he smeared me. The reason he discredited me was to justify his takeover of PTL.[30]

Falwell aide Mark DeMoss added fuel to the fire when he told the *Los Angeles Times* in April 1987 that Falwell certainly was considering using the PTL satellite network for his *Old Time Gospel Hour.*[31] Falwell himself continued to deny any such designs, but to Bakker hard-liners it was a power grab that had more to do with satellites than allegations of Jim's misdeeds.

Pat Robertson

Robertson, the president and founder of the Christian Broadcasting Network in Virginia Beach, Virginia, and host of the popular *700 Club,* tried to keep his head down as Gospelgate erupted and the Holy Wars began. He had good reason for doing it—he was running for president using his tufted chair on the *700 Club* as his launching pad. The Jim Bakker scandal could not have come at a worse time for Robertson, with the presidential election the following year and early primary and caucus dates just a few months away. As one of the nation's best known religious broadcasters and, like Bakker, a Pentecostal, Robertson was undeniably suffering from guilt by association with other televangelists whom the public was rapidly coming to regard with skepticism. How far behind could Robertson be from the rest of the crowd? As he was loading cartons of bumper stickers in his station wagon, he must have been seething as he saw his White House dreams go up in smoke.

The emergence of the Religious Right as fundamentalist Christians got heavily involved in politics in the late 1970s had been phenomenal. Spurred to action by a host of social issues, including their strong stand against abortion, millions of evangelical Christians registered to vote and got involved in the political campaigns of Ronald Reagan and other conservatives. They were instrumental in defeating twelve liberal incumbent Democratic United States senators in the 1980 elections and claimed credit for throwing eight other Democratic senators out of office two years before.[32]

The fires of the Religious Right were fanned by the television evangelists, most prominently Jerry Falwell and Pat Robertson. Jim Bakker was much less political than the others and one could watch him for weeks and never discern any political bent on his part. Bakker was never really a member of the go-go politically lighted crowd of religious broadcasters.

The others were doing the work without him, with such jarring success that *Newsweek* magazine declared 1976 "The Year of the Evangelicals" for the emergence of so many millions of them into the political arena.[33] They had enormous voting power and dwarfed the power that liberal preachers like the Reverend Jesse Jackson had, and the votes that Jackson could deliver. Evangelical Christians accounted for one-fifth of Ronald Reagan's total vote in the 1980 elections.[34] Robertson was banking on riding that wave until the Bakker sex and money scandal in 1987 and 1988 made national laughing stocks of the profession.

University of Virginia professor Jeffrey Hadden, a biographer of several televangelists, had it right: "Pat Robertson has got to be thinking, 'Oh, Lord, why does this have to happen now?' "[35]

On his *700 Club,* Robertson stuck mostly to other news stories and gave the PTL scandal short shrift. But he did attempt to hang Bakker with the problem. Said Robertson on the air, "I think the Lord is house cleaning a little bit. I am glad to see it happen."[36] Right. On his March 25, 1987, broadcast, he threw up his hands and muttered, "I'm just not involved in this at all."[37] Finally, his campaign press secretary, Connie Stapp, tried a different tack when nothing else seemed to be working. She offered critical reporters a correction while her boss was campaigning in the New Hampshire Republican primary. "Pat has been labeled a TV evangelist, but he's not," she said. "He's a religious broadcaster, a businessman, a newscaster."[38]

But Robertson's campaign speeches raised questions among the Republican rank-and-file. It surfaced that a few years before he had gone around telling people that the world would end in 1982 and told his CBN staff to come up with ideas for telecasting it. He unabashedly claimed to possess, through God, the power to effect miracles, such as the time he "prayed away" a hurricane that was about to strike the Virginia seashore. Robertson did not seem quite as uptight about sex as Falwell, but did raise some eyebrows recently by warning that AIDS could be spread by sneezing.[39]

He did invite the antagonists arrayed against Bakker to be guests on his program and they minced no words in attacking the fallen PTL leader. Swaggart. Falwell. But it was Robertson in the final analysis who delivered the unkindest cut of all to Bakker, when a scathing letter he wrote his former protégé in 1977 was used by the prosecutors in Bakker's fraud trial in 1989. In that letter, Robertson wrote:

. . . you continue to make untrue claims about it [that PTL would have a 24-hour-a-day satellite network to compete with CBN] to the public. This is a totally uncalled for waste of the money of God's people merely for the purpose of gratifying your personal ego and unbelievable competitive spirit.

Jim, God does not bless falsehood, and the Bible says He resists the proud. This competitive spirit and financial wastefulness has brought about many of the troubles you are now in. Unless you face reality and ask God's forgiveness, He is going to bring you down.[40]

George Bush

Vice President George Bush consciously moved to the right politically during Ronald Reagan's second term in order to better position himself for the battle for the 1988 Republican presidential nomination. The millions of born again and evangelical voters were one of his priority groups. Not only did he need them to win the 1988 general election, it was imperative that he garner a large percentage of those votes in the primaries as he fought Pat Robertson and others for the nomination itself. It was obvious enough to Bush strategists that the Vice President had to at least neutralize the evangelical vote and deny Robertson a lock on those voters.

One of Bush's first moves, in November 1985, was to call Jim Bakker and ask to meet privately with him that month in a VIP suite at the Charlotte Plaza. Bush told reporters that he watched the *PTL Club* "from time to time,"[41] and that as far as viewers around the country contributing to televangelists like Jim and Tammy, he "certainly wouldn't be opposed to it."[42] Bush flew to Charlotte to meet with Bakker and according to the Vice President's press secretary, Marlin Fitzwater, the two of them "discussed their shared Christian beliefs and the possible 1988 candidacy of evangelical Pat Robertson."[43] Bush was obviously seeking Bakker's endorsement, which President Reagan had received the year before in his landslide 1984 reelection win. Said Bakker of the meeting, "I spent an hour with him" and he impressed me as "a regular guy."[44] Bush characterized the meeting as "very enjoyable, very friendly, [and a] no-agenda kind of a meeting."[45]

In fact, the two got along so well and Bakker's support was so important to Bush that Tammy Faye was invited to meet privately with Barbara Bush in Washington two months later. She did, and put $8,300 on PTL's Master Card for her hotel bill and other expenses during her brief stay in the nation's capital.[46]

The *Washington Post* reported that at the same time, Bakker wanted three Washington insiders with connections to Bush to handle PTL lobbying and other chores in D.C. There was nothing illegal or improper about it from either end, certainly, and its truest significance was in Bakker's attempt to become more politically visible. The *Post* claimed that Doug Wead, the Bush campaign's religious liaison, was to write a book entitled "Anatomy of a Smear" to tell Jim Bakker's side of the FCC investigation (it was never published); Pete Teeley, Bush's former press secretary, was to be PTL's Washington lobbyist; and Dean Burch, the former chairman of the FCC and a Bush confidant, was going to advise Bakker on his relations with the FCC.[47]

The *Post* reported that Doug Wead held several meetings with Jim Bakker over the course of more than a year for the purpose of securing Bakker's endorsement of Bush in 1988. In the "very difficult to believe" category, Don Hardister, Bakker's personal bodyguard who was present at many of those meetings, told *Post* reporters that Wead discussed the possibility of Bakker being named a White House aide if Bush were elected president. Right. As Hardister explained it, "Jim Bakker would have been the new Billy Graham, and he would have gotten [a White House position] without any question. I was looking forward to working at the White House also,"[48] Hardister remembered. Wead denied any discussions of the sort. So did an emphatic Marlin Fitzwater in a White House press briefing as soon as the *Post* exposé hit the fan.

Certainly, however, Bush was courting Bakker and Bakker was responding affirmatively. No one visiting Heritage USA, for instance, could fail to notice a huge autographed picture of Bush in the lobby of PTL's headquarters. But when the Hahn scandal broke and Bakker resigned, the Vice President kept his distance. After his indictment, Bakker was asked whether Bush wanted to forge a political alliance with him. "He did before," Bakker said, "he doesn't now."[49]

Ronald Reagan

Before Bakker became damaged goods, he could count Ronald Reagan as a friend. In fact, at the 1982 national convention of the Religious Broadcasters Association in Washington, D.C., President Reagan praised Jim Bakker and PTL for the hundreds of People That Love centers around the country that provided clothing and food for needy people.

Reagan sent Bakker a congratulatory telegram a year later for the dedication of PTL's new broadcast studio at Heritage. "On this notable occasion, you begin a new chapter. . . . By reaching out with hope and concern for those leading troubled lives, you help many Americans endure and triumph . . . ,"[50] wrote the President.

In a 1984 speech, Reagan spoke glowingly of PTL as one of the "miracles of the entire broadcasting industry."[51]

> **Jim Bakker in prison:** The action of the Justice Department [in 1988 and 1989] in indicting and prosecuting me is hard to understand because I was so close to President Reagan. I had dined at his home in California, at candlelight dinners. I had spent time with him. I knew him.[52]

It was a fact that Bakker had been one of Ronald Reagan's conduits to the millions of evangelical Christians in the country. Reagan had appeared on the *PTL Club* and been very friendly to Bakker over the years.

At this point, no one seems to know whether the decision to impanel the federal grand jury in Charlotte which eventually indicted Bakker was ever reviewed by then–Attorney General Edwin Meese or if Meese mentioned it to Reagan. It is fascinating speculation, though, whether Bakker had been subjected to such enormous derision by the national press that he was beyond even Ronald Reagan being politically able to intervene on his behalf and override one of the Justice Department's U.S. attorneys in the field.

Norman Roy Grutman

While the nation's other high profile televangelists kicked Bakker in the teeth, the last person in the world he expected to join in the attack was Norman Roy Grutman, the flamboyant New York attorney whom Bakker retained with a $50,000 PTL check just before his resignation. The law, like politics, makes strange bedfellows and Grutman had earned his stripes as a python in several cases that touched the evangelical community.

First and foremost, the fifty-nine-year-old New York lawyer had for years represented *Penthouse Magazine* and its publisher, Robert Guccione. In fact, Grutman defended *Penthouse* in a libel suit brought by Jerry Falwell when that skin magazine published a picture of a nude body with Falwell's head attached to it. Grutman won the case for *Penthouse,* and Falwell apparently was sufficiently impressed with his adversary's trial skills that he hired him himself.

Grutman, a high flyer who often wore suspenders with likenesses of nude women on them, was an unlikely mouthpiece for the Virginia Baptist. But when it comes to attack lawyers, you don't hire the nicest attorney you can find. You go to the pound and ask for the toughest.

So, when Jim Bakker felt Jimmy Swaggart and the *Charlotte Observer* closing in on him in March of 1987, Bakker turned to Norman Grutman and asked that he help. Grutman was paid a $50,000 retainer on March 13, 1987 and immediately persuaded the *Observer* to hold its Hahn story for one week in return for an exclusive interview with Bakker. Three days later, it would be Grutman who flew with Richard Dortch and Jerry Falwell to the Palm Springs summit with Bakker which ended in the transfer of power at PTL.[53]

Soon after the resignation, Grutman denied that Bakker was his client. Instead, he claimed he represented PTL, then headed by Falwell. Grutman was reportedly also paid another $440,000 out of PTL funds to represent the ministry as its general counsel.[54] In that capacity, Grutman became one of Jim Bakker's most quotable and outspoken accusers. In fact, it was Grutman who later took credit for uncovering Jim and

Tammy's extravagances when he first reviewed PTL's books. "I was the person who discovered the crimes Jim Bakker has just been convicted of,"[55] he preened after the verdict came in later, contending that Bakker had preyed on the public's gullibility for years before he was caught.

The specter of the man he thought was his own attorney leading the charge against him was too much for Bakker to take, and he asked Melvin Belli if something could be done about it. Belli found Grutman's conduct reprehensible and quickly filed a lawsuit alleging conflict of interest and breach of the duty of loyalty that an attorney owes a client. Belli explained the lawsuit to the press, "What he [Grutman] did was go to Bakker's home and tell him he was going to be his lawyer and help him, but he had just come from Falwell's place and he and Falwell were conspiring to take over Bakker's ministry."[56]

As Bakker recounts it, and even Grutman admitted, it was Grutman who urged Bakker to resign and who actually wrote out the resignation statement. As far as exactly whom Grutman represented, it is interesting to note that in an earlier letter to the *Charlotte Observer,* Grutman himself wrote, "I represent Jim Bakker, Richard Dortch and the PTL."[57] Later, in press conferences and interviews he reiterated that Bakker was one of his clients.[58] Bakker sure thought so. He trusted Grutman and relied upon his counsel in resigning from PTL.[59]

Grutman later called Bakker's confusion about whom Grutman represented "hogwash."[60] Said he to the *New Yorker,* "Oh come on now. I did not represent Bakker. I represented PTL. Any Christian minister who is guilty of either rape or adultery and of being a tax fraud and a cheat certainly should resign. But I did not force him to resign—it was his idea."[61] As Grutman remembered it, "[t]he only time I spent alone with Mr. Bakker was when he asked me to come and pay a social visit to Mrs. Bakker and tell her to stop crying. The woman is an incessant cataract."[62]

Reacting bitterly to Bakker's lawsuit against him, Grutman blasted the fallen televangelist, "Jim Bakker thinks lawsuits are like cosmetic plastic surgery—something he can resort to to lift his face."[63]

On top of that, Grutman complained that by filing the lawsuit Bakker was violating his own earlier pledge never to sue a brother in Christ.[64]

Belli quickly set him straight: "Grutman isn't a brother in Christ," snorted Belli from San Francisco, "We don't have any problem in suing him. We'll just go after that son of a bitch."[65]

George Davis, who replaced Belli as Bakker trial counsel, convinced Bakker to drop the lawsuit against Grutman. So, a jury never got to decide who was right, and Bakker never proved his allegations against Grutman.

Oral Roberts

Roberts, the Pentecostal tent revivalist and faith healer whose religious beliefs most closely resembled Bakker's, was the only televangelist who had anything good to say about Bakker during the media frenzy that ensued for the two years after Bakker resigned. On his own television program, Roberts defended Bakker from Swaggart's attacks by rebuking the Louisianan: "You are sowing discord among the brethren, because somehow you think you're holier than thou. Somehow Satan has put something in your heart that you are better than anybody else. Move back, and treat Jim Bakker like what he is, an anointed man, a prophet of God."[66]

Roberts claimed that Swaggart, the *Charlotte Observer*, and the bureaucratic hierarchy in the Assemblies of God church had "formed an unholy alliance . . . creating an atmosphere for a hostile takeover of PTL and our brother and sister Jim and Tammy Bakker."[67] Then, in a stunning prophecy, Roberts predicted that "the hand of the Lord will fall upon" all of those who had conspired against Bakker and he urged his own viewers to "go to your checkbook" and build a "wall of protection around Jim and Tammy."[68]

Yet, after standing up for Bakker, Roberts's support wavered after the later revelations of financial self-dealing by the Bakkers were reported. "We do not enter the ministry to become rich,"[69] Roberts scolded.

David and James Taggart

During the weeks immediately before the August 28, 1989 start of his trial in Charlotte, the news Jim was getting was all bad, as his closest friends jumped ship and ran to save their own skins rather than stand up for the boss.

David Taggart, Bakker's thirty-two-year-old confidential secretary and personal aide, and his brother James, PTL's own in-house interior decorator and lodging planner, were both convicted by a federal jury on July 26, 1989 of income tax evasion. In its case against the Taggarts, the government proved that the brothers took $1.1 million from PTL for their own use, including the purchase of a $600,000 condominium in the luxurious Trump Plaza in New York City and a matching pair of $40,000 Jaguar automobiles. The brothers, of course, failed to report PTL's cash as income on their tax returns and that sealed their fate with the jury. They were convicted flat out.[70]

But Judge Potter, who would be presiding over Jim Bakker's trial a few weeks later, delayed sentencing the Taggart brothers until after they testified against their former boss at his trial. The incentive for them to do everything they could to help the prosecutors could not have been more obvious.

Don Hardister

Few of those who were in Bakker's inner circle at the height of his power and popularity remained loyal when things really started going south. One of the most shocking defectors was long-time bodyguard Don Hardister. The PTL security chief was like family to Jim and Tammy. He was inseparable from Jim for years, was very close to Bakker's children, and was Jim's "go to" man when he needed help.

Even before Bakker's trial, the *Washington Post* was reporting that Hardister was bad-mouthing Jim. In one interview with reporters from his home in Tega Cay near Jim and Tammy's abandoned house, Hardister was asked about the infamous air-conditioned doghouse. It seems he was its architect.

I just got tired of Jim and Tammy calling me at 3:00 a.m. like it was high noon to check on those idiot dogs. [So I installed a window air conditioner.] We put the dogs inside but they didn't like it. You're talking about a couple of St. Bernards who can suffer a little cold.[71]

It is definitely a bad sign for anyone when their bodyguard starts entertaining the Washington, D.C. press corps with kiss and tell stories, but things were just not going at all well for Bakker.

Richard Dortch

The most devastating blow to Bakker was the one that Richard Dortch dealt him on August 8, 1989, when he entered Judge Potter's courtroom in Charlotte and told the judge that he was pleading guilty to the fraud charges for which both he and Bakker had been simultaneously indicted. Dortch, who had been the PTL's vice president and Bakker's second in command, had been Bakker's alter ego for years and had staunchly defended him against all charges of wrongdoing even long after Bakker resigned. It was Dortch who joined Bakker on his television program to promote the lifetime partnerships which were at the heart of the government's case against the two men.

No one knew more about the operations of PTL than did Richard Dortch, and no one had more contact with Bakker on an ongoing daily basis. Bakker had confided in Dortch and trusted him with every personal and business thought. So, when Dortch walked into that courtroom to remove himself as Bakker's co-defendant in the trial that would be starting three weeks later, it broke the case wide open.

Dortch, dressed in a black suit, stood before Judge Potter with his shoulders hunched and his hands clasped in front of him. His wife, Mildred, and son Richard Dortch, Jr., sat behind him. The judge asked: "Are you in fact guilty of the crimes charged?" Choking back tears, Dortch replied: "In the last few years, I have had a lot of time for reflection, and I am not proud of myself. And I plead guilty." Judge Potter then asked, "You want this court to accept your plea of guilty?" Dortch, "Yes, your honor."[72]

The plea agreement with the prosecutors was straightforward. Dortch agreed to plead guilty to two counts of wire fraud, one count of mail fraud, and a count of conspiracy to commit fraud which are felonies that normally carry a twenty-year prison sentence and fines of over $750,000. The plea bargain required Dortch to testify in the upcoming trial and provide "truthful, complete and forthright information" about all that he knew. Naturally, the prosecutors were most interested in what he would say about any conspiracy he and Bakker entered into, and what he knew about the lifetime partnerships. The government's part of the deal was that it would agree that Dortch would be sentenced to no more than ten years in prison or have to pay more than $500,000 in fines.[73]

When asked for her reaction to Dortch running up the white flag and leaving only Bakker remaining to be brought to the bar of justice, Jessica Hahn told reporters: "I pray they have hell to pay."[74]

Jim and Tammy's response was to plead with what television viewers they had left and try to raise a $1 million defense fund before the start of Jim's trial. On the program, Jim said solemnly that those who were arrayed against him were "using the very lowest moment of my lifetime to destroy me today."[75] Tammy told viewers: "My Lord spoke to me and He said the battle is not between flesh and blood. He said, 'It's between me and the devil, and I'm going to win!'"[76]

> **Jim Bakker in prison:** If we [Dortch particularly, and to a lesser extent the other national televangelists] had only stood together, the prosecutors would never have been able to do this.[77]

NOTES

1. Williams, "Jim and Tammy Rise Again—With Plan to Build a $2B Jerusalem," *Star,* April 19, 1988 at 9.

2. Jim Bakker, interview by author, in Rochester, Minnesota, September 25, 1992.

3. Stille, "The Legal Fight for an Evangelical Empire," *The National Law Journal,* September 28, 1987 at 41.

4. Frank and Grove, "The Raging Battles of the Evangelicals; Swaggart Confirms Investigation of Bakker, Denies Takeover Plan," *Washington Post,* March 25, 1987 at 1-A (Nexis printout); Associated Press, "Billy Graham

'Reserves Comment' on Furor over TV Preachers," *Los Angeles Times*, March 27, 1987 at 22-A, col. 3; Ostling, "Now It's Jimmy's Turn; The Sins of Swaggart Send Another Shock through the World of TV Evangelism," *Time*, March 7, 1988 at 46.

5. Perkinson, "Domestic News," UPI [wire story], March 25, 1987, PM Cycle.

6. "PTL Officials Say Theme Park Not for Sale," UPI [wire story], August 5, 1987, AM Cycle.

7. Dart, "Denies Takeover Attempt; Swaggart Admits a Role in Going after Bakker," *Los Angeles Times*, March 25, 1987 at 1–1, col. 1; Frank and Grove, *supra*, n. 4.

8. Dart, *id.*

9. Jim Bakker, interview by author, in Rochester, Minnesota, September 25, 1992.

10. "Swaggart Cites Proof of New Sex Charges against Bakker," Reuters [wire story], April 26, 1987, AM Cycle.

11. Greenberg, "Swaggart Decries 'Corruption' of Church Leadership," UPI [wire story], March 29, 1987, BC Cycle.

12. *Id.*

13. "Swaggart Cites Proof of New Sex Charges against Bakker," *supra*, n. 10.

14. Dart, *supra*, n. 7.

15. Perkinson, "Domestic News," UPI [wire story], March 24, 1987, AM Cycle.

16. Frank and Grove, *supra*, n. 4.

17. Ostling, "TV's Unholy Row; A Sex-and-Money Scandal Tarnishes Electronic Evangelism," *Time*, April 6, 1987 at 60.

18. Frank and Grove, *supra*, n. 4.

19. "Regional News," UPI [wire story], August 22, 1987, AM Cycle.

20. *Id.*

21. Perkinson, *supra*, n. 5.

22. Chandler and Dart, "Great Opportunity, Great Risk Seen for Falwell as PTL Leader," *Los Angeles Times*, April 11, 1987 at 3-M, col. 4.

23. "Falwell Plans Sweep of Ministry's TV Network," UPI [wire story], May 24, 1987, AM Cycle.

24. Dart, "Could Be a Jolt to TV Ministries; Repercussions Seen in Bakker Scandal," *Los Angeles Times*, March 21, 1987 at 1-M, col. 1.

25. "Heaven Can Wait," *Newsweek*, June 8, 1987 at 58, 61–62.

26. Preston, "Regional News," UPI [wire story], December 5, 1988, BC Cycle.

27. "Heaven Can Wait," *supra*, n. 25 at 58, 61.

28. Craig, "Domestic News," UPI [wire story], October 9, 1987, PM Cycle.

29. Preston, "Vandals Toss Cinnamon Buns at Bakker's PTL," UPI [wire story], October 7, 1989, BC Cycle.

30. Jim Bakker, interviews by author, in Rochester, Minnesota, September 25, 1992; April 4, 1993; and May 29, 1993.

31. Chandler and Dart, *supra*, n. 22.

32. "Windfall in the Senate," *Economist,* November 8, 1980 at 24 (Nexis printout).

33. "Year of the Evangelicals," *Newsweek,* October 25, 1976 at 68.

34. Malone, "Bush and the Bakker Connection; On His Way to the White House, the Vice President Wooed the Preacher," *Washington Post,* December 18, 1988 at 1-C (Nexis printout).

35. Grove, "Scandal Shakes Bakkers' Empire; Followers Fear Widespread Impact on Evangelicals," *Washington Post,* March 21, 1987 at 1-A (Nexis printout).

36. Ostling, *supra,* n. 17.

37. "God and Money," *Newsweek,* April 6, 1987 at 18.

38. Lord, "An Unholy War in the TV Pulpits," *U.S. News & World Report,* April 6, 1987 at 58.

39. Van Deerlin, "Religious Right Gloms onto the Perils of Paula," *San Diego Union-Tribune,* May 20, 1994 at 5-B (Nexis printout).

40. Trial transcript, *United States of America v. James O. Bakker,* Docket C-CR-88-205-1, U.S.D.C. (W.D., N.C.), October 2–5, 1989, vol. 10 at 1833.

41. Malone, *supra,* n. 34.

42. *Id.*

43. *Id.*

44. *Id.*

45. *Id.*

46. *Id.*

47. *Id.*

48. *Id.*

49. *Id.*

50. "Regional News," UPI [wire story], July 4, 1983, AM Cycle.

51. "NRB Finds Hope and Hard Talk in Washington," *Broadcasting,* February 6, 1984, at 152.

52. Jim Bakker, interview by author, in Rochester, Minnesota, May 29, 1993.

53. Stille, *supra,* n. 3 at 40.

54. *Id.*

55. "Regional News," UPI [wire story], October 6, 1989, BC Cycle.

56. Van Dyke, "Regional News," UPI [wire story], March 16, 1988, AM Cycle.

57. Stille, *supra,* n. 3 at 40.

58. *Id.*

59. Jim Bakker, interview by author, in Rochester, Minnesota, September 25, 1992; "Regional News," UPI [wire story], August 28, 1987, AM Cycle.

60. Preston, "Regional News," UPI [wire story], April 7, 1990, BC Cycle.

61. *Id.*

62. Stille, *supra,* n. 3 at 40.

63. Van Dyke, *supra,* n. 56.

64. *Id.*

65. *Id.*

66. Dart, *supra*, n. 7.

67. Perkinson, *supra*, n. 15.

68. *Id.*

69. "TV Preacher's Testimonial on Hill: To Right the Wrong of PTL," *Broadcasting*, October 12, 1987 at 74.

70. Preston, "Bakker Trial to Stay in Charlotte," UPI [wire story], July 10, 1989, BC Cycle; Harris, "$$$ and Sins: Jim Bakker's Case Hits Court; In Charlotte, a Sordid Saga Nears Its Spicy Conclusion," *Washington Post*, August 22, 1987 at 1-E (Nexis printout).

71. Harris, *id.*

72. Wright and O'Neill, "PTL's Dortch: 'I Plead Guilty;' Ex-Top Aide Will Testify against Bakker," *Charlotte Observer*, August 9, 1989 at 1-A (Westlaw printout).

73. *Id.*

74. Wright, "The Bakker Trial: Jim and Tammy," *Charlotte Observer*, August 20, 1989 at 6-A (Westlaw printout).

75. Applebome, "2 Years After Fall of PTL Empire, Bakker Trial Begins," *New York Times*, August 22, 1989 at 14-A, col. 3.

76. Preston, "Jury Selection Proceeds in Bakker Trial," UPI [wire story], August 21, 1989, BC Cycle.

77. Jim Bakker, interview by author, in Rochester, Minnesota, June 26, 1993.

Part Two

THE TRIAL

Chapter 9

A Jury Is Quickly Chosen

Bad Breaks for Bakker

Jury selection for Bakker's trial began Monday, August 21, 1989. Jim had left for Charlotte that weekend, leaving Tammy at home in Orlando where son Jamie was still in grade school. Tammy also drew host duties in Jim's absence on their new daily TV program. Their daughter, nineteen-year-old Tammy Sue Chapman, would be with her father for most of the trial and walk with him to court each day. But as his last weekend before zero hour, Bakker was rocked by two more pieces of shattering news.

First, Judge Potter denied a defense motion for a change of venue which would have moved the trial outside Charlotte and the Western District of North Carolina to some other location in the state where jurors might not have been exposed to the repeated pounding that Bakker took in the *Charlotte Observer*. The judge ruled that the press accounts, while voluminous, would not likely inflame any jurors to the extent that they couldn't fairly weigh the actual evidence of Bakker's innocence or guilt as it would be introduced in court.[1]

In many respects, it was at this juncture that Bakker's trial was lost. School was out. The *Charlotte Observer* had won a Pulitzer Prize, after all, for exposing what it saw as Bakker's wrongdoing two years before any jury ever convicted him. Their reporting, much of it negative about Bakker, had been prominent and extensive. In fact, Bakker's attorneys counted

999 articles that had been published about him and PTL in the year before the trial began.[2] That averages 2.7 articles per day for twelve solid months. When one considers the fact that the *Charlotte Observer* was the primary printed source of news for most people who lived there, the newspaper's potency was overwhelming.

"I don't believe any human being in this century has been treated as badly by the media as we have,"[3] groused Tammy before the trial. Her sense of history is subject to disagreement, of course, but the Bakkers did feel that they had already been tried and convicted in the press before the first juror was seated.

The other bad news that hit Bakker in the face that last weekend was the *Observer*'s publication of a full-page board game about his upcoming trial, which it entitled "Down the Tubes." Bakker's heart must have sunk as he saw the fun the paper was having presaging his defeat. The game consisted of several true-false questions about the lives of Jim and Tammy. If you answered correctly, you moved around the board. The object was to go down the water slide and reach the air conditioned doghouse. But there were pitfalls. If you landed on Jimmy Swaggart's face, you had to "return to start and sob your heart out."[4]

Tammy, despite appearances, knew what was up. She was in constant communication with Jim and, more than that, she was a tougher customer than he in some situations. For instance, she had violently opposed his resignation two years before, arguing that he should never give up PTL and instead should use the power of his TV program to fight it out. And during the broadcast of the *Jim and Tammy Show* that she hosted on the day the jury was being chosen, she told the live audience in Orlando, "I don't know how possibly Jim can get a fair trial in Charlotte, North Carolina."[5] Then, looking straight into the camera, she blew a kiss to her husband and sent him this message: "I love you, sweetheart. Be a brave soldier. Don't you dare give up."[6]

It was her last admonition that particularly intrigues me and, I think, provides further evidence of Bakker's unwillingness or inability to stand up and really fight when he is cornered. That is one of the themes that I have detected from the outset in this case and which explains virtually everything that happened to Bakker over the course of the last seven years. He's just not a fighter. That is not his makeup. He avoids confrontation. And that is why he resigned from PTL rather than confronting that situation and fighting it out. That's why he spent the next two years of his life rebuilding his television ministry and even staking out a new Christian theme park with his bare hands, rather than confronting the legal tidal wave that was moving toward him. That is surely why his wife, who knew him better than anyone else, would have cautioned him not to give up as he emerged for his trial after so many weeks of bad turns in his case.

The answer to the question of whether Jim Bakker really had the intestinal fortitude to fight for his life in a federal courtroom would come within the first three days of his trial.

But that was a week away. Today, a jury had to be selected.

How to Insure That a Celebrity Gets a Fair Trial

Special precautions must be taken by judges, and to a lesser extent attorneys, in high-profile criminal cases to seat jurors whose opinions on the defendant's guilt or innocence have not already been formed on the basis of the publicity to which they have been exposed prior to trial. It is a problem limited to those few cases where the crime is newsworthy enough to warrant extensive coverage, and those cases where the accused is a celebrity or public figure who attracts media attention. What all high profile cases have in common is a torrent of television or newspaper publicity about the case before it goes to trial. The extent to which a potential juror might have been contaminated by watching or reading those press accounts of the case impacts whether that juror will be able to judge the case solely on the testimony and evidence that is presented in the courtroom.

Media reports of notorious crimes and famous defendants are often sensationalized and inaccurate. Potential jurors exposed to them are at risk for developing preconceptions about the crime itself and the guilt or innocence of the defendant. In that way, those prospective jurors are tainted. They are biased rather than impartial and open-minded. And with someone like that on the jury, the defendant could never get a fair trial.

So, in high profile cases, judges are very careful in the jury selection process to go the extra mile to make sure that no juror has been affected by the media blizzard surrounding the case. It is hard work and it takes time.

Jury selection in the O.J. Simpson double murder case in 1994 was a textbook example. A jury pool of one thousand Los Angeles County residents called to the courthouse was subjected to five weeks of prolonged and detailed questioning before twelve were selected as jurors in that case. Then, it took another month to choose twelve alternates to sit with them. At the outset, 304 prospective jurors were required to complete a lengthy questionnaire and then face further questions in court by Judge Lance Ito and attorneys for both sides.[7]

Jury questionnaires are extensively used in highly publicized cases as a means to go beyond the verbal assurances of prospective jurors that they have not formed opinions about the case. The questionnaire Judge Ito used was seventy-five pages in length and consisted of 301 essay-type questions. Potential jurors were required to answer questions like: "What is your impression of Nicole Brown Simpson based upon what has been reported or published in the media?" "How big a problem do you think racial discrimination against African-Americans is in Southern California?" "Which of the following best describes how you would describe the media coverage overall (accurate, sometimes accurate, not accurate)?"[8]

After the judge and the attorneys studied the answers to those questions, the prospective jurors were questioned in the courtroom. They were pushed and they were probed. They were challenged. It was never enough for any of them to say that they had not formed any opinions about the case based on its publicity. The judge and the attorneys were suspicious of everyone and kept digging. Both the prosecution and the defense employed professional jury consultants to help them spot jurors who were lying about not having opinions about O.J.'s guilt or innocence. That some potential jurors would not tell the truth in answer to questions was fully recognized by both sides and those additional steps were taken to respond to it. And in the final analysis, after nine weeks of work, there were twelve jurors and twelve alternates who both sides thought were untainted.[9]

Similar care has been taken in other highly publicized cases. It took eight days to select a jury in Oliver North's 1989 trial in which he was charged with illegally funneling money to Iran-Contra rebels in Nicaragua.[10] It took two weeks of hard-nosed questioning of prospective jurors in 1993 before twelve of them were chosen to hear the case against the two Los Angeles rioters who attacked truck driver Reginald Denny.[11] In the Rodney King criminal case in Simi Valley, California, it took nearly a month to select a jury[12] and in King's Los Angeles federal civil rights suit it took twenty-one days to choose twelve people who had not been contaminated by the media.[13] Even the first Lyle and Erik Menendez murder trials required five weeks to select juries because of the intense publicity those twin cases generated.[14]

Judge Robert Potter chose Jim Bakker's jury by himself in a day.

Choosing the Jury

At exactly 9:30 A.M. on Monday, August 21, 1989, Judge Potter strode into his courtroom to face the sixty-five potential jurors he had ordered to appear for jury duty. He gingerly took his seat and looked out at the motionless crowd. "We are here for the matter of *United States v. James O. Bakker*,"[15] he began. He then briefly explained what the case was about—whether Bakker conspired with Dortch to "create and continue a lavish and extravagant lifestyle by obtaining money from PTL lifetime partners by means of false and fraudulent pretenses . . . using the money received from partners for personal benefit and PTL operating expenses without reserving sufficient funds to construct the facilities promised. . . ."[16]

At that point, he immediately launched into his questioning of the potential jurors. He did it all himself. Neither prosecutors nor defense attorneys were allowed to ask questions. And he did it quickly. By nighttime, twelve jurors and six alternates were in the box. His questioning of those people seated before him was in sharp contrast to the time-consuming methods taken by judges in other recent high profile cases.

For starters, Potter refused the request by Bakker's attorneys to require potential jurors to complete questionnaires designed to gauge latent bias. His oral questioning of jurors in the courtroom was a lot like a homeroom teacher introducing himself and talking to his class on the first day of school. He was folksy and conversational. No questions were too confrontational or embarrassing. It never got very personal. No one was put on the spot.

There was little individual examination, Potter preferring to question them en masse instead. He repeatedly interjected his own personal opinions regarding the subjects of his questions, and he invited jurors to agree with him. He took most answers at face value and downplayed jurors' admissions of having seen or heard news coverage.

Prospective jurors were typically questioned about general information and attitudes as a group, often with a request for a show of hands in response to each question. Then, he would sometimes pose more specific questions to individuals. He dealt with the issue of pretrial publicity early on.

Judge Potter: . . . there is no secret about the fact there's been a great deal of publicity about this trial and I want each of you as you are sitting there today to consider this. If you were a defendant in this trial or any trial, would you be willing to have your case decided on the publicity surrounding this case? Assuming it had publicity like this one has had.[17]

Now criminal trials . . . should and are not conducted in the newspapers and on TV and radio . . . the media, you know, is largely keyed to entertain you.[18]

I want you to ask yourselves the question. I'm not going to ask you the question. You ask yourselves this question. If you were a defendant in a criminal case, would you be willing to have the jury decide your innocence or guilt based on newspaper and TV publicity or would you require the government to prove your guilt beyond a reasonable doubt by evidence and exhibits submitted in a criminal trial?[19]

Now does anyone have any opinions or beliefs whatsoever about the case such that you could not render a verdict in the case based on the evidence . . . and nothing else? If you have, let me know. Now is the time to tell me, not after you get back in the jury room. . . .[20]

Potter then called for a show of hands of those who could not render a fair verdict. A Mr. Johnson raised his hand.

Judge Potter: All right, sir. Let's see. You're not just trying to get out of sitting on the jury, are you?
Mr. Johnson: I knew you'd say that.[21]

Nancy Summey, who would eventually be selected for the jury, was also individually questioned regarding her exposure to publicity or conversations with other people before the trial about Jim Bakker. Several people had actually expressed opinions to her. No matter.

Judge Potter: You have heard opinions expressed about this case, is that right?
Ms. Summey: Yes, sir.
Judge Potter: And in spite of the fact that you've heard opinions expressed about the case, you are telling us now that you would be willing to decide the case based on the evidence presented in court and from nothing you've heard from anyone else, is that right?
Ms. Summey: Yes, sir.
Judge Potter: Now, again, just tell us the person who expressed the opinion to you. Was that a relative—don't tell us the name, but was that a relative or a friend or somebody you worked for or what?
Ms. Summey: All of them.
Judge Potter: Pardon?
Ms. Summey: All of them.
Judge Potter: All of them, okay, all right, everybody's got an opinion. Okay. Move on down. . . .[22]

That was the way Potter, without criticism, dealt with certain answers. He did it all day.

He asked general questions about each potential juror's educational level, their jobs, and their families. He asked if they used credit cards. He asked if any had special training in the ministry or in law, banking, and business. He asked about their religious affiliations and some of them identified themselves as born-again Christians. Most of them had some church affiliation and professed to regular attendance at church. He asked which of them subscribed to the *Charlotte Observer* and many of them did.

The judge clumsily attempted to find out about their television viewing habits and ended up telling them more about his own.

> **Judge Potter:** Do you ever watch or listen to anything like Phil Donahue or Oprah Winfrey or Larry King or Sally Jesse Raphael?
> **Ms. Summey:** No, I don't have the time.
> **Judge Potter:** You don't have the time? I don't either. In fact, I don't even know when they come on.[23]

> **Judge Potter:** Do you ever watch any of those shows I mentioned before . . . ?
> **Mr. Funderburke:** Maybe once in a while. See, I leave one job and go to another one.
> **Judge Potter:** I see. Too busy earning a living and paying taxes. That's the way most of us are.[24] [Note the Judge's opinion and his seal of approval.]

> **Judge Potter:** . . . all right. You ever watch Phil Donahue, Oprah Winfrey or Larry King?
> **Mr. Hill:** I try not to.
> **Judge Potter:** I don't blame you.[25] [Note that juror Hill would be a guest on Larry King Live after the trial.]

But the point is, of course, would any potential jurors sitting in that courtroom ever admit to watching those shows after exchanges like that between the judge and other jurors? In another important area, whether prospective jurors watched religious programming on TV, there were similar odd exchanges.

> **Judge Potter:** Any of you have cable TV . . . all right, the last thing, Mrs. Boardman, do you watch CBN or PTL . . . or any cable network program I have mentioned?

Mrs. Boardman: I don't watch too much TV.
Judge Potter: You don't watch it at all. [Note his overstatement.] Well, you're like I am on that.[26]

Potter's questioning on the specifics of the Bakker trial was terse.

Judge Potter: Now has anyone on the jury seen or otherwise heard about any other criminal proceedings, criminal or civil, involving James O. Bakker, Richard Dortch, . . . or Jessica Hahn? I assume everybody has heard something. . . .
　　Anybody who has not heard, I guess, . . . ?[27]

The judge also raised the issue of Bakker's roll in the hay with Jessica Hahn.

Judge Potter: Now, the defendant Bakker is charged in this case only with mail and wire fraud and conspiracy which are federal crimes and not with any adultery or any other conduct.[28]

Throughout the day, only six potential jurors were excused by Potter after indicating they had opinions which they could not set aside. Not all who had opinions were cut.

Judge Potter: Do you have an opinion?
Mrs. Boardman: Not one that I couldn't set aside.[29]

――――――――――――

Judge Potter: . . . and probably don't read the newspaper much, do you?

――――――――――――

Judge Potter: Have you read much about this case?
Mrs. Dalley: No, I haven't had the opportunity.
Judge Potter: Have you formed an opinion about the case before you came here?
Mrs. Dalley: I don't think so.
Judge Potter: Have you expressed an opinion to anyone else about this case?
Mrs. Dalley: I may have. Years ago, I may have.
Judge Potter: Well, are you telling me now then that you do not have an opinion about the case at this time?

Mrs. Dalley: I don't think so.

Judge Potter: You don't think so or you know you don't have an opinion?

Mrs. Dalley: Well, to say you don't have any opinion at all is like a blank slate.

Judge Potter: Well, I understand that.

Mrs. Dalley: I don't think I have a blank slate.

Judge Potter: You don't have a blank slate up there in your head, do you. You've got to think?[30]

Judge Potter: And have you expressed your opinion to anyone else?

Mr. Newton: Jokingly.

Judge Potter: Pardon?

Mr. Newton: Jokingly.

Judge Potter: Well, you've never—whatever it was, it was insignificant in a sense. What I'm asking, is it insignificant what you've said?

Mr. Newton: Yes, sir.[31]

Unsurprisingly, given his methods, Judge Potter succeeded in strapping twelve jurors and six alternates in the box in his courtroom by 7:10 P.M. that night.

This would be the only audience that counted for Jim Bakker's last performance. The curtain would go up in one week.

Final Roll Call

The Bakker jurors were seated in this order:

1. Nancy Summey [a Registered Nurse and Baptist from Charlotte who said she'd been "saved"]

2. Rick Hill [a technical services representative for Fiber Industries (formerly Celanese), married to a nurse, and a Southern Baptist who said he'd been "saved." He lived outside Monroe, a town forty miles north of Charlotte]

3. Roscoe Jones [a data processor with IBM for ten years, and a Methodist]

4. Naydeen Coffey [formerly an employee of Delmar Photography in Charlotte, who had no formal church affiliation]

5. James McAlister [a retired Chester Chemical Company salesman, and a Methodist]
6. Gwendolyn Morrison [a machine operator at National Metal Fabricators in Charlotte, and a Methodist]
7. Buddy Howell Dyer [a liquor store clerk at the ABC Store in Monroe, he lived in the country ten minutes from town. He was a Methodist]
8. Catherine Boardman [a Charlotte resident who worked for Technical Development Corporation, and an Episcopalian]
9. Ray Love [an electrician from Monroe, who was not a churchgoer]
10. Vivian Ferguson [a retired domestic worker, and a Baptist]
11. Thomas Teeples [a home builder and electrical contractor]
12. Barbara Dalley [a Monroe homemaker with five children, and a Roman Catholic]

The alternates:

1. Mickey J. Bolin [a plastics company supervisor from Belmont, North Carolina, and a Presbyterian]
2. John D. Clayton [a planner at Duke Power, also from Belmont, North Carolina, and a Baptist]
3. Shirley M. Wise [an office worker at Cherry-Line Oil Company in Cherryville, North Carolina, and a Presbyterian]
4. Robert E. Thornberry [a systems analyst with Belk Store Services in Davidson, North Carolina, twenty miles north of Charlotte, and a Presbyterian]
5. Mr. Myers [a maintenance technician at Phillip Morris in Concord, North Carolina, and a Lutheran]
6. Mrs. J.B. Grier [a physical plant supervisor at Johnson C. Smith University in Charlotte, and a Presbyterian]

NOTES

1. Wright and Garloch, "Jurors Selected—Questions Focus on Publicity Issue," *Charlotte Observer*, August 22, 1989 at 1-A (Westlaw printout).
2. Jim Bakker, interview by author, in Rochester, Minnesota, September 25, 1992.
3. "It's Jim and Tammy Time Again!" *People*, July 4, 1988 at 34.

4. Johnson, "Newsmakers," *Los Angeles Times,* August 20, 1989 at 2-A, col. 1.

5. Wright and Garloch, *supra,* n. 1.

6. *Id.*

7. "Subtle Issues in Jury Selection," *Des Moines Register,* September 26, 1994 at 3-A, col. 3; Cobb, "Simpson Jury Questions Probe for Bias," *Des Moines Register,* October 1, 1994 at 4-A, col. 5.

8. Cobb, *supra,* n. 7 at col. 6.

9. "Ito Wary of 'Hermits' in Simpson Jury Pool," *Des Moines Register,* October 13, 1994 at 3-A, col. 4; "Simpson Jury Selection Ends," *Des Moines Register,* December 9, 1994 at 6-A, col. 3.

10. Moran and d'Errico, "The Law," *Boston Globe,* February 12, 1989 at 18-A (Nexis printout).

11. "The Denny Beating Trial: The Verdicts; Sequence of Events," *Los Angeles Times,* October 19, 1993 at 19-A, col. 2.

12. Price and Taylor, "The Rodney King Verdict," *Washington Times,* April 18, 1993, at 6-A (Nexis printout).

13. *Id.*

14. Abrahamson, "To Retry, or Not to Retry, Is the Question," *Los Angeles Times,* January 27, 1994 at 1-B, col. 2.

15. Transcript of jury selection, *United States of America v. James O. Bakker,* Docket C-CR-88-205-1, August 21, 1989 at 2.

16. *Id.* at 19.

17. *Id.* at 12.

18. *Id.* at 19.

19. *Id.* at 20–21.

20. *Id.* at 33.

21. *Id.* at 34.

22. *Id.* at 39–40.

23. *Id.* at 58.

24. *Id.* at 61–62.

25. *Id.* at 80.

26. *Id.* at 211–12.

27. *Id.* at 116.

28. *Id.* at 157.

29. *Id.* at 189.

30. *Id.* at 302–3.

31. *Id.* at 192.

Chapter 10

Bakker's Last Stage— Courtroom 112

The Scene at the Courthouse

Before dawn on the first day of Jim Bakker's trial—Monday, August 28, 1989—the news media moved into position to secure the federal courthouse in downtown Charlotte. Engineers from CNN in Atlanta erected a huge eight-foot-wide satellite dish on an adjacent parking lot and pitched a massive tent to cover all of the uplink equipment from the searing North Carolina sun. When asked for an example of the last time they set up this mobile studio, the technicians said it was in Washington, D.C. for the 1987 Reagan-Gorbachev summit.[1]

While there was plenty of room on the courthouse grounds for the one hundred reporters who would keep the Bakker vigil throughout the trial, Judge Potter's small, windowless courtroom had only eighty seats for visitors. The Judge reserved eighteen of those for Charlotte-area reporters and twenty-four for members of the public, many of whom were pro-Bakker. A few were not. Another eighteen seats were reserved for out-of-town journalists, who were required to begin signing up for them at 5:00 A.M. each day. On this first day, reporters for the *Washington Post* and *Chicago Tribune* were at the top of the list because they paid local teen-agers to stand in line before dawn for them. Reporters for the *New York Times*, the *Los Angeles Times* and other major American newspapers covered the trial, as did correspondents for the *Daily Telegraph* of London, the

Associated Press, United Press International, and all major television networks.[2]

By the time Bakker arrived at the courthouse at 9:00 A.M., reporters and photographers who did not have seats inside had formed two lines along the steps leading up to the seventy-nine-year-old stone, sand-colored building. Many photographers stood on ladders for a better view. A black BMW was driven up to the curb and a tanned Bakker emerged. An attorney on each arm, he was quickly escorted through the press phalanx. "Have a nice day"[3] was his only response to the questions that were shouted at him. With that, he bounded in the door.

Shut out of the courtroom action, reporters turned their attention to the spectators milling around behind the police barricades. Vernon Hines, a seventy-two-year-old gas station owner from Atlanta, was interviewed and said that he had left his home at 4:00 A.M. to drive to Charlotte in order to support Bakker. "I'm going to go in there and pray for Jim Bakker,"[4] he said. Standing next to him was C. W. Dawkins, from Columbia, South Carolina, who told the press that he had been saying his prayers, also. "I've been praying he gets 20 years,"[5] Dawkins scoffed.

The Combatants

As the jury filed into the cramped first floor courtroom, the stage was set for action. It didn't look that much different from Judge Ito's relatively small Los Angeles courtroom. From the perspective of a seat in the spectators' section, the twelve jurors and six alternates were taking their seats in a jury box that took up most of the left side of the front of the courtroom. At the center of the room and atop the traditionally elevated bench, Judge Potter, robed, sat patiently but intensely, his eyes searching the entire courtroom. There was no doubt that he was in control and that this was his domain.

Robert D. Potter, sixty-six, was nominated to the federal bench in 1981 by North Carolina's senior U.S. senator, Jesse Helms. With his white hair and dark eyebrows, he looked like Judge Wapner but had pronounced jowls and Lyndon Johnson–size ears.

Potter had made a name for himself in the 1960s when, as a conservative on the local county board of commissioners, he reamed other politicians for supporting anti-poverty programs. To Potter, they were just "buy[ing] off the militants"[6] and it would "bring about a completely socialistic government if it is not stopped."[7] He was a Helms soul-mate for sure.

As a judge, Potter was crusty and short-tempered. Some called him a loose cannon. Quickly earning a reputation as one of the toughest judges in the country by slapping convicted defendants with harsh sentences and heavy jail time, he was known everywhere as "Maximum Bob."[8]

A strict Catholic, Potter could be very moralistic in criminal cases and was typically pro-prosecution, according to defense lawyers.[9] His severe sentences were his trademark and to defendants sitting petrified in his courtroom waiting to be tried or sentenced, he was the Grim Reaper.

There were two long tables for the attorneys who would try the case, one for the prosecution and one for the defense. At the defense table, on the right side of the room, sat a subdued forty-nine-year-old Jim Bakker. Throughout the trial, he would furiously take notes on what every witness said. He looked like a college student in a lecture class trying to get down every word the professor said each day.

To Jim's left was Charlotte attorney Harold Bender, a forty-seven-year-old criminal defense attorney who was no stranger to this building. Bender was a local boy who epitomized the Deep South, with a courtly manner, deep Southern accent, and toughness in his gut. Quick-thinking on his feet, Bender was charming when speaking to the judge and jury. He was healthy and in shape, with tousled hair showing a glint of gray and bright blue eyes. On weekends in the fall, he was a college football official for the Southern Conference, refereeing NCAA games between schools like Vanderbilt and Duke.

To Bender's left sat Bakker's lead attorney, Californian George Davis, who at eighty-two years old had left semi-retirement and his hundred-acre Hawaiian cattle ranch to lend his grit as the country's best known "last chance lawyer" to a Bakker case that had been rocked with setbacks for weeks.

Defending more than one hundred death penalty cases, Davis made national headlines the five years he spent representing Caryl Chessman, California's Red Light Bandit, for whom Davis engineered several impressive appeals and delays before Chessman was finally executed in 1960. He quickly became a champion of the world-wide movement to outlaw the death penalty.[10]

Davis had also represented Alfred Krupp, the heir to the German munitions empire, Philippine opposition leader Benigno Aquino, and several other celebrity clients throughout five dramatic decades of practicing law. Warner Brothers made a movie about his defense in the first sodium pentathol trial in history and Davis earned international acclaim with a stunning series of acquittals in tough, hard criminal cases. A heavyweight in California politics, Davis managed President Harry Truman's 1948 come-from-behind presidential campaign in that state.[11]

Davis had been introduced to Bakker by a mutual friend, a Texas minister, on the day Bakker was indicted. A large man with white hair and bushy eyebrows, he had a presence in the courtroom not unlike that of Clarence Darrow. Accustomed to being given wide latitude by trial judges to weave often unconventional theories in his celebrated cases, Davis hit a brick wall in Judge Potter. This judge was strict and unyielding. Nor did Judge Potter show deference to Davis's reputation as one of the nation's best-known lawyers. The two clashed from the first day of the trial to the last.

The plan was for Davis to examine Bakker and the other major defense witnesses. The goal was to persuade the jury that despite all the negative things the government would be saying about PTL and its money, Bakker himself never intended to defraud any contributors nor was he personally involved in any wrongdoing. Bender's role would be to cross-examine the government's witnesses with the vigor necessary to discredit or neutralize the testimony of each.

Davis was a maverick and one of the last of the old courtroom gunslingers. His methods were unorthodox at times.

George Davis: I always try my cases a little differently. Let's just leave it at that. [The defense of Jim Bakker] is one of my 'cause' cases. I've always been motivated to help people. This case is complicated and it's difficult. It just fits into what my whole lifetime motivation has been.[12]

At the government's counsel table, on the left side of the courtroom and just a few feet from the jury box, two Justice Department attorneys paged through files of documents in last-minute preparation. To the right sat Assistant Attorney General Deborah Smith from the department's Washington, D.C. fraud division who had been assigned to pilot the case against Bakker. Fraud was Smith's specialty and she knew what she was doing. Formerly, she had prosecuted multimillion dollar white-collar fraud cases in Alaska and earned a reputation as a tough-nosed, sharp trial lawyer. She had grown up in Florida, and before going to law school in Boston had worked a year as a reporter for the *Fort Lauderdale News*.[13]

A taller woman with long auburn hair, Smith spoke confidently and sternly. She was very serious in the courtroom and it was clear she had strong personal feelings about Bakker's guilt. She believed in her case.

To her left was Assistant United States Attorney Jerry Miller from the U.S. Attorney's Office in North Carolina. Miller, as the area's local federal prosecutor, was a battle-trim veteran of Judge Potter's courtroom. More than six feet tall, the forty-one-year-old former football star at North Carolina State was the quintessential good old boy. Most often friendly, humble, and low-key in his treatment of witnesses and jurors, he was like a comfortable, old shoe in front of the jury. He spoke their language. And, the fact that Miller was a devout Baptist made him the ideal choice to present the case against Bakker and cross-examine Bakker's followers.[14]

Between the judge's dais and the defense table, court attendants had positioned a television set and VCR to permit the jury to view the hours of PTL programming that would be introduced into evidence during the trial. Easels and an overhead projector were also located nearby for what promised to be a trial that would come to life with charts, graphs, photographs, and enlargements. Five feet behind the lawyers' tables was a three-foot-high partition which ran the width of the courtroom and separated the eight rows of benches for spectators and the press from the front of the courtroom where the fireworks would soon begin.

The space between the counsel tables and the partition was crammed with dozens of boxes filled with hundreds of documents and exhibits which would be introduced into evidence. The witness stand was attached to the judge's dais, on the left side closest to the jury, and the desk for the court reporter who would be transcribing every word of testimony was directly in front of the Judge. Witnesses would enter and exit through a swinging gate at the center of the partition, and federal marshals were stationed both inside and outside the courtroom.

As the two and a half years of unprecedented upheaval since Jim Bakker's resignation wound down and the last juror took her seat, Judge Potter had a small, brown sign posted outside in the hallway which read, "Quiet—Court in Session."

Potter glanced once more from right to left, saw that all was still, brought his gavel down loudly, and began the trial by directing the attorneys to deliver their opening statements to begin the first week of what the media called the trial of the century in the South.

NOTES

1. Smith, "TV Crew Camping Out for Coverage," *Charlotte Observer,* August 28, 1989 at 6-A (Westlaw printout).

2. Garloch, "Spoofs, Sellers Hold Court Outside; Bakker Impersonators among Faces in the Crowd," *Charlotte Observer,* August 29, 1989 at 1-A (Westlaw printout).

3. *Id.*

4. Leland, Wright, and the Associated Press, "On the Scene," *Charlotte Observer,* August 30, 1989 at 12-A (Westlaw printout).

5. *Id.*

6. Nichols, "Bakker's Fate Rests with Tough Judge," *Gannett News Service,* October 23, 1989.

7. *Id.*

8. *Id.*

9. Chase, ed., *Almanac of the Federal Judiciary,* vol. 1 (Aspen Law & Business, Englewood Cliffs, N.J.: 1996) at 29.

10. Abrams, "Last-Chance Lawyer Heats up Bakker Defense," *Los Angeles Times,* August 24, 1989 at 1-V, col. 1.

11. *Id.*

12. Nowell (Associated Press), "Bakker Picks Colorful Lawyer to Defend Him," *Richmond (VA) News Leader,* January 23, 1989 at 9 (Westlaw printout).

13. Page, "PTL Trial Promises Not to Be Boring; Opposing Attorneys Have Opposite Styles, Manners," *Columbia (S.C.) State,* August 20, 1989 at 1-A (Nexis printout).

14. *Id.*

Chapter 11

The Trial—Week One

Opening Statements (Monday, August 28, 1989)

Prosecutor Jerry Miller addressed the jury first, and gave a smooth, matter-of-fact, thirty-five-minute overview of the government's case against Bakker. The evangelist used his television ministry to "cheat people out of their money" by using "untruths" and "half-truths" to deceive his viewers, Miller contended.[1] Bakker's fraud, the prosecutor argued, was in overselling tens of thousands of $1,000 lifetime partnership lodging and vacation deals which he knew could not be honored. The government promised to prove to the jury that, rather than spend the money raised on the construction of the necessary hotels at Heritage USA, Bakker diverted it to other uses including the payment of rich bonuses to himself and his wife.

His motive, Miller insisted, was to keep the donations pouring in so the Bakkers would have plenty of money to spend on themselves. The guts of the crime was that Bakker deliberately failed to disclose to those who were buying partnerships that the packages were oversold and there was not room for everyone who was buying them. "This case is about tricking people out of their money. The motive was opulence. The motive was extravagant living,"[2] sneered Miller, who vowed to take the jury behind the scenes at PTL and show them a minister gone bad.

George Davis's eighty-five-minute opening statement on

Bakker's behalf, by contrast, was punctuated with controversy. He told the jurors that the vacation packages were not real estate sales at all but were voluntary donations to the ministry which were not covered by the fraud statutes Bakker was charged with breaking. The only thing Bakker did here was to accept free-will donations to his ministry. "We will prove there wasn't a sale of one single membership,"[3] he emphasized.

He explained that Bakker had acted innocently and in good faith in all of his partnership fund-raising, and that he never entertained a criminal thought. "He was a creative, religious genius,"[4] roared Davis, and it was Jim Bakker who was the victim in this case, betrayed by trusted lieutenants Dortch and Taggart, who were "confessed and convicted felons,"[5] whose testimony against Bakker should not be believed.

But the jury took an early negative reading of George Davis during his lengthy argument when he and Judge Potter clashed dramatically. On several occasions during Davis's opening, Judge Potter interrupted and scolded him for making inappropriate comments. What Davis was doing that so angered the judge was arguing his case, which is supposed to be done at the end of the trial in a lawyer's closing arguments. The judge was madder than a hornet and kept telling him to toe the line. "I'm not going to warn you again,"[6] admonished Potter.

But Bakker's attorney stuck to his guns when prosecutor Deborah Smith began her direct examination of the government's first witness an hour later. Davis repeatedly interrupted Smith's questions and objected to her use of the word "sale" in discussing the PTL partnerships. With each objection, he would attempt to make the point for the jury that those lodging packages were not really sales but were instead gifts to the ministry. That infuriated the judge who lectured Davis to keep his objections short and to the point. But when Davis refused to remain silent while statements were made to which he objected, Potter erupted, "Mr. Davis—be quiet."[7] A few minutes later with Davis's objections continuing, Potter growled, "You don't have to make a speech. Now sit down."[8]

Bakker, sitting wide-eyed as his attorney was being ground up in a fight with the judge during the first hour of the trial, was horrified at the spectacle and knew that he was in deep trouble.[9]

The Government's First Witness

The prosecution started with a bang by calling David Taggart to the stand, who for eight years had been Bakker's personal assistant and confidant. Wearing an expensive suit and designer glasses, and with his slightly receding light hair smartly styled, the thirty-two-year-old Taggart looked like a young stock-broker. His facial features were soft, but he brought the hammer down hard on his former boss. Deborah Smith would spend the rest of the entire first day of the trial asking Taggart questions about everything he had seen at Bakker's side, and his answers painted a very unflattering picture of the fallen evangelist.

One of Taggart's most jarring admissions was that Bakker, on a daily basis, received reports on the number of lifetime partnerships that had been purchased (to use the verb George Davis found objectionable) the day before.[10] He was also briefed on the amount of money the ministry was receiving each day in contributions. The cashier's office would prepare those figures for Bakker and record them in a book which he would retain on his desk. The government had seized that book from Bakker's office and Smith had Taggart identify it. She then introduced it into evidence.[11]

Even when he would be traveling, Bakker would stay on top of the money the ministry desperately needed. He called in and asked about the "tray for that day," Taggart remembered, a three-foot-long tray of mail containing the previous day's donations.

The bulk of Taggart's testimony concerned how Bakker spent PTL's money. Responsible for all of Bakker's travel arrangements, he reviewed bills that PTL had paid for recent Bakker vacations. A three-week visit to Hawaii in January 1984, with a stop in Palm Springs, California on the way back to Charlotte, cost $100,000 for Bakker and his ten-member entourage. They stayed at the Halekulani Hotel on Waikiki in an oceanfront condo at a daily room rate of $1,675, took along an assistant to do Tammy's laundry on vacation, and flew first class all the way.[12]

Taggart also explained that Bakker did not have to wait for a vacation to live in luxury because he and Tammy occupied several sumptuous homes. The ministry purchased a $900,000 lakeside parsonage for the couple at Tega Cay, South Carolina, and staffed it with three maids and several security guards for the Bakkers and their children. PTL paid the Bakkers' utilities, too, including the electric bill which they often ran up to $2,000 a month by heating the pool to a comfortable 90° every day.[13] In 1982, the ministry bought a $375,000 condominium for the Bakkers on Florida's Atlantic coast, north of Miami, and spent $150,000 to decorate it. But after three weeks there, Tammy complained that it was nothing more than a hotel room. It was sold.[14] In 1984, they bought a $400,000 home in Palm Desert, California, which was sold in 1987 so that the Bakkers could move up to a $600,000 spread in nearby Palm Springs.[15]

When Taggart dropped the bomb that Bakker "had compared himself to being paid like Johnny Carson,"[16] Deborah Smith unveiled two huge charts for the jury showing what Bakker and his top aides had received. In 1986 alone, Jim was paid $313,000 in salary and $790,000 in bonuses. That same year, Tammy received $99,000 in salary and $265,000 in bonuses.[17] Nowhere near Carson's level, to be sure, but the point the government was making for the jury was that there was something suspicious about any minister accepting income of a million dollars a year. Taggart knew even more about bonuses, too, because he was the one who kept the minutes of the meetings of the PTL board of directors. He explained that whenever the board would vote a bonus of $50,000, for instance, Pastor Dortch had told him to always double it to take taxes into account. So, Taggart would record in the minutes that it was a $100,000 bonus.[18]

Taggart also disclosed that Jim had plastic surgery for himself and Tammy in 1982, which PTL paid, and that Jim spent plenty of his own money on Tammy over the years surprising her with such gifts as a $5,720 mink coat, a $10,000 diamond ring, and the most fashionable clothes money could buy. But Taggart was quick to add that wealth didn't bring happiness to the Bakker family and that in early 1987, PTL paid nearly $1,900 so that he and Vi Azvedo, a friend of Tammy's, could go through the Betty Ford Center's outpatient drug abuse program with Tammy and Jim to give Tammy moral support.[19]

> **Jim Bakker in prison:** It [the trial] was all driven by symbols— the dog house, the gold plated faucets in the presidential suite.[20]

The other major PTL expenditure about which Taggart testified was the $165,000 that was earmarked for Jessica Hahn to buy her silence. "Mr. Bakker did not want to pay Jessica Hahn. Mr. Bakker made the statement that he didn't believe in paying blackmail money, but he also said do whatever—he told Richard Dortch to do whatever he had to do. . . ."[21] Taggart also confirmed that Dortch did handle the deal and that Bakker was unaware of where Dortch got the money.[22]

Ms. Smith kept poking Taggart for information about what kind of man Jim Bakker really was. Taggart finally chipped in that Bakker didn't like to hear bad news from anyone and that many of the vice presidents were afraid to directly give him any. Instead, they would ask Taggart or Shirley Fulbright, Jim's executive secretary, to pass on bad news for them.[23] And, Bakker had a habit of carrying around a hand-held tape recorder with him each day when he would walk the Heritage grounds and he would dictate a daily list of things for his staff to do. The government had obtained those lists from Bakker's files, too, and Smith asked Taggart to read several entries for the jury:

> June 25, 1985. Tell Joyce I need shampoo at home. [Also some gray rinse for my hair.] I guess it's Fanciful Rinse Number 12.
> July 12, 1985. Make sure that they are putting flea powder on our dog, all the dogs, and take care of the cats. I must find my bifocal glasses. Please have anybody look for them. I can't even find one pair of them now.
> July 7, 1985. Find out why they took the air conditioning out of Jamie's tree house and get them to put it back in immediately.[24]

As the first day of the trial drew to a close, and David Taggart left the stand, the die was cast. Who on the jury could possibly have felt anything but unease at the way Jim Bakker had consumed ministry contributions on an opulent Hollywood lifestyle for himself and Tammy? The signal that had been flashed to the jury was that Bakker had selfishly profited from his own ministry. The government was off to the races.

Bakker knew he had been wounded by Taggart's testimony. Tammy attempted to cushion the blow for followers by telling her television audience on that day's show, "What you see on the tube, folks . . . take with a grain of salt. Don't believe everything you hear."[25] She also offered a rather unusual prayer: "Lord, I know you will squelch and quash any courtroom loss."[26] They knew that they were in for the fight of their lives.

The Second Day of Trial (Tuesday, August 29, 1989)

David Taggart returned to the stand when court reconvened Tuesday morning to face cross-examination by Bakker attorney Harold Bender, who employed some tough love on young Taggart. In a series of nonconfrontational and friendly questions, the attorney extracted several admissions that cast Bakker in a much more positive light than Taggart had been willing to allow the day before. Particularly noteworthy was the fact that Jim Bakker was breaking his back at Heritage and that PTL's board was genuinely concerned for his health. Taggart, who was with Bakker virtually all the time, testified that "he worked on a 24-hour basis."[27] He admitted that Bakker was the one who single-handedly raised every penny of PTL's $150 million budget each year, and that Bakker was everything from television performer to groundskeeper at Heritage.[28]

And on his trips around the grounds with his tape recorder, the actual daily transcripts revealed that Bakker's primary concerns were for others.

January 20, 1986. Elders and pastors are to have a room that they pray with salvation people after an altar call.
December 18, 1986. Shirley, get a little gift for Frances, the retarded lady that comes to the show every day. Her and her

mother live at Heritage USA and just get a Christmas card and put with the package and tell her that Tammy and I love her and thank her for coming to the show so often and being an encouragement to us.[29]

Bender also forced Taggart to admit that the PTL board regarded Bakker as the corporation's primary, irreplaceable asset and paid $857,791 a year for premiums on a $50 million life insurance policy it took out on him.[30] Jim Bakker *was* PTL. The former Bakker aide also acknowledged that the board was concerned for several years that Jim and Tammy were not being adequately compensated considering all the exhausting work they were doing. The pricey bonuses were "love gifts" from the board to make up for it.[31]

In fact, Taggart revealed, he attended meetings of the board "in which each of the board members expressed to Reverend Bakker his or her concern for the health and welfare of the Bakker family"[32] and that it was the board that purchased the Florida condominium in an effort to force Bakker to take some time away from Heritage. Taggart, who handled much of Bakker's money, also admitted that he knew personally that Bakker had reimbursed PTL from his own pocket for the time that Bakker spent in that seaside condo at its fair market rental value.[33]

As far as all of the time Jim and Tammy were spending each year in Palm Springs, the full story was that there were so many tens of thousands of PTL followers in California that Bakker was there to purchase land for a West Coast Heritage.[34]

So, what the prosecutors attempted to characterize as Bakker jetting to California to enjoy the lifestyle of the rich and famous in reality bore closer resemblance to David Letterman taking his New York–based *Late Show* to Hollywood for a week during the year. Not that Bakker didn't live well while he was on the road, but it had a business purpose. And, nobody ever said business travel had to be painful. Or that if you didn't stay at Motel 6, you'd go to prison for forty-five years for living too high on the hog.

On a less congenial note, Bender attempted to damage Taggart's credibility with the jury in a flurry of sharp exchanges. He probed not only the fact that Taggart stood to gain points with his own sentencing judge if he testified well against Bakker, but also that Taggart had himself been convicted a few weeks before in that same courtroom.

Mr. Bender: So if the prosecution likes your testimony, they are going to tell the Judge, is that your understanding? ***
Mr. Taggart: To the best of my knowledge, yes.

Mr. Bender: You embezzled from your company $2500 and had it paid to your close personal friend, didn't you, Mr. Taggart?
Mr. Taggart: To my recollection, no.
Mr. Bender: And you have embezzled other funds from PTL, have you not?
Mr. Taggart: No, I have not. I was charged with income tax evading.
Mr. Bender: I have no further questions.[35]

Lois Chalmers, a senior writer at PTL who was responsible for brochures and direct mail letters, was the government's next witness. As she spoke about each of the lodging partnership programs, from the Heritage Grand to the Towers to the Bunkhouse, the actual letters she had written explaining those programs were introduced into evidence and blow-ups of them were shown to the jury. She then read key sentences from each letter and implied that Bakker, who signed them, had been less than honest in representing that people who purchased lifetime partnerships would be guaranteed lodging for life because he wasn't using all of the money he raised to build the promised hotels.[36]

But on cross-examination, the weakness of the government's case was exposed. Harold Bender asked this witness to read lines and paragraphs from the letters that the prosecutors had skipped over a few minutes earlier. Among them were these: "Your gifts are used to support PTL and all its programs."[37] Another one read: "Please fill out the special form I am enclosing and send it today with your gift of $500 for the PTL ministry."[38] And in yet another one: "Yes, Jim, I want to become a PTL lifetime partner. I am enclosing my $1000 gift to help build the new PTL Partners Center and keep PTL preaching the gospel."[39]

It doesn't take an English teacher to see that in the letters with which the government was attempting to hang Bakker, he and his writers had used language to allow them to spend donations not just on the hotels but on "PTL and all its programs," "the PTL ministry," and [to] "keep PTL preaching the gospel." Nothing in those letters said that every dollar contributed for lifetime partnerships would be spent on the hotels at Heritage. But that was the key government evidence of fraud on Bakker's part.

So after two days of testimony, the only really damning thing against Bakker was not smoking gun evidence of him misrepresenting things to his contributors in the letters that the government kept waving before the jury, but the way he spent his salary and bonuses on the good life. But—he wasn't indicted for living the good life, he was indicted for fraud.

The government called Richard Ball, a PTL vice president, to the stand. He had worked with Jim Bakker to duplicate thousands of plaster replicas of an original statue of David and Goliath by well-known Italian sculptor Yacov Heller. Even if the representations in Bakker's fund-raising letters didn't scream fraud, it was the government's contention that he tried to con people with these eight-inch statues by mass producing them for $10 each and then implying to viewers that they were worth $1,000. So, David and Goliath would become one of the themes of the government's case and those statues would clank around that courtroom for five weeks.

First, the government had seized the original statue from Bakker's desk, which he had used as a "source of strength" as he described it. It was introduced into evidence and Miller asked the judge for permission to pass it to the jury so they could examine it. Potter replied: "Okay, let it be admitted, and don't drop it on your toe over there. It looks like it's kind of heavy."[40]

Then, Miller introduced into evidence one of the replicas and got this witness to confirm that it only cost $10 to make. But as Miller passed the replica to the jury, its craftsmanship didn't pass the test and the witness yelled out: "You just lost the sword. It always broke off."[41] But as the jury was looking at it, the questions continued:

> **Mr. Miller:** Now would there be any way that you could ascribe a value of $1000 to that copy?
> **Mr. Ball:** I don't believe so.
> **Mr. Miller:** That would be a pretty fair markup on a ten dollar piece, wouldn't it?
> **Mr. Ball:** I believe so.[42]

And with the government having fired that big artillery against Bakker, the day drew to a close and the jury was sent home at 6:00 P.M.

The Third Day of the Trial
(Wednesday, August 30, 1989)

This was the day the earth opened up and swallowed Jim Bakker alive.

Steve Nelson, the thirty-nine-year-old former PTL vice president from Franklin, Tennessee, offered some of the most damning testimony of the trial against his former boss. Nelson, responsible for PTL's telethons, said that he became angry when more lifetime partnerships were sold in the Grand Hotel than there was room to ever accommodate them. The hotel was built for 25,000 partners, but 66,683 partnerships were sold.[43] Two or three times during 1985 and 1986, he took the numbers straight to Dortch and Bakker and told them they were in real trouble.

> **Mr. Nelson:** I specifically went to Pastor Dortch . . . [and I said:] We've got big time problems, we're not going to get these people in there. . . . *** I specifically said to Pastor Dortch at the second meeting that someone could go to jail for this. *** And it was then that I went and actually met in Jim's office and talked with Jim saying there was a problem. He said, "Look, you know, the Lord's

done a miracle for us here and there is not anything for you to be worried about or concerned about, you know, we can get room, we can have room for these people to get in here."[44]

Nelson also revealed that he was under instructions from Dortch and Bakker to keep two sets of lifetime partnership tallies at the phone bank as his fifty to a hundred operators took calls from around the country. The sheet with the real numbers went to Bakker and Dortch. The second, sham tally showing far fewer lifetime partnerships was shown to the television audience.[45] Jerry Miller zeroed in.

> **Mr. Miller:** So you had two sets of numbers?
> **Mr. Nelson:** Yes, sir, we did.
> **Mr. Miller:** And how frequently during the telethons did these numbers get reported to Mr. Bakker and Mr. Dortch?
> **Mr. Nelson:** Every few minutes they would call, especially when they were promoting the offer.[46]

But in early 1987, when the roof started caving in, Nelson was ordered to destroy the evidence.

> **Mr. Nelson:** Well, I got a call from Pastor Dortch too. Told me to destroy the reports—destroy everything, but it was regarding— they thought there was an IRS agent on the property, they wanted to make sure to get rid of all of it.
> **Mr. Miller:** Did Mr. Dortch himself tell you that?
> **Mr. Nelson:** Yes, sir.[47]

His testimony against Bakker lasted only an hour, but Nelson showed signs of discomfort and stress throughout it. He whispered many of his answers and had to be told by the judge to lean forward and speak into the microphone in front of him. At another point, he asked the judge for a drink of water before continuing. But he got through it, delivering a series of body blows to Bakker and a recess was taken from 11:00 to 11:25 A.M. for him to compose himself before cross-examination.[48]

When Nelson returned to the stand, Harold Bender tore into him like a tiger. The savvy attorney smelled blood, and saw an opening to make Nelson out as an ingrate and liar to the jury. First, Bender got the witness to admit that his gloomy lodging forecasts did not take into account the one-hundred-unit Heritage Inn Motel which was also available for partners in the event the Grand filled up. That was what Bakker was referring to when he kept telling Nelson that there was nothing to worry about. Also, Nelson was forced to admit that his figures didn't include the thousands of campsites that were available for people who preferred to stay in their RVs when visiting Heritage.[49]

Nelson then admitted that he thought that the church services at Heritage were "stupid."[50] And that he had called Norman Bakker, Jim's handicapped brother who walks with a severe limp, "the assistant to the village idiot."[51]

Mr. Bender: Would you describe him that way today?
Mr. Nelson: Yes, I would.[52]

Then, Bender really turned up the heat by brandishing a copy of an affidavit that Nelson had signed under oath to avoid liability in another lawsuit. In that affidavit, Nelson claimed that he had received a $10,000 bonus from PTL in 1987. But Bender had the facts. What he got was a $20,000 bonus and Bender made him admit that to the jury.[53] On top of that, the attorney surprised him with something else he had failed to acknowledge in his affidavit—a $30,000 loan given him by PTL which he never had to repay. Then Bender jabbed him with the question, "You received a $30,000 bridge loan from the ministry that maintained stupid services . . . ?"[54] The only response he could offer was, "That deal was cut with Pastor Dortch."[55]

Nelson was on the ropes, and Bender kept charging.

Mr. Bender: You remember Mr. Woodall, you remember him, don't you? I'm sorry, if you answered?[56]

Nelson slumped in the witness chair and then his head dropped against his chest. A spectator called out, "He's just died!"[57] Bender, staggered that he might have caused it, clasped his face with his hands and stepped backward uneasily to sit with Bakker. Juror Nancy Summey, the nurse, jumped from her seat in the jury box and ran over to Nelson. Another nurse sitting in the spectators' section rushed forward. U.S. marshals lifted Nelson out of the witness chair and laid him on the floor. Bakker himself jumped from his chair to kneel next to Nelson and pray quietly.[58]

Nelson was still alive, and was carried by paramedics out of the courtroom on a stretcher. He was taken to Presbyterian Hospital, where it was determined that he had collapsed from malnutrition and dehydration, apparently not having eaten for two or three days before the trial. He was treated at the hospital for three hours with intravenous feedings of glucose, and then released.[59]

But back in the courtroom, his fate was still very much in doubt. Shortly after noon, Judge Potter told the attorneys that Nelson "apparently has had a heart attack,"[60] and granted Harold Bender's motion to recess until the next day at 9:30 A.M. The jury, which had been ushered out as the paramedics attempted to revive Nelson, again took their seats. The Judge told them:

Judge Potter: Mrs. Summey, first of all, we want to thank you so much. I think we should always have a nurse on the jury. Mr. Nelson may or may not be able to come back, but whether he does or doesn't, I think we probably ought to recess today because I am sure that the attorneys and everyone else may be a little upset about this. So we are going to recess until tomorrow morning at 9:30.[61]

Pandemonium erupted in the courtroom as reporters ran to flash the story to their newsrooms. Bakker stood at the side of the courtroom, alone, crying. Bender held hands and prayed with two Bakker supporters in the back of the courtroom, and he was teary-eyed too. When Bender started to walk out the double doors at the back of the courtroom by himself, Bakker called out: "Harold, don't leave me here."[62] At that, Bender returned and, with George Davis, escorted their shaken client away from the swarming reporters and photographers.

As they passed by, Bakker's supporters in the courtroom said that God had struck Nelson down on the stand because he was lying. "Sometimes, God softens people's hearts in this way,"[63] said Virginia Mack of Jacksonville, Florida. "This can help turn the trial,"[64] she said.

But not the way the press reported it that afternoon. The second paragraph in the *New York Times* story that ran the next morning read: "Steve Nelson, a former PTL vice president, collapsed after testifying he had warned Mr. Bakker that 'someone could go to jail' over the ministry's fund-raising practices."[65] That, of course, was incorrect chronologically and is one of hundreds of examples of the way the media sensationally reported the testimony and evidence in the trial, absent nuances that would have portrayed Bakker more positively or sympathetically. Nelson did not collapse immediately after testifying about warning Bakker of jail, he collapsed after Bakker's attorney had scored several points off him.

Everything about this unbelievable turn of events broke against Bakker. The press used it against him; the jury probably blamed his attorney; and as several spectators told me, it appeared to rock Bender himself. It changed the whole trial.

Mrs. Loretta Mays was in the spectators' section for three solid weeks of the trial. At Jim's request, she sat with her husband, a Jacksonville, Florida, minister and other long-time friends of the Bakkers in the benches reserved for family just behind the defense table. Mrs. Mays says today that "there was no question about it" that after Nelson's collapse, the trial was never the same.[66]

But beyond all of that, the person most affected was Bakker himself. It pushed him over the edge.

NOTES

1. Shepard and Wright, "Bakker Portrayed as Victim," *Charlotte Observer*, August 29, 1989, p. 1-A (Westlaw printout).

2. *Id.*

3. Page, "Lack of Criminal Intent Emerging as Bakker's Defense," *Columbia (S.C.) State*, September 17, 1989, p. 1-B (Nexis printout).

4. "Bakker Fraud Trial on at Last—Tales of Greed Open Proceedings," *San Jose Mercury News*, August 29, 1989, p. 2-A (Nexis printout).

5. Shepard and Wright, *supra,* n. 1.

6. *Id.*

7. *Id.*

8. *Id.*

9. Jim Bakker, interview by author, in Rochester, Minnesota, October 31, 1992.

10. Trial transcript, *United States of America v. James O. Bakker,* Docket C-CR-88-205-1, U.S.D.C. (W.D., N.C.), August 28, 1989, vol. 1 at 25.

11. *Id.* at 23–25.

12. *Id.* at 31–36.

13. *Id.* at 69–70, 210–11.

14. *Id.* at 91–92, 105.

15. *Id.* at 93, 131.

16. *Id.* at 87.

17. *Id.* at 178–82.

18. *Id.* at 114–16.

19. *Id.* at 121–23, 129–31, 184–86.

20. Jim Bakker, interview by author, in Rochester, Minnesota, October 31, 1992.

21. Trial transcript, *supra,* n. 10 at 102.

22. *Id.* at 103.

23. *Id.* at 75–77.

24. *Id.* at 65–68.

25. Leland and Wright, "On the Scene," *Charlotte Observer,* August 30, 1989, p. 12-A (Westlaw printout).

26. *Id.*

27. Trial transcript, *supra,* n. 10 at 225–26.

28. *Id.* at 228–29.

29. *Id.* at 232, 235.

30. *Id.* at 281–82.

31. *Id.* at 264, 266.

32. *Id.* at 260.

33. *Id.* at 263.

34. *Id.* at 272.

35. *Id.* at 227, 296–97.

36. *Id.* at 335–74.

37. *Id.* at 381.

38. *Id.* at 382.

39. *Id.* at 393–94.

40. *Id.* at 432.

41. *Id.* at 433.

42. *Id.* at 434.

43. Trial transcript, *United States of America v. James O. Bakker,* Docket C-CR-88-205-1, U.S.D.C. (W.D., N.C.), August 28, 1989, vol. 2 at 468.

44. *Id.* at 477–78.

45. *Id.* at 492–93.

46. *Id.* at 493.

47. *Id.* at 489.

48. *Id.* at 497–99.
49. *Id.* at 509–11.
50. *Id.* at 515.
51. *Id.* at 516.
52. *Id.*
53. *Id.* at 516–17.
54. *Id.* at 518.
55. *Id.*
56. *Id.* at 520.
57. Shepard and Wright, *supra,* n. 1.
58. *Id.*
59. *Id.*
60. Trial transcript, *supra,* n. 43 at 520.
61. *Id.* at 521.
62. Shepard and Wright, *supra,* n. 1.
63. *Id.*
64. *Id.*
65. "An Ex-Bakker Aide Collapses in Trial," *New York Times,* August 31, 1989, p. 17-A, col. 1.
66. Loretta Mays, telephone interviews by author, July 27, 1993 and February 22, 1995.

Chapter 12

Bakker Snaps and Judge Potter Racks Him

Bakker Breaks (Thursday, August 31, 1989)

Bakker was so distraught at what he saw in the courtroom Wednesday that he was unable to regain his composure. It was horrifying for Jim to see Nelson be struck down and feared dead after testifying against him. As Tammy told friends, "He began to cry and could not stop. . . . The weight of what he had suffered the last two years had finally become more than one man could bear [and] his nervous system could just take no more trauma."[1] He was having a panic attack. He had had them before, including a major one while working with Pat Robertson at CBN, and he was having one now. Late Wednesday night, Jim's attorney called in Dr. Basil Jackson, a psychiatrist from Milwaukee, and pleaded with Jackson to fly to Charlotte that night to care for Jim. He agreed.

When he arrived, Jackson administered several milligrams of Xanax, a tranquilizer, to Bakker in hopes of calming him. But, as Bakker explained to me, even today his system is extremely sensitive to medication and instead of relaxing him, the Xanax "greatly accelerated my stress and panic, and caused the most frightening experience a human being could ever have."[2] He awakened at 4:00 A.M. Thursday, took more Xanax, and went back to sleep for a couple of hours. He later awakened groggy and disoriented, but dressed and made his way to Harold Bender's office to begin the day.[3]

Jim had another panic attack there, bursting into tears and crawling under a couch where he cowered in the fetal position. Earlier, he thought that the reporters lining the sidewalk outside the courthouse looked like bugs—"frightening animals, which he felt were intent on destroying him, attacking him, hurting him."[4] Bender and Davis, seeing that Bakker was in no condition to even walk over to the courthouse, decided they would ask Judge Potter for a one day delay so that Jim could get the treatment he needed for his panic episode.[5] After all, Bakker wasn't making it up. Panic attacks strike tens of thousands of people in this country each year. It's a medically recognized illness and is treatable with the right kind of medication.

Potter would have none of it. He warned the attorneys that Bakker was under a federal criminal indictment and had to be in court to face the music whether he was ready or not. The judge flew into action and ordered seven U.S. marshals to immediately apprehend Bakker at his attorney's office, take him into custody, and forcibly bring him to the courthouse. Minutes later, the officers reached Bender's office. Bakker was grabbed, his hands and feet were bound, and he was dragged out of the building. The press had learned of it, and was there to record every move as Bakker was forced into the police car and rushed to the courthouse where he was thrown into a holding cell.[6]

For the next three hours, Potter wielded every ounce of power that he possessed against Bakker. For the first time in his life, Bakker found himself inside a jail cell. And with Bakker caged one floor below and the jury excused, Potter strode in to the courtroom and turned up the heat by conducting a full-blown competency hearing. Maybe Bakker really was mentally unfit to stand trial. Or, was he faking it to gain some kind of advantage? Potter was going to find out . . . and fast.

The Competency Hearing (Thursday, August 31, 1989)

George Davis rose and made the motion that the hearing be postponed until Dr. Jackson and others could treat Jim Bakker and restore him to competency so that he could proceed with the trial.[7] The judge saw red.

Judge Potter: We'll determine his competency in this court, and if it's not determined today, we're going to send him over to Butner. Do you understand that, Mr. Davis?[8]

Dr. Jackson was quickly called to the stand and ordered to report on Jim's condition.

Dr. Jackson: Mr. Bakker at the present time is manifesting evidence of a severe psychiatric emotional regression, which in my medical judgment is related to the stress that he has experienced. When I left him 10 minutes ago, he was laying in a corner of his attorney's office, with his head under a couch hiding, expressing thoughts that someone was going to hurt him. Yesterday he was actively hallucinating after the court appearance here . . .[9]

Jackson also emphasized that if Bakker were sent to the jail environment of a state mental hospital, rather than being treated by a private physician there in Charlotte, his condition would definitely be aggravated.[10] The doctor pleaded that Bakker, like anyone suffering a panic attack, should be treated gently and civilly, instead of being pushed around like a slab of meat in some prison.

But Dr. Jackson's medical credibility was dashed when Deborah Smith got him to admit on cross-examination that he was one of Bakker's supporters and had actually helped select the jury a week before. Jackson readily acknowledged that one of his areas of specialty was juror assessment and that he had sat in the courtroom and told the defense attorneys which potential jurors would be good ones for Jim.[11]

Perfect. What a medical witness. On top of that, Smith showed Judge Potter what she had found out about the doctor's research published in the *Journal of the American Medical Association*—entitled "Catnip and the Alteration of Consciousness."[12] It was true, he was an authority on catnip! Of course, all of this gave the prosecutors the opening to tell the judge that Jackson was nothing more than a hired gun who couldn't be trusted to either diagnose or treat Bakker. Instead, Bakker should be sent to a facility controlled by the federal government where objective psychiatrists could determine whether he was mentally fit to continue the trial.

Davis shouted that Bakker was not a guilty man and shouldn't be taken into custody.[13]

The gavel came down and Potter announced his ruling without hesitation from the bench.

> **Judge Potter:** I will have to find that there is, by a preponderance of the evidence at this time, he is suffering from mental disease, and I am going to commit him to the custody of the Attorney General, with the direction he be taken to Butner. I will ask the marshals to take care of that shortly after this proceeding.
> **George Davis:** I will ask you, sir, will you give us—
> **Judge Potter:** No, sir, I'm going to send the marshals down there. If you want to go down with them, you can, but they're going down to get Mr. Bakker. I told you what we are going to do here.[14]

The judge immediately signed an order committing Bakker to the federal psychiatric hospital and prison at Butner, N.C. Under the law, he could not be released until the director there certified that he was well enough to proceed with the trial. Potter dismissed the jury for six days without telling them about Bakker's incapacitation or the reason the trial was being delayed. They left the courtroom smiling, happy to have a few days off.

That was definitely not the expression on the disheveled Bakker's swollen, puffy face. He was dragged, sobbing, in handcuffs and shackles to a waiting vehicle for his trip to the bowels of hell. Startled spectators could hear Bakker begging the marshals who were manhandling him, "Please don't do this to me!"[15] Of course, news cameras captured it all.

> **Tammy Faye, from Orlando:** What Judge Potter has done to my husband is a disgrace to the Constitution—[parading Jim] like a freak at a carnival show.[16]
> **Pat Clark-Kitts, waitress at Charlotte's Providence Road Sundry Shop:** They [customers] laughed when they took him to the nut house. Everyone thinks he's doing it because he doesn't want to go to prison.[17]

The Road to Butner

Butner, one of a handful of federal prisons which boasts a psychiatric hospital, is located two and one-half hours from Charlotte. Tammy said that Jim was "so out of it that he thought they were taking him to [Charlotte's Butler] animal hospital."[18]

> **Jim Bakker in prison:** They drove me clear across the state while I was chained up, laying me over sideways in the back of the police car. They wouldn't stop to let me go to the bathroom and my kidneys were almost exploding. [When we finally arrived] it seemed like hundreds of photographers were there and I was still in a state of shock. I was in a stupor. They wouldn't even tell me where I was being taken.[19]

With Bakker behind bars, the chief of psychiatric services at Butner, Dr. Sally Johnson, held a news conference. Meeting with reporters for half an hour, she said that Bakker would be under twenty-four-hour-a-day supervision and confined alone in a cell. He would be able to receive occasional visitors. Years before, Dr. Johnson had been the psychiatrist who evaluated Reagan assailant John Hinckley, Jr. in that case in which a jury found him not guilty by reason of insanity. She promised the press that the evaluation of Bakker would be exhaustive and that they would get to the bottom of whether he was mentally well enough to continue with the trial.[20]

Local WRFX deejays Billy James and John Boy Isley, who were sure Bakker was faking, began airing a parody of Lou Reed's pop hit "Walk on the Wild Side." Their version, "Walk on the Weird Side," quickly became the talk of the town.

> A witness passed out right there on the stand, and Jimmy hatched a brand-new master plan: /Severe depression, mental pain. He's not guilty, he's insane./Hey, judge, take me off to the nut house. . . .[21]

In response to one reporter's question, which reflected the prevailing skepticism, Dr. Johnson acknowledged that some people can fake mental illness. "It's not easy, but it can happen,"[22] she said. Her assurances about the considerate care Bakker would be given, however, were sharply disputed by a frantic Tammy Faye who told Jim's supporters that he was being abused.

Tammy Faye's letter to supporters: They took Jim into another room and once again asked him to take off all of his clothes. They took more pictures. These were pictures for her [the psychiatrist's] file. Why would she demand naked pictures (front, back, and side) for a psychiatric file?

The cell consisted of a metal bed, a toilet, and a shower. There was no bathroom tissue and they would not even allow him a pillow. [He was] put in a psycho ward—a prison insane asylum. Shackled like an animal.

I was out of my mind . . . someone called and told me they had taken Jim to a hospital in Butner, N.C. I turned on the TV and saw them taking my husband away. I looked out the window and the news media was gathering in front of our house. TV cameras and huge satellite trucks were pulling up and parking. I began to sob and cry. I could think of no one else so I dialed 911 and told them I needed help. I was frantic! I had to get to Jim, he would need me. I finally got a few clothes together and left, with Jim's sister Donna and my friend Fran Moore, for Butner, N.C. We arrived 14 hours later, dropped off our suitcases at a little Day's Inn Motel, in Durham, N.C., and headed for the prison in Butner.

The woman psychiatrist came to meet me and made me talk to her for nearly two hours before she would allow me to see Jim. Finally, after filling out papers and being searched, they let me go to him . . . I heard the bars closing shut behind me. He was standing there in his prison uniform as I walked in. They had just taken off his handcuffs. On his uniform were the letters in SECL—which means seclusion. They had him in solitary confinement.

I cannot tell you the look on Jim's face . . . it was so terrible, so hopeless . . . I put my arms around him, 'we are not supposed to touch,' he said. His hair was all plastered to his head and he had no brush. I was standing there looking at a broken, beaten man. We talked and cried . . . it was time for me to leave, so that they could strip search him again, handcuff him and take him back to his cell.

For days Jim suffered in that prison cell. He underwent days of psychiatric testing . . . hours with the woman psychiatrist, asking him the same questions over and over. He could not sleep as the guards talked all night long just outside his cell. He could not eat as the stench from his backed-up toilet kept him sick to his stomach.[23]

Jessica Hahn, filming a television spot in Los Angeles, was also asked for her reaction and it differed markedly from Tammy's: "Jim Bakker pulled this with me in a hotel room in Florida. This time, the public can see it with their own eyes instead of having to take my word for it. I only hope they won't fall for it. He is a master of manipulation, and this is simply a sympathy stunt."[24]

She was referring to the statement she made in her 1987 *Playboy* interview about Tampa revivalist John Wesley Fletcher, who arranged the rendezvous between Hahn and Bakker in Clearwater in 1980. Fletcher told her just after she and Bakker did whatever they did that Jim was sobbing in a fetal position on the floor of his room.

Federal psychiatrists would spend the next six days testing Hahn's theory.

Bakker Redux—Back from Butner

At 6:30 P.M. Tuesday night, September 5, officials at Butner notified Judge Potter that Jim Bakker was well enough to be released.[25] And at 8:30 A.M. the following morning, still in leg irons and handcuffs, Bakker was led back to the Charlotte courthouse by U.S. marshals where he would face a two-hour hearing to determine whether he was mentally competent to resume the trial. Bakker himself appeared exhausted and withdrawn. Tammy Faye arrived a short time later, her first appearance at the courthouse, carrying an armload of clean clothes for her husband. As she walked inside, reporters asked how her husband was, and she shouted back: "I don't know. That's what I am here to find out."[26]

Dr. Johnson took the stand to report the results of her observation and testing of Bakker the past week. Her conclusion was that he wasn't crazy at all, but had just suffered a panic attack from which he was sufficiently recovered to resume the trial.

Dr. Johnson: [M]edically Mr. Bakker's pretty stable and psychiatrically he's pretty stable. *** I think he has the capacity to get through it [the trial].[27]

She explained that she had interviewed him extensively about his attack and he gave her a very different picture from that which had emerged earlier. For instance, Bakker told her that he never really thought any reporters were insects. He told her he was very frightened when he left the courthouse after Steve Nelson had been taken away by paramedics, and when he looked out at the horde of reporters and technicians, many with headphones and other equipment, he thought they resembled large ants with antennae but that he never lost touch with the reality that they were not. So, she rejected Dr. Basil Jackson's characterization that Bakker had been hallucinating.[28]

She said that when she interviewed Dr. Jackson, he told her that when he was summoned from Milwaukee that night that it was Jim Bakker's own attorney who told him that Bakker "had flipped out."[29]

Dr. Johnson went on to say that what really happened to Bakker was that Nelson's collapse precipitated a panic attack, and that the medication he subsequently took and the lack of sleep all combined to temporarily incapacitate him. She was asked specifically if Bakker had been faking it and she replied, "I have not said in my report nor in here . . . that I perceived him as faking."[30]

She found that the breaking point for Bakker was the fear that Nelson had died while testifying against him. What particularly hurt Bakker was that Nelson had been a close friend and he found it very difficult to listen to him, as Bakker explained it, lie about Bakker on the witness stand.

Dr. Johnson: He very much wanted his attorneys to be vigorously cross examining the witness and discrediting his testimony and he believed that his attorneys were succeeding at doing that. [But at the same time], he was not wishing for anything harmful to come out at the trial for anyone as he describes and so when the person fainted, his immediate perception was that he had dropped over dead . . . and the fact that maybe he had got his wish [that Nelson would somehow be taken away by somebody or something] and I think that that was just a very frightening experience or shocking experience for him and the other folks who observed it.[31]

As she saw it, that was the panic attack he experienced in the courtroom which grew worse later in the day.

> **Dr. Johnson:** For the first time in the last three years, the whole situation really came home to him and he just started to cry and he cried a lot. *** The weight of all of those events just seemed to coalesce and he began to cry. *** It's a very frightening cycle to be in. So I think it kind of snowballed through Thursday morning.
>
> [What kept haunting him as he thought about it was] all of the events that had happened in the last two and a half to three years leaving the PTL ministry . . . the loss of his involvement in Heritage USA, the impact that the financial problems and legal problems had had on his family, on his privacy, on his children. . . .[32]

But, over all, Dr. Johnson was satisfied that Bakker was in no danger of any more panic attacks in the immediate future and she was sure that he could get through the trial.[33]

At that, Tammy Faye, sitting on the spectator's bench behind her husband, broke into a coughing fit and raced up the aisle to the exit, a white chiffon designer caftan billowing behind her and a silver bracelet jangling loudly. When she regained her composure and returned a few minutes later, she leaned forward and asked Jim what she had missed. "I was in a mental institution. Everybody was crazy. They said I wasn't," he whispered.[34]

With that, Judge Potter turned to Harold Bender and confirmed that he had had an opportunity to visit with Bakker for a few minutes that morning.

> **Judge Potter:** And based on your conversations with him, do you have an opinion as a lay person whether the defendant has sufficient present ability to consult with you as an attorney with a reasonable degree of rational understanding?
>
> **Mr. Bender:** I have such an opinion.
>
> **Judge Potter:** And what is that opinion, sir?

Mr. Bender: That he has recovered sufficiently, that he will be able to assist in his own defense.[35]

At that point, the judge turned to Jim Bakker and spoke directly to him.

Judge Potter: Mr. Bakker, do you understand what you are on trial here for today?
Jim Bakker: Yes, sir.
Judge Potter: And do you understand that you must be able to consult with your lawyers in order that they may properly defend you?
Jim Bakker: Yes, sir.
Judge Potter: And do you presently feel that you are able to consult with your attorney and understand what they're saying to you?
Jim Bakker: I'm very tired, but I believe I can do that, sir.[36]

Potter then ruled that Bakker had recovered sufficiently to resume the trial, that Bakker was mentally competent to stand trial, and that he was no longer under any mental condition which would justify delaying the trial. He ordered the U.S. marshals to immediately discharge Bakker from custody, but did require him to take any drug tests necessary to insure that he did not take any medications which might trigger any more panic attacks.[37]

George Davis stood up to complain that "this entire proceeding has been unconstitutional"[38] and that he would file papers later to prove it. Harold Bender then asked the judge for a three-day continuance arguing that since Bakker had been incarcerated for several days he needed some time to work with his client before the trial resumed. Bender told the court, "I think forcing us to go to trial in an hour and a half to defend these very serious charges, taking into account what has transpired in the last week, I think is asking just a little much of us, so I ask you to continue."[39] Deborah Smith strongly resisted, arguing that the week's delay had been "caused by Mr. Bakker's behavior and problems"[40] and that he wasn't entitled to any more breaks. The judge was certainly not going to give him any, either, and snorted, "I've already had a great deal—too much delay in this case."[41] With that, he instructed the clerk to call the jury members and have them report to the courtroom at 2:00 P.M. that afternoon so that the trial could continue.

The dazed Bakker was given ninety minutes for lunch, and as he left the courtroom was asked by reporters how he felt. "I just got out of an insane asylum," he said, "and I'm just getting used to being back."[42]

NOTES

1. Tammy Faye Bakker, letter to New Covenant Partners, September 1989.

2. Jim Bakker, interview by author, in Rochester, Minnesota, September 25, 1992.

3. *Id.*

4. Trial transcript, *United States of America v. James O. Bakker,* Docket C-CR-88-205-1, August 28, 1989, vol. 2 at 522 [appended supp. page 12].

5. *Id.* at 522 [appended supp. pages 2–3]; Tammy Faye Bakker, letter to New Covenant Partners, September 1989.

6. Wright, Shepard and Leland, "Bakker May Be Back in Courtroom Today," *Charlotte Observer,* September 6, 1989 at 1-A (Westlaw printout); Tammy Faye Bakker, letter to New Covenant Partners, September 1989.

7. Trial transcript, *supra,* n. 4 at 522 [appended supp. page 3].

8. *Id.*

9. *Id.* at 522 [appended supp. pages 6–7].

10. *Id.* at 522 [appended supp. pages 7–8].

11. *Id.* at 522 [appended supp. pages 10–11].

12. *Id.* at 581.

13. *Id.* at 522 [appended supp. page 22].

14. *Id.* at 522 [appended supp. page 23].

15. Drescher and Shepard, "Bakker Better, May Return for Trial, Wife Says," *Charlotte Observer,* September 2, 1989 at 1-A (Westlaw printout).

16. Wright, Shepard and Leland, *supra,* n. 6.

17. Leland, "Talk of the Town," *Charlotte Observer,* September 6, 1989 at 1-A (Westlaw printout).

18. Wright, Shepard and Leland, *supra,* n. 6.

19. Jim Bakker, interview by author, in Rochester, Minnesota, September 25, 1992.

20. Drescher, "Butner Assessing Competency," *Charlotte Observer,* September 1, 1989 at 13-A (Westlaw printout).

21. Leland, *supra,* n. 17.

22. Drescher, *supra,* n. 20.

23. Tammy Faye Bakker, letter to New Covenant Partners, September 1989.

24. "The Bakker Trial," *Charlotte Observer,* September 1, 1989 at 12-A (Westlaw printout).

25. Trial transcript, *supra,* n. 4 at 523.

26. Harris, "Jim Bakker, Fit to Be Tried," *Washington Post,* September 7, 1989 at 1-C (Nexis printout).

27. Trial transcript, *supra,* n. 4 at 551, 553.

28. *Id.* at 532–33.

29. *Id.* at 534.

30. *Id.* at 557.

31. *Id.* at 538.

32. *Id.* at 538–39, 550.

33. *Id.* at 551–52.

34. Harris, *supra,* n. 26.

35. Trial transcript, *supra,* n. 4 at 584.

36. *Id.* at 584–85.

37. *Id.* at 586–87.

38. *Id.* at 588.

39. *Id.* at 590–91.

40. *Id.* at 592.

41. *Id.* at 596.

42. Harris, *supra,* n. 26.

Chapter 13

Week Two—The Trial Resumes

Wednesday Afternoon (September 6, 1989)

As the jury took their seats for the first time in six days, a very much alive Steve Nelson returned to the witness stand. Pressed by Judge Potter to explain why he fainted the week before, the young former PTL executive said that he had the flu and had been "sweating real bad"[1] that day.

> **Mr. Nelson:** [Then, in the courtroom] I remember . . . it just got real hot in here and at one of the questions, you know, I just— blacked out, yes.
> **Judge Potter:** Did Mr. Bender's cross-examination in any way cause your collapse?
> **Mr. Nelson:** No, sir, it did not.[2]

The judge then asked the jurors whether any of them felt any sympathy for Nelson because he had collapsed on the witness stand, or whether they blamed Bakker or his attorney for causing it. The jurors shook their heads "no."[3] But, Bender was not about to risk it and when the judge told him he could resume his cross-examination the attorney replied, "Your honor, we have further questions, but under the circumstances, we will not cross-examine Mr. Nelson."[4]

With Bender's hands tied, prosecutor Miller seized the opportunity to himself ask more softball questions of his witness to make sure the jury hadn't lost the scent during the one week delay.

Mr. Miller: Was there a point in time when you were out at PTL that you knew that you were involved in illegal conduct?
Mr. Nelson: Yes, in my opinion, it was.[5]

Mr. Miller: Did you go to Mr. Dortch or Mr. Bakker and tell them of any problems . . . [concerning overbooking]?
Mr. Nelson: Yes, sir I did. . . .[6]

The remainder of the afternoon's testimony came from three former PTL employees, each of whom claimed that lifetime partners had great difficulty reserving rooms at the Heritage Grand. Connie Brennecke, employed in partner relations, said that she eventually resigned from PTL "because I could not stay at this ministry knowing that partners were having a hard time getting reservations and yet there were still more memberships being offered."[7] But on cross-examination, she admitted a startling fact:

Mr. Bender: And do you know or not whether Reverend Bakker, Pastor Bakker had given explicit orders . . . that when a partner wants a refund, I want it paid?
Ms. Brennecke: Yes, sir, I do recall that.
Mr. Bender: So that was his policy?
Ms. Brennecke: Yes, sir.
Mr. Bender: If anybody was disgruntled, they want a refund, they get a refund?
Ms. Brennecke: Yes, sir, I have heard him say that.[8]

So, what is the deal here? Since when does a hotel commit fraud if people wishing to stay there have "a hard time getting reservations"? Is it fraud if they are told the hotel is booked on the exact date at peak season they want? Is it fraud if they have to stay there a different day? Is it fraud if they get a busy signal when they call the reservations number? If they have to call back, and because of that they "have a hard time"?

On top of that, if someone possessing a lifetime partnership has difficulty getting a reservation exactly when they want it, and they can obtain a full refund of their contribution, how in the world have they been harmed? Poor lambs, as the government sees what it must consider the helpless, idiot citizenry of the country. Can't get a reservation on the Fourth of July at their favorite hotel? Call the cops! Prosecute!

The troublesome thing about it, legally, is that the prosecutors kept emphasizing that this was a real estate scam case and not one about Jim Bakker personally or what the jury might have thought of him. But, when it came to the government's real estate fraud case, it was built on the testimony of witnesses like Ms. Brennecke and its foundation shook like Jello.

For a different take on Jim Bakker, put yourself in the jury box. As you read the testimony of all of the witnesses, keep your eyes firmly focused on the evidence of real estate fraud. Not that you ignore everything else, but it was Jerry Miller himself in his opening statement who emphasized that this was a real estate case. So, don't let anyone switch apples and oranges on you, leaving you watching something other than real estate fraud. Bakker's attorneys should have signaled the real jury to watch for the same thing.

Jerry Miller's next witness was J'Tanya Adams, a partner troubleshooter at PTL.

> **Mr. Miller:** Now with respect to lifetime partners, what sort of problems, if any, were you having with respect to lifetime partners?
> **Ms. Adams:** I had some reservation problems getting people placed. Occasionally a few disgruntled partners and then some pleased.[9]

That was it as far as the fraud went, but the big hit in her testimony was the revelation that Jim Bakker promised a new Cadillac to the PTL telephone operator who signed up the most partners. She called it "the Cadillac meeting"[10] where Bakker offered that incentive. And then, after a few more inane questions, she was off the witness stand. Harold Bender didn't cross-examine her at all. And what did she accomplish as the government's fourth witness in its batting order? Anything about real estate fraud? Not much. Anything to turn the jury against Jim Bakker personally? Well, what minister offers a Cadillac for bringing in more money?

Carol Price was the government's next witness. She had supervised the telephone operators at PTL and dealt with partners who called in to make special requests. If they wanted someone to pray with in the middle of the night, she would often get on the line. And if they couldn't get reservations at the Grand because it was filled on the dates they wanted, she would attempt to help them by personally calling her friends at the hotel and seeing if they could make an accommodation. She was often able to do that. "Sometimes it was possible and they [the hotel reservations people] would make exceptions for us and sometimes they couldn't,"[11] she said.

Mr. Miller: But could you always accommodate a partner?
Ms. Price: No. No. Many times we could not.[12]

Incredibly, the example she used was the time a couple who had obtained a lifetime partnership got a divorce. The partnership was not allocated in their dissolution decree. Each of them remarried and, amazingly, one morning all of them showed up at the Grand wanting to use the membership at the same time.

Price explained that she was urgently called to arbitrate the dispute and that she actually had to physically separate them in the lobby. Yet, in the final analysis, there were rooms enough for all of them and the crisis was resolved.[13]

The question, then, after this testimony: so what's the big deal? How is this evidence of the inability to accommodate anyone? Where is the fraud in this example?

Price told the jury that she was so disheartened by the problem and Jim Bakker's reassurances to her that there really was enough room that she took matters into her own hands.

Mr. Miller: Now did you personally ever discourage anyone from purchasing a lifetime partnership? ***
Ms. Price: Yes I did discourage people. If a person called in and related to me circumstances that I believed was beyond their means . . . I had a lady who described herself as being in her seventies. She and her husband, excuse me [the witness started crying and was unable to continue for a minute].
Mr. Miller: Upon the basis of talking to her, what did you tell that woman about purchasing the lifetime partnership?
Ms. Price: I told her that I felt selling a burial policy to get $1000 when she was in her seventies was not something she should do.[14]

Wham. Now the jury sees Bakker as a rat preying on people like that. But that wasn't the only damage Price did to her former employer. Later, her partner relations office was combined with another and she and nine of her employees lost their jobs. She told the jury that she went straight to Steve Nelson. Through her tears on the stand, she relived their encounter:

> **Ms. Price:** I went in to him and I said to him, "Steve, I just want to know why." *** And he leaned back in his chair and he looked at me and he said, "Carol, . . . that's the price you pay for knowing too much and not keeping your mouth shut." And I looked at him and I said, "Okay. I can understand that because yes, indeed, I fought tooth and toenail for these partners and, yes, every opportunity that I had to tell Mr. Bakker what the situation was, I took it. . . ." And thus ten people lost their jobs because my conscience would not let me keep my mouth shut. It would not let me keep from trying to do everything I knew to do to give the partners what we were promising and I have carried that on my head since that day.
>
> **Mr. Miller:** Those are all of my questions of the witness, your honor.[15]

And after a fifteen minute recess, Carol Price stepped back to the witness stand to face cross-examination and Harold Bender obviously decided that she was real trouble and could do even more damage with a few more minutes on the stand. "We have no questions, your honor,"[16] and that was that. But there was absolutely no doubt that Price had landed several stinging blows to Bakker and greatly diminished him in the eyes of the jury.

Christy Howe, who had supervised thirty reservation operators at the Grand Hotel, explained that most partners wanted reservations in the summer months and those times would fill up early. After that, she said that there were still rooms available during the other times of the year but that some people only wanted to take their vacations in the summer. She said that dealing with so many thousands of requests for reservations was so stressful on her operators that most of them didn't work longer than three months in those positions.[17]

Then, after showing her a chart that calculated 66,683 Grand Hotel partnerships sold which according to his numbers represented 104 percent occupancy of the hotel if every room was used every night of the year, the prosecutor put the ultimate question to her:

> **Mr. Miller:** Was there any way that you in reservations could possibly have accommodated 104% occupancy in the hotel with 50% of the rooms?
> **Mr. Bender:** Objection.
> **Judge Potter:** Overruled.
> **Ms. Howe:** No, sir.[18]

With that testimony, the judge recessed for the evening at 5:20 P.M.

Thursday, September 7, 1989

This sixth day of testimony marked a turning point in the trial as prosecutors, for the first time, called to the witness stand five former PTL lifetime partners who claimed they were defrauded, a former member of the PTL board of directors who said that Bakker kept his own directors in the dark, and a number of sales clerks who described how quickly Jim spent PTL's money.

The two most powerful witnesses of the day were Dana Angel and her eighty-nine-year-old mother, Lila, who lived together in Atlantic Beach, Florida. Dana, with an enlarged heart, was on Social Security disability and her elderly mother lived on Social Security retirement checks each month. They bought a lifetime partnership in the Heritage Grand in 1984.[19]

The plain fact of the matter is that every one of the 158,000 who purchased a lifetime partnership eventually lost their money when Jerry Falwell put Heritage USA into bankruptcy and the place was sold. After that, the lifetime partnership lodging packages were never again honored. In all fairness to Jim Bakker, it must be said that during all the years that he was at Heritage the lifetime partnerships were either honored or the contributions refunded, if the partner for any reason didn't feel that they were receiving what they had paid for. What these two star witnesses represented, then, were all of the people in the country who had purchased lifetime partnerships expecting to be able to use the hotels at Heritage for the rest of their lives, and now could not.

But what Dana Angel said on the stand was quite tame. Her mother's testimony was more hard hitting, but something just wasn't right. The big question that Jerry Miller put to Dana was whether they tried to use their membership in 1984.

Dana Angel: Yes. I had reservations, but they canceled them.[20]

But later, she admitted:

Dana Angel: We had made them for Christmas of 1984. When they canceled them because of the Grand not being completed, I think they made them then for 1985.[21]

She's complaining about not being able to stay in a hotel that wasn't finished yet? And when the rest of the story eventually spilled out, still a different picture emerged. The truth was that once the hotel opened its doors, she and her mother made reservations in advance and used their partnership when they wanted. They were there at Christmas 1985 the following year, and again in September of 1986. They enjoyed their stays so much that they asked for an extra day even at those peak times and they were given it.[22] More than that, in terms of the true substance of her testimony, she answered two of Miller's questions in ways that made Bakker's whole case.

Mr. Miller: Did you expect to be . . . guaranteed a specific three days each year?
Lila Angel: No, it was whenever available space was for the partners.
Mr. Miller: But did you expect . . . there would be four days and three nights available for you sometime during the year?
Lila Angel: Sometime during the year, yes, or campground or someplace on the retreat there.[23]

Of course, the jury didn't pick up the significance of what she was saying. But she had just confirmed what Bakker had always said—a partner could not claim they had been denied their yearly lodging rights just because they could not get a reservation at the Grand on the exact date they preferred. And, there were other lodging and RV sites on the premises which some partners might choose rather than the Grand.

What the jury understood was that these two people on Social Security were testifying against Jim Bakker and the government was claiming that they had been defrauded. Not that the Angels said so from the stand, but that was the heartrending picture the government was conveying.

Next up was Dana's mother, Lila Angel, who of course melted the hearts of the jurors. The first thing that Miller extracted from her was her age, and when she told him she was eighty-nine the judge burst in, "You ought to be proud of that."[24] She thanked his honor and Miller rode the good vibrations for the ten minutes of her testimony.

What she said was, "We enjoyed coming up here very much [to Heritage],"[25] in fact to the point that they bought a second lifetime partnership in 1986 for the Towers Hotel. That would give them two weeks a year at Heritage. So, they split the $1,000 cost and the mother charged her $500 share to her Visa card and let her daughter keep the new partnership in her own name so that she would have it the rest of her life. Then Miller asked the questions that seared the jury:

Mr. Miller: Was that a lot of money for you?

Lila Angel: Yes, it is because I worked until I was 77 and I saved my pennies. I still do. Have to. And $500 was quite a bit of money for me.

Mr. Miller: Now would you have sent that money in if you weren't going to get something in return for it?

Lila Angel: No. No, I wouldn't.

Mr. Miller: My question to you is was that a gift to the ministry or did you expect to get something?

Lila Angel: No, it wasn't a gift to the ministry at all.

Mr. Miller: And if you had known when you sent that money in that you might not be able to get into the hotel because too many people were trying to get in, too many memberships were out there, would you have liked to have known that?

Lila Angel: If I had known it, I wouldn't have sent the money. . . .[26]

The emotional impact of her grandmotherly testimony was so obvious that Harold Bender didn't ask her one single question on cross-examination. The jury would have thought he was picking on her.

Jerry Miller's questions to Lila Angel dealt with the Angels not being able to get into the Towers Hotel, which of course was not yet completed. Once the Grand Hotel had opened earlier, the Angels never had a problem staying there. Despite the issuance of 66,683 Grand partnerships, the Angels came when they pleased and even stayed additional days.

The truth about the Grand was that even though it had been oversold by more than 30,000, still for the two years and three months that it was open during Bakker's tenure, it was never one hundred percent full twelve months of the year. Later government witnesses would confirm the fact that there were always rooms available at some time during the year.[27]

So, how could it be said with certainty that a similar overselling of the Towers would have necessarily resulted in the Angels not being able to get a reservation there? It was speculation which was surely not based on the experience that the Angels had with the Grand Hotel.

But who in the jury is going to get too technical about sticky real estate facts when you've got an eighty-nine-year-old grandmother on the stand telling about how she saved her pennies to purchase a second partnership?

Next, the government turned the knife with the testimony of Lamar Kerstetter, a retired coal miner from Pennsylvania, who testified that he bought a Towers partnership in March, 1987 with some of his black lung disease disability benefits. And of course, in the final shakeout of things, he ended up with nothing.[28] Interestingly, he contended that he wouldn't have bought the membership if he had known the Towers was not yet finished.[29] Well, how could he not be aware of that given the fact that Bakker had a live camera every day on the construction site showing workers topping out the hotel with a huge boom crane that towered 200 feet above the ground? Would reasonable people in the country watching that program or hearing anything Bakker ever said about the new hotel have understood that the Towers was open for business?

With this witness, then, the prosecutors used as a representative victim of Bakker's alleged fraud a person who missed the most obvious of details about the transaction. The only fair standard should have been that of the reasonable person— would a reasonable person have been misled by Bakker into believing the Towers was built? It's another example of the paucity of the government's evidence against Bakker that dealt with the core real estate issue.

But again, the substance of Kerstetter's testimony was not as memorable to the jury as the fact that he was a hardworking manual laborer who had black lung disease and was being ripped off by a smooth televangelist who tanned himself in Palm Springs every other week and paid himself $3.7 million in salary and bonuses over three years' time.

The former general manager of the Heritage Grand, William Mabrey, took the witness stand to explain to the jury some of the mathematics of the government's case. He told his story against Bakker one step at a time.

Mabrey was employed by the Brock Hotel Corporation, which managed the Heritage Grand on PTL's behalf for a fee.

He was the head man at the Grand from the time it opened during Christmas 1984 until he left a year later.

Brock's deal with Bakker was that half of the 504 rooms in the hotel would be set aside for lifetime partners, who would not have to pay for them when they used them. The other half would be rented out at an average of $63 a night to walk-ins and other visitors to Heritage who wanted to stay there overnight.

Even if one hundred percent of the hotel was used for partners each day of the year for 365 days, there weren't enough rooms for all 66,683 who had purchased Grand packages. When that fact became clear to Mabrey, on August 13, 1985, he sent a memo to Jim Bakker to that effect. And, he reported to Bakker the news that the half of the hotel set aside for partners was completely booked, with not one room left, for the next four and a half months. He told Bakker that his "reservations department is beginning to receive many abusive phone calls from many irate lifetime partners."[30] A copy of that memo was enlarged and shown to the jury.

But on cross-examination, this intriguing exchange:

> **Mr. Bender:** During all of this time and all the problems that you have alluded to with your reservations and over bookings . . . in the hotel out there, there were times, months of the year when the occupancy level of that hotel was not one hundred percent, wasn't it?
>
> **Mr. Mabrey:** We did not run one hundred percent occupancy year round.[31]

One could argue vigorously that there was no fraud here. There would not be fraud until there was 100 percent occupancy and one single partner was told he or she could not use their membership at any time during the year. Mabrey admitted, however, that despite everything that had been said by the prosecutors to the contrary, the Grand Hotel was not overbooked. It had rooms left over several months each year. It was underbooked.

The prosecutor's last big gun of the day was former PTL board of directors member Ernie Franzone from Ft. Lauderdale, Florida. He portrayed the board as spineless yes-people completely controlled and kept in the dark by Bakker. At the time, and not coincidentally, he was a heavy in the Brock Hotel Corporation with some thirty years' business experience. But to hear him tell it, the board just rubber-stamped everything Bakker wanted and let him lead them around by the nose.

Franzone testified that he never knew what salary was being paid either Bakker or Dortch and that he didn't realize Bakker's bonuses were being doubled for tax purposes. He said that the only information the board got from Bakker was positive, and that they didn't know that more than 25,000 Grand Hotel partnerships had been sold or that partners were having difficulty obtaining reservations. He said that Bakker always represented to the board that there were no financial problems at PTL, and that the board was never told of any cash flow crises.[32]

Franzone testified that he was never informed that any

money was paid to Jessica Hahn out of PTL funds, that he didn't even know that she existed, and that he might well have resigned if he had been told. He said the board was never permitted to take financial reports or audits home with them, and instead those documents were just passed around the table at the meetings for five or ten minutes. He also revealed that the board was not allowed to take copies of the minutes home with them. He remembered that he was surprised after his first board meeting when he folded up his copy of the minutes to put it in his coat pocket and was told that he wasn't allowed to do that.[33]

On cross-examination, Harold Bender scored a few points, including the fact that at every board meeting that was held at Heritage, Bakker invited all board members to go anywhere on the grounds they desired by themselves. They were encouraged to see anything they wanted and individually talk to any employee or visitor. Many times, Bakker took them on tours himself, but he always urged them to go out on their own anywhere they wanted and talk to anybody.[34]

The thing about Franzone's testimony that seems odd is that anyone in the country who watched Jim and Tammy Bakker for more than ten minutes on any one of their television programs knew that there was always a financial crisis at PTL. If so much money wasn't raised by Friday, they wouldn't be able to pay for the broadcast time on all their stations. If money wasn't received in the next twenty-four hours, PTL wouldn't be able to meet its payroll. It was always something like that. They lurched from financial crisis to financial crisis and talked about it all the time on the air to prompt more contributions. Why wouldn't the board have known about PTL's money problems if everyone else in the country did? But, Franzone did real damage and, in combination with all of the other witnesses, this was a bad day for Bakker.

Jerry Miller topped it off by calling in rapid fire order a few more witnesses with quick jabs to end the day. An airplane charterer testified that PTL paid $101,736 to fly Bakker by private jet to Palm Springs and back in 1984.[35] The owner of an aircraft dealership confirmed that PTL later bought its own jet for just under a million dollars.[36] A salesman from a local luxury automobile dealership testified that he sold Jim Bakker three Mercedes in December 1986—one for $59,000, another for $61,000, and the last for $28,000.[37] The bookkeeper at Arnold Palmer Cadillac testified that Bakker bought a Caddy there for $28,300.[38]

And on that happy note, Bakker was driven from the courthouse in Harold Bender's new BMW to get some rest that evening to face more revelations the next day.

Friday, September 8, 1989

"TGIF" must have had special significance for Bakker after all he had been through this week, but the prosecutors didn't slow down for a second.

First up was Mark Burgund, the former PTL budget director, who reported that he was asked by Jim Bakker to calculate the value to an average family of lifetime partnerships in the Towers Hotel. After working it out, Burgund reported back to Bakker that over thirty years' time, a family of four would receive $84,735 in vacation benefits. That would be primarily the savings to them not having to pay for a hotel room each year. But he remembered Bakker as dissatisfied with the figure. In fact, Bakker told him that he wanted to be able to tell his television audience that one of those memberships would be worth a million dollars to a family.

> **Deborah Smith:** He told you he wanted you to show it would be worth a million dollars and then sent you back to do the figures to reach that figure?
> **Mr. Burgund:** Yes.[39]

So, Burgund did what his boss wanted and recalculated it using a family of five who would be staying at Heritage for fifty years and participating in virtually every activity for which a daily fee was charged. That would include miniature golf, the Passion Play, ice skating, and use of the water park. Then, to get the number up close to what Bakker wanted, Burgund had to factor in the value to that mythical family of several mythical facilities, like the bowling alley and health spa which were on the drawing boards but not yet built.

Still, he wasn't coming close to the $1 million figure so he had to project that family using all of the Heritage fee-charging activities not just for the one week stay they got with their lifetime partnership, but for a month each year. That answer drew surprise from Deborah Smith, who asked him how in the world he figured somebody from out of town could have done that.

> **Ms. Smith:** They'd have to live within driving distance of Heritage Village, isn't that true?
> **Mr. Burgund:** They'd have to be here 30 days.
> **Ms. Smith:** So they'd either have to stay in a hotel off the grounds for 30 days or they'd have to live within driving distance?
> **Mr. Burgund:** Yes, Ma'am.
> **Ms. Smith:** They'd be very busy on those 30 days, wouldn't they?
> **Mr. Burgund:** Yes, Ma'am.
> **Ms. Smith:** Be attending the Water Park all five members?
> **Mr. Burgund:** Yes.
> **Ms. Smith:** And they'd be attending all the recreational facilities?
> **Mr. Burgund:** Yes.
> **Ms. Smith:** They would have to do this for a solid 50 years in order for this to be worth a million dollars?
> **Mr. Burgund,** Yes, ma'am.[40]

Then, she emphasized to the jury that the Towers Hotel was never completed, and no lifetime Towers partner ever got a nickel in lodging value.

> **Ms. Smith:** Did any family of five ever stay in the Towers Hotel?
> **Mr. Burgund:** No, ma'am.
> **Ms. Smith:** Did any family of five ever go bowling at Heritage USA?
> **Mr. Burgund:** No, ma'am.
> **Ms. Smith:** Any family of five ever use the health spa at Heritage USA?
> **Mr. Burgund:** No, ma'am.[41]

As Burgund testified, Tammy Faye Bakker was sitting in the

spectators' section for the first time while the jury was present. She repeatedly shook her head in disbelief as he was speaking. But, really, his testimony was not all that one-sided. On cross-examination, he actually helped his former boss with some extremely significant testimony going to the substance of the charges against Bakker. However, it was subtle and dry compared to the story he told for the government about the value of the Towers partnerships.

Burgund confirmed that six million people visited Heritage in 1986 and that Bakker ministered to all of them. In fact, he said, Bakker did everything at PTL and was so important to it that the ministry insured his life for $50 million because that's what it would take to replace him if something happened to him.[42]

Burgund also corroborated that one of the nation's largest accounting firms audited PTL's books each year, including the executive payroll account and that those audits were, in CPA terminology, "not qualified." He said that term meant everything was okay.[43]

He also was familiar with Jim's policy that if any partner was unhappy with PTL, their money would be refunded. Burgund explained that there were times when Bakker had him go back over several years and return a donation simply because people wrote years later that they didn't like PTL anymore. That was Bakker's philosophy. He used to say that there were enough people that loved PTL and believed in what it was doing.[44]

Burgund testified that, as finance director and based on everything he knew about PTL's finances, there was no chance PTL could go bankrupt as long as Jim Bakker was there. In fact, he felt it was very wrong for Jerry Falwell to put PTL into bankruptcy in June 1987. It had substantial assets, including all of its land and buildings, which far outstripped any bills it owed.[45]

Importantly, Burgund acknowledged that Bakker told his television viewers that the money raised from the sale of lifetime partnerships was not considered restricted funds. Instead, he told them that those were donations for the entire ministry. It was not money only to be used for the construction of those hotels.

> **Mr. Bender:** Reverend Bakker when he went on television would on occasion tell people that these are not designated funds. They are your donations for the ministry?
> **Mr. Burgund:** Yes, sir.
> **Mr. Bender:** And you knew them to be donations, didn't you?
> **Mr. Burgund:** Yes, sir. ***
> **Mr. Bender:** Never considered designated funds?
> **Mr. Burgund:** No, sir.[46]

As Mark Burgund stepped down from the witness stand, both sides could claim points were put on the scoreboard. But the government's next witness, minister Alan Foor of the United Church of Christ in Beavertown, Pennsylvania, scored a touchdown for the prosecution. In response to Jim Bakker's promotion of the Victory Warriors partnerships in 1986, Reverend Foor bought one for $1,000 and put it on his Mastercard. But ten months later, after the Christian world was rocked by the revelations out of PTL about Bakker's million dollar salary, the Jessica Hahn scandal, and the shifting of funds from the actual construction of the Towers Hotel, Foor demanded his money back in a scathing letter to Bakker. As Bakker sat motionless listening a few feet away, Reverend Foor read the three-page letter to the jury.

> I believed so much in what he was doing that I borrowed $1000 for the Towers and Silver membership. The response was so great that they received more than enough to pay for the Towers. . . . Now after almost a year, the Towers is still unfinished. . . . Now here you are asking for more Towers memberships to finish the Towers. A year ago the Towers was to be paid for and membership closed forever and ever. ***
> Now I've had it. I feel robbed and cheated. While Jim and PTL spent over a quarter of a million dollars for a sexual coverup, plus it has been revealed that Jim and Tammy own at least four properties amounting to millions of dollars and gold fixtured bathrooms, expensive jewelry, mink coats, limousines, Rolls Royces, plus the thousands of dollars spent on big birthday

extravaganzas for Jim and Tammy with tuxedos and fine furs and so on, and still beg every day from these struggling, working people of America to sacrifice for—"the Lord's work"—and send in hundreds of thousands of dollars. Now enough is enough. I for one am through. ***

I discontinued my support of all TV ministries until they come out with a yearly financial statement, along with salaries and expenses paid and no dumb excuses like Jim made about the millions of dollars unaccountable for and said "—the devil got in the computer—". How dumb does he think people are? It's really easy just to blame everything off on the devil, isn't it?[47]

Foor had drawn blood.

With just a few minutes left in the day, the prosecutors decided to leave the jury with a couple of other images to think about over the weekend. First, Brenda Dryden was called to the stand.

Mr. Miller: And what is your occupation?
Ms. Dryden: I sell Mercedes.
Mr. Miller: Where?
Ms. Dryden: At VIP Motors in Palm Springs.
Mr. Miller: If you would, tell the jury, please, the type of vehicle again, date of the transaction and purchase price and who the purchaser of the vehicle was?
Ms. Dryden: 1984 Mercedes Benz, 380SL, purchase price . . . $48,524.98. The date of the transaction was June 11, 1984.
Mr. Miller: And who was the purchaser?
Ms. Dryden: Jim Bakker was the purchaser.
Mr. Miller: And did Mr. Bakker himself personally participate in that transaction?
Ms. Dryden: Yes.
Mr. Miller: And would you point him out for the jury, please, the person that you dealt with?
Ms. Dryden: Right over there. [The witness pointed to Jim Bakker just a few feet away.][48]

The last witness of the day was Lenton Brown, PTL's former pilot who flew the ministry's million dollar Sabre Liner corporate jet. He described the plane as a typical corporate jet, seating eight passengers, traveling at speeds of 500 miles an hour, and equipped with such amenities as air conditioning and a galley.

Ms. Smith: There was a galley in it?

Mr. Brown: Uh-huh.

Ms. Smith: For anyone who may not know, can you tell us what a galley is?

Mr. Brown: Airline had facilities to have food in it, trays, coffee, snacks, little sink to clean it up with.

Ms. Smith: Can you tell us who controlled the use of the plane?

Mr. Brown: I think Jim Bakker was the bottom on line on the control of the airplane.[49]

Then, the pilot acknowledged that Bakker had him fill up the jet in California with just clothes and the Bakkers' personal belongings and fly it back to Charlotte, without any passengers.

Ms. Smith: What volume are we talking about? Two or three boxes, suitcases?

Mr. Brown: There was a lot of stuff in the airplane.

Ms. Smith: Can you estimate for us about how many items or boxes?

Mr. Brown: Oh, gosh, 15–20 boxes. Just suitcases, boxes, shopping bags. Just all kinds of things.[50]

And with that, the second week of the trial was over with the government still flying high and continuing to make Bakker look like a heel.

NOTES

1. Trial transcript, *United States of America v. James O. Bakker,* Docket C-CR-88-205-1, U.S.D.C. (W.D., N.C.), August 28, 1989, vol. 2 at 626.

2. *Id.*

3. *Id.* at 626–27.

4. *Id.* at 628.

5. *Id.* at 632.

6. *Id.* at 634.

7. *Id.* at 646.

8. *Id.* at 650.

9. *Id.* at 656.

10. *Id.* at 657.

11. *Id.* at 663.

12. *Id.* at 664.

13. *Id.* at 682–85.

14. *Id.* at 671–72.

15. *Id.* at 703–4.
16. *Id.* at 705.
17. *Id.* at 710, 722–23.
18. *Id.* at 726–27.
19. *Id.* at 907, 909.
20. *Id.* at 909.
21. *Id.* at 910.
22. *Id.* at 926–29.
23. *Id.* at 911.
24. *Id.* at 930.
25. *Id.* at 931.
26. *Id.* at 932–33.
27. *Id.* at 840.
28. *Id.* at 894, 904.
29. *Id.* at 902.
30. *Id.* at 825–26.
31. *Id.* at 840.
32. *Id.* at 849–53, 869.
33. *Id.* at 851–52, 859–60.
34. *Id.* at 882–83.
35. *Id.* at 937.
36. *Id.* at 940.
37. *Id.* at 979–85.
38. *Id.* at 990.
39. *Id.* at 1001.
40. *Id.* at 1005–6.
41. *Id.* at 1012.
42. *Id.* at 1035–36.
43. *Id.* at 1045.
44. *Id.* at 1048–49.
45. *Id.* at 1049.
46. *Id.* at 1046.
47. *Id.* at 1079–82.
48. *Id.* at 1089–92.
49. *Id.* at 1094.
50. *Id.* at 1095–96.

Chapter 14

The Trial—Week Three—And the Prosecution Grinds On

Monday, September 11, 1989

The government kicked off the week by providing jurors a behind-the-scenes look into Bakker's personal life. Donald Hardister, Jr., the chief of security at PTL and Jim's bodyguard for several years, was called to the stand by Jerry Miller. He proceeded to do something that he had previously been paid handsomely to prevent—put a bullet right through Bakker's head with his testimony.

He told the jury that he and Jim were inseparable, and that he was responsible for transporting Bakker wherever he needed to be. When Bakker was home, Hardister drove him from his residence to Heritage and accompanied him everywhere he went on the grounds. He also traveled with Jim and Tammy on many out-of-town trips, including those to Hawaii and California, occupying a room connected to the one occupied by the Bakkers.

He disclosed that there were actually six PTL parsonages. In addition to the million dollar Tega Cay home in which the Bakkers lived, residences were also provided for Pastor Dortch, Norman Bakker, the Goodman family, Vi Azvedo, Doug Oldum, and Dr. and Mrs. Nichols.[1] Miller got him to admit that not all of those people were ministers, suggesting that parsonages, as property privileges of a ministry, should be used only for clergy. Hardister acknowledged that his boss really didn't like to hear bad news and that he would often ignore someone or change the subject if approached with any. But, once anybody got his attention, "he would act on it."[2]

And it was mostly good news that filled Bakker's life, borne on the wings of the PTL cashier. Hardister said that Bakker always liked to carry $1,000 in cash in his wallet, and that he didn't hesitate to spend it. Bakker had his guards build a two-story tree house for Jamie, which Hardister described as very nice, with doors that closed and locked. It was wired for electricity and had a window air conditioner. But it didn't stay there long.

> **Mr. Miller:** So there was an air conditioner in it?
> **Mr. Hardister:** Yes, sir.
> **Mr. Miller:** Who had taken it out?
> **Mr. Hardister:** I took it out, and put it in the dog house.[3]

Hardister also remembered one trip to Anaheim, California, in which the Bakkers asked him to buy $100 worth of cinnamon buns to make their Marriott Hotel rooms smell like a bakery. He explained that there were so many rolls that it took two security guards to carry them back to the hotel.

> **Mr. Miller:** And tell the jury what happened to the cinnamon rolls when you left?
> **Mr. Hardister:** I threw them out.
> **Mr. Miller:** Any of them eaten?
> **Mr. Hardister:** No, sir.[4]

Hardister hurt Bakker, too, by revealing that before several PTL board meetings Bakker had conferred with David Taggart about the bonuses that Bakker and others should be paid. Hardister explained that in a roundabout way, the two men would discuss the amounts that the bonuses should be.[5]

Judge Potter's impatience showed through during Hardister's testimony. Asked, "Were there other items that Mr. Bakker would ask you to purchase secretly for him?" Hardister responded, "There's some things I'm probably really not proud of."[6] Potter interrupted and told him, "Whether you're proud of it or not, answer the question."[7]

At that instant, Harold Bender jumped up and objected. Potter allowed Bender to approach the bench out of the hearing of the jury to argue his point. Whispering to the judge, Bender apparently explained that the answer he feared would be embarrassing to any minister and would make Bakker look extremely foolish. When he heard that, Potter took off his glasses, rubbed his face in disbelief and put his hand over his mouth to hide a huge grin. The judge then granted Bender's objection to prevent the prejudicial testimony.[8]

Harold Bender cross-examined Hardister, and got him to admit that providing security for the Bakker family was a very serious job because there had been several threats made on Bakker's life. In fact, it was Hardister who kept pushing Bakker to stop riding around in his Buick and get a Mercedes because they're built like tanks. Bakker was a security problem, too, because he was always out on the grounds at Heritage, greeting people and moving around. He worked very long hours and kept a frenetic pace.[9] But the witness had less flattering things to say about some of the others at Heritage. Reverend Dortch? To Hardister, he seemed very secretive.[10] The *Charlotte Observer*? "They were always on our case,"[11] he complained.

The day's other major witness, James Taggart, also took jurors on a journey into the outwardly materialistic world of Jim and Tammy Bakker. The former assistant music director at PTL, Taggart was singing like an opera star today. Of course, there was every motivation to do so as he looked at a long prison sentence of his own.

For the last several years, Taggart had been PTL's own in-house, full-time interior decorator, responsible for everything from the buildings at Heritage to Bakker's own private homes. Showing photographs to the jury, he described each of the rooms of the 11,000 square foot Tega Cay parsonage which he had decorated. Since Jim liked looking out over the water, his private office in the home was right on the lake. Tammy had a closet the size of an average person's living room. Jim's favorite color was blue and he loved mirrors in every room. Tammy always wanted flowers or plants in each room. There were pillows everywhere. "The Bakkers are both very small people and Mrs. Bakker especially. She likes to feel very cozy . . . she likes the coziness of pillows,"[12] he explained. Overall the home was quite regal, he confided.

But, despite the elegance of Jim and Tammy's different venues, Taggart resigned himself to the fact that "the Bakkers had a tendency to grow very bored with whatever they had."[13] And so, they had Taggart remodel and redecorate their home many times as they went through different phases from contemporary to country. Each time, Taggart would purchase new furniture and draperies to capture the changing mood.

Jerry Miller then asked Taggart to narrate a video the government had made of the Grand Hotel's presidential suite. Happy to oblige, the witness pointed out everything to the jury as the tape rolled—four thousand square feet all lavishly appointed . . . four bedrooms . . . a suite for each child . . . gold-plated swan fixtures in the bathroom . . . a piano in the living room . . . a fireplace in Jim and Tammy's bedroom.[14]

But how much more blatant could it be that Bakker was being prosecuted for his lifestyle and wealth? A government camera going through his bathroom? His closets? The drawers?

To get an even closer look, the government called Bakker's insurance agent to the stand. While the jury peered at a full-size enlargement of the complete listing of all of Bakker's personal property, the agent read the list of their possessions: "natural mink stole $3,000; full length Blackglama mink $10,000; natural brown Russian sable shirt $6,500. . . ." Tammy's $6,800 diamond watch. Her diamond rings, insured for $6,000. One strand of cultured pearls, $2,750. The total personal property insured in the home was valued at $134,000. On top of that, they listed another $158,000 for miscellaneous items.[15]

Then, some of the area retailers and crafts people who had served the Bakkers were called to trace where the duo spent their money. A jeweler testified that Tammy bought a Rolex watch for herself for $10,910.[16] A custom drape maker said that she was paid $2,984 to make twelve pillows and some drapes for Tammy Sue's bedroom.[17] Darlene Irwin, an interior decorator in Charlotte, raised the most eyebrows with the revelation that she had been paid $570.35 for a shower curtain she made for Tammy Sue's bathroom.

> **Ms. Smith:** Was it necessary to keep the water from coming out of the tub?
> **Ms. Irwin:** No, it's strictly for looks. ***
> **Ms. Smith:** Can you describe for us what a $570 shower curtain is and what it looks like?
> **Ms. Irwin:** It had like a pouf and it was puddled down at the bottom. There were either five or seven very small ribbons in sherbet colors to make it, you know, especially nice looking and then the streamers came down into the puddles.[18]

Then, the prosecutors scored a clothesline tackle on Jim by calling three contributors whose money was used to help bankroll the grandeur in which Bakker was ensconced. Floyd Hines, a Towers partner, ripped into Bakker for overselling the partnerships and never finishing the hotel.

> **Mr. Hines:** When I paid $3,000 for my membership, how did I know the whole thing was a lie. How could decent people, even if not a Christian, lie to the Christian public in such a blatant manner. This is sick! *** If I'd a knowed Jessica Hahn deal would have been there, I'd a never joined anything over there.[19]

Rebecca Rabon, a Grand Hotel partner from Salisbury, North Carolina, was also angered.

> **Ms. Smith:** Did you have occasion to stay at the Grand?
> **Ms. Rabon:** No, I did not.
> **Ms. Smith:** Can you tell us if you intended to make reservations?
> **Ms. Rabon:** Yes, I did in 1985. It was around May or June. I wanted to go in July and they were filled up.[20]

But on cross-examination she admitted that she had received a newsletter from Jim Bakker explaining that not every partner could stay at the hotel at the same time.

> **Mr. Bender:** And you knew from reading that it was on the first come, first served basis reservations?
> **Ms. Rabon:** Right.

Mr. Bender: And you also knew that because you'd seen it on TV? Reverend Bakker and perhaps Mr. Dortch and Sam Johnson, some of the others have always said it's on a first come, first served basis.
Ms. Rabon: Yes, sir, that was said on TV.[21]

Then, she confirmed that she never tried to make a reservation for an alternate date. When she didn't get the exact day she wanted the first time she called, she never called back.

Mr. Bender: You didn't even attempt to try in the year 1986? Never even made a phone call?
Ms. Rabon: That's true.
Mr. Bender: And in 1987, you made no attempt to use your membership, didn't even attempt to try, did you?
Ms. Rabon: No, I did not.[22]

While many people would dismiss Rebecca Rabon's complaints as extreme, it should not be overlooked that this was exactly the evidence of fraud upon which the government's case rested. That is, the testimony of witnesses like Ms. Rabon who could not make reservations on the dates they preferred is what the government relied on to convict Bakker. Couldn't the same case be made against every Holiday Inn in the country that was booked on one particular night but could accommodate the guest later? Why wasn't the Bakker jury more skeptical of this evidence?

As the day wore down, it started to look like the class warfare that was associated with Leona Helmsley's trial. David Sisler, a PTL mailroom employee, was on the witness stand testifying about how he would leave Charlotte late Friday night and drive a PTL truck all the way to Ohio to pick up computer forms so that they would have them on Monday morning. He didn't get paid overtime for it, and to save money he ate at McDonald's along the way. After recounting his own sacrifices, he was asked this about Jim Bakker.

Ms. Smith: Were you aware of the type of home and the type of cars Mr. Bakker drove?
Mr. Sisler: I had never seen his home and I seen him in different

cars, had no way of knowing whether those were his cars or donated cars or rental cars or whatever.[23]

A question like that was less expensive than putting up a billboard outside the courthouse or erecting a neon sign, but the effect was the same—the jury couldn't have missed it. No one could tell whether Bakker was stung by it, as he bundled up his papers for the evening recess. He remained tight-lipped. But a few blocks away, at the television studios of WSOC, channel 9, the only major character in this drama who was not subject to Judge Potter's gag order appeared as a guest on the Phil Donahue program which was being broadcast from Charlotte. In the hour-long interview, Tammy Faye lashed out at Judge Potter for treating her husband like a dog and sending him to the Butner house of horrors. She also said that prison doctors even watched Bakker taking showers. They stripped him of all his dignity, she sobbed. Donahue asked what she and Jim would do if he was acquitted and she replied, "I think we will probably build another ministry but we will always be very careful to remember not to forget this time from whence we came."[24]

Tuesday, September 12, 1989

Tuesday was a bad day for Jim Bakker. It started with Judge Potter threatening to jail him for failing to personally report to his probation officer that he was taking prescription medication for the flu. Scowling and raising his voice at Bakker, the judge bellowed: "Being on bond is a privilege that can be revoked."[25] Harold Bender rose to defend Bakker, telling the judge that he had volunteered to report the medication to the probation officer to save his client the trip. "If your honor feels I have done something wrong, then blame it on me and not my client. I told him that I would do that. I apologize to the court. It is my fault. If there's any contempt or jail sentence, I'll serve it."[26] Potter decided to give Bakker a break this time, but warned him that he'd go to jail if it ever happened again.

Then, former PTL attorney John Yorke took the stand and

shelled Bakker for two straight hours. Yorke had been an associate in the well-known local law firm headed by former Charlotte mayor Eddie Knox. The Knox firm had served as general counsel to PTL for years, going back to the ministry's humble beginnings in an abandoned Charlotte furniture store. They had walked the walk with Bakker, but when PTL broke into the stratosphere as the nation's largest television ministry in the early 1980s Bakker and Dortch started ignoring their local attorneys' advice.

Yorke testified that after 1982, no attorneys were allowed to attend and observe PTL board meetings and that he was actually evicted from one such meeting by Pastor Dortch who didn't want him anywhere around. After that, Yorke warned Bakker that the board should be more fully apprised of the financial details of the ministry, that new people with solid business backgrounds should be named to the board, and that PTL's attorneys must be present at board meetings to insure that nothing unlawful was undertaken. All of that advice was rejected.[27]

Later, a real estate attorney wrote Yorke to express his fears that the Grand Hotel partnership promotions just being launched could be "fraudulent or misleading."[28] Yorke asked Dortch to delay the mailing of hundreds of thousands of solicitations, but Dortch refused.

In a 1984 memo to senior partner Knox, Yorke wrote, "I don't think you are aware of how quickly the benefits to Jim and Tammy have accelerated in the past 18 months."[29] He noted that in 1983, Jim and Tammy earned more than $700,000 in income but only earned $600 in interest, meaning that they were going through money so fast they didn't have time to draw interest on it. He expressed concern at the huge bonuses that were being paid the Bakkers from contributions received. "The alarming thing to me is that the suspect expenses are growing exponentially."[30] He explained that he and the tax lawyers had spoken directly with Bakker about their fear that his escalating compensation could cost PTL its tax-exempt status.

Nonprofit organizations, including ministries, are permitted to avoid paying taxes on the income or contributions they receive as long as those involved in the ministries aren't using their organizations for their own personal benefit. The IRS calls that practice "private inurement" and if a charity's contributions are funneled to its leaders rather than for charitable purposes, that's a violation of the tax laws. That is not to say that charities are not permitted to compensate those who lead them. What the IRS permits is normal, reasonable compensation. It does not allow the payment of excessive salaries or bonuses.

What particularly frustrated Yorke was that the IRS was already at Heritage conducting an on-site audit to determine if Jim and Tammy were personally benefiting from exactly that kind of private inurement. Yet, with IRS agents invading the place and combing the books, Bakker and Dortch kept heaping enormous bonuses and salary increases on themselves. Wrote Yorke, "I do think that we need to try to keep the IRS from going any further."[31] But that advice, too, was ignored.

Yorke said that "a constant rationale"[32] put forward by both Bakker and Dortch in defense of their escalating salaries and bonuses was that other ministers were doing the same thing. Other nationally known televangelists had vacation homes, earned large salaries, and flew in their own jets. "Reverend Dortch even brought up the Pope at one point,"[33] Yorke revealed.

When the attorney persisted in confronting them about their salaries, and criticizing them for rushing into so many new construction projects without finishing the old ones, he started hearing many derogatory comments about lawyers and accountants from top management at PTL. They obviously didn't like what their attorney was telling them.

Yorke also advised them that if they exceeded the original 25,000 limit on the Grand Hotel, they should go back to the 25,000 people and tell them that they were going to sell more and give them the chance to get their money back if they wanted it. That advice was disregarded.[34]

On November 26, 1985, as PTL was spinning out of control, Eddie Knox himself sent a personal note to Jim Bakker bemoaning the fact that Bakker was disregarding the counsel of his lawyers. Prophetically, Knox wrote:

> The bottom line is that you just can't afford not to get a legal opinion in situations like that. The punishment meted out by the law is often great for you not to afford yourself the opportunity to know the consequences of your acts beforehand.[35]

Yorke ended his testimony on a bizarre note, when he was asked to recount meetings that he and Eddie Knox had with Bakker in the PTL offices.

> **Mr. Miller:** Did you ever have occasion to go to any meetings where Mr. Bakker was present and Mr. Knox passed along some bad news to Mr. Bakker?
> **Mr. Yorke:** He didn't necessarily react the same way all the time, but sometimes—Jim didn't like to hear bad news, and on several occasions when Eddie got kind of stern with him, he'd turn around and wouldn't look at us.
> **Mr. Miller:** For how long?
> **Mr. Yorke:** Until we left.
> **Mr. Miller:** Would he talk to you?
> **Mr. Yorke:** Yes.
> **Mr. Miller:** He wouldn't look at you until you were gone?
> **Mr. Yorke:** Right.[36]

On cross-examination, Yorke did offer the impression that he didn't think Bakker himself resented the legal advice that was given, although he ignored it. It was Dortch who was often very angry when lawyers would tell him that he shouldn't do something that he wanted to do.[37]

The rest of the day went no better for Bakker. The government called Sarah Combs, the wife of a disabled coal miner from Spanishburg, West Virginia, and she told the jury that her family of thirteen children lived on $400 a month in disability benefits. Yet, they watched *The PTL Club* every day on television and were so excited about the Grand Hotel that they took $1,000 out of her husband's black lung disability payments to buy a partnership. But, she could never get reservations despite trying three or four times a year. She got so mad that she telephoned and asked to speak to Bakker himself, but was denied the chance. At that point, she sent Jim a certified letter saying that he had misrepresented the partnerships on the air and she couldn't believe that he had done it.[38]

Barbara Schmidt, who worked in a school lunchroom in Florida serving 725 students hot lunches every day, testified that she never would have purchased her Bunkhouse partnership if she had known that Bakker was not setting that money aside to build bunkhouses.[39]

And, in a shot from the mailroom, PTL mailroom employee Terry Innis told the jury that at first he was a monthly contributor, but stopped giving. "I felt like the people that were what you call higher up in management was living highly and the people that were like working for me in the mailroom and other parts of the ministry, they were making a lot less, real small salaries, some made $4.00 an hour."[40] He also criticized Bakker for being very demanding of his staff and expecting PTL employees to work overtime.

Wednesday, September 13, 1989

September 13 was the money day in the Bakker trial. With veteran PTL finance director Peter Bailey on the stand, the government cracked open PTL's books and financial records. Through dozens of internal financial memos and letters the government seized from Jim Bakker's files, the jury saw how contributions were quickly spent at PTL.

Bailey, a certified public accountant, was a knowledgeable and serious witness who commanded the jury's attention. A very religious man, he retained an emotional attachment to the ministry which he had served for so many years. That continuing loyalty to PTL, and to an extent, to Jim Bakker as well, made him an even-handed and credible witness. He had plenty to say.

In a January 14, 1985 memo to Bakker, Bailey reported that they had been forced to divert $20 million from the Towers Hotel partnership account to pay for construction and expenses at the Grand Hotel, for television time, payroll, and the Water

Park; and that there remained only $2 million in the Towers account. He expressed his concern in that memo that they would never be able to construct the Towers if the account continued to be invaded in that way.[41]

Other Bailey memos showed that payroll, including the healthy executive salaries paid Jim and Tammy and Pastor Dortch, were being covered by the Towers and Grand Hotel accounts. "To me, we are in a false euphoria. We must cut back on spending or continue to use Tower funds to maintain operations,"[42] he wrote Bakker. In an October 17, 1984 report, Bailey traced how the most recent $5.2 million in Towers partnerships had been spent: $2.6 million on the Grand Hotel; $2.2 million on television time; $450,000 on the Water Park; and $450,000 on payroll, leaving a balance of $500,000.[43] By November 9, 1984, $8.6 million had been received from people expecting to stay in the Towers and all of that had been spent on those other expenses and none remained in the account marked for construction of the hotel.[44]

Deborah Smith walked Bailey through a flood of memos he sent to Bakker reporting seriously past due bills and looming financial disaster. In one, it was revealed that PTL owed American Express $85,000 and that until they paid it the company had cut off its card. Bailey insistently sounded the alarm that spending at PTL was dangerously out of control. "I have great concern for the size of our payroll. We cannot keep going. We need to be in prayer for our next payroll,"[45] he wrote.

What Deborah Smith then did was to show the jury that Bakker had received many of those warning memos from Bailey within a few days of the times he had received enormous bonuses and salary increases from the board of directors. Bailey admitted that he was never asked to appear before the board to explain the bleak financial condition of the corporation. He reported only to pastors Bakker and Dortch, and kept them fully informed in weekly memos of the horrendous cash flow problems at PTL. He also prepared memos for them weekly on the money that was being received from lifetime partners.[46]

The figures in his memos were frequently staggering. One

accounting showed that PTL was spending $50,000 a day to buy television time. It cost another $185,000 a day to operate Heritage. At one point, PTL was spending $700,000 a month more than it was bringing in.[47]

But Bailey wasn't going to let Smith put her own spin on his statistics:

Ms. Smith: Do you know, Mr. Bailey, what a pyramid scheme is? *** Isn't that, in fact, what happened here? ***
Mr. Bailey: No, it wasn't a scheme. I mean, it really wasn't a scheme. It was a great plan.[48]

With a question that should have made Bakker's attorneys jump to their feet in protest, Smith asked the witness whether Bakker was really any kind of minister at all.

Ms. Smith: Is it, in your opinion, a religious thing to do or an act that would indicate that someone was keeping their eyes on Jesus to accept a bonus of $500,000 shortly after being informed by the finance director that only checks that were strict emergencies were being approved?
Mr. Bailey: I will not judge his heart. It might have been a poor decision on his part, poor business decision.[49]

In answering Harold Bender's questions on cross-examination, Bailey attempted to maintain his objectivity and give Jim Bakker his due. He admitted, "I have a lot of deep feelings about PTL. It was a great organization."[50] He said Bakker "put his life's blood into that place."[51] He recounted that when bankers or accountants visited who had never seen Heritage before, their reaction was always the same: "Nothing but awe and admiration for the place, and there is, there is no place like PTL."[52] People said that Bakker was a genius for putting it together. Jim was a workhorse, too, spending hours each day in the studio doing his television program and, after that, working on the grounds from one end of the property to the other. He didn't sit in his office—he was always out working.

Bailey revealed that Bakker had given more than 6,000 free hotel rooms to people who couldn't afford them during 1985 alone. He said that everybody at PTL, including the 3,000 employees who worked at Heritage, depended entirely on Jim Bakker. Jim had an uncanny ability to raise the money to support the ministry's activities. And when Falwell took over, promising to save the ministry? "He wasn't a Jim Bakker. He couldn't hold a stick to him as far as raising money."[53]

A few eyebrows were raised when Bender showed Bailey the same memos that he had quoted from in answering Deborah Smith's questions. Interestingly, some of what he had written in many memos was helpful to Jim Bakker, but he had not been permitted to read those lines to the jury earlier. So, Bender asked him to.

> **Mr. Bailey (from July 20, 1984 memo):** "I know, with Jesus's help, we will make it."
> **Mr. Bender:** And you believed that?
> **Mr. Bailey:** With all my heart. ***
> **Mr. Bailey (from June 30, 1985 memo):** "I know Jesus will see PTL through. *** We will make it."
> **Mr. Bailey (from November 18, 1985 memo):** "In spite of all this, we will make it and Jesus is coming soon."[54]

Bailey finished his testimony by telling the jury how shocked he was that Jerry Falwell had placed PTL in bankruptcy. The witness explained that the value of the 2,200 acres of prime real estate and all of the buildings that had been erected far exceeded the debts that PTL owed. And he emphasized that his earlier gloom and doom memos to Bakker should not be misconstrued—PTL might not have been run like a Wall Street bank, but it was getting the job done in its own way.

> **Mr. Bailey:** Just because you have a cash flow problem doesn't mean you aren't a going concern. *** I've had more hand wrenching and discussion with people on the finances of PTL while I was there [8 years], with bankers, lawyers, my fellow workers, and the bottom line seems to always be, he [Jim Bakker] raises the money. He delivers.[55]

Other witnesses added the finishing touches this day. Arthur Borden, a minister and the president of the Evangelical Council for Financial Accountability, an accrediting agency for evangelical Christian churches, testified that his organization was concerned about PTL's erratic spending. He thought Bakker needed to make sure that money that was raised for a particular purpose was spent on it, and not thrown anywhere it was needed at the time.[56]

Another of Jim's former attorneys took the witness stand and did some major damage. Charles Chapel, a tax attorney from Tulsa, Oklahoma, testified that he had advised Bakker not to treat proceeds from the sale of Grand Hotel partnerships as general gifts to the ministry. He told Bakker to segregate that money and use it solely on the hotel. But, when Bakker refused to follow his advice, he withdrew his representation and explained his dissatisfaction in a letter which was shown to the jury.

> I have repeatedly attempted to convince you all of the seriousness of the tax problem. [Including the private inurement issue] *** You have been entrusted with the care, custody and control of hundreds of millions of dollars. You have an extremely high responsibility and we have not seen the kind of commitment required for us to continue to represent the church. *** You have got to take charge and get your business under control, otherwise your church will be lost.[57]

Kathleen David, a Victory Warrior partner from the Virgin Islands, testified that Bakker always represented on the air that his family was greatly sacrificing and that everything he received in the way of compensation was turned back to the ministry. She said that he represented that he "was living a very frugal life and really sacrificing his own personal comfort for the sake of the ministry."[58] She contended that had she known that he was receiving salary and bonuses in the seven figure range, she would never have purchased any partnership.[59]

The last witness of the day was Pastor J. Don George of the Calvary Temple Church in Irving, Texas, who had been a member of the PTL board of directors from 1985 until he resigned two years later. He told the jury that he was unaware of Bakker's salary but believed that he was living on a rather meager one. He said he was never aware that when the board voted a bonus, plus taxes, that the amount would be doubled because he didn't understand that Bakker was in that high a tax bracket. And as far as the $500,000 bonus that Jim received on November 3, 1986 and the $50,000 bonus he received a month later, Reverend George said he didn't remember the board ever discussing those.[60]

He also confirmed that the board was largely uninformed about the inner workings of the organization. The board was never told that PTL checks were being floated and written on insufficient fund accounts, never told that more than 25,000 Grand Hotel partnerships were going to be sold, and never told that the money raised from those partnerships was going to be spent for other purposes. They were never told of any cash flow problems at PTL, never informed that the IRS proposed to revoke PTL's tax exempt status in 1985, and never told that PTL funds were going to be paid to Jessica Hahn. He said if he had known any of those things, it definitely would have affected how he voted on the bonuses that were proposed so frequently for Jim and Tammy.[61]

On cross-examination, Pastor George did admit that the PTL board operated about the same as other church boards that he had served on in his life: "I would say that the review of the financial documents while I served as a board member at PTL was very similar to the review of financial documents that I made while serving on other church boards."[62]

He also stressed that he didn't think that Jim Bakker was undeserving of the bonuses that were given him because "without Jim Bakker there would have been no PTL."[63] The same was true of Tammy because she had given herself so untiringly to the ministry and deserved her bonuses too.

But the damage was done, and George left the stand.

Thursday, September 14, 1989

The next day, September 14, the government rolled out its biggest cannon—Richard W. Dortch.

Jim Bakker's long-time co-pastor, his second in command at

PTL and Pentecostal blood brother, did more damage to Jim than any other single witness during the trial. In five hours of solemn and measured testimony, Dortch recounted several instances of wrongdoing on Bakker's part over the years, and sealed his fate. No witness was more damning. None was more powerful.

Dortch was, after all, indicted along with Bakker for the same fraud on contributors. Dortch hosted *The PTL Club* broadcast in Bakker's absence, and appeared with him as a guest on numerous other programs encouraging viewers to purchase lifetime partnerships. They were in it together. The difference was that Dortch pleaded guilty and agreed to testify at his boss's trial, leaving Bakker the only target in the shooting gallery. Dortch squeezed off the most direct hits. He would look at Bakker only once in five hours of testimony.

At the outset he confirmed that he and Bakker justified exceeding the limits they first announced on the Grand and Towers partnerships because so many partnerships had been purchased by people living in California who were unlikely to make the 3,000 mile trek to use their benefits.[64]

> **Mr. Miller:** Now, what other reasons can you recall Mr. Bakker used for continuing the promotion or reopening the promotion of lifetime partnership programs . . . [which he had earlier said were] closed?
> **Mr. Dortch:** The fact that we needed money.[65]

> **Mr. Miller:** Now, knowing that [it was theoretically impossible to fit all the partners in the Grand] did you continue to participate in the offering of lifetime partnerships there at PTL?
> **Mr. Dortch:** Shamefully so, yes.[66]

Dortch also corroborated Steve Nelson's testimony that there were two sets of partnership totals—the real ones and smaller totals used on the air.

> **Mr. Miller:** What did Mr. Bakker tell you about it?
> **Mr. Dortch:** He asked me not to use those numbers and not to announce what those numbers were.

Mr. Miller: Which numbers?
Mr. Dortch: The real numbers.[67]

When the two spoke privately, Bakker was bullish on the partnerships.

Mr. Dortch: He stated to me he felt that the concept was a gold mine and it was something that we could be able to use in whatever kind of projects we had.[68]

Dortch confirmed that the board had not been told everything. He admitted he had given instructions not to include in the board's minutes any references to the delicious bonuses that were bestowed.

Mr. Miller: Well, were you concerned about people finding out about what the bonuses were?
Mr. Dortch: Yes.[69]

He explained that the minutes were sometimes made available to banks and other lending institutions and he didn't want the largess to be seen by inquiring eyes. PTL's own board was also kept in the dark.

Mr. Miller: Now, did you at those board meetings, when these bonuses were being mentioned . . . did you tell the board of directors about the content of those Bailey memoranda and say that Mr. Bakker may be needing this [bonus] but the ministry can't afford to give it to him?
Mr. Dortch: Regretfully, no.
Mr. Miller: You should have done that, shouldn't you?
Mr. Dortch: Yes, sir, I should have.[70]

That wasn't the only thing they kept from the board.

Mr. Miller: Did it turn out that PTL money was paid to Jessica Hahn . . . without the board of directors ever being asked about it, ever being consulted about it, or ever being advised that it might be done or had been done?
Mr. Dortch: Yes, sir.
Mr. Miller: [And why was that?] What was Mr. Bakker's status there under the bylaws . . . ?

Mr. Dortch: He [Bakker] was president for life except in certain cases—incapacitated, convicted of some crime, immorality, a number of those issues. I don't remember exactly each one of them.[71]

The incident between Bakker and Hahn would definitely have constituted immorality and so it had to be handled.[72]

Mr. Miller: Tell the jury, please, the first time that you ever had any communication with Mr. Bakker about Jessica Hahn, what you said to him and what he said to you. ***
Mr. Dortch: His response was that, "Brother Dortch, I've never assaulted or kidnapped or done anything like that in my life," and my response was, "I know that and I believe that." And he asked me where this person was from, and I said "New York." He said to me, "What is her name?" And I said, "Jessica Hahn." And in a reflective way, he turned toward the window and for a period of time said nothing and I remained silent. And after a period of some expanded time he turned around and looked at me and said, "I have not done those things. I have not raped anybody or assaulted anybody, but there is a problem."[73]

Mr. Dortch: When I realized the problem was not going to go away, I was getting telephone calls from Jessica Hahn and her pastor and other individuals, I then, in Palm Springs, California, during a time Mr. Bakker was there, sent someone to call him out of a meeting . . . and told him that a sum of money was going to have to be paid to her, and his response was, "I hate to give them anything. I hate to give them a dime, but do what you have to do to get it solved."[74]

Dortch then borrowed $265,000 from Roe Messner and asked him to simply pad his monthly PTL bill by showing that amount as labor and materials for the Passion Play and the amphitheater.[75]

Mr. Miller: With respect to this money you sent to—had Mr. Messner send to Jessica Hahn, did you ever have a conversation with Mr. Bakker about what you had done? ***
Mr. Dortch: When we were walking down Main Street USA and I approached Mr. Bakker and explained to him what had transpired in the California transaction and told him the amount of money

that we had settled the matter for, and his response was, "I don't want to know it. I don't want to know it. I don't want to hear it." And I responded and said, "Well, you will hear it because for us to do something like this, this is something you will know," and explained to him how the transaction took place.[76]

He also admitted concealing from the board of directors the results of the IRS probe and that agency's attempt to revoke PTL's tax exempt status. Bakker did not like hearing what PTL's own lawyers had to say about it, either. Dortch remembered that at one meeting with PTL tax counsel Lloyd Caudle over the IRS audit, things got pretty heated and Bakker slipped Dortch a note on a yellow pad: "See if there is some way you can get these jerks out of here."[77]

With those bombs, Dortch's direct examination came to an end. There really wasn't much that Harold Bender could do cross-examining the good pastor because he certainly wasn't going to recant anything that he had already said. So Bender settled for a couple of smaller bones. First, Dortch acknowledged that there was never a single month during all the years that he was at PTL that the Grand Hotel had been one hundred percent occupied.[78] Second, he said that he believed to this day that Bakker cared deeply about the partners and loved them.[79]

Jerry Miller seized the opening on redirect examination and popped Bakker again.

> **Mr. Miller:** Did Jim Bakker care enough about those partners for Jim Bakker to tell them the truth about what was going on in the solicitation of those partnerships . . . ?
> **Mr. Dortch:** No.
> **Mr. Miller:** Was he being open and honest with them?
> **Mr. Dortch:** No, sir; nor was I.[80]

With that, Dortch stepped down and the trial recessed for the night. The significance to Bakker in what Dortch had said the last several hours could be summarized in two words: hello prison. Bakker was cooked, and all that really remained was for the prosecutors to turn him over a few more times on the rotisserie to make sure that he was done to perfection. They began the first thing the next morning.

Friday, September 15, 1989

Two PTL board members were called as government witnesses on September 15. Evelyn Carter Spencer, a minister from Oakland, California, testified that during her years on the board she was never told anything negative about the financial condition of PTL. She did not know that it was having cash flow problems or was floating checks. She also said that she was left uninformed about everything from Bakker's salary to the number of lifetime partnerships he and Dortch were actually issuing in the two hotels.[81]

Board member Charles Cookman, Bakker's superior in the Assemblies of God hierarchy, said that it was his understanding that the money raised from the partnerships would be spent on the construction and operation of the hotels. He also lamented that if he had known that PTL was in financial distress, he would not have voted for bonuses for Bakker. He would not have voted for the Florida condo for Bakker. And he would have resigned the board if PTL didn't stop spending more than it was bringing in.[82] Not only that, there were some shenanigans with the minutes of past board meetings which referred to him.

Ms. Smith: "Reverend Cookman made a motion that the salary of the president of the corporation [Jim Bakker] be raised . . . 91.2%. And a second motion was made by Reverend Cookman that Tammy Bakker's salary be increased by 53.8%." Do you recall ever doing that and providing those percentages to the board?
Rev. Cookman: No, I do not. I don't recall it, doing that.
Ms. Smith: Can you imagine any circumstance where you made a motion for a salary increase of 91.2% for Mr. Bakker?
Rev. Cookman: No, I cannot.[83]

To give the jury one more reason to detest Jim Bakker on a personal level and to give them a chance to think about it all weekend long, prosecutors called Joanie Aimes as one of their last witnesses to wrap up the week. Aimes was a single parent who was raising two small children on her own. She worked as a payroll clerk at PTL and was paid $4.50 an hour until she was laid off in November 1985, the day before Thanksgiving.

Ms. Smith: Can you tell us what impact that had on you and your family, please? ***

Ms. Aimes: *** It was really traumatic for me because I had young children in grade school and so I got them together and I told them, I said, "I'm really sorry to tell you this," I said, "but we just may not have Christmas until after Christmas because the [unemployment] checks just won't be here."[84]

Of course, the rest of the story was that a year later she was rehired by the same supervisor at PTL and continued to work there over the years and was, at the time of the trial, making $18,000 a year as the administrative assistant to the general manager of the Grand Hotel.[85] But the image of Bakker the Terrible, cashing his $100,000 bonus checks at the Bloomingdale's customer service counter in Palm Springs while this $4.50 an hour employee was axed the day before Thanksgiving, was vividly etched in the jury's mind.

With the third week of the trial behind him, Bakker was seven days closer to being convicted by a jury which was fast making up its mind that he was dishonest and contemptible.

NOTES

1. Trial transcript, *United States of America v. James O. Bakker,* Docket C-CR-88-205-1, U.S.D.C. (W.D., N.C.), August 28, 1989, vol. 4 at 1327–28.

2. *Id.* at 1340.

3. *Id.* at 1345.

4. *Id.* at 1347.

5. *Id.* at 1344.

6. *Id.* at 1341.

7. *Id.*

8. *Id.* at 1341–42; Preston, "Judge Threatens to Jail Bakker during Trial," UPI, Domestic News, BC Cycle, September 12, 1989.

9. Trial transcript, *supra,* n. 1 at 1352.

10. *Id.* at 1353.

11. *Id.* at 1354.

12. *Id.* at 1265.

13. *Id.* at 1259.

14. *Id.* at 1361–68.

15. Trial transcript, *United States of America v. James O. Bakker,* Docket C-CR-88-205-1, U.S.D.C. (W.D., N.C.), August 28, 1989, vol. 3 at 1143–44.

16. *Id.* at 1159.
17. Trial transcript, *supra*, n. 1 at 1167.
18. *Id.* at 1203.
19. *Id.* at 1184–85.
20. *Id.* at 1209.
21. *Id.* at 1213.
22. *Id.* at 1215–16.
23. *Id.* at 1310.
24. Perlmutt, "Spotlight on Tammy Bakker," *Charlotte Observer,* September 11, 1989, at 1-A (Westlaw printout).
25. Trial transcript, *supra*, n. 1 at 1417.
26. *Id.* at 1416.
27. *Id.* at 1498, 1507–8.
28. *Id.* at 1518.
29. *Id.* at 1521.
30. *Id.* at 1504.
31. *Id.* at 1521.
32. *Id.* at 1523.
33. *Id.* at 1524.
34. *Id.* at 1546.
35. *Id.* at 1543.
36. *Id.* at 1549.
37. *Id.* at 1563–64.
38. *Id.* at 1394–96.
39. *Id.* at 1430.
40. *Id.* at 1475–76.
41. Trial transcript, *United States of America v. James O. Bakker,* Docket C-CR-88-205-1, U.S.D.C. (W.D., N.C.), September 13 and 14, 1989, vol. 5 at 1666–67.
42. *Id.* at 1651–52.
43. *Id.* at 1652–53.
44. *Id.* at 1654–55.
45. *Id.* at 1643.
46. *Id.* at 1613, 1626.
47. *Id.* at 1627, 1632.
48. *Id.* at 1805–6.
49. *Id.* at 1800.
50. *Id.* at 1777.
51. *Id.* at 1789.
52. *Id.* at 1784.
53. *Id.* at 1798.
54. *Id.* at 1782, 1784–85.
55. *Id.* at 1792.
56. *Id.* at 1853, 1859–60.
57. *Id.* at 1874–75.
58. *Id.* at 1897.
59. *Id.* at 1898.
60. *Id.* at 1915, 1920–22.

61. *Id.* at 1923–24.

62. *Id.* at 1929.

63. *Id.* at 1942.

64. Trial transcript, *United States of America v. James O. Bakker,* Docket C-CR-88-205-1, September 14–18, 1989, vol. 6 at 24.

65. *Id.* at 26.

66. *Id.* at 95.

67. *Id.* at 31.

68. *Id.* at 47–48.

69. *Id.* at 61.

70. *Id.* at 71–72.

71. *Id.* at 72.

72. *Id.* at 73.

73. *Id.* at 73–74.

74. *Id.* at 79.

75. *Id.* at 80–82.

76. *Id.* at 83–84.

77. *Id.* at 85.

78. *Id.* at 109.

79. *Id.* at 121.

80. *Id.* at 148.

81. *Id.* at 188–89.

82. *Id.* at 290–91, 305.

83. *Id.* at 308.

84. *Id.* at 213–14.

85. *Id.* at 215.

Chapter 15

The Trial—The Government Rests Its Case after Four Weeks

Three Days of Television

Prosecutors concluded their case against Jim Bakker with a dramatic three-day flurry that included only brief testimony. Actor Efrem Zimbalist, Jr., best known as Inspector Lewis Erskine on TV's *The FBI* but also a PTL board member from 1981 through 1986, was called to the stand by the government. He remained loyal to Bakker in many respects. Although Zimbalist did confirm that the board was never told of any financial problems at PTL, he explained that it was a church board and not a board of directors like one would find governing a business or corporation. It was a group of like-minded Christians who always acted by affirmation and consensus, and did not get into the financial end of the ministry at all.[1] When prosecutors put the bonus question to him, he stood his ground.

> **Mr. Zimbalist:** I would have assumed it [the bonuses] would have been plus tax anyway. *** They weren't going to give him a bonus and then have it cut in half. *** I don't think the thing that ruined it [PTL] was the Bakkers' bonuses. I mean, financially, that certainly would not have ruined it. *** Had it [Heritage USA] been finished, had it gone on, it probably—and had the financial management of it been a good one . . . I think it could have very well run on its own. I think that the income that it would have generated from all of the buildings and so forth, could have run it without any appeals for funds. I always felt that.[2]

When repeatedly pressed by Jerry Miller to dump on Bakker, Zimbalist finally arched his back and retorted:

Mr. Zimbalist: But I don't see it as the great malfeasance that I think you wish me to. . . .[3]

Not that the prosecutors needed Zimbalist's testimony, anyway. The rest of the board had already done all the damage necessary. But Zimbalist's view did cast doubt on the party line against Bakker that the other board members had taken.

Next, U.S. postal inspector Robert Dash took the stand for a few minutes to report the results of his review of PTL's books. In the thousands of pages of documents that he scrutinized, one thing in particular stood out. Jim Bakker's March 1984 bonus of $195,000 was not issued in the form of a check. Instead, the cash was wired to Bakker's personal checking account. Five days later, Bakker used it to make the down payment on his $449,000 Palm Desert, California vacation home. What caught Dash's eye was that the $195,000 was taken from the Grand Hotel lifetime partnership deposit account.[4]

If that wasn't bad enough, the next witness lugged two big charts in for the jury which made Bakker look increasingly greedy and self-indulgent. IRS agent Leon Bowman testified that he had carefully examined Jim and Tammy's tax returns from 1983 through 1986 and had prepared charts to show the jury the income and spending information contained in those returns.[5] The spending chart listed the Bakkers' major acquisitions during those years: $158,000 in jewelry and furs; the Palm Desert home for $449,000; the move up to the Palm Springs spread for $600,000; Mercedes and Cadillacs and Rolls Royces (and one lowly Dodge); plastic surgery for both Jim and Tammy; and $43,000 to remodel Tammy's kitchen in North Carolina.

Agent Bowman explained that the Bakkers' lavish lifestyle was made possible by million dollar salary packages in each of those years. On his second chart he detailed the salary, bonuses, and retirement ("MBA") investments each of the Bakkers was paid.

Jay Leno, on The Tonight Show: All week long, they've been showing videotapes of the Bakkers' lavish lifestyle. I got an idea. . . . We should show these tapes to the Colombia drug lords. When they see how much money they can make they'll quit selling cocaine and become TV evangelists.[6]

Next, the prosecutors kicked Bakker in the teeth with his own shoes. They called Eleanor Berthold to the stand, who owned a small plastics business in Charlotte. PTL paid her $1,800 to take a pair of Jim Bakker's shoes, which had mud on them, and preserve the mud and shoes in a custom designed airtight plastic case to commemorate the Crystal Palace ground-breaking ceremony. She brought the shoes with her, looking museum-ready in an acrylic box with mud and history intact. The shoes were admitted into evidence and the judge allowed Jerry Miller to pass them to the jury.[7]

Before wrapping it up, Rose Ellen Baker was asked to take the stand. A long-time PTL employee, her job had been to take detailed notes during each day's television program about what was broadcast that day. If Jim delivered a sermon for ten minutes, that would be logged. The same if the PTL singers were on for eight minutes—she would log it. If Jim promoted the lifetime partnerships for fifteen minutes, she'd write that down too.

Through her, the government introduced the logs for twelve *PTL Club* programs aired between 1984 and 1987. On each of them, Bakker spent the majority of the program talking about Heritage, the hotels, the campgrounds, and the partnerships.[8]

Jim Bakker in prison: Of all the witnesses who testified against me, Ellen Baker was the most painful. I hired her when we first started out, in the old furniture store. She had worked for me so long. I thought she was my friend. But now she was working for the bankruptcy trustee. It broke my heart—like a knife going through it to see her up there.[9]

The government's last witness, veteran FBI agent John Pearson, took the stand on Monday afternoon. He finally stepped down on Wednesday and actually he didn't do that

Major Items Obtained by or on Behalf of the Bakkers

	Date On or About	Approximate Cost
Two Dogwood Condos (SC)	February 28, 1983	$109,800
Ring (Tammy Bakker)	December 10, 1983	10,000
Palm Springs Home	January 30, 1984	449,000
Convertible Auto (Tammy Bakker)	April 19, 1984	13,700
Mercedes Auto (CA)	June 6, 1984	48,500
Two Rolls Royce Autos	June 11, 1984	93,000
Jeep Vehicle (CA)	August 14, 1984	14,600
Cadillac (NC)	December 4, 1984	28,600
Rolex Watch	December 10, 1984	11,900
Cadillac (CA)	January 16, 1985	27,850
Mazda RX-7 (Tammy Sue Bakker)	June 19, 1985	12,500
Gazelle Auto	July 2, 1985	24,100
Misty Plum Condo (SC)	November 8, 1985	97,000
Fur Coat	January 16, 1986	6,100
Boat	April 30, 1986	21,000
Gatlinburg, TN House Renovations	August 14, 1986	149,500 340,000
Record Production (Tammy Sue Bakker)	September 1986	97,000
Three Mercedes Autos	December 18, 1986	150,000
Palm Desert Home	February 1, 1987	600,000

Agent Bowman's chart showing the Bakkers' spending

Salaries, Bonuses and Contributions Paid By PTL on Behalf of the Bakkers

Jim Bakker

Year	Salary[1]	MBA	Bonuses	Total
1984	$ 270,822	$121,690	$ 640,000	$1,032,512
1985	314,673	145,348	550,000	1,010,021
1986	313,567	132,500	790,000	1,236,067
1987 (Jan.-May)	121,017	55,208	450,000[2]	626,225
	$1,020,079	$454,746	$2,430,000	$3,904,825

Tammy Bakker

Year	Salary	MBA	Bonuses	Total
1984	$ 94,355	—	$ 100,000	$ 194,355
1985	99,034	—	148,512	247,546
1986	99,951	—	265,000	364,951
1987 (Jan.-May)	39,550	—	170,000	209,550
	$ 332,890	—	$ 683,512	$1,016,402

Combined

Year	Salary[1]	MBA	Bonuses	Total
1984	$ 365,177	$121,690	$ 740,000	$1,226,867
1985	413,707	145,348	698,512	1,257,567
1986	413,518	132,500	1,055,000	1,601,018
1987 (Jan.-May)	160,567	55,208	620,000[2]	835,775
	$1,352,969	$454,746	$3,113,512	$4,921,227

Notes: 1. Includes Salary, Housing and/or Automobile Allowances, 1099 Items, Etc.
2. Includes an Unexplained Payment of $150,000 to Jim Bakker in 1987.

Agent Bowman's chart showing the Bakkers' income

much talking. But by the time Pearson finished, Bakker was dead.

The murder weapons were videotapes of Jim and Tammy on television hawking lifetime partnerships. Agent Pearson prepared nine videocassettes of Jim and Tammy on three of their shows—*The PTL Club, The Jim and Tammy Show,* and *The Jim Bakker Show*—that aired from February 20, 1984 through April 1987. He traced the on-air evolution of each of the lifetime partnership programs, from the first time each one was unveiled by Bakker, through several later broadcasts when Bakker would report the progress of each campaign, to the final programs where Bakker would close off the promotion.

Before he got to play his first tape for the jury on the TV monitor in the center of the courtroom, however, Pearson was criticized by Harold Bender for using only a minute or two from many hour-long PTL programs. He had also excised the religious content from each show. Agent Pearson had only included the fund-raising representations made by Bakker about the lifetime partnerships, and had omitted Bakker's preaching, the testimonials by born-again Christians which were featured on most programs, Bible study, and gospel singing which made up the bulk of each day's programs.

The judge jumped in.

Judge Potter: Are you suggesting we look at 2000 hours of TV, in excess of 2000 hours?

Mr. Bender: Sure, sure. I don't have any problem with that at all because the burden is on the government. Not on us.

Judge Potter: Mr. Bender, the defendant was on TV. Now whether it was on a five percent or one hour program, he was on TV saying these things. Now, that to me is sufficient, certainly, evidence. *** If you're going to bore this jury with 500 hours of tapes, that's fine with me. We'll sit here for 500 hours. Ok. Let's go.[10]

For the next three days, the jury's viewing of those composite tapes was punctuated only by Deborah Smith occasionally stopping the tapes and asking Agent Pearson to verify representations that Bakker was making on the air. Pearson was armed with PTL's own computer records which showed the true number of lifetime partnerships in each of the different lodging plans that had been sold on each date. Time and time again, Pearson would contrast the true number of partnerships sold to what Bakker was saying on television. For hours and hours each day, the jury saw tapes of Bakker representing facts about the partnerships which the ministry's own records refuted.

The first composite tape played was of highlights of Bakker's promotion of the Grand Hotel partnerships which he unveiled on February 20, 1984, in a special program complete with a full orchestra. On that show, Bakker enthused that the Grand Hotel was "the most exciting project probably undertaken in the whole history of Christianity."[11] He urged viewers to act quickly because "when the 25,000 memberships in the Grand are gone, we cannot have any more . . . we'll have to refund your money if they are all gone. . . ."[12] Repeatedly, on numerous broadcasts, Bakker urged supporters to act quickly before the Grand was sold out. When calling on the special 800 number, Bakker didn't want his partners tying up the lines, either: "Don't ask them any questions, just give them your credit card and say good-bye."[13]

In May 1984 Bakker told his audience that he had used his own Visa card instead of cash to buy a lifetime partnership because "I really don't have the funds to do it. Uncle Sam got to me first. . . . It took everything we could get, we could scrape together to pay our taxes. . . ."[14] PTL payroll records showed that eleven days after that, $195,000 in cash was wired to Bakker to make the down payment on his new Palm Desert getaway.

At another point on the composite tape, from the December 3, 1985 television program, Bakker looked into the camera and told viewers: "I've never asked for a penny for myself. . . . God had always taken care of me."[15] The year before, on the December 21, 1984 broadcast he emphasized that no criminal activity of any kind would be tolerated at Heritage USA: "If I ever see anyone at this place robbing or stealing, they are going to jail."[16] At that instant, a spectator from the back of the courtroom shouted, "Amen."[17]

The videotapes the jury watched were collages of misstatements and exaggerations about the different lifetime partnerships. It could not have been more blatant or obvious than when Deborah Smith stopped the tape after the excerpt of Bakker's July 8, 1985 TV show in which he announced with great fanfare that Lulu Roman of *HeeHaw* had just purchased the last two lifetime partnerships in the Grand Hotel. Agent Pearson testified that on that day, Bakker had already received 58,748 fully paid Grand Hotel partnerships. Beyond that, Bakker kept selling them until May 1, 1987 when there were 66,683 in the final tally. Lulu never knew that she wasn't, after all, the last Grand Hotel partner.[18]

Bakker's urgent promotion of the Bunkhouse partnership program far outpaced construction. He repeatedly invited viewers to purchase and use them to enjoy the rustic beauty of the eight-room bunkhouse chalets. By the end, according to the government, he had received $6,681,961 from Bunkhouse partners but had fully constructed only one bunkhouse, which all 42,162 Bunkhouse and Eleven Hundred Club members would have to use.[19]

He and Tammy said some other amazing things on the tapes.

Tammy (on August 1, 1984 with Jim standing next to her): [The lifetime partnership revenue] is being used to build the Grand, it's not being used to pay the bills. So now we need some paying-the-bills money.[20] [Jim didn't correct her misstatement even though most of the money raised from Grand partners was being used to pay for television time and the other expenses of PTL.]

Jim (in a 1984 broadcast): I'm sincere. I would not lie to you about anything.[21]

On Wednesday, after three days on the stand, Pearson concluded his video barrage and was briefly cross-examined by Harold Bender. Bakker's attorney kept up his attack that nine videocasettes edited and cut from 3,000 TV programs unfairly represented the PTL television ministry.

It didn't matter. The jury had seen enough. At the conclu-

James Albert and Jim Bakker during one of their many prison interviews spanning two years

Jim Bakker recalls his first TV program, Come On Over, *a 1965 religious puppet show for children on Pat Robertson's CBN.*

Heritage Grand Hotel—"the scene of the crime"

Main Street, Heritage USA

The imposing lobby of the Grand Hotel

*Dale Evans and
Roy Rogers at
Heritage USA*

*Pat Boone at
Heritage USA*

Jamie Charles Bakker and his father interview Art Linkletter.

Kevin's House

Jerry Falwell, at Heritage USA at the time of his takeover

Celebrating 32 Years of Spirit-Filled Ministry

The Evangelist

THE VOICE OF THE JIMMY SWAGGART MINISTRIES   NOV. 1988 • VOLUME 20 NU

DON'T MISS
Thanksgiving

Camp
Meeting
'88

Death, Burial, And Resurre
by Jimmy Swaggar
See page 4

Jimmy Swaggart, around the time of the PTL scandal

The federal courthouse in Charlotte, North Carolina, where Bakker's trial roared on for five weeks in 1989

Fundraising brochure for Jim Bakker during his trial

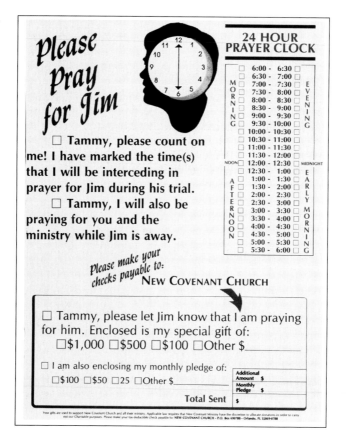

Jim Bakker was escorted to the Charlotte courthouse each morning by his attorneys George T. Davis (right) and Harold Bender (left).

Judge Robert D. "Maximum Bob" Potter

Making an appearance during Jim's trial, Tammy Faye blows a kiss to the press and spectators.

Jim Bakker, immediately after suffering a nervous breakdown during the first week of his trial, seized and shackled by U.S. marshals to be taken back before Judge Potter, who then incarcerated Bakker in a mental institution for one week before resuming the trial

Prosecutors Jerry Miller and Deborah Smith talking to the media immediately following their victory

Bunkhouse #2 as it stood at Heritage USA, when the federal court of appeals upheld Bakker's conviction for such frauds as building only one bunkhouse for visitors

The other "scene of the crime": Heritage Grand Towers Hotel, as it stood when Jim Bakker resigned as president of PTL

KARL GARMAGER

U.S. District Court Judge Graham C. Mullen, who reduced Bakker's sentence from 45 years to 18 years and later to eight years

Roe and Tammy Faye Messner

Today Bakker lives on a rented farmhouse in Hendersonville, North Carolina.

sion of Agent Pearson's testimony, and after ninety-one witnesses over four weeks time, Deborah Smith rested the government's case.

After Agent Pearson stepped down from the stand, Harold Bender made a motion to dismiss the case against Bakker, a legal maneuver common in criminal trials when a defendant disputes the sufficiency of the prosecution's evidence of guilt. Bender pursued a slightly different tack, however, arguing that Bakker's constitutional right to freedom of religion was being violated.

> **Mr. Bender:** Your honor . . . what we have tried to establish is that we have a minister, we have a religious entity that—and that everything that it did was religious in nature, as some of my cross-examination hopefully has pointed out, and that the Constitution prohibits government interference in a religion. *** For the government to come in here and impose its laws and its regulations on a ministry that's operating as a ministry and a religious organization violates the Constitution, and on that basis, we ask that you allow our motion. . . .
>
> **Mr. Miller:** This is not a case about religion. This is a case about lying to people over television to cheat them out of their money.
>
> **Judge Potter:** It has nothing whatever to do with religion. I'm going to let it go to the jury. *** We don't have to spend any time on that.[22]

And with that, after a short recess, it was Jim Bakker's turn to begin to try to undo the serious damage that the government had done in four weeks of methodical pounding.

But even Tammy realized things had not gone well up to that point. She abruptly left Orlando to join her beleaguered husband in Charlotte as he prepared to mount his defense, and her mood was definitely not upbeat. Reporters asked Tammy's secretary what the former first lady of televangelism was doing then. Shirley Balmer's reply: "she's praying a lot."[23]

NOTES

1. Trial transcript, *United States of America v. James O. Bakker*, Docket C-CR-88-205-1, U.S.D.C. (W.D., N.C.), September 14–18, 1989, vol. 6 at 338.

2. *Id.* at 351, 354.

3. *Id.* at 357.

4. *Id.* at 368.

5. *Id.* at 398–403.

6. Leland and Shepard, "Trading One Storm for Another," *Charlotte Observer,* September 21, 1989 at 15-A (Westlaw printout).

7. Trial transcript, *supra,* n. 1 at 442–44.

8. *Id.* at 447, 472.

9. Jim Bakker, interview by author, in Rochester, Minnesota, April 4, 1993.

10. Trial transcript, *supra,* n. 1 at 492; trial transcript, *United States of America v. James O. Bakker,* Docket C-CR-88-2051-1, U.S.D.C. (W.D., N.C.), September 19–25, 1989, vol. 7 at 617.

11. Shepard and Wright, "Jury Sees Bakker on Video—Prosecution Argues He Lied on TV," *Charlotte Observer,* September 20, 1989 at 1-A (Westlaw printout).

12. *Id.*

13. *Id.*

14. *Id.*

15. *Id.*

16. *Id.*

17. *Id.*

18. Trial transcript, vol. 7, *supra,* n. 10 at 517–18.

19. *Id.* at 543–45, 556, 577.

20. Shepard and Wright, *supra,* n. 11.

21. *Id.*

22. Trial transcript, vol. 7, *supra,* n. 10 at 622–24.

23. Leland, "Tammy Goes to the Mall," *Charlotte Observer,* September 20, 1989 at 11-A (Westlaw printout).

Chapter 16

The Trial—Bakker's Defense
Begins with a Bang

Hitting the Blocks

Harold Bender got the defense off to an all-television start by playing two solid hours of unedited videotapes of old PTL broadcasts. This was at the end of the day Wednesday when the government rested its case after playing several hours of Jim Bakker videos itself. Better hope the jury liked the show to make them watch a whole day of it.

The programs Bender chose were not exactly cliff-hangers, though. Tammy Faye was featured singing a medley of patriotic songs; Dale Evans spoke of her faith and led the studio audience in prayer; and PTL baritone Doug Oldham belted out "The Impossible Dream." The first hour-long program dragged so much that when Judge Potter took a break to let Bender load the second videotape, reporters and spectators fled from the courtroom as fast as they could. The *Charlotte Observer* reporters who didn't escape later wrote that without a doubt this was the "most boring day" of the trial.[1]

Interesting strategy. After ninety-one government witnesses pummeled Bakker over fifteen days, the defense just played a couple of programs that had nothing to do with much of the testimony against Bakker.

Surely, the defense attorneys were saving their fire for the next day when they would have the entire day to themselves.

Thursday, September 21, 1989

Outside the courthouse, the carnival atmosphere reached its height as both Bakker supporters and detractors excitedly waited for sparks to fly from Jim's gunslingers. To be right in the middle of the action, WRFX deejays Billy James and John Boy Isley told their listeners that they would broadcast live from the lawn of the courthouse all morning. They would bring a sofa and award prizes, such as Tammy Faye albums, to spectators stopping by who would fit their heads under the sofa. The scornful deejays also promised they'd have $100 worth of cinnamon buns with them, a station producer explaining "[t]hese aren't for eating, they're just for air fresheners."[2]

As Harold Bender made his way through the crowd, he confidently told a reporter, "You're going to get a hefty dose of God before this is over."[3] What exactly did he have in his kit bag to save his client?

Inside the courtroom, anticipation was at a fever pitch as Jim's defense was unveiled. Bakker loyalists who had been agonizing in the spectators' section as the government vilified their pastor, arrived early to see some of the prosecution's fire returned.

Bakker's very first witness was Vicki Liddell, who worked at the Heritage House home for unwed mothers. She testified that Bakker built the home to provide pregnant mothers with lodging free of charge. They received spiritual guidance, accredited high school classes, and vocational training while waiting for their children to be born. Then, they would be given help in placing their children for adoption or help so that they could keep their children themselves. She said the home was at full capacity and a very vibrant part of Heritage USA. She also explained that she bought a lifetime partnership to support all of the ministry, including the girls' home and adoption program.[4] Cross-examination turned this testimony of Bakker's good deeds right around to the government's issues.

> **Mr. Miller:** If another $3 million [Bakker's salary and bonuses] had been added to your budget, you would have been able to help a lot more young women and girls, wouldn't you?

Ms. Liddell: Yes.

Mr. Miller: Now, were you personally aware that during the years that you were there that Mr. Bakker was receiving bonuses in the amount of a half a million dollars, a quarter of a million dollars on a regular basis?

Ms. Liddell: No.[5]

Bakker's second witness was Michael Elder of Goodwill Industries in Charlotte who testified that Jim Bakker once donated $20,000 in PTL funds to Goodwill and gave the dedication prayer at a Goodwill ceremony. On cross-examination, the government did it again:

Ms. Smith: If you had received $2.4 million from 1984 to 1987 from PTL, would that have really enabled you to do some very good work for the people of this community?

Mr. Elder: Yes, it would have.[6]

Louise Grimes, who owned a gas station in Hopton, South Carolina, and had purchased a Grand Hotel partnership, said that she never had any trouble using her lodging privileges as long as she made reservations in advance. If they were filled up on the day she wanted, she was told when there were vacancies on other days. She loved it at Heritage and went to Bible classes and spent time praying in the Upper Room with Christians from all over the country who, like her, were there to seek the Lord. She said it was as close to heaven as you could imagine and that you could feel the presence of the Lord there. Camp meetings and church services were always packed. People couldn't wait to get there to talk and think about Jesus with like-minded believers. And there was something else that made Heritage special—"You didn't get smoke blowed in your face and you didn't get alcohol blown on you and people didn't curse and that's—it was just a good environment."[7]

On cross-examination, she got the treatment.

Mr. Miller: Now, do you have any knowledge about how many people had Grand partnerships?

Ms. Grimes: No.

Mr. Miller: Do you know how many of the people that had Grand partnerships were never able to use them?

Ms. Grimes: I don't know any of those, no, sir, I don't.[8]

Builder Sam Gasaway from Atlanta testified that the lifetime partnership he bought was a gift to the overall ministry, not just to build a hotel. Cross-examination was quick.

Ms. Smith: Has Mr. Bakker during his conversations with you ever indicated to you how he and his wife spent the $3.1 million bonuses they received in 1984 through 1987?

Mr. Gasaway: No, I never asked him about that.[9]

The very best defense witness this first day was James Johnson, a computer programmer for AT&T in Winston-Salem. He testified that when he mailed in his lifetime partnership contribution, he understood that it could be spent for any ministry purpose and not just for the construction of the hotel.

Mr. Johnson: He [Jim Bakker] explained that he would use the money not only for the building but for other uses also. *** Jim had explained this time and time again.[10]

But harm was done on cross-examination.

Mr. Miller: Did Mr. Bakker ever come on television or tell you in person or send any letter to you telling you that he had decided to exceed [the limit on the Grand] and go as high as 66,000?

Mr. Johnson: I'm not familiar with that. ***

Mr. Miller: Well, did he ever tell you he was exceeding those limits?

Mr. Johnson: No.[11]

Constance Martin, who did not purchase a lifetime partnership but was a monthly contributor to PTL, offered some testimony that reflected the Pentecostal tenet that God maintains a daily, personal relationship with believers. The witness said that she didn't contribute anything to Jim Bakker for a while but "then when the Lord spoke to me, because I don't do nothin' until he tells me I am supposed to do something, and when he told me that I was supposed to start having a relationship with PTL, then I did it, and I started giving to the monthly partnership $15.00 a month. . . ."[12]

Of course, there were no Pentecostals on the jury and so testimony about God speaking to people may have seemed bizarre to some, and may have made it look like Bakker was leading people with rather extreme religious views.

A veteran PTL employee of ten years who rose to the rank of vice-president of lodging, Priscilla Sherrill, testified that she had an office in the Grand Hotel and there were always rooms available there. She bought a lifetime partnership for herself and never had any trouble making reservations because she didn't try to reserve a room during peak seasons. She also was adamant that her $1,000 partnership gift was for the entire ministry and not just to build the hotel.[13]

Some of Ms. Sherrill's credibility was questioned on cross-examination when Jerry Miller got her to admit that since leaving PTL she had opened a pricey boutique in Denver and that Tammy Faye was one of her customers.[14] But what did her friendship with Tammy have to do with whether there were rooms available at the Grand?

Helen Headley, who was responsible for the Bakkers' TV audiences for ten years, said that their programs were so enormously popular that she had to have twenty-five people working under her to do the job each day. A thousand people would attend *The Jim Bakker Show* which aired at 11:00 in the morning, and they would start lining up at 7:00 A.M. for a chance to sit in the audience. She also made the point that Jim and Tammy never hid their lifestyle from their contributors. He televised several programs live from his own home. He showed people his luxury automobiles. He had a camera crew walk through his home. It was all out in the open.[15]

Deborah Smith's cross-examination refocused the testimony of this witness back to the government's misuse of funds issue:

Ms. Smith: When you sent money in for the Bunkhouse partnership, did you intend for that money to be used in any way to assist in paying Jessica Hahn $265,000?

Ms. Headley: I did not know about Jessica Hahn.

Ms. Smith: But when you wrote that check and arranged for this payroll deduction, that certainly wasn't your intent, was it?

Ms. Headley: Well, nobody would support that knowingly.[16]

Bakker's star witness of the day was Betty Sacco. A staunch Bakker loyalist and former PTL employee whose job it was to write down everything Bakker said on his television programs from her vantage point in the church choir, she was PTL's permanent mouse-in-the-corner and had seen it all. She was so infuriated by the indictment and prosecution of Bakker that she strode defiantly to the witness stand to set the record straight and fight back.

In response to questions from Harold Bender, she explained that Bakker was very sensitive and had deep feelings for others. She remembered that he had built Fort Hope after receiving a letter from a woman whose father had become an alcoholic and was languishing in a skid row section of town. That lady's comment to Bakker was: "That wasn't a bum, that was my father."[17] Bakker was so touched by her story about how people would laugh at her father and demean him that he vowed then and there to build a place for people like that to live in dignity.

Sacco remembered being in a meeting where Bakker "broke down and cried"[18] when he learned that the twenty or thirty correspondence clerks who read mail from viewers were losing some letters and were not answering the mail quickly. He demanded that his staff get on the ball so that not one single letter was ever lost or unanswered. He reminded them that they must never forget the lonely people without families, people who were shut in and whose only link to religion was through PTL. He implored his workers: "[Don't say] . . . it's only one letter. . . . Every time I see a letter, I see a person. That's why I'm so broken. Because we hurt so many people. My driving force is blessing and touching people from the baby to the elderly, bringing them dignity and love."[19]

She remembered a frazzled Bakker late in his PTL tenure admitting that "things were happening in the ministry that he was not aware of, the vice presidents and the managers are not telling him."[20] Bakker had told his staff:

> The problem is I'm one person. There's unbelievable demands and I can't be everywhere. 2800 employees. The sheets and reports many times never get to me. They go through a chain of command. People protecting their jobs, they hid, they're afraid to tell me. *** I was getting positive reports that everything was fine. On top of things, we must dig out, restructure, totally rebuild everything.[21]

Sacco wanted the jury to understand that a person really could feel the spirit of God moving on the grounds of Heritage like nowhere else in the world. She testified that looking out at the huge congregation from her place in the choir, she saw unwed mothers from the girls' home and former street people from Fort Hope and they would all be smiling. The congregation would smile at them, too. They were treated with genuine respect there.

There were Catholics and every Protestant denomination imaginable in Bakker's audiences, all worshipping God together. She said it was like a sale at Macy's when they would open the doors to the church at 9:30 in the morning because people would jam in and fill the place to the rafters. There were so many who wanted to attend his services Bakker always had to send people away. He even had to build an overflow auditorium next to the church. He was that popular a preacher.[22]

Right up until the time Bakker left, Sacco continued to make a monthly tithe to PTL. "I continued to faithfully support it until that fateful spring time when that fat man came from the north, you know, and it wasn't Santa Claus [Falwell]."[23]

Jerry Miller's cross-examination of this witness was a replay of Little Bighorn, however. It turned into a contentions fiasco that shook all the good Sacco tried to do with her choir-spy testimony. The judge was right in the middle of it.

Judge Potter: Ms. Sacco, listen to the counsel's questions. Answer the question.

Ms. Sacco: I'm sorry, your honor.

Mr. Miller: You have a lot of enthusiasm. You want to come here and tell what you want to for Mr. Bakker, don't you? You have a lot of enthusiasm—

Ms. Sacco: I'm part Italian. I can't help it. It comes out.

Mr. Miller: You have a lot of allegiance to Mr. Bakker, don't you?

Ms. Sacco: My first allegiance is to God.

Mr. Miller: Do you have a lot of allegiance to Mr. Bakker? Can you answer that question?

Ms. Sacco: Yes, I do. I am proud of it.

Mr. Miller: What's difficult about answering that question, Ma'am?

Ms. Sacco: Nothing.

Ms. Sacco: I feel loyal because I've seen what this man has built. A greedy man does not build what this man built. A greedy man doesn't turn gray in five years because he doesn't pour his sweat, blood and tears into a place.

Mr. Miller: Well, he turned gray sort of from week to week, didn't he?

Ms. Sacco: That man aged an awful lot. I wouldn't have taken his job for $10 million a year. It was a terrible job.

Mr. Miller: Ms. Sacco, it would be gray one week and brown the next, wouldn't he?

Ms. Sacco: No. Oh, one time Tammy Faye wanted him to color it, because she didn't want him to be gray and he did, and it turned red and it was terrible, and he tried to get the red out and it turned blond and he looked like, you know, he was becoming a punk rocker and . . . he just said, Tammy, I'm just going to be gray, I'm just going to be myself.

Mr. Miller: Ms. Sacco, since you say he was being himself, do you know that he went to a plastic surgeon to have his facial appearance changed? Is that being himself?

Mr. Bender: Objection.

Judge Potter: Overruled.

Mr. Miller: Do you know that?

Ms. Sacco: Yes, I know he went. *** His eyes were closing up. He had these things here, that can be very annoying. I see nothing wrong with that.

Mr. Miller: Well, is there anything else, it sounds like you want to get something off your chest about the government? Would you like to do that?

Ms. Sacco: I love the United States of America more than any country in the world. I would never leave it. But I tell you, when I was sitting there and Jerry Falwell came in with his people, I felt like I lived in communist Russia. All we needed was barbed wires and tanks. The media came on the—

Judge Potter: Just a minute. That's not necessary.

Ms. Sacco: Well, it was terrible.

Judge Potter: You don't need to make a political speech. Just answer the questions.

Mr. Miller: Now, can you tell us how Mr. Bakker then was being himself . . . having plastic surgery and coloring his hair and all those things, now how is that compatible?

Ms. Sacco: What in the world. *** You know, my mother colors her hair. Does that make her wicked? Are you wicked because you color your hair? These earrings, you know, they're gold. Does that make me wicked?

Judge Potter: Just a minute.

Ms. Sacco: I don't understand.

Mr. Miller: Your testimony is that Mr. Bakker loved the partners?

Ms. Sacco: Yes, he most certainly did.

Mr. Miller: Did you ever hear Mr. Bakker love the partners enough to go on the air and tell them, folks, we have sold more lifetime partnerships in the Grand than we had originally advertised?

Ms. Sacco: No, I did not hear him say that. Now, can I explain? *** Why would a man who worked so hard, why would he do something to fleece his partners and to destroy the place that he built? It doesn't make any sense.

Mr. Miller: Would it have anything to do with Rolls Royces and a half-a-million-dollar homes? ***

Mr. Miller: How many [homes] was he entitled to, Ms. Sacco?

Ms. Sacco: Probably—I don't know. How many is anybody entitled to? That's something I can't answer.[24]

Of course, what really hurt was that this witness was unprepared to answer the $64,000 question about whether Bakker ever went on the air to tell his viewers that he was going to offer more than 25,000 partnerships in the Grand Hotel. In fact, he did and a videotape of it existed. All of Bakker's witnesses should have been informed of it before taking the stand.

The next witness called by the defense was Bill Sacco, Betty's father. He was a retired electrical engineer who had moved to Heritage USA and had seen Bakker build it from a pile of dirt. The highlight of his testimony was the cross-examination by Deborah Smith which reflected the government's strategy to focus the jury's attention on Bakker's salary and bonuses.

> **Ms. Smith:** OK. Did you know at the same time there were very large, extremely large overdue bills, in the millions of dollars that Mr. Bakker accepted bonuses up to as much as a half a million dollars. Did you know that?
>
> **Mr. Sacco:** I didn't know the exact bonuses or how much Mr. Bakker received. *** I know entertainers that make $100 million a year.
>
> **Ms. Smith:** Now, those are entertainers now. A pastor in charge of the church, you think he should make, what, $50,000 to a million dollars a year?
>
> **Mr. Sacco:** If he's worth his salt. He's better than someone that gets paid a dollar a year and destroys a place, which has been done by three administrations after Bakker.[25]

As Judge Potter gaveled the proceedings to recess for the evening, it was clear it had been a bad day for the defense. Betty Sacco knew it as she left the courtroom. She tangled with reporters outside on the steps: "Two and a half years of garbage—a man going to prison for gold faucets and cinnamon rolls. They're nit-picking him to death."[26]

On the lawn a few feet away, David Steinbeck of Annandale, Virginia held a hand-lettered placard which he hoped Bakker would see as he exited for the day. The sign read, in large black and white letters, "PTL—Prison Term Likely."[27]

The *Charlotte Observer,* in reporting the day's events, noted with some surprise that Bakker's attorneys "never mentioned the 24 charges against Bakker"[28] during the first full day that they had to clear their client.

For Bakker, the horizon looked bleak in more ways than one.

Friday, September 22, 1989

In the darkness of the early morning hours on Friday, September 22, Hurricane Hugo roared up the Carolina coast and struck far enough inland to hobble Charlotte. Powered by 150-mile-an-hour winds, the fierce storm killed eleven people, hit historic Fort Sumpter with $1 million in damage, and heaped destruction and terror throughout its path. Trees in the city of Charlotte were uprooted, buildings were crushed, and the power was knocked out.

"It looks like we've been bombed," a saddened River Hills resident explained, "there's trees on houses [and] trees through windows."[29] Channel 3, WBTV, was knocked off the air and WSOC-TV's huge tower was blown right into the studios. "It twisted over like somebody bending a paper clip,"[30] said general manager Greg Stone. The governor called out 2,500 National Guard troops to provide emergency services and restore order.

As dawn broke, the crippled city struggled to cope with the destruction. With no power, few businesses were able to open. That certainly applied to the federal courthouse. Bakker jurors were notified in a recorded message from the clerk of court's office with these words: "Attention district court jurors, the Bakker trial has been postponed until Monday due to the extreme weather."[31]

On her TV program in Orlando, Tammy saw God's wrath in the hurricane: "I said I believe the storm hitting Charlotte was a warning to Charlotte. I said it had nothing to do with Jim and Tammy Bakker, but it did have to do with the way the people in Charlotte, N.C., have treated God's people."[32]

Like it or not, for the third time during this unusual trial, proceedings were halted. The first time was when Steve Nelson collapsed at noon on the third day and the jurors were given the day off. The second time, of course, was when Jim Bakker suffered a panic attack the following day and the trial was postponed nearly a week. Hurricane Hugo left its own mark on the trial by forcing the third delay.

Would the defense attorneys use that extra day and the

weekend to prepare a come-from-behind finish to win the case in the last inning? Would Judge Potter use the three-day break to lighten up, relax, sleep in, and replenish his patience? Would Hugo lift up the government's remaining witnesses who were being saved for rebuttal and throw them all the way to Kansas so that they couldn't do any more harm to Bakker?

Jay Leno, guest hosting the *Tonight Show:* They stopped the Jim Bakker trial again today. I guess they had to call a recess when the court artist ran out of colors trying to draw Tammy's face. . . .[33]

NOTES

1. Leland and Shepard, "Trading One Storm for Another," *Charlotte Observer*, September 21, 1989 at 15-A (Westlaw printout).

2. *Id.*

3. Preston, "Defense Tries to Show Bakker Not a Con Man," UPI [wire story], September 22, 1989, BC Cycle.

4. Trial transcript, *United States of America v. James O. Bakker*, Docket C-CR-88-205-1, U.S.D.C. (W.D., N.C.), September 19–25, 1989, vol. 7 at 637.

5. *Id.* at 639.

6. *Id.* at 645–46.

7. *Id.* at 695.

8. *Id.* at 696–97.

9. *Id.* at 714.

10. *Id.* at 718.

11. *Id.* at 721–22.

12. *Id.* at 765.

13. *Id.* at 781.

14. *Id.* at 789.

15. *Id.* at 791, 793, 799.

16. *Id.* at 806–7.

17. *Id.* at 649.

18. *Id.* at 651.

19. *Id.* at 652–53.

20. *Id.* at 651–52.

21. *Id.* at 652.

22. *Id.* at 656.

23. *Id.* at 654.

24. *Id.* at 666–73.

25. *Id.* at 681–82.

26. Wright and Associated Press, "Bakker's Witnesses Tell a Very Different Story," *Charlotte Observer*, September 22, 1989 at 1-A (Westlaw printout).

27. *Id.*

28. *Id.*

29. "Hugo Takes Top Honor as Standard for Destruction, Awestruck Survivors Tell Stories of Damage, Hope," *Charlotte Observer,* September 23, 1989 at 1-Y (Westlaw printout).

30. Haight, "TV News Broadcasts to City without Power," *Charlotte Observer,* September 23, 1989 at 9-B (Westlaw printout).

31. Wright, "Hurricane's Chaos Gives Bakker Trial Delay No. 3," *Charlotte Observer,* September 23, 1989 at 1-B (Westlaw printout).

32. Shepard and Wright, "Defense Team Presents Jim Bakker as Man of Faith, Good Works," *Charlotte Observer,* September 27, 1989 at 1-A (Westlaw printout).

33. Leland and Shepard, *supra,* n. 1.

Chapter 17

The Trial—Week Five and the Defense Struggles

Monday, September 25, 1989

The three day hiatus didn't do anything to improve Bakker's plight. As the new week opened and Jim fought for his life, Judge Potter's impatience with Bakker's attorneys and witnesses seemed even more obvious. After the four weeks the government had spent with its ninety-one witnesses, the defense had barely begun and already the judge was pushing Bakker's attorneys to speed up their case.

Bakker's best witness of the whole trial opened the week, but was cut up by prosecutors on cross-examination as they continued the pattern set the week before. Roe Messner, who in thirty-three years had designed and built more than 1,200 churches in forty-seven states and was the largest church contractor in America,[1] told the jury that Bakker deserved a lot of credit as a creative genius who was delivering on his promise to build a whole town for Pentecostal fellowship.[2] Nor was PTL's financing all that suspicious, Messner said.

Messner explained that very few churches have money up front for new construction, and that instead they raise money as they go along. In all the years he worked for Bakker, he was never worried about the fact that Bakker didn't have cash in the bank. He told the jury, "Churches pay their bills slow, I am sorry to say, and they raise money through contributions and gifts and I understand how it works, and so I wasn't alarmed by it, myself, personally."[3] Bakker always managed to raise the cash sooner or later.[4]

The PTL money trail led George Davis to ask Messner about the Jessica Hahn scandal, and he was involved in it up to his hard hat. He told the jury that Dortch had approached him and asked for a $265,000 loan to settle Hahn's threatened lawsuit. Messner explained that as a member of the Assemblies of God church he was concerned that Hahn might also sue the church itself and that he was prepared to do what was necessary to prevent that. Dortch had told him that he was acting on his own and that Bakker didn't know that this request was being made, but that Messner should simply add $265,000 to the following month's invoices and be repaid by PTL in that way for the loan.[5]

> **Mr. Messner:** He asked me to make up an invoice for brick and block and labor and, you know, materials and labor as if I was doing work, this specific amount of work out in the field, and I said, I won't do that, Brother Dortch. I will not create an invoice but I will loan you the money.[6]

Messner did just that and some of his cash was wired to Jessica Hahn's representatives. She was satisfied and agreed not to file her lawsuit.[7]

The rest of Davis's examination of Messner was unexciting. An enormous amount of time was spent going through the detailed blueprints of different buildings at Heritage. Messner argued vehemently that if Bakker had been allowed to remain there he would have finished the construction of every one, including all the hotels.[8] But, of course, that didn't have anything to do with the charges of fraud and it missed the mark.

As Davis's questioning of Messner continued, Judge Potter's patience again wore thin. For instance, at the end of Messner's direct examination, Davis made a routine request of the judge:

> **Mr. Davis:** Judge, would you allow us to take the recess at this time and here is my thought. I don't have anything else—
> **Judge Potter:** You don't need to tell us your thoughts. Let's go ahead and take a recess anyway.[9]

After the break, Deborah Smith cross-examined the builder and he admitted that he had received a total of $66 million from PTL for all of the construction work he had undertaken there in the last ten years.[10] She moved him through her questions quickly and didn't give him any room to deny harmful facts.

> **Ms. Smith:** Now, if you had received that $74 million [raised by PTL by partnerships sold for the Towers], you could have built two-and-a-half Towers Hotels couldn't you have, Mr. Messner?
> **Mr. Messner:** Yes.[11]
> **Ms. Smith:** If you had received $164 million [the total raised from the sale of lifetime partnerships in all the hotels and bunkhouses], could you have finished the Towers Hotel as well as fifty bunkhouses, the Heritage Grand Mansion, the Eleven Hundred Club, the campground building and the Country Farm Inn?
> **Mr. Messner:** Yes.[12]

But then Messner showed some spunk when Smith tried to bore even deeper.

> **Ms. Smith:** In fact, if you had even received a portion of that, you could have completed all of those buildings. Isn't that fair?
> **Mr. Messner:** Yes, it is, but I don't know how the ministry would have sustained itself.[13]

Messner explained, based on his experience building churches all over the country, that when a church raises money for a building project, "the ministry has to go on, too."[14] Smith's retort turned the point around, though, back to the Bakkers' salaries:

> **Ms. Smith:** Well, the partnership funds as far as you know were being used to pay the operating expenses at PTL, that included the salaries of the management and bonuses to the management and things of that sort?
> **Mr. Messner:** That was my understanding.[15]

As Messner stepped down from the stand, it was clear that he had scored some points for Bakker. What no one could gauge was whether the jury was buying it.

The remainder of the day was spent trying to portray Bakker in a good light, but the prosecutors ambushed every single witness with questions about salary, bonuses, and lifestyle.

Peggy Johnson, the head of the local Bethel African Methodist Episcopal Zion Church, was a classic example. On Bakker's behalf, she testified that when her church burned to the ground, Bakker helped rebuild it and even gave them new pews.[16] She estimated the total gift from PTL to be between $30,000 and $35,000.[17] That was the extent of her testimony on direct examination, but on cross Jerry Miller hit her with a question about Bakker's $3 million in bonuses.

Mr. Miller: Now . . . would you give this jury some kind of idea about how many people you all could have helped if you would have had, say, $3 million to have used towards helping needy people?[18]

Bakker was doomed. He couldn't even get credit for a good deed like rebuilding a burned-out church because his salary, bonuses, and lifestyle overshadowed everything. And the government made sure virtually every day of that trial that an eye was kept on Bakker's wealth and the good life he was living.

Given how effectively the government kept scoring with it, one must wonder whether this prosecution strategy ever could have been thwarted. He was being killed by it.

Undaunted by the failure of their character witnesses to get any traction, Bakker's attorneys kept pouring on evidence of his good deeds.

PTL correspondence department employee Carolyn Williams broke some new ground by telling the jury that hundreds of checks payable personally to Jim and Tammy were received as love gifts. They would be sent by viewers for the Bakkers' birthdays or their anniversaries. It was money meant for them personally, but Jim had a strict policy that he was never to receive any of it. Every dime was turned back to the ministry. Even money that was sent for his children. Whenever the Bakkers received gifts in the form of boxes of Mary Kay cosmetics or cologne or handmade afghans, Bakker insisted that everything be donated to charity with much of it going to the PTL Girls Home.[19]

Kenneth Coopersmith, a partner from Arizona, told the jury that he supported Jim Bakker financially because he had seen results.

> **Mr. Coopersmith:** There had been a youth concert [at Heritage USA] and about 1:00 in the morning I heard some noise and I got up to look out, and here was about 500 young kids right out in the parking lot having a prayer meeting. There was hundreds of people that night who had given their hearts to the Lord. This is people who were not out doing drugs. They were not out robbing or mugging people. This is people who decided they wanted to clean up their life. This is the ministry that I wanted to support.[20]

Karl Garmager, the technical director at the ABC-TV station in Detroit and a long-time partner, robustly defended the role of televangelism in modern life. He said that "the application of what is taught on the air from scripture . . . gets me through another day."[21] He said there were many people in the country who felt left behind by local churches in their home towns and who turned to Bakker for their religious nurturing.

> **Mr. Garmager:** I got glued to it [the PTL program]. I found it very uplifting to me. I couldn't wait to get home at 9:00 P.M. to watch it.
>
> **Mr. Bender:** Is this sort of a busman's holiday? Do you look at television when you go home or do you try to get away from it?
>
> **Mr. Garmager:** Well, the Christian television helps me when I'm shot, when I'm worn out and I need an uplifting. As many of the media that are here today, they know the pressures. . . . The demands are massive and I get home and I live by myself. I don't have anybody else and this was sort of helping me along and continues to this day.[22]

But on cross-examination, Deborah Smith asked him right off the bat if he had ever heard Jim Bakker on his television show tell the public that he and Tammy had received over a million dollars in combined salaries. "No, I never heard that,"[23] Garmager had to admit. Then, she asked him if he had ever heard Bakker say on television that he and Tammy had received over $3 million in bonuses. "No"[24] was the only answer Garmager could honestly give.

Lochie Schuessler, a former schoolteacher from California with four college degrees and four lifetime partnerships, strode to the stand to take on the prosecutors with straight talk and razored responses. She said that she and her husband had stayed at the Grand seven or eight times and never had any trouble making reservations.[25] "It was a marvelous experience to be there around Christian people,"[26] she said. "To have a Christian atmosphere to go for a vacation time without having to worry about safety, alcohol, smoking . . . it seemed like a paradise to us and in actuality we found it to be true."[27]

Suffering from rheumatoid arthritis, she was housebound later in her life and explained, "I came to live for those days [when PTL would come on TV in the morning and in the evening] for the simple reason that I was too ill to get out of my home to go anywhere . . . I loved it. It was beautiful."[28]

And when Jerry Miller tried to put a negative spin on what she had said, she struck back:

Mrs. Schuessler: I was being ministered to. Don't forget that. I was ill and I was being ministered to twice a day on a daily basis. ***[29]

Mr. Miller: Now, to use the campsites, you'd have to have some sort of camping equipment, wouldn't you?

Mrs. Schuessler: Yes . . . by the way we have an R.V., we have a motor home.[30]

And look at what Miller asked her then and how the judge got involved:

Mr. Miller: How much did you pay for that?

Mrs. Schuessler: I'm sorry. I don't think that's relevant to this case.

Judge Potter: Mrs. Schuessler, will you please answer the question. I'll decide what's relevant.

Mrs. Schuessler: How much I paid for my motor home?

Judge Potter: Yes.[31]

Suddenly, it was not only Bakker's wealth but that of his

contributors that was fair game. Now the jury could be unsympathetic to both Bakker and his witness.

The day ended on an odd note for Bakker when Joe Haviland of Atlanta was called to the stand. He was the president of the Association for PTL Partners, an organization of Bakker loyalists who opposed Falwell. He identified himself as holding a law degree—a juris doctorate—and having been employed as an investigator for a Georgia prosecutor at one time.[32] After that, he owned and managed a campground. His grammar, however, seemed somewhat unlawyerly. In response to a question about when he got involved, he said: "It was when, I think just after Jim had went to California."[33] And on cross-examination Jerry Miller subtly probed the fact that Haviland apparently was not licensed as a lawyer:

> **Mr. Miller:** Well, as a lawyer, you probably know that an account—
> **Mr. Haviland:** No, sir, I'm not a lawyer. I have a degree but I'm not a lawyer. I don't want to get caught on that one.[34]

That's a great line for any juris doctor's credibility, and with that testimony school was out and the trial recessed for the night.

Tuesday, September 26, 1989

Bakker's attorneys played two more videotapes for the jury on Tuesday, September 26, of past *PTL Club* programs. In one of them, Jim and Tammy welcomed Gavin MacLeod, the *Love Boat's* Captain Stubing. MacLeod and his wife, Patti, are born-again Christians and they discussed their faith during that 1985 broadcast. One of the interesting stories they recounted for the Bakkers was their own divorce and subsequent remarriage after they found God. That prompted Tammy to launch into a spontaneous stream of consciousness about marital fidelity, and she told the skipper that if a wife ever caught her husband cheating on her, "I'd go after her and knock her head off."[35] After that, the topic was dropped.

After the video, it was back to live witnesses taking the stand on Bakker's behalf. Suddenly, they started scoring points for their man.

Bakker's witnesses offered solid testimony this day that cast Jim in a light quite unlike that urged by the prosecution. Iva May Gravenor from Portland, Maryland, drove a battery-powered scooter into the courtroom and was helped to the witness stand.[36] She explained that she had been disabled for thirty-four years with polio and had paid for her $1,000 lifetime partnership by canning fruits from her wheelchair and selling them for a few dollars each.[37] She told the jury that she and her husband never had any trouble getting reservations at the Grand. "We have never been denied. Mr. Bakker didn't promise us anything he didn't give us, and I don't say that in defense of Mr. Bakker. I'm saying it in defense of Mr. Gravenor and I. I listened to him on television over and over and over again, and everything he told us he was going to give us he gave us,"[38] she said.

Partner Marjorie Grey told Jerry Miller flat out that one couldn't expect PTL to put every penny of the lifetime partnership proceeds into building hotels because it cost big money to keep Heritage USA open. Without that, the hotels would never be necessary in the first place.[39] She was referring to streets, utilities, and maintenance. Miller shot back, "bonuses?"[40]

Ms. Grey: Well, yes, bonuses. Oprah Winfrey makes $32 million for running one show a day. He ran two. I think he is one of the most grossly underpaid men in America today.

Mr. Miller: Now, what is the ministry of Oprah Winfrey?

Ms. Grey: Well, you know the show don't you?

Mr. Miller: Well, I'm just trying to understand your analogy here since you are saying how Mr. Bakker is entitled to be compensated the same way Oprah Winfrey is.

Ms. Grey: Well, I am saying she spends one hour a day on a TV show. Mr. Bakker spent—he and Tammy together had two hours a day on TV shows. Not only that he was working 18–20 hours a day trying to develop things and get that place going.

Mr. Miller: Now, you're pretty enthusiastic of your support of Mr. Bakker, aren't you?

Ms. Grey: Right. I am still supporting him and many others are. We feel like this case is an attack on us. It's our ministry.[41]

But in the final analysis, after all the sparks, Grey's testimony was stricken from the record because it was discovered during the noon recess that she had been sitting in the courtroom for four days rather than being sequestered as the court ordered prior to her own testimony.[42] But, the jury heard it anyway. No rebuttal from Oprah on her show the following day, however.

George Davis called Dr. Earl Phillips, a Douglasville, Georgia, chiropractor and PTL partner, who extolled the virtues of the Christian fellowship that awaited everyone at Heritage USA. But on cross-examination, Ms. Smith gave his testimony a serious adjustment and turned him into a spectacular witness for the prosecution.

> **Ms. Smith:** You are one of about 25,000 people here who sent money to PTL expecting to go to help build the bunkhouses. Is that right?
> **Dr. Phillips:** That's right.
> **Ms. Smith:** You weren't aware that there was 50,000 people in line here expecting to use that bunkhouse?
> **Dr. Phillips:** No ma'am.[43]

Soon after that, Judge Potter grew noticeably impatient and called for a ten-minute recess. He excused the jury and confronted Harold Bender. First, Deborah Smith complained that virtually all of Bakker's witnesses were testifying to "non-issues in this case. The issue is whether or not Mr. Bakker lied on TV to get them to send him money, . . ."[44] she said. Judge Potter took it from there.

> **Judge Potter:** We've got to put a limit on this thing [the number of PTL partners testifying on Bakker's behalf] some way. . . . ***
> We're going to have to put an end to this sometime, to just come in with the same thing over and over. The jury knows and everybody in the courtroom knows what they are going to say before they get up here. They love the place and it gives them the spirit of the Lord and they just think it's great, but when are we going to end it, that's what I'm asking you.
> **Mr. Bender:** Well, I would just hope that we would finish our evidence by Friday.
> **Judge Potter:** Well, today is Tuesday. You've got two more days of people saying the same thing over and over?

Mr. Bender: No, not necessarily.

Judge Potter: It's getting ridiculous now. . . . I'll let it go a bit longer.

Mr. Bender: Your honor, I take issue with your honor's comment. Your honor is conveying to me at least, that our defense is ridiculous and I hope—

Judge Potter: I didn't say anything about your defense. I'm talking about the cumulative effect of these people coming in here and saying the same thing over and over. Let's go ahead a little longer, but I am going to get tired of it after a while, Mr. Bender. *** Call the jury.[45]

With that, Bakker's second best witness of the entire trial took the stand. Lee Albert Stillwell told the jury that Jim had saved his life.

Mr. Stillwell: I never did have no trade or nothing. Couldn't work at doing nothing because I lived on the street all my life. *** Twenty-some years out there where nobody didn't want me. Dranked all my life. Growed up in it. *** My mom put some of us in the orphans' home. *** [But I stayed with my father] and my daddy done the best he could to raise me, really. But I wouldn't go to school or nothing. I only got a five education, fifth grade, you can't learn that much in five years, going to school, I'll tell you. When I got big enough to hit the road, Jack, I hit the road.

Harold Bender: Did you ever get in trouble with the law?

Mr. Stillwell: I've been in jail all my life, in and out, in and out of jail for one reason, drinking, drinking and drugs. *** [When I was in a halfway house, a custodian talked to me about Jesus Christ and PTL. He told me about a farm there at PTL where people would care about me.] . . . and he led me to the Lord there. *** I called mom. I was crying. She thought I was hurt again. I wasn't hurt. I was glad happy to believe somebody could care for me. *** [And after I got out of the halfway house, I got a ride to PTL].

Mr. Stillwell: When I got to PTL, this place called Opportunity Farm, they was waiting for me, open arms, just loving me right on in there. God knows, buddy, I didn't have nothing to give them 'cept me. I didn't have nothing. I didn't have two pennies to put in my pocket and a pair of old shoes the church gave me to come down here on. ***

Mr. Stillwell: And I know without a doubt, there's not a doubt in my mind that if the Lord hadn't used Mr. Bakker, give him a vision for people like me on the street, . . . *** because if it wasn't for the Lord using Mr. Bakker to build a place for me to come to, it isn't no doubt in my mind, I would have been a dead person. ***

Mr. Stillwell: And I learned how to run a bulldozer. . . . It means a lot when you've got a warm bed to lay in and a pillow to put under your head instead of a cardboard box. And they didn't ask me nothing. They didn't ask me for nothing, that's simple there. *** My mom told me last night on the phone . . . one of these days she might get to see him [Jim Bakker], she wants to just shake his hand and say thank you for helping my son that he ain't dead.[46]

Stillwell's testimony was so overwhelming that Deborah Smith asked him absolutely no questions on cross-examination. But, despite the passion that Stillwell showed in speaking from his heart, some people in the spectators' gallery were laughing at his broken English.[47]

But, all in all, this had been a good day for Bakker.

Wednesday, September 27, 1989

At 9:30 A.M. on September 27 the jury returned and Potter asked his standard morning question. Had any juror seen or read anything about the case overnight? Juror Ricky Hill, who would later be named foreman, said that he was watching the local *Eyewitness News* at 11:00 P.M. the night before. As they went to a commercial break, the announcer said that coming up next Tammy Faye Bakker was going to blame Hurricane Hugo on this trial. Hill said that he immediately turned off the television. The judge asked if that was going to make any difference to him and he said that it would not.

Then, this intriguing exchange occurred. It was not pursued by Bakker's attorneys.

Harold Bender: Would you be able to set that aside, whatever you might have heard?
Juror Hill: Yes. I thought it was crazy.[48]

Great. Juror Hill obviously thought that Tammy Faye Bakker's idea was crazy that the hurricane was God's wrath. And it probably was. But if Tammy Faye Bakker is crazy, how far behind is her husband? If she is irrational, and the two of them are a television and religious team, can Jim Bakker possibly be rational? What were the jurors thinking?

That was the least of Bakker's worries. The trial, like a runaway freight train, left the track this day. And with it, any chance Bakker had for acquittal.

The fireworks started when Deborah Smith asked the judge to cut off the partners who were testifying for Bakker because "their views of PTL or their personal relationships with the Lord, things of that nature . . . are of questionable relevancy to the issue of whether or not Mr. Bakker did, in fact, appear on TV and lie. . . ."[49] Harold Bender bristled that Bakker's supporters were "entitled to come in here just as the government's witnesses are entitled to come in."[50]

> **Judge Potter:** Well, now, Mr. Bender, I am being extremely lenient with you, and I'm going to let you put some more [witnesses] on, but I'm not going to sit here the next three or four days to listen to the same thing over and over. I don't think I'm required to.
>
> **Judge Potter:** Ms. Smith, I agree with you . . . that what they're doing is bringing in people that know very little about what they are talking about, but I feel like they're entitled to put on whatever defense they feel like is appropriate, and I'm going to let it continue for awhile, but we're going to finish today, Mr. Bender. Do you understand that? You have all your witnesses of this nature here today?
>
> **Mr. Bender:** No, sir.
>
> **Judge Potter:** You plan on bringing some more tomorrow?
>
> **Mr. Bender:** Yes, sir.
>
> **Judge Potter:** You'd better get them here, because we are going to finish today. Call the jury.
>
> **Mr. Bender:** Judge, these people are from Michigan, they're from California.
>
> **Judge Potter:** I'm not going to sit here, Mr. Bender, forever on this thing. I can tell you that right now. *** I'm going to hear from the government tomorrow on this, Mr. Bender. We may or may not listen to those witnesses [that you plan to call tomorrow]. Call the jury.[51]

The irony of it was the blatant double standard in grousing

that Bakker's witnesses were all saying the same thing. The very same could be said of the stock cross-examinations of the prosecutors. They asked variations of the same questions of virtually every Bakker witness for days on end—sure he might have rebuilt your burned down church, but couldn't you have really been in the gravy if he'd given you his $3 million in salary and bonuses over four years?

Bakker's witnesses were doing everything they possibly could to try to help him. Bea Martin, Bakker's longtime housekeeper, told jurors that Tammy Faye designed a Susie Moppett doll which sold for $50 and became a national hit. Tammy would use the dolls on television, like puppets, and people just loved them. PTL manufactured 100,000 of them, they sold like hotcakes, and more than $10 million was made. Every penny of it went to the ministry, not to Jim or Tammy personally.[52]

Mrs. Martin also remembered that Bakker's daughter, Tammy Sue, recorded an album when she was sixteen years old that made $2 million. All of that money was turned over to the ministry.[53]

There was also plenty of testimony about the religious nature of Heritage USA. Barbara Garber of Florida said that "we felt the presence of the Lord as soon as you drove onto the grounds."[54] Francis Moore, a retired schoolteacher, said that she took her nine-year-old grandson to stay at Heritage and "the child gave his heart to the Lord at the Passion Play watching that Passion Play. There was a minister. I wanted him to talk to my grandson. He went down on his knees on the concrete, put his arms around my grandson and my grandson is a Christian today because of PTL and Rev. Bakker."[55]

Sam Sandifer of Wilson, North Carolina, who ran a Buick-Oldsmobile dealership and supported Bakker, was grilled by Deborah Smith. She asked him if it made any difference to him how Bakker spent PTL money. He replied straight away, "I had no objection when they spent it (money) for the Heritage Grand, Jessica Hahn, unwed mothers, that was their decision."[56]

Ms. Smith: Do you have any objection to lifetime partner funds being used to pay Jessica Hahn $265,000 . . . ?

Mr. Sandifer: None whatsoever.

Ms. Smith: Do you think chartering a $100,000 jet as opposed to taking a commercial liner coach at $3,000, is that somehow helping the needy and assisting in bringing Christianity to people, you see that as furthering the goal of the ministry, do you?

Mr. Sandifer: I'm sure there was a good reason for it.

Ms. Smith: How about the purchase of half a million dollar vacation home in Florida with PTL funds? Is that a good and wise investment of the money people send in to do the Lord's work, do you think?

Mr. Sandifer: I'm sure there was a reason for the purchase, yes, ma'am.[57]

But when partner Carlotta Blackmun from New Jersey emphasized that she never had any trouble making reservations to stay at the Grand, she ran into a buzz saw. After Smith asked her three different times whether she had encountered any problems while at the Grand and after she responded three different times that she did not, Deborah Smith kept coming at her.

Ms. Smith: Did you have any conversation with Mr. Mabrey, the general manager, as to whether or not they were having to close down rooms to repair mildew damage caused by leakage in the hotel?

Ms. Blackmun: Young lady—

Judge Potter: Ms. Blackmun—

Ms. Blackmun: I have no knowledge of mildew, no, ma'am.

Judge Potter: Just a minute. Ms. Blackmun, you answer the prosecutor's questions. Do you understand that?

Ms. Blackmun: I thought I was answering them.[58]

This was one tough judge, as several of Bakker's witnesses learned.

A rather emotional story about Jim Bakker was told by Vance Hartsell, who drove a bulldozer at PTL for ten years. He recounted that when he and Bakker were clearing trees from some remote acres of PTL property to build campsites and bunkhouses, Bakker discovered an elderly black couple living in a shack just off the edge of the property. The man had only one arm and his wife was bedridden. They didn't have running water. The man was cutting wood with a chain saw with his one hand, and they used that wood in a stove to cook their meals. Without saying anything, Bakker had a new trailer pulled in for them to live in. Then, he had the trailer hooked up to a septic tank and had a well drilled for them so that they would have running water.[59]

But on cross-examination, the government wouldn't let even that act of kindness stand without challenge.

> **Mr. Miller:** You can provide a lot of trailers and a lot of septic tank hookups and well hookups for $4 million couldn't you?
> **Mr. Hartsell:** I suppose you could.[60]

But the highlight of the day was the prosecution's belittling of the Pentecostal religious beliefs of two of Bakker's key witnesses. Even more jarring was the fact that Judge Potter allowed it to happen. Not that Bakker's own attorneys were objecting, but judges still have the duty to ensure that trials are fair and that witnesses are treated respectfully.

I have personally interviewed both of those witnesses at length and their stories tell a great deal about Bakker's trial. Arnold Santjer, the businessman from Florida who had purchased seventy-six lifetime partnerships, more than any other person in the country—took the stand to go to bat for Jim Bakker.

First, Santjer, age seventy, explained that just because somebody bought a partnership, or multiple partnerships, didn't necessarily mean that they would be banging on the door of the two hotels that Bakker built. Even with all his partnerships, he preferred to park his 35-foot Airstream RV in the PTL campgrounds and stay there for weeks at a time.[61] Santjer also testified on direct examination that he was not angry with Jim Bakker. The way Arnold looked at it, the Lord gave him the money to begin with and he was well satisfied with what Bakker had done with it. His strong conviction was that Jim had used the money as Arnold intended—for Heritage and its eighty-six religious services each week, its forty pastors, and the best gospel music in the country.[62]

The trial took a noticeable turn with Jerry Miller's cross-examination.

Mr. Miller: The shipping business, obviously treated you pretty well?

Mr. Santjer: The good Lord took care of that.

Mr. Miller: I don't guess he signed the check?[63]

Arnold swears he saw jurors giggling.[64] Santjer then attempted to explain that God had given him his health and the wisdom to do well in business, but Miller kept boring in. When Santjer said that Jim Bakker was an honest man, Miller asked if Santjer would believe anything that Bakker said.

Mr. Miller: Now, if Mr. Bakker told you he could fit me inside of that pitcher, would you still believe him?[65]

Santjer, whose beliefs about baptism and the use of water for that sacrament went to the core of his religion, thought that Miller was overstepping his bounds. But Bakker's attorneys didn't object. So Santjer was left to fend for himself and he protested: "I think it's a silly question."[66] The judge ordered him to answer the question. Santjer eventually said: "Well, if he thinks you could get it in, fine."[67]

Santjer himself remembers how shocked he was when the judge ordered him to answer the question. "My religion was being questioned and I was being belittled in my religion. They were trying to make it seem like we were a Jim Jones cult. I think they carried it a little far myself."[68]

Today, Santjer looks back on the trial and wishes he would have had the chance to help Jim with his testimony, rather than try to defend his own evangelical beliefs. "I wanted to tell them what was going on. Jim is a wonderful man of God. I was his usher on Sundays. People would flock to those church services. Every denomination was there. He would bring in the best speakers and the best music. He worked daylight until long after dark."[69]

Arnold, putting Fort Hope on the list of Bakker achievements, says, "I can still see street people carrying their Bibles. They're not street people any more. They are working. Jim's the one who brought them up."[70]

Santjer also minces no words in describing how Jim didn't have a chance in that trial. "That trial wasn't right. From what I saw from the witness stand, it was a joke."[71]

Arnold Santjer wasn't the only one whose religious beliefs were belittled by the prosecution. Celeste Montgomery of Concord, North Carolina, an early ministry volunteer, also took the stand on Bakker's behalf. Midway through her cross-examination by prosecutor Miller, she commented that Jesus had surely been good to her.

Ms. Montgomery: Praise God, he's been good to me.
Mr. Miller: Can you answer that question? Ok, if you're through with acting, can you answer the question for me? Mr. Bakker also had a pretty good knack of spending money on himself, didn't he?[72]

Celeste was stunned.[73]

Of course, she wasn't acting. Those were her religious beliefs. She went to Heritage for church every Sunday and took her parents. Even though she believed very strongly in the PTL ministry, Celeste told me that she "wasn't going to go up on that witness stand and lie for Bakker, but the whole problem with reservations at the hotel was that they all wanted to go at the same time. And you can't do that at Myrtle Beach or Dollywood."[74]

And what about Jim's attorneys? "They didn't give me any advice for answering questions from Miller and, let me tell you, he let me have it with both barrels. Both of those prosecutors were tough and made me feel like I had broken a federal law for believing in PTL. Miller treated me like an uneducated woman, like a cult member, like I'd been brainwashed in what I said. I think the judge should have stepped in and told Miller not to ask that kind of question. Really, he treated me like a slab of meat on the witness stand."[75]

Jim Bakker in prison: They made all of us look like wide-eyed fanatics in that trial. That was the U.S. attorney's strategy. They tried to make us look like Jim Jones fanatics. And when the judge said that he didn't want to hear from any more of my witnesses, those who represented the Lifetime Partners who were standing with me and claiming that they weren't defrauded, he was really sending a signal to the jury that those people were programmed just like Jim Jones's followers.[76]

Another prime example was Jerry Miller's response to some emotional and helpful testimony Celeste gave about blankets. She said Jim told his TV audience in the mid-1980s that he wanted every street person in Charlotte to have a blanket so they wouldn't be cold at night. He raised enough money to buy several tractor trailer trucks full of blankets.

She went with him one night to deliver them and remembered what he said:

Ms. Montgomery: [There was] Jim Bakker kneeling down beside a man, and he said—I heard exactly what he said— . . . "I want you to use this blanket to warm your body and I want you to draw strength from Jesus, because . . . through the Holy Spirit, you don't have to live like this. You can be a productive person and be on fire and change your whole life around." ***
Mr. Miller (on cross): Now, at the time you say that Mr. Bakker went out with the blankets and giving to the homeless people—do you know how many houses Mr. Bakker himself owned at that point in time?
Ms. Montgomery: No, sir, I don't know that.[77]

Apparently the government was taking the position that Jim Bakker was the only national TV star who should be paid nothing for his work, or at least that this Charlotte jury had the right to decide whether his salary was too high. Do members of the cast of *Friends* have to answer to similar authorities for their million-dollar salaries?

Thursday, September 28, 1989

Finally on September 28, after twenty days of Bakker bashing, evidence was offered that could easily have cleared Jim. But it was too late. The die had already been cast.

The evidence that finally emerged this day went to the heart of the government's money-raising charges against Bakker. It was financial evidence—technical, boring, and subtle. It wasn't evidence like the payoff of a young woman after a sexual encounter. It wasn't juicy dirt or another litany of Bakker excesses and indulgences.

No, this was a letter that Jim Bakker had mailed to PTL contributors on January 9, 1984. But the jury never got the point that it was a smoking gun.

Partner Ronald Smith of Columbus, Ohio, was called to the witness stand. Thinking it might help Jim, he brought his copy of that letter with him. Amazingly, on direct examination by Bakker's attorney, he wasn't asked much about it. He talked about the other things that every other defense witness had talked about—how great the Grand Hotel was, and how wonderful Heritage was for Christians. It was only on cross-examination by Deborah Smith that the letter was even read for the jury.

The absolutely staggering thing about it is that it arguably destroyed one of the government's major indictments of Bakker. Prosecutors had been telling the jury day in and day out that Bakker defrauded lifetime partners by not spending their contributions on the construction of the hotels and bunkhouses, and had instead used it for just about anything else he wanted to keep the ministry going including the purchase of millions of dollars of television time.

But this is what the fund-raising letter from Bakker said:

> How would you like to spend four days and three nights at the brand new Heritage Grand Hotel every year for the rest of your life . . . ! The Lord has given me a vision to do what no one in the Christian world has ever done before. I wanted you to be one of the first to invest in a unique lifetime partnership with the PTL ministry. For a gift of $1,000 today to help us build this beautiful center of Heritage USA *and continue our worldwide ministry,* you will become a lifetime partner and will be afforded some very special privileges. [emphasis added][78]

That's it. It couldn't be any clearer. From the very beginning in that first letter soliciting partnerships, contributors were on notice that their $1,000 would be used to build Heritage USA and continue PTL's ministry. There was absolutely no representation that all of the money raised would be spent on constructing those hotels or the other buildings in the so-called partner center at Heritage. And without such a representation, there simply could have been no fraud if Bakker used the money for purposes other than building the hotels. But the jury did not see it as evidence of his innocence at all. Instead, they believed there was overwhelming evidence of the overselling of the partnerships.

There were some other good witnesses for Bakker that day, too.

Patricia Harrison, one of Bakker's secretaries at PTL, testified that she handled Jim's personal checking account for years and never saw him write one check. His executive secretary, Shirley Fulbright, had signature authority for him. Jim himself never knew how much he had.[79]

Harrison did recall Jim having checks sent as donations to PTL. He made a $5,000 personal contribution to Kevin's House, $200 to $250 monthly gifts to PTL, and $300 to the Assemblies of God. Jim also bought one Towers partnership.[80]

She distinctly remembered three other checks. One, for $400, was drawn on Jim's personal checking account and paid the worker who built the infamous air conditioned doghouse.[81] That was Jim's money. Second, she was instructed to write out two last PTL checks three days before Bakker resigned in March, 1987—one for $50,000 to Attorney Roy Grutman and one for $25,000 to Jerry Falwell's ministry.[82]

A last witness actually offered testimony that portrayed Bakker as a good man—not the greedy, conniving person that government witnesses had for so long described. Joyce Cordell, who operated the beauty shop at Heritage, told the jury that Bakker was out on the grounds all the time and that he was really nice to everybody. People just loved him. He would frequently ask her to do favors for partners in her beauty shop, especially for mothers whose children were ill. She specifically remembered one mother's daughter who was terminally ill and

Bakker asked her to do something very special for them, to give them a nice style or permanent and to send him the bill for it.[83]

Jim Bakker would have one last chance to do something special for himself in fifteen hours, like save his own hide, because he was the only witness left. He would take the stand the next morning at 9:00 A.M.

NOTES

1. Trial transcript, *United States of America v. James O. Bakker*, Docket C-CR-88-205-1, U.S.D.C. (W.D., N.C.), September 19–25, 1989, vol. 7 at 809.

2. *Id.* at 819.

3. *Id.* at 837–38.

4. *Id.* at 837.

5. *Id.* at 847.

6. *Id.* at 848.

7. *Id.* at 850–51.

8. *Id.* at 858.

9. *Id.* at 855.

10. *Id.* at 865.

11. *Id.* at 872.

12. *Id.* at 890–91.

13. *Id.* at 891.

14. *Id.* 872.

15. *Id.* at 891.

16. *Id.* at 919–20.

17. *Id.* at 923.

18. *Id.* at 924.

19. *Id.* at 928–30.

20. *Id.* at 942–43.

21. *Id.* at 954.

22. *Id.* at 952–53.

23. *Id.* at 961.

24. *Id.*

25. *Id.* at 969.

26. *Id.* at 970.

27. *Id.* at 971.

28. *Id.* at 974.

29. *Id.* at 979.

30. *Id.* at 983.

31. *Id.*

32. *Id.* at 987.

33. *Id.* at 990.

34. *Id.* at 993.

35. Shepard and Wright, "Defense Team Presents Jim Bakker as Man of

Faith, Good Works," *Charlotte Observer*, September 27, 1989 at 1-A (Westlaw printout).

36. *Id.*

37. Trial transcript, *United States of America v. James O. Bakker*, Docket C-CR-88-205-1, U.S.D.C. (W.D., N.C.), September 26–27, 1989, vol. 8 at 1013.

38. *Id.* at 1014.

39. *Id.* at 1046.

40. *Id.*

41. *Id.* at 1046–48.

42. *Id.* at 1050–51.

43. *Id.* at 1090–91.

44. *Id.* at 1117.

45. *Id.* at 1118–21.

46. *Id.* at 1158–63.

47. Trial transcript, *United States of America v. James O. Bakker*, Docket C-CR-88-205-1, U.S.D.C. (W.D., N.C.), October 3–5, 1989, vol. 10 at 2102.

48. Trial transcript, *supra*, n. 37, at 1180–81.

49. *Id.* at 1250.

50. *Id.* at 1252.

51. *Id.* at 1252–55.

52. *Id.* at 1191–93.

53. *Id.* at 1195.

54. *Id.* at 1184.

55. *Id.* at 1224.

56. *Id.* at 1287.

57. *Id.* at 1287–89.

58. *Id.* at 1262.

59. *Id.* at 1293–94.

60. *Id.* at 1294.

61. *Id.* at 1360–61.

62. Arnold Santjer, interview by author, in Bradenton, Florida, January 14, 1993.

63. Trial transcript, *supra*, n. 37 at 1365.

64. Arnold and Dorothy Santjer, interview by author, in Bradenton, Florida, January 14, 1993.

65. Trial transcript, *supra*, n. 37 at 1369.

66. *Id.* at 1370.

67. *Id.*

68. Arnold and Dorothy Santjer, interview by author, in Bradenton, Florida, January 14, 1993.

69. *Id.*

70. *Id.*

71. *Id.*

72. Trial transcript, *supra*, n. 37 at 1245.

73. Celeste Montgomery, telephone interview by author, February 8, 1993.

74. *Id.*

75. *Id.*

76. Jim Bakker, interview by author, in Rochester, Minnesota, September 25, 1992.

77. Trial transcript, *supra*, n. 37 at 1240–41.

78. Trial transcript, *United States of America v. James O. Bakker,* Docket C-CR-88-205-1, U.S.D.C. (W.D., N.C.), September 28–29, 1989, vol. 9 at 1445–46.

79. *Id.* at 1570–73.

80. *Id.* at 1575.

81. *Id.* at 1571.

82. *Id.* at 1578.

83. *Id.* at 1514.

Chapter 18

The Trial—Jim Bakker Takes the Stand, Tells His Story, and Scores Some Points

Friday, September 29, 1989

In his first five hours on the witness stand Friday, September 29, while calmly answering questions from George Davis, Jim Bakker soared like an eagle. But after two hours of cross-examination later in the day, Deborah Smith shot him down like skeet.

Dressed in a gray tailored suit, Bakker was composed and fluent when answering questions put to him by George Davis. The gallery was hushed. The jury listened intently to what he was saying. Reporters, hostile for years, were impressed with his businesslike demeanor and the coherence of his answers. Spectators marveled at how relaxed and confident he was on the witness stand as he spoke directly to the jury.[1]

Even Judge Potter stayed his hand for the first few hours. Bakker began by talking about his background.

Mr. Bakker: I was born in Muskegon, Michigan in 1940. . . . I was quite a bashful boy, and I failed a couple grades in those early years but then we moved . . . to a wonderful school where a photo teacher took interest in me and I began to work in something that I could excel in and I began to study journalism. . . . ***

And in my senior year I felt the call of God to go into the ministry. . . . *** So I went to North Central Bible College in Minneapolis, Minnesota, and there I met Tammy Faye, and I met her in the second year. *** And we were married at North Central after being there two years [1961]. *** Tammy and I traveled for several years in our denomination [Assemblies of God] in church evangelism and we had revival crusades in churches every night. And we then began to develop a children's ministry . . . and that's when we developed a puppet family called Susie Moppet and her family.[2]

Bakker explained it was because of those floppy puppets that he and Tammy got into television. In 1965, Pat Robertson asked the young duo to join his fledgling Christian Broadcasting Network (CBN) to star in a children's program featuring their puppet family. Jim agreed on the condition that Robertson also let him develop a Christian talk show based on the format of Johnny Carson's *Tonight Show*. Bakker told the jury that when he and Tammy would come home after a long day and turn on television, some of the language and jokes on *The Tonight Show* just weren't "compatible with the church world, and I said, why can't there be something for Christians like this?"[3] The idea was alternative TV programs for Christians. They called their program *The 700 Club*.

> **Mr. Bakker:** Television is the most powerful medium in the world today and I felt that the most important message, the message of the gospel of Jesus Christ should be propagated over that medium.[4]

And that's how it all began. For eight years on CBN, they broadcast *The Jim and Tammy Show* every day in front of a clean scrubbed audience of 200 Christian children (many of whom were probably home schooled or in kindergarten and glad to get out of there for a couple of hours). At night, they hung up their puppets and hosted *The 700 Club*. The innovative show was a surprise hit.

> **Mr. Bakker:** I always call it [the Christian talk show that he invented] a sermon that is done in a more relaxed atmosphere, because I believe that television is a medium that is better talking because people are in their home, and even though we do use preaching . . . when people are in their homes, I felt they didn't always want somebody shouting in their ear, that they would like

to have someone talk to them. And so that formula of Christian talk show was born.[5]

He explained that in the earliest days of his CBN program, the show was two hours long. But he would often extend it on any given day to ten or twelve hours if people were "coming to the Lord to accept Christ as savior."[6] He would simply stay on the air as long as people were calling and coming to Christ. Sometimes he would be on the air until 5:00 A.M.

But after eight years on *The 700 Club*, "I felt the voice of God speak to my heart that I was to leave, and I resigned. . . ."[7]

That was in 1972 and he spent the next year in California getting a new Christian television station on the air in Los Angeles and forming the Trinity Broadcasting Network. While with Trinity, he was asked to travel to Charlotte, North Carolina, to help raise money for a local Christian station. He did and the response was so overwhelming that he and Tammy decided to stay in Charlotte. It was there that they launched PTL in 1976.[8]

At first, they built a little studio and prayer room in a building on Independence Boulevard in Charlotte that for years had been used as a furniture store. Within a short time, they outgrew that and paid $200,000 for an old estate on twenty-five acres where they built a studio and church. But Jim and Tammy were absolutely made for television and their audience was growing so rapidly that their whole ministry was exploding. One computer run showed that in eighteen months they grew 7,000 percent in church membership and viewership. It got to the point that there weren't enough seats in the TV studio to accommodate all the people who wanted to be in the audience.[9]

So, in 1978, Bakker bought 2,200 acres of mostly undeveloped timber and flatland on the North Carolina–South Carolina border to build what would be Heritage USA. His vision for it was clear.

Mr. Bakker: It would be large enough to fulfill the vision that God had laid on my heart, and the vision for a people place, a place that would be like the old-fashioned campgrounds, only be modern and up-to-date.[10]

It would cost millions. His attorney diplomatically asked whether he was up to the task of managing that kind of money.

Mr. Davis: I guess you went to Bible College and that's about it, isn't it?
Mr. Bakker: Yes, two years.
Mr. Davis: Did you finish high school?
Mr. Bakker: Yes, I did.
Mr. Davis: But you didn't have any other college training?
Mr. Bakker: No, sir.
Mr. Davis: Now, did you up to that time ever have any training in bookkeeping or accounting?
Mr. Bakker: No.[11]

A key question was how Jim intended to raise the necessary money and put the package together.

Mr. Bakker: I've never worked with a ministry or known of a ministry that literally had money in the bank and didn't have to believe God by faith that the money would come in every month. *** I call it living by faith. ***
Mr. Davis: You didn't have the money at that time?
Mr. Bakker: No.
Mr. Davis: Did you have confidence in your ability to raise it?
Mr. Bakker: I had confidence in God supplying it.[12]

Bakker then emphasized to the jury that those people who would travel to Heritage for Christian fellowship wanted to stay on the grounds overnight. Like the old Assembly of God camps.

Mr. Bakker: They didn't come to be at a motel on the highway . . . in the middle of the night or in the night I woke up and it was like a vision or a dream—I don't know what it was, but the concept, God gave me the concept of the Heritage Grand Partner Center and the Lifetime Partners. And I got up and I began to sketch and write it all down. . . .[13]

It worked. Millions of dollars began pouring in to build the Christian Disneyland of Bakker's dreams. He explained to the jury, though, that he was more than just the planner and dreamer. He ended up doing everything there and he often worked eighteen to twenty hours a day, joking on the stand that it only felt like twenty-four hours.[14] For almost an hour, he gave the jury details of all the work he did at Heritage. As he calculated it, he really held seven different jobs there every day—school superintendent, pastor, administrator of the grounds and buildings including Fort Hope and the Girls' Home, executive in charge of the worldwide PTL satellite network, television personality, producer of virtually all of his wife's records and of many other television shows, and fund-raiser.

Mr. Bakker: I think fundraising was my most burdensome job. *** You never ever, ever get away from the pressure that you have to raise the funds for the next week, the next month, the next year. ***

Our budget [which I had to raise] for the last year that I was there, which was 1986 . . . was close to . . . $160 million, which is, I think it boils down to something like $3 million a week.[15]

He recalled humbler beginnings when he and Tammy were starting out and their total income the first two years was $50 a week. But that was then and this was now, and $160 million was what Bakker had to raise yearly to keep Heritage USA and his television program afloat. "It was a real responsibility to carry that load of fund-raising,"[16] he admitted with some pain.

Mr. Bakker: In faith you live by faith in God, not by fact. You don't say, "I'm going to build a church because we have money in the bank." You say, "I'm going to build because I feel this is what God would have us to do."[17]

One of Davis's strategies was to suggest to the jury that Bakker was not overpaid given all that he was doing each day. That same point was also attempted in a series of questions about how much it would have cost PTL to hire a professional fund-raiser to raise that kind of money each year. Bakker replied that some charities pay from 25 to 95 percent of the money that is raised to those who raise it. Davis then noted that Bakker was never paid anything for his fund-raising at PTL other than the salary and bonuses he received.[18] Yet, as they went through all of that, the poker-faced jury was hard to read. It would be several days before anyone would know whether this strategy was working.

The most noteworthy aspect of Jim's testimony on direct was the maddening lack of clarity with which he discussed the question of whether he oversold the two hotels. Appearing unprepared and unrehearsed, he spoke in stream of consciousness fashion at length about the hotel partnership programs but never really directly refuted the contention that he oversold the hotels without telling his viewers.

He didn't get down to brass tacks, look the jury straight in the eye, and tell them, by God, he sure did go on the air and tell his viewers he was going to go over 25,000 partnerships in the Grand. He didn't slam his fist on the witness stand and say that he absolutely notified contributors in writing that their hotel partnership contributions could be used for purposes other than only building the hotels. Instead, his attorney had him talk around the edge of the issue.

> **Mr. Bakker:** The original partnership was the Heritage Grand partnership program, originally announced it would be 25,000 lifetime partners for fifty percent of the Grand, and then the next development was we expanded the Heritage Grand partnerships program to include other areas, the rest of the facilities at Heritage USA, including the Fort Heritage campground, the Heritage Inn, and the other facilities there at Heritage USA. The response was overwhelming. People kept wanting to come.[19]

So, what is it? Did he tell them or didn't he? That's what the jury wanted to hear.

Then, George Davis asked Bakker if he had made a chart showing the total number of rooms that were available with each partnership program. Bakker said he had and reached down to show them to the jury. At that point, Deborah Smith objected, claiming that the numbers on those charts had been cooked.[20] The judge sent the jury out of the room and a battle royal ensued between all attorneys over whether Bakker would be able to use the two charts he had prepared.

Jerry Miller was allowed to ask him several questions about his figures and the wheels fell off Bakker's case as he tried to answer them. Bakker's math showed that there were accommodations on the Heritage grounds for 211,000 PTL partners each year—three times the number that prosecutors had been using during the first three weeks of the trial. He arrived at that number by including campgrounds and the Heritage Inn Motel in addition to the two big hotels. It was his reliance on accommodations other than hotels that the prosecutors claimed unfairly spiked the numbers and gave a distorted picture of how many rooms were actually available for people who thought they were receiving hotel accommodations.

> **Mr. Miller:** My question is when was Wilderness Camping ever announced to the Grand partners who was being promoted to join the Grand partnership program?
>
> **Mr. Bakker:** I don't know if that was actually worded in a brochure.
>
> **Mr. Miller:** Or on the air?
>
> **Mr. Bakker:** No, but because it was just automatically used for the overflow of Fort Heritage, we used Wilderness Camping. The Lakeside Lodges would be the units of timeshare which are here, and we used the unsold units for lodging. The overflow from the Grand was used in those areas.
>
> **Mr. Miller:** As to Lakeside Lodges, when were any announcements made as part of the Grand partnership promotion that Lakeside Lodges would be relied upon for housing Grand Hotel partnerships?
>
> **Mr. Bakker:** To my knowledge, I don't know of any official announcement.
>
> **Mr. Miller:** When was that announced to anyone?
>
> **Mr. Bakker:** I don't know if it was announced. It was just part of our facilities that we had . . . that we used. . . . ***
>
> **Mr. Miller:** When as part of any Grand Hotel's partnership promotion was it ever announced . . . that Lakeside Lodges were part of what you were relying on to make everybody fit in?
>
> **Mr. Bakker:** I don't believe we actually announced it. That's part of—if you come to the Grand and the Grand is full, you get into all of these other facilities. It's just like having one big hotel with auxiliary units on the grounds. And then that adds up to 69,142 lifetime units in that [Grand] program. ***[21]

Convinced that the charts would mislead the jury into thinking that contributors were actually told that they might end up at a lodge or campsite if the Grand couldn't hold them, Judge Potter refused to allow Bakker to introduce them into evidence. However, he did permit them to be kept at the witness stand for Bakker to glance at to refresh his memory as he was concluding his testimony.[22]

But Bakker was dazed by the refusal of the judge to allow those charts into evidence. For weeks, he had sat quietly and been beaten over the head with an unending deluge of charts, diagrams, and transparencies that the government used to hang him. In response, he drew up two little charts of his own to try to crawl out of that hole and now the judge wouldn't let him use them.

> **Jim Bakker in prison:** When the judge refused to allow me to speak from my lodging chart, I was devastated because I had built my whole defense on the facts that I had detailed on that chart. The judge ordered me to put the chart at my feet, behind the low wall where I was sitting. To present my case, I had to look down to the floor to get the figures. I had planned to have them on an easel and present them to the jury. So, I lost eye contact with the jury.
>
> At that point, I gave up and lost all hope. I . . . [felt] the judge was totally against me.
>
> As a side point here, the judge ruled that my chart was not built on previous facts entered into the record . . . [but] I had carefully built it myself from blueprints and the publications. . . .
>
> I knew it was over.[23]

Those charts were cap guns, anyway, compared to the visual aids the government had been using against him. It was no big deal, either, because whether in or out the charts didn't speak to the key question of whether contributors had ever been notified that the 25,000 limit on the Grand was going to be exceeded. Those charts had nothing to do with that.

So the jury came back again and Bakker resumed his testimony, simply glancing down at the charts as he went through his own math about how many rooms were really available at Heritage during the year for partners who bought lodging plans.

These were his calculations: he told the jury that the Grand Hotel and its four backup facilities would accommodate 69,142 lifetime members each year. That would be 25,000 people who could stay three nights and four days at the Grand, 14,554 who could stay at the Fort Heritage Campground, 12,075 who could stay at the Fort Wilderness Campground, 2,555 who would be housed in the Lakeside Lodges time-shares, and 4,380 partners who would stay at the Heritage Inn. And that, he calculated, was more than enough accommodations for everyone who bought a Grand Hotel partnership.[24]

And, with respect to the Towers Hotel, he explained the rest of his math. The Towers itself would accommodate 31,207 partners a year, the Crystal and Grand Mansions would hold 7,300 a year, the Mayor's House would accommodate 3,041, and the Jerusalem Inn would kick in an unspecified number of rooms for a grand total of 53,714 for the year.[25]

Adding all of those Grand and Towers accommodations together, there would be room for 122,856 partners each year to stay a minimum of three days and four nights each. Bakker then added to that number 45,625 partners who would be housed in the as yet unbuilt bunkhouses and others who would stay in lodging that was still on the drawing board. Adding all of it together, he calculated that 211,000 partners could be housed at Heritage each year.[26]

It was a confusing jumble. How many people could have been crammed onto those grounds in campsites and hotel rooms anywhere there wasn't even the question in the case. The question, of course, was whether people buying hotel partnerships had ever been told that they might have to stay someplace other than in a hotel. So, the total number of accommodations was irrelevant unless Bakker first showed the jury that he had informed hotel partners that they might be placed elsewhere on the grounds.

That was not done and so all of his testimony about this important part of the case simply missed the target and didn't help a bit.

> **Mr. Davis:** Did you communicate the figures with reference to how many partnerships there were, the number of partnerships, or was that a secret?
>
> **Mr. Bakker:** It was never a secret.

Mr. Davis: Did you communicate that information?
Mr. Bakker: I tried to.[27]

Then, George Davis handed Bakker dozens of photographs of facilities and activities at Heritage and asked that Jim describe them for the jury. His point was that each represented the fulfillment of a promise that Bakker had made on television. Each was the wise expenditure of contributors' money. There were pictures of the Grand Hotel, the Towers Hotel, the Water Park, a youth concert, the petting zoo, the farm, the train, and holiday celebrations at different times of the year. Also photographed were partners canoeing, partners in paddleboats, partners in double decker buses, children skating at the youth center, and partners picnicking. There were shots of the tennis courts, restaurants, the candy store, an all night gospel sing, a big camp meeting, the television studio, musical productions, antique cars, baptismal services in the pool, the Upper Room, the Girls' Home, and the eighty-six church services a week. Other Bakker pictures showed Billy Graham's home, the dinner theater, an Easter service, the passion play, and numerous shops and stores. ("I learned that from my wife, that no woman wants to go on vacation where she can't shop a little bit, and so we put the shops in here. . . ."[28])

And after nearly five hours of testimony, Bakker ended on a strong note.

Mr. Davis: [Did you ever do anything] where you were intentionally committing or trying to commit a criminal act?
Mr. Bakker: Absolutely not. ***
Mr. Davis: Did you ever intentionally, knowingly commit in any way or by any reference a fraud and an intentional criminal act with reference to the subject of conspiracy?
Mr. Bakker: I absolutely did not.[29]

Jim was done and had acquitted himself impressively. It was 3:00 in the afternoon and the judge let the jury take a recess before cross-examination commenced.

Bakker, after five hours on the stand, was ready for a break, too. He would need it.

NOTES

1. Shepard and Wright, "Bakker Challenges Charge He Oversold Partnerships," *Charlotte Observer*, September 20, 1989 at 1-A (Westlaw printout).

2. Trial transcript, *United States of America v. James O. Bakker,* Docket C-CR-88-205-1, U.S.D.C. (W.D., N.C.), September 28–29, 1989, vol. 9 at 1599–1601.

3. *Id.* at 1602.

4. *Id.* at 1607.

5. *Id.* at 1603–4.

6. *Id.* at 1604.

7. *Id.*

8. *Id.* at 1606–7.

9. *Id.* at 1607–9.

10. *Id.* at 1612.

11. *Id.* at 1614–15.

12. *Id.* at 1610, 1627.

13. *Id.* at 1624–25.

14. *Id.* at 1640.

15. *Id.* at 1649.

16. *Id.* at 1651.

17. *Id.* at 1718.

18. *Id.* at 1655.

19. *Id.* at 1665.

20. *Id.* at 1667.

21. *Id.* at 1670–71.

22. *Id.* at 1682.

23. Jim Bakker, interview by author, in Rochester, Minnesota, September 25, 1992; Jim Bakker, written answers to questions from the author, September 1992.

24. Trial transcript, *supra,* n. 2 at 1685–87.

25. *Id.* at 1687–89.

26. *Id.* at 1689–90.

27. *Id.* at 1707.

28. *Id.* at 1702–3.

29. *Id.* at 1720–21.

Chapter 19

The Trial—Cross-Examination? Five Words: General Custer, Meet Reverend Bakker

Bearing the Cross

Veteran trial attorneys say that no matter how well a witness does responding to the questions posed by his or her own attorney, the real test in the eyes of the jury is how that witness holds up under cross-examination. This is especially true with criminal defendants because juries typically gauge the truthfulness of a defendant's version of the case only after it is subjected to a stiff and challenging cross. Is the defendant's explanation or alibi still persuasive after that kind of scrutiny? Or has the prosecutor punched so many holes in it that it is unbelievable to the jury?

To avoid that trap being sprung, cautious defense attorneys will exhaustively prepare their clients for cross-examination. Hours or even days will be spent steeling their clients to the gale force winds of cross to which they will surely be subjected. Defense attorneys will meticulously anticipate questions that the prosecutor will ask and work with the client in preparing answers to the most dangerous of them. The client will be put through his paces, sometimes even by taking that client to the courthouse at night, putting him in the witness chair, and bombarding him with tough questions to give him some experience in fielding them.

Los Angeles Police Detective Mark Fuhrman was reportedly prepared for his O. J. Simpson testimony by a battery of assistant district attorneys. Those attorneys, it was claimed, peppered Fuhrman with tough questions in mock trial sessions days before he ever got on the witness stand. When he did, he was ready for even the most hostile questions on cross-examination which the venerable F. Lee Bailey put to him. (These reports of Fuhrman's rigorous preparation were later disputed, which would only go to corroborate the ineptitude of the prosecution.)

The point is that there is much to be done in preparing a witness for cross-examination. They are simply not to be left up there on the stand to fend for themselves. And, of course, witnesses themselves must give thought to their stories and do their part to be in command of the facts of their case so they can answer questions put to them. But during his cross-examination, Bakker seemed unready.

Friday, September 29, 1989

Deborah Smith, in keying up for one of the most important cross-examinations of her career, must have thought a television star would be tough to shake. But after Bakker had shocked reporters and spectators with five hours of compelling testimony on direct, he was pummeled on cross-examination and kept falling backwards. For three hours Friday afternoon until the judge finally recessed the trial for the weekend at 6:00 P.M., Smith bombarded him with a torrent of rapid-fire questions, many of which he was largely unable to answer.

She hit him early and kept him reeling for all of Friday afternoon. As she turned up the heat, Bakker became very quiet and answered her questions guardedly, in sharp contrast to his emphatic testimony earlier in the day. When pressed about memos from Peter Bailey about the overselling of hotel partnerships, he could only reply, "So many of these figures that I am hearing, I'm hearing them for the first time in these sessions."[1] When she asked him about the $390,000 bonus he was paid in early 1984, he said he couldn't remember it. Nor could he remember any warnings from PTL attorneys about private inurement and other threats to the ministry's tax exempt status. He said he couldn't remember PTL employees complaining to him that partners were having difficulties making reservations in the Grand.[2]

And, over and over again, he professed not remembering meetings in which anyone told him the partnerships were being oversold.

In fact, he disputed PTL's own computer printouts which the government had introduced into evidence showing sales in the Grand: "If you believe the computer records of Heritage USA, I could sell you land under water in Florida,"[3] he quipped.

Astonishingly, he did not have an answer for the most profound question in the case which anyone could have anticipated. When asked whether he diverted funds from the Grand and Towers partnerships to meet other operating expenses at PTL, he said he was unaware of it.[4]

Asked whether former aide David Taggart had told the truth, Bakker doubted it: "I believe there's a lot of people lying because they have motives behind it."[5] He said Steve Nelson lied or was absolutely mistaken when he testified that Bakker ordered the destruction of weekly reports confirming overselling of the partnerships.[6]

He showed little tenaciousness at all in responding and no interest in sparring with Smith. After an hour of cross, it was clear enough that he simply wasn't fighting back. With one jab after another, she would push him clear across the ring into the ropes and he wouldn't counterpunch. It was a rout.

Smith's unmistakable strategy was to destroy his credibility by casting him as an unscrupulous television huckster who was willing to lie on the air in order to milk more money from his viewers. She said that when he gave his television audience reports on the number of partnerships that had been issued, he knew the real figures and he knew he was lying. That was the linchpin of her case, the crucible of her cross-examination and he had no plausible retort to offer.[7] So she just trampled him.

He wouldn't even return her fire when she attacked his explanation that God gave him the idea for the hotel partnerships.

Ms. Smith: So actually you did not initially get this vision for the Grand Hotel in the fall of 1983.

Mr. Bakker: No, that is not . . . like the Grand membership. *** I don't think so, no.[8]

What kind of answer was that? As weak as it could be, of course. Instead, he should have stood his ground and answered, "Like I said before, God gave me the plan. That's exactly how it happened. It wasn't the first time He spoke to me either. Millions of us Pentecostals have a personal, daily relationship with God. That's the way it is. Whether you like it or not."

She hung him with the statement he made on his March 22, 1984 broadcast that the reproduction of the Yacov Heller sculpture of David and Goliath that partners also received was "something that's worth, I think, a thousand dollars alone."[9] She reminded him sternly that the government had introduced evidence earlier in the trial that he got those plastic reproductions for ten dollars each.

Ms. Smith: That's a bit of an overstatement there, in fact, wouldn't you say, Mr. Bakker?

Mr. Bakker: I believed that when I said it and it was a limited edition, and I think the spiritual value—I don't see how you can put a value on a Biblical inspirational piece. ***

Ms. Smith: This is what you described to your viewers who were trusting you to tell them the truth as being worth a thousand dollars. Is that right, Mr. Bakker?

Mr. Bakker: As a collector's item, it's a numbered edition, and I think it's beautiful, but I can understand that you don't.

Ms. Smith: Well, you certainly understood that it was worth ten dollars. PTL was paying ten dollars for it. *** Isn't that correct?

Mr. Bakker: I think it's an absolute phenomenon that it could be manufactured that cheap.

Ms. Smith: So you're not troubled by the fact that you didn't tell the people who were trusting you for full information that this was costing PTL ten dollars—you felt comfortable announcing to them that this was worth a thousand dollars?

Mr. Bakker: I was talking about lifetime membership. They were receiving the Grand membership and partnership for their gift and I'm sure in my exuberance I said this alone could be worth a thousand dollars because it's a beautiful piece. *** I stand by whatever I said on the record. ***

Ms. Smith: It's all right to tell the public it's worth a thousand dollars when, in fact, you paid ten for it? ***

Mr. Bakker: I don't believe it's ever right to deceive the people. *** I felt I was being honest when I said that.[10]

She hammered him with the videotape of his September 17, 1984 television program where he announced that the Grand partnerships were closed forever. Then, on his April 11, 1985 broadcast he announced they were open again because 900 checks had bounced. She showed him PTL's own computer records which revealed more than 5,000 partnerships in the Grand were sold between those two dates.

Ms. Smith: So you, basically, continued to sell them regardless of the representations you made on the air?

Mr. Bakker: You keep using the term "sold," and I didn't sell any partnerships.

Ms. Smith: Promoted. You continued to promote them. You promoted more than 5,000. Isn't that true?

Mr. Bakker: I used the figures that were given to me. . . . *** If that's what I said on the tape, then I said it.[11]

When she tried to get him to admit that he never went back on television to tell his viewers how many total partnerships had been sold, he answered quietly.

Mr. Bakker: Oh, I believe I did.[12]

But throughout his cross-examination, Bakker was unable to identify specific dates of programs where he would have told his viewers the truth about the partnership numbers.

Ms. Smith: You never announced to the public that because you were including the Heritage Inn and the campground that you felt justified going beyond the 25,000? You never told the public that, did you?

Mr. Bakker: I'm sure I discussed that with the partners.

Ms. Smith: Again, can you give me a date?

Mr. Bakker: No. There is so many tapes, I couldn't—I don't know what day I did anything.

Ms. Smith: Mr. Bakker, you've known for at least a year that you—well, you've known for two years you were being investigated by the grand jury. You've known for at least a year that, in fact, you would be someday sitting where you are now answering these charges. *** And you're telling us since that time, on an issue of this importance, you haven't bothered to locate in a tape run to be able to provide a date of when you made these various statements, supposedly?

Mr. Bakker: I have not had the tapes.[13]

She got him to admit that he said on television that the Towers rooms were worth $250 a night, but that the hotel manager had testified earlier that the cost for that type of room would be between $70 and $90.

Ms. Smith: That's quite a jump from that to telling people the room was, in fact, worth $250 isn't it, Mr. Bakker? *** That's just the Yakov Heller sculpture, you really—

Mr. Bakker: You really don't like that piece, do you? ***

Ms. Smith: Well, you typically inflated the value of these partnerships when you would promote them on television, didn't you?

———————

Mr. Bakker: I really believed that. . . .[14]

Toward the end of his three-hour free-fall, Smith accused him of being greedy and heartless. She introduced PTL documents into evidence that showed Bakker trimmed the organization's payroll in 1986 by laying off 283 people in order to save $3,613,000. Then, she asked him if it wasn't true that the combined bonuses he and Tammy received over the years was $3,113,512.

Ms. Smith: So, basically, if you had foregone those bonuses . . . these 283 people wouldn't have had to have been laid off from November and Christmas of 1985 and 1986. Isn't that true?

Mr. Bakker: No, my take home pay in 1986 was . . . $500,000, and that would maybe operate PTL for one day, but that would have very little impact on a payroll of 30 million dollars. ***

Ms. Smith: Did you hear the testimony of Joannie Aimes in this courtroom who described her Christmas and her family's Christmas, or rather lack of it, in 1985 due to being laid off at PTL?

Mr. Bakker: I believe so.

Ms. Smith: And you yourself enjoyed bonuses of $790,000 in the year 1986 alone, Mr. Bakker. Now, let's see, Ms. Aimes made $13,200 annual salary. So, in fact, had you foregone your bonus of that year alone, you could have kept 100 people on, more than 100. *** Is your testimony you were doing the best for PTL accepting these huge bonuses at the same time you are slashing the budgets and firing people at Thanksgiving and Christmas?[15]

Her voice strong, she reminded him of the $500,000 bonus he was paid in November 1986 just before another $50,000 a month later. He answered that he didn't remember receiving the December bonus.

Ms. Smith: Had your lifestyle become so extravagant at that point that you would not notice a $50,000 deposit in your checking account? ***

Mr. Bakker: I did not look at my checkbook for many years, and I know you are smiling. You find that hard to believe, but it is the truth.[16]

———————————

By then, it was 6:00 P.M. and Deborah Smith suggested to the judge that it would be a good time to stop for the weekend. Judge Potter obliged; Bakker made his way down from the witness stand; and the jury was excused after a very long and tumultuous week. So much damage had been done to Bakker the last three hours that, as the jurors filed out and headed toward their cars, they could not have thought anything good about him on their drive home or as they relaxed over the weekend in preparation for the last day of the trial.

Some of them may have begun making up their minds at this time, having heard Bakker's side of it and seeing the government challenge it. Bakker would have one more chance on Monday to save his skin. As a charismatic, he had preached and believed in miracles his whole life. He would need one now.

Monday, October 2, 1989

Deborah Smith was ready for Bakker on Monday morning, October 2, and tore into him with a vengeance when he returned to the stand. She stayed on the attack for three-and-a-half hours, until mercifully his personal ordeal ended just after lunch and he was allowed to leave the witness stand.

Right off the bat with her first questions, she deftly planted and then detonated a time bomb that did as much to destroy his credibility as anything else during the trial. She began by reminding him that he had told the jury on Friday that he got his start in Christian television on CBN with Pat Robertson. Then, she asked if he enjoyed a good relationship with Robertson and Bakker responded, "I believe so."[17] At that point, she produced a letter Robertson had written to Bakker in September 1977 which sternly rebuked Bakker for making "patently false and misleading"[18] statements on television. In that letter, Robertson ripped into Bakker for wasting money contributed by God's people in order to gratify his own ego and competitive spirit. Bakker said he didn't remember receiving the letter.

After that, she asked him if it wasn't true that the Assemblies of God had defrocked him in 1987 for wrongdoing. He quietly acknowledged it.[19]

She grilled him on the hefty bonuses he accepted from PTL at times the ministry was in financial distress, establishing that many of them were used by the Bakkers to purchase vacation homes around the country. She showed him PTL's own records that he and Tammy received bonuses of $150,000 in July of 1983, $150,000 in September of that year and $150,000 in December. The books also showed PTL $2.1 million in the red in November of that year and she asked him flat out if he revealed that fact to the board of directors when he accepted his December bonus. "I don't know if I did or not,"[20] he answered.

She brandished the PTL records that revealed it was $13 million behind in paying overdue bills at a time in 1984 when he accepted a $390,000 bonus which he used to make a down payment on his Palm Desert home. Did he tell the board of directors that PTL had no cash to pay its creditors when they voted that bonus? Bakker replied, "I do not know what I told the board at that meeting."[21] Three months later, in July of 1984, the board again voted a $150,000 bonus for Jim and Tammy.

She directed him to a 1985 memo from PTL finance director Bailey that the cash flow crisis had reached an alarming point and that payroll needed to be cut by 40 percent. Yet, he and Tammy accepted bonuses of $300,000 on November 12, 1985 from the board. She asked him if he had told them that PTL was strapped for money when they voted him such a sizable bonus. "I always told them, you shouldn't do this,"[22] he argued.

But when he insisted that he should not be blamed for the bonuses, she cut to the core.

> **Mr. Bakker:** But I did say to them, please don't give me any more bonuses. I said that many, many times.
> **Ms. Smith:** And then you cashed the check and used it to buy houses many, many times, didn't you?[23]

> ———————
>
> **Ms. Smith:** You received $3.7 million dollars of bonuses . . . between you and your wife, from '84 to '87. Now, if you had used that money to build bunkhouses, [at $350,000 each] . . . you could have built nine additional bunkhouses for your partners. Isn't that true?
> **Mr. Bakker:** Yes, I'm sure that would be close, but I would like to say that I raised $425 million for the work of the Lord during that same period of time. If I had not been there, where would that $425 million have come from?[24]

She pressed him, demanding an explanation of why he didn't tell the board of directors that PTL was in financial trouble.

> **Mr. Bakker:** Well, I spoke faith, of course. *** Because that's what I am, a minister of the gospel, and we have to teach and preach faith. When we don't have anything, we say, by faith, God is going to supply the need.
> **Ms. Smith:** How about truth, Mr. Bakker? Did you tell them the

truth . . . ? You never told them the truth of what the financial condition was, did you?
Mr. Bakker: I absolutely did.[25]

Bakker did show some spunk in a furious exchange with Smith when she finally made him mad. What sparked him was her contention that his own tally that 211,000 partners could be housed at Heritage in a year's time was "a very recent fabrication." Bakker bristled.

Mr. Bakker: That is a lie. That is absolutely not true.[26]

Jim vigorously denied that partners like Mrs. Angel and her eighty-year-old mother, in Deborah Smith's words, would have to buy a pup tent and stay in the campgrounds if they couldn't fit in the Grand. "She would not be put in the camp-ground, . . ."[27] he argued. Instead, if there weren't rooms at the Grand, she could stay at the Heritage Inn Motel where there were always rooms available. And, beyond that, he stressed that "if Mrs. Angel . . . had been unhappy for any reason with her lifetime membership, I would have given her a refund. If she . . . didn't like that the trees had turned too soon in the year, she could come up and say, I want my funds returned, and my policy was and always was to return anyone's gift if they wanted it returned."[28]

He was adamant that he had also refunded regular, non-lifetime partner contributions even after fifteen years if people for any reason wanted their money back. He remembered one occasion where an elderly contributor's grandchildren told him that their grandmother would like a refund on money that she had given years before in order to buy a wheelchair. He gladly refunded it.

Jim shot back that she had it all wrong about Heritage USA being a pyramid scheme or a house of cards.

Mr. Bakker: One of the things that I think you're missing is that this is a church camp. This is not the Marriott Hotel.[29]

He protested that just because the Towers or the Bunkhouses

weren't finished on time didn't mean that it was a scam. He said he hadn't met deadline on any building that had ever been erected at Heritage. PTL would always run out of money. They didn't have money in the bank before they built any of them. They just started building and waited for God to move enough people to contribute the money necessary to finish each one. Sometimes, it would take longer than Bakker anticipated but that didn't mean that those buildings weren't constructed and it didn't mean that the Towers or the Bunkhouses wouldn't be constructed, either.

He argued that he had not defrauded anyone. PTL was up and running with contributors' dollars. His plan was to phase out his contractual relationship with the Brock Hotel Company which was running the Grand to open up one hundred percent of the hotel to his partners. Once that was done and the Towers was built, those two hotels alone would accommodate 171,000 partners every year. PTL's later money troubles and eventual bankruptcy, he said adamantly, were the doing of Jerry Falwell, not Jim Bakker.[30]

Bakker showed Smith a statement that Richard Dortch had made in his pretrial deposition that he and Jim never had any meetings or agreement at all to oversell the hotel and not tell the public. There was never a conspiracy, he pleaded.

He maintained that what he was doing in building Heritage USA was no different from the federal government's own deficit spending.

Mr. Bakker: I do know the federal government uses, basically, the same system.
Ms. Smith: What system, sir?
Mr. Bakker: Paying for old debt with new income.[31]

With that, Bakker was ushered down from the stand to rejoin his attorneys at their table. Whether the jury was swayed by his version of events would be known soon enough. Bakker himself didn't think he had a prayer. Even though he was able to make some points, he felt he had been put through the meat grinder during his ten hours on the stand over two days. He realized that Deborah Smith had been effective. She had been a tiger in cross-examining him. She was good. He knew it.[32]

As Judge Potter recessed for lunch, word spread quickly in the courthouse that the trial was rapidly drawing to a close. Tension was high as everyone realized that the jury would soon have the case. There was an emotional edge piercing the courtroom, as Deborah Smith and George Davis clashed openly.

> **Ms. Smith:** Your honor, I would object to this constant mischaracterization of various questions that are made. I mean, if I'm the one to be cross-examined—
> **Mr. Davis:** Well, I may just call you before we get through.[33]

The afternoon session was brief. Without fanfare, the defense rested. Then, the government called six rebuttal witnesses to contradict several statements that Bakker had made on his own behalf earlier in the day. Two of them stood out.

M. C. Benton, Jr., the court-appointed trustee in PTL's bankruptcy, disputed Bakker's claim that PTL was on a sound enough financial footing that had he remained there and continued his fund-raising, everything would have been fine. Not so, said Benton, whose own review of the records showed PTL to be hopelessly in debt tens of millions of dollars during Bakker's tenure. He reviewed for the jury the statistics showing that at the time Jim left PTL he owed $50 million in secured and unsecured debt. Since that time, the IRS revoked PTL's tax exempt status and slapped it with a tax bill of up to $79 million, and the state of South Carolina got in line for another $12 million in back taxes. To Benton's eyes, Heritage USA was leaking like a sieve.[34]

But rather than bore the jury with any more dry financial details from the complicated PTL bankruptcy proceeding, the prosecutors called their hottest rebuttal witness—Christy Howe, a former PTL employee. And she told the jury about hot dogs.

Mr. Miller: [were you] . . . in the vicinity where Mr. Bakker was attending a meeting when food was ordered out from the McMoose Restaurant?

Ms. Howe: They [PTL executives] had a private meeting in the general manager's office that particular afternoon. They sent out for sandwiches because they had been in there for a lengthy time. When the sandwiches came back, Mr. Bakker became outraged with the fact that the cook had neglected to put mustard on his sandwich and demanded that that employee be terminated, and I heard it from outside of the office.

Mr. Miller: You could hear Mr. Bakker's voice?

Ms. Howe: Yes, sir.[35]

The perfect climax to a "real estate fraud trial." Testimony about what a mean person Jim Bakker was. Giving the jury that one last low blow snapshot of Bakker, the government rested for the final time.

Closing arguments would be delivered the next morning.

NOTES

1. Trial transcript, *United States of America v. James O. Bakker,* Docket C-CR-88-205-1, U.S.D.C. (W.D., N.C.), September 28–29, 1989, vol. 9 at 1738.
2. *Id.* at 1811, 1823, 1742.
3. *Id.* at 1748.
4. *Id.* at 1828.
5. *Id.* at 1828.
6. *Id.* at 1772.
7. *Id.* at 1747–51, 1769–73.
8. *Id.* at 1726–27.
9. *Id.* at 1743.
10. *Id.* at 1743–46.
11. *Id.* at 1760–61.
12. *Id.* at 1763.
13. *Id.* at 1793–94.
14. *Id.* at 1787–89.
15. *Id.* at 1807–10.
16. *Id.* at 1815–16.
17. Trial transcript, *United States of America v. James O. Bakker,* Docket C-CR-88-205-1, U.S.D.C. (W.D., N.C.), October 2–5, 1989, vol. 10 at 1833.
18. *Id.*

19. *Id.* at 1834.

20. *Id.* at 1870.

21. *Id.* at 1872.

22. *Id.* at 1874.

23. *Id.* at 1869.

24. *Id.* at 1909.

25. *Id.* at 1866.

26. *Id.* at 1895.

27. *Id.* at 1907.

28. *Id.* at 1908.

29. *Id.* at 1902.

30. *Id.* at 1903 and trial transcript, vol. 9, *supra,* n. 1 at 1798.

31. Trial transcript, vol. 10, *supra,* n. 17 at 1859–60.

32. Jim Bakker, interviews by author, in Rochester, Minnesota, October 31, 1992 and April 4, 1993.

33. Trial transcript, vol. 10, *supra,* n. 17 at 1924.

34. *Id.* at 2014–18.

35. *Id.* at 2043–44.

Chapter 20

The Trial—Closing Arguments—The Attorneys Make Their Final Pleas

Tuesday, October 3, 1989

The $570 shower curtain closed on the Bakker trial today with each of the four attorneys delivering closing arguments to the jury. After the lawyers spoke, Judge Potter instructed the jury on the law to apply in the case. The jurors were then sent home for a good night's sleep before beginning deliberations the next day.

Deborah Smith

Deborah Smith, in a powerful and driving presentation, told the jury that what they'd seen the last five weeks was a minister gone bad.

> What has unfolded before you . . . is a tale of immense corruption.[1]

She argued that the videotapes of Bakker's programs proved that the PTL empire had been built on false representations and half-truths. She quoted Alfred Lord Tennyson: "A lie which is half a truth is ever the blackest of lies."[2] Looking straight at the jury, she scolded Bakker.

> Mr. Bakker is a world class master at half truths. [He's] an accomplished con man.[3]

His misrepresentations, as she listed them, were promoting lifetime partnerships in the hotels long after he knew there was no more room, and concealing PTL's dire financial condition from its own board of directors.

She complained that the partnership contributions went to operating expenses and into the pockets of the Bakkers. She brought out the charts that she had used earlier in the trial— one showing the 66,000 eventual Grand partnerships dwarfing the originally announced 25,000 limit, another tracing the meager 15 percent of Towers partnership money that was ever spent constructing that hotel. It was like Ross Perot's infomercial during the 1992 presidential campaign in which he used a chart with a map of the state of Arkansas with a big chicken superimposed on it—simple, graphic, and memorable. Smith and Perot both knew the same thing about charts— they help explain complicated things and people remember them.

So, Smith shuffled her charts like a deck of bridge cards and reiterated for the jury the basic facts about the lifetime partnerships and the money that Bakker was earning and spending, which the prosecutors had been emphasizing throughout the trial.

Smith hit Bakker hard on the Hahn cover-up, reminding the jury that $265,000 of the lifetime partnership contributions collected by Bakker in the name of God were earmarked for Jessica Hahn to keep her silent.

> There may have been a time years ago when Mr. Bakker was a good man. You heard people testify to his good works in the '70s, but he changed and fell in love with worldly goods and schemed to raise money for that lifestyle.
> The way he did this was he lied to people. The federal law is simple—you cannot lie to people, get them to send you money.[4]

Put it all together, she said, and you have nothing less than a crooked pyramid scheme built on lies made even more egregious by the fact that it was all perpetrated in the name of religion.

It's gone on too long. It's your job and your time to let the world and the victims know what went on.[5]

George Davis

George Davis began his remarks with a lengthy dissertation on history, philosophy, and physics. Some jurors appeared noticeably perplexed at where he was going. He didn't mention Bakker by name for the first thirty minutes.[6]

Davis talked at length about the Bill of Rights and the beauty of the American system of justice. He argued that the government had violated several of Bakker's constitutional rights. Specifically, he railed against the prosecutors and federal agents for subjecting Bakker to unlawful, unreasonable searches, refusing to honor the separation of church and state, and subjecting the evangelist to cruel and inhuman punishment.

> He's facing the most serious moment I am sure he will ever face in his life. He doesn't expect you to give him pity. . . . But he does have a right to expect justice under the law.[7]

The judge was visibly angered by what was being said, believing that it went beyond the evidence presented during the trial. Potter actually interrupted Davis eight times during his remarks.[8]

To some, it appeared that Davis was making an oblique reference to a mistrial when he emphasized that if any juror had doubts, that person should hold out.

> If it turns out that just one of you does not agree . . . you have the sworn duty to adhere to that. *** [e]ven if it's one versus eleven.[9]

When Davis spoke of the jury's right to nullify the fraud by wire statute if it didn't agree with it, Judge Potter stopped him. What set him off was the fact that juries in America absolutely may not refuse to follow a statute even if they don't agree with it, and the judge ripped into Davis for suggesting it.

Judge Potter: Mr. Davis, stick with the evidence. I will instruct the jury.[10]

*** [A few moments later, when Davis continued hammering at it] Do you want me to have you removed from the courtroom?[11]

Davis then attempted to diminish the evidence against Bakker.

He [Bakker] was the victim of a lot of circumstances. I think 95% of the evidence in this case by the government is circumstantial. It is reeking with it.[12]

On top of that, said Davis, prosecutors never proved that Bakker intended to commit any criminal act.

You didn't hear one person in this case say that. You didn't hear it because it isn't true.[13]

The real villains in the case, Davis told the jury, were Jerry Falwell, the Devil, and Richard Dortch. "Dortch did it all,"[14] he railed. Davis's theory was that it was Bakker who was the victim in this case—the victim of Satan and jealous rival ministers.

Davis also complained that the whole case against Bakker was an unfair intrusion into the religious activities of PTL. He argued it wasn't right for Bakker to be questioned about his salary and bonuses.

I don't recall ever hearing anything about how much the Pope of Rome got for bonuses or housing allowances.[15]

Davis ended with a plea to the jury:

Let him go. He's not going to go back to anything he did before. He's stripped. He doesn't even have a name. But he's a human being.[16]

Harold Bender

After Davis had his turn at bat, Harold Bender stepped up to the plate to deliver his own closing argument. He made several good points. But by that eleventh hour, the train had already left the station. Bender should be awarded debating points, however, for putting the best possible face on five weeks of damage. Within his remarks, there really was the outline of a scenario or some logic by which any juror so inclined could find some reasons to vote to acquit.

If any juror had wanted to reach out to save Bakker, there actually were some things in Bender's argument to justify it. But, no juror was willing to reach quite that far.

Bender began by casting the government's case in context. Sure, there were thirteen partners who testified against Bakker that they had been defrauded, but that left 159,987 who didn't feel that way. He noted that the FBI had interviewed hundreds and hundreds of partners in their own homes with a questionnaire, and that only those who were critical of Bakker were ever asked to testify before the grand jury or there in Charlotte. All the rest, the ones who were fully satisfied that they had not been defrauded, were left home alone by the government. His point was that the prosecutors were presenting testimonies of members of a very small militant fringe, and in the process distorting what the vast majority of partners thought.[17]

Bender argued that by using only excerpted blurbs of Bakker's television programs, the government presented an unfair and unrepresentative picture of what Bakker really did on television. He told jurors that it was like taping the services of their own ministers in their hometown churches and using only those parts of the services where the offerings were taken. To a person who had never been to that church, it would look as if all the minister did was ask for offerings.

> Wouldn't you say, wait a minute, there is more that goes on at my church than that?[18]

He maintained that the government had not proved any criminal intent on Bakker's part, nor had it proved that there was any criminal conspiracy between Bakker and Dortch to defraud anyone of anything. He reminded them of Dortch's own testimony in which he confirmed that he never had a meeting or a discussion with Jim Bakker where they discussed overselling lifetime partnerships. It never happened. That was

Dortch's own testimony. So, where was the conspiracy and where was the intent to commit a crime?[19]

But Bender himself knew how the government had turned Bakker into damaged goods during the trial, a *persona non grata* for whom no juror would want to advocate in the jury room. He addressed it head-on.

> This case is not about cinnamon buns. This case is not about mustard on hamburgers. This case is not about shoes in glass cases. This case is about criminal charges, criminal charges that involve an element of specific intent. *** Specific intent to defraud the partners.[20]

He emphasized that the televangelist had acted in good faith, honestly believing that God had given him the vision to build a city for Christians and erect hotels for them to stay in. Bender quoted Efrem Zimbalist, Jr., whom the government brought all the way from Spain to testify in their case, and who said that he couldn't find the malfeasance in the way Bakker ran PTL that the government wanted him to find. He said that there was no bad purpose to Bakker's deeds.[21]

And PTL finance director Peter Bailey, whose memos of doom and gloom the prosecutors enlarged into huge charts throughout the trial for the jury to see? Bailey said there was no intent on Bakker's part to defraud the partners. Those were his words. He said that the partnerships were a great plan and that Heritage USA was God-given.[22]

Bender reminded jurors that Bakker was doing a tremendous amount of good at PTL, and that his show was a bright spot in the lives of tens of thousands of shut-ins around the country who watched him every day on television. And those viewers knew PTL was no fraud. He told the jurors to remember Lee Albert Stillwell, from Fort Hope.

> And, yes, he doesn't talk like you and me, and you may have laughed about it. I know some in this courtroom did. You tell him that your life has no meaning because of Fort Hope and that man who came off the street, you did something for yourself, but it has

no meaning anymore. You tell him. [because Bakker gave it to him through a fraud] ***

And you tell the old black guy, the man with one arm trying to cut wood, his wife in bed sick, that the mobile home that was brought in here one day and set and put in, so they could have a place, you tell them that it was obtained by fraud.

And, yes, you are going to hear about what a small percentage was used for this and what a small percentage was used for that. Well, folks, I know in my religion we don't do enough. We should do more. I hope yours is not like mine. If one life is changed, if somebody that is hurt is helped. It was going. It was continuing.[23]

He attempted to refute the most damning of all the evidence against his client by arguing that what the jurors had heard about cars, boats, watches, furs, bonuses, and California vacation homes was nothing but an attempt to inflame them against Bakker. Bender told them that the real question should be—did Bakker earn that money? Was he worth it? Well, the board of directors had Bakker insured for $50 million. He was worth $50 million dead and the board paid more than $800,000 a year in premiums on that policy. Wasn't he worth at least that in salary and bonuses each year? Isn't everyone worth at least the amount of premiums that are paid on their life insurance each year?[24]

Bender asked them to look at the compensation that other television performers earned in determining whether Bakker was worth what he was paid. Because, after all, he was a television star. Oprah Winfrey made $5 million a year. And Bakker was entitled to be compensated for what he did on television, too.[25]

Bakker gave millions of dollars in royalties back to the ministry. Would a man with criminal intent to defraud do that? Would a man who was intending to rip off the ministry's partners reach into his own pocket and pay for people to get their hair fixed at the beauty shop so that they could go to a funeral? Is that someone who would defraud those partners?[26]

Nor did Bakker ever conceal his lifestyle from his contributors and his television audience. He showed his homes on TV. He even put a camera in the Rolls Royce that he bought and drove it around on one of his programs. That's being devious? That's an example of someone who is attempting to defraud contributors?[27]

Bender got right to the heart of it with one question: What was the fraud? The fact that somebody couldn't get in to one of the hotels when they wanted? The fact that the Towers was never built? But the evidence in the case was that there was never one year at Heritage when the place was one hundred percent booked.[28]

Lastly, Bender attempted to put the best possible light on his own witnesses, recognizing that when all was said and done many of them had actually ended up damaging Bakker's chances. He looked straight at the jury and told them that maybe some of them were uncomfortable with Jim's evangelical witnesses because of the jurors' own very different religious backgrounds.

> But in spite of my uncomfortable feelings, or your uncomfortable feelings, these people are alive, they're on fire, they tell you what it means to them and what it meant to them to be there, to walk that place, and no, and it's not the holy of holies, it was just South Carolina red clay but it was red clay transformed into a special place by that man [Bakker], by God, and wanted to do something for him and he did. . . .[29]

Jerry Miller

Prosecutor Jerry Miller was the last attorney to address the jury. He began with a provocative comment.

> My personal hope for each of you . . . we [the government] can't bring religion into the case as something to be relied upon, but what I can ask each of you to do is to make contact with your own personal beliefs, with your own maker, with your own concept of religion, and I ask right now that you have your eyes open and you be able to see past personalities and be able to see past confusion and find the truth because that is what your search is for, is the truth of this case.[30]

What Miller meant by the admonition that jurors "make contact with your own personal beliefs, with your own maker, with your own concept of religion . . ." is unclear. It could be subject to different interpretations. How any of the jurors understood it is unknown.

Some people, hearing it, might interpret it as a request that they seek the guidance of their own maker in finding the truth in the case. But it wasn't said that directly. There was more to it.

The question is whether it was a request for the jurors to determine the truthfulness of what Bakker and his witnesses said by evaluating it from the standpoint of their own religious beliefs.

Did "mak[ing] contact" with their own concept of religion mean they were to judge Jim Bakker's religious practices against their own? If in a juror's own religion God didn't speak to you, would Bakker probably be lying if he claimed that God gave him the vision for the lifetime partnerships? If a juror's religion rejected the Pentecostal belief in miracles, including financial miracles and the faith ministry which Bakker claimed financed PTL from the beginning, did that mean Bakker's statements to the contrary during his own testimony were of questionable truthfulness?

Miller then launched into a critique of the PTL partners who testified for Bakker during the trial.

> First of all, you've seen these people. They're victims, too. They have been deceived even to this day. They have been deceived to the extent that their allegiance to this man, their loyalty to that man overcomes their ability to even deal with reality. It's come to a point where they almost worship this man. They give him the deity to where if he says something, no matter what it is, they'll accept it as true. *** Don't be distracted by this argument about whether or not they were defrauded.[31]

That's right. Don't believe those contributors who claimed they were not defrauded. Because they were religious extremists untethered to reality.

> It matters not what the people who were potential victims of it think about it. The people who were defrauded, some of them don't realize it to this day. They just won't accept it.[32]

How arrogant can you get? In other words, the government knows better than the people who sent their money in about whether those people were really defrauded. The opinions of those people don't count, even though they represented the landslide majority of PTL partners. Because they just don't know. Only the government's opinion is the correct one.

Miller moved on to other arguments. He emphasized that jurors should weigh very heavily the fact that Richard Dortch pleaded guilty to the same crimes with which Jim Bakker was charged. He said that there was no surer evidence of Bakker's guilt than the fact that the person with whom he acted pleaded guilty.[33]

Importantly, Miller responded directly to the defense theory that Bakker did not possess criminal intent. Miller told the jurors that intent to defraud can be proved by evidence that Bakker purposely misled contributors into purchasing lifetime partnerships long after he exceeded the limits he announced in the beginning. If the jury was satisfied that the government had proved that much, it could presume that Bakker possessed criminal intent. Miller argued that Bakker had demonstrated his knowledge that the partnership limits had been surpassed and that he had shown the jurors a "fraudulent mind in operation."[34] Miller stressed that Bakker knew full well how many partnerships had been sold because his staff was briefing him with daily and weekly memos on the sales. So, he had full knowledge of the overselling.

Miller also argued that even if Bakker actually, in his own mind, didn't know that the limits on the two hotels had been exceeded, he should have known it because everybody around him was alerting him to the disaster. Peter Bailey, Richard Dortch, and even lower-ranking PTL employees had attempted to get his attention on the physical impossibility of fitting 66,000 Grand Hotel partners into the Grand during a year. Miller reminded the jury that Bakker had told them that he didn't know all that went on at PTL. Miller's response—that's the same reaction Bakker had when his attorneys gave him advice that he didn't like. He would just spin his chair around and look out the window until the attorneys left.

That's because this man is demonstrating to you he is turning his blind eye to the facts that are right there. *** The element of knowledge may be satisfied by inference drawn with proof that the defendant deliberately closed his eyes to what would otherwise have been obvious to him.[35]

Miller ripped into Bakker, telling the jurors that he "was not truthful to you when he took this stand."[36] Jim Bakker filled his pockets from the PTL treasury. He raised the money to build Heritage USA with a fraudulent scheme. It was fraudulent because he wasn't telling people the whole truth. He didn't tell contributors the truth about the number of partnerships, he didn't tell partners the truth about where their money was being spent, and he didn't tell even his own board of directors the truth about the financial condition of PTL.

Miller responded to Harold Bender's criticism that it wasn't the government's business how Bakker spent his money. It sure was, the prosecutor argued, because Bakker elected "to hide behind the tax exempt status of a religious organization."[37]

Oprah Winfrey doesn't have to answer to show [how] she spends her money because she doesn't have her organization hiding behind a tax exempt status to where they get the support of the taxpayers to carry on that business. The organization that promotes her show pays its taxes, pays its way as it should.[38]

And he had some harsh words about Bakker's luxurious lifestyle.

The lavishness. Folks, you've heard enough about that. I don't need to tell you any more about it. You can understand this. *** To some extent this case is about that. . . . This man has been so numb and so callous to the ministry of the needs of people that he could do something like the sweet rolls incident. He could do something like the mustard incident. Those are relevant. . . .[39]

Bingo. You bet this case is about that. It's exactly about it.

Miller closed with some critical words about George Davis. He wasn't the only one with things to say, either.

Mr. Miller: Have you noticed that in four lawyers in this court-room, there was only one who ever had problems obeying the rules of the court? If you folks think that Mr. Davis accidentally transgressed those rules, then we've got some swamp land in Florida, better yet, we've got a membership in the Towers to sell you. Folks, what he was doing was deliberately, deliberately provoking this court . . . trying to create in your mind that there is something improper about Judge Potter keeping order in this courtroom. *** [T]hat was calculated and he is trying to play that into this mean, old government routine, this is the mean old government picking on him. That somehow this court is against him. ***

Mr. Davis: Your honor, that's an entirely false statement.

Judge Potter: Mr. Davis, you're out of order.

Mr. Miller: You know, in our part of the country they say stuck pigs squeal. I must have just stuck him.

Mr. Davis: I object to that also.

Judge Potter: Mr. Davis, if you want me to, I'll have you removed from the courtroom. Now, you're out of order.[40]

With those fireworks, Jerry Miller's argument drew to a close. Tammy Faye, in a bright red cashmere suit with oversized black earrings, was awash in tears as she listened to Miller's clubbing. As the jury watched, tissues were passed back to her from the defense table. Jim remained solemn as he continued to scribble notes, only occasionally looking up.

After a brief recess, it was Judge Potter's turn to instruct the jury on the law that was to be applied in determining Bakker's guilt or innocence. It had been a long day. It was 6:45 P.M. when Potter began reading the instructions, but the jury paid rapt attention.

The Jury Is Instructed

Potter read each of the four laws Bakker was charged with violating—mail fraud, fraud by telephone, television fraud, and conspiracy. In the process, he explained the elements of each offense and what the government was required to prove.

To find Bakker guilty of fraud, the jury would have to find that he "knowingly and willfully and with specific intent devised a scheme . . . to defraud or [obtain] . . . money and property by means of false pretenses, representations or promises."[41] He then explained:

> A statement or representation is false or fraudulent within the meaning of these statutes if it relates to a material fact and is known to be untrue or is made with reckless indifference as to its truth or falsity and is made or caused to be made with intent to defraud. A statement or representation may also be false or fraudulent when it constitutes a half truth or effectively conceals a material fact with intent to defraud.[42]

He also told them that it was not necessary that the government prove that "the alleged scheme actually succeeded in defrauding anyone." Instead, what must be proved beyond a reasonable doubt was that Bakker knowingly devised a scheme to defraud.[43]

The judge admonished the jurors that they had to apply the law that he gave them, even if they disagreed with it. For instance, if they didn't like the judge's instruction on the intent necessary to convict or the fact that no one had to be defrauded in order to send Bakker to prison, they didn't have any choice.

> And you must follow all of my instructions as a whole. You have no right to disregard or give special attention to any one instruction or to question the wisdom or correctness of any rule I may state to you.[44]

The instructions were lengthy and complicated. They were heavy with complex legal definitions and read more like Black's *Law Dictionary* than anything to which nonlawyers would ever be exposed. It is clear that several instructions were heavy with legal nuances and subtleties. One stood out.

Potter explained what the jury would have to find in order to convict Bakker for conspiracy.

> [That Bakker and someone else] came to a mutual understanding to try to accomplish a common and unlawful plan as charged in the indictment. Second, the defendant willfully became a member of such conspiracy. Third, that one of the conspirators during the

existence of the conspiracy knowingly committed at least one of the means or methods or overt acts described in the indictment. . . .[45]

The government, of course, had alleged that Bakker's co-conspirator was Richard Dortch. Bakker himself certainly denied that he and Dortch ever reached such a mutual understanding. In his testimony on the government's behalf, Dortch denied it too. But Bakker was soon convicted of conspiracy nonetheless.

Potter concluded with standard admonitions that signaled the very end of the trial.

> A verdict must represent the considered judgment of each juror. In order to return a verdict, it is necessary that each juror agree thereto. In other words, your verdict must be unanimous. ***
>
> It is your duty as jurors to consult with one another and to deliberate in an effort to reach an agreement if you can do so without violence to your individual judgment. *** In the course of your deliberations, do not hesitate to reexamine your own views and change your opinion if convinced it is erroneous, but do not surrender your honest conviction . . . for the mere purpose of returning a verdict. ***
>
> The first thing you want to do . . . select one of your members as the foreperson who will preside over the deliberations.[46]

The jurors had been sitting for hours on end listening to four attorneys make lengthy closing arguments, and to the judge's own ponderous instructions. It was 8:00 P.M. The trial was recessed until the following morning, when it would finally be the jury's turn to speak.

Wednesday, October 4, 1989

At 9:15 A.M. sharp Wednesday morning, October 4, the jury returned to receive their final marching orders before walking down the narrow hallway to the small jury room where they would determine Jim Bakker's fate. Judge Potter, in an attempt to neutralize the sting still resounding in the courtroom from his bitter exchange with George Davis the day before in which he threatened to have Davis bodily removed from the courthouse during his closing argument, told the jurors that they shouldn't hold anything that happened against Jim Bakker.

> **Judge Potter:** That's something that sometimes comes up in the heat of a trial, and . . . any comments I make to the attorneys . . . should not affect your decision any way whatever.[47]

Right. Like that could erase the indelible impression that was made the day before, and which indeed had been made throughout the trial, about the clash between Judge Potter and Bakker's lead attorney.

At that point, Potter excused the six alternates from further service and sent them home. They had sat in the jury box throughout the lengthy trial so that if any of the first twelve jurors had been unable to make it to the end of the trial and participate in the deliberations, they could sub for them. But that didn't happen and the alternates were sent home.

Potter then turned to the jury and reminded them that if during their deliberations they needed anything, including any further instructions or clarification on any point, "Just press the buzzer and let us know and we'll see if we can accommodate you."[48] It was 9:25 A.M. and as the marshal prepared to escort the jury back down the corridor, the judge put the punctuation point on the end of five long weeks: "Now . . . it's up to you."[49]

With the jury gone, George Davis and Judge Potter fought one last time. Davis was furious at what had happened the day before.

> **Mr. Davis:** You made a statement right in this court, right in front of that jury, that I felt, I felt was totally unfounded and I felt was almost irrational. *** You said "I'll have you removed from the courtroom." Now, that was a very intimidating statement to me, to me. *** It was a very threatening statement and it certainly indicated to me, from all the other things in this case, has been a bias and prejudice on your part thinly veiled but clearly conveyed to the jury. . . .[50]

Deborah Smith responded that Davis had been out of line in his closing argument in telling the jury that it could disregard those laws on fraud and conspiracy with which it disagreed. But Judge Potter was in no mood to spar with Davis. He cut him off quickly.

Judge Potter: Well, there have been improper matters all the way through this trial, Mr. Davis. I think I've tried to use as much restraint as I could under the circumstances. Now, I've got other matters to handle besides your case and we're going to start them right now. It's 9:30 A.M.[51]

And with that stick-it-in-your-ear Valentine from the robed one, George Davis was brushed away. He and his party then left to huddle in a small anteroom on the top floor of the courthouse to sweat out the jury's deliberations. There was an eeriness to it all and an unsettling feeling descending on Bakker's supporters that the trial had not gone well and that these could be Bakker's last hours as a free man.

NOTES

1. Applebome, "PTL Fraud Case Goes to the Jury," *New York Times,* October 4, 1989 at 26-A, col. 1.

2. *Id.*

3. Preston, "Domestic News," UPI [wire story], October 3, 1989, BC Cycle.

4. *Id.*

5. Applebome, *supra,* n. 1.

6. *Id.*

7. Preston, *supra,* n. 3.

8. *Id.*

9. Applebome, *supra,* n. 1; Harris, "Jim Bakker Case Goes to Jury," *Washington Post,* October 4, 1989 at 1-B (Nexis printout).

10. Preston, *supra,* n. 3.

11. Trial transcript, *United States of America v. James O. Bakker,* Docket No. C-CR-88-205-1, U.S.D.C. (W.D., N.C.), October 2–5, 1989, vol. 10 at 2131.

12. Associated Press, "Closing Arguments End in Bakker Trial," *Florida Sun Sentinel,* October 4, 1989 at 4-A (Nexis printout); Digby, "Bakker a World 'Master of Half Truths,' Prosecutor," Reuters [wire story], October 3, 1989, AM Cycle.

13. Applebome, *supra,* n. 1.

14. Harris, *supra,* n. 9.

15. Applebome, *supra,* n. 1.

16. Harris, *supra*, n. 9.
17. Trial transcript, *supra*, n. 11 at 2072, 2081.
18. *Id.* at 2083.
19. *Id.* at 2084–85.
20. *Id.* at 2104.
21. *Id.* at 2105.
22. *Id.* at 2105–6.
23. *Id.* at 2102–3.
24. *Id.* at 2091–92.
25. *Id.* at 2089–90.
26. *Id.* at 2090, 2104–5.
27. *Id.* at 2095–96.
28. *Id.* at 2100–2101.
29. *Id.* at 2099.
30. *Id.* at 2107.
31. *Id.* at 2125.
32. *Id.* at 2126.
33. *Id.* at 2114.
34. *Id.* at 2118.
35. *Id.* at 2129.
36. *Id.* at 2144.
37. *Id.* at 2136.
38. *Id.*
39. *Id.*
40. *Id.* at 2130–31.
41. *Id.* at 2158.
42. *Id.* at 2159.
43. *Id.* at 2160.
44. *Id.* at 2145.
45. *Id.* at 2163–64.
46. *Id.* at 2174–76.
47. *Id.* at 2181.
48. *Id.* at 2182.
49. *Id.*
50. *Id.* at 2187.
51. *Id.* at 2188.

Chapter 21

The Jury Deliberates—Bakker Is a Dead Man

The Courthouse Scene

It took the jury a day and a half to decide Bakker's fate, and while those deliberations continued everyone else played a waiting game. The pack of reporters, which had swelled to seventy, stuck close by since the jury might return at any minute. For stories, they interviewed the Bakker followers, who were also maintaining a courthouse vigil, and other passersby. There were so many reporters that several were forced to huddle on staircases in the building to type their dispatches, while others sat in groups on the floor and talked. They searched the corridors like hawks for any sign of Jim and Tammy, the attorneys, and members of the jury. But there wasn't much action, and stories were hard to come by.

For instance, the big news reported during the first day was that the local Shoney's delivered the jury's lunch to the courthouse. Eager reporters jumped on the story, found reliable sources and learned that the jurors had ordered hamburgers, reuben sandwiches, shrimp, strawberry pie, and hot fudge cake. The biggest sighting the first day was at 1:00 P.M. when Jim and Tammy came downstairs for something to eat. Reporters scrambled to get a quote and asked Jim if he was worried. Replied Bakker, "No, I'm trusting God." They asked Harold Bender where the entourage was going for lunch and he drew a laugh when he told them, "Chez Hardee's." Tammy joined in the tense humor and said that she might prefer "La

McDonald's." As it turned out, the group just went back over to Bender's office a few blocks away and had spaghetti.[1]

After eating, the Bakkers and their attorneys returned to the second floor conference room in the courthouse where they would spend every hour while the jury did its work. Nearly a dozen relatives and close friends spent those two days in that room with the Bakkers reading the Bible, singing, and praying.

Bakker loyalists who had converged on Charlotte to support him during the trial stood defiantly outside the courthouse, many of them with placards denouncing the government's prosecution of the evangelist. "Enough is Enough" read one large banner hoisted by a group of churchwomen from Florida. Helen Gordon of Winston-Salem, North Carolina had a bumper sticker with Jim and Tammy's faces on it on her Cadillac. "I've had people look at me, holler at me," she admitted. But she couldn't believe that the government had gone after Bakker. "Jim and Tammy loved everybody. They would give you the shirt off their backs," she argued to reporters. Gordon said that the Bakkers were different: "I never knew God loved us. I went to church all my life. I always thought God was up there with a big stick until I heard Jimmy and Tammy tell it different."[2]

Gordon was joined by about forty other Bakker supporters who prayed and commiserated on the courthouse steps. Others rested in lawn chairs on the grounds and knitted under stately oaks.

Inside the courthouse, the jury was hard at work. Throughout the first day, they sent notes to Judge Potter asking for several exhibits that had been introduced into evidence so they could take one more look at them. Mostly, they asked for government exhibits. The memos from PTL's finance director to Jim Bakker, the internal PTL weekly tallies of the lifetime partnerships, and even the charts of Bakker bonuses the government had used throughout the trial were at the top of the jury's list.

At 5:30 P.M. on Wednesday, when handing over another document to jury foreman Ricky Hill, Judge Potter asked him if the jury might be able to reach a verdict yet that first day. "If we get that [document], we may,"[3] replied Hill. But within half an hour, the jury returned to tell the judge that they wanted to go home, sleep on it, and return the next morning.

Harold Bender was savvy enough to read trouble in the requests the jury made, however, and he sensed it was not going well for his client. After all, the jury was obviously being drawn back to the government's evidence and the documents that supposedly showed that Bakker had knowledge of the overselling of the partnerships. So that night, as Bakker remembers, Bender called Jim and Tammy to his office. He told them that the signals from the jury were very negative and that Bakker should prepare himself that night for the possibility of being convicted the next day and being immediately incarcerated. Bakker was flabbergasted that this could be his last day as a free man.

> **Jim Bakker in prison:** That was the first time he told me something like that could happen. I couldn't believe what I was hearing.[4]

But when the dozen Bakker intimates regrouped the following morning in the second floor conference room to await the imminent verdict, Tammy was upbeat. Dressed in a fire engine red suit, with red high heels and huge white earrings, she told the group that God had spoken to her that morning and told her, "There are only twelve jurors, but I am the thirteenth one and don't give up."[5]

At that, they all knelt on the floor together and prayed. They didn't have long to wait.

Inside the Jury Room

Suzan Brooks, my research assistant, spent months locating and then interviewing every juror and alternate we could find. Through in-depth interviews with all who were willing to talk, the picture emerges of what really took place in the jury room.

The jurors who took their seats at the secluded courthouse conference table to debate Bakker's guilt or innocence were:

1. Nancy Summey, an R.N. from Charlotte Memorial Hospi-

tal who tried to revive government witness Steve Nelson
when he collapsed on the third day of the trial.

2. Rick Hill, a representative for the old Celanese Corporation who attended Sunday School regularly and read the
   Charlotte Observer faithfully.

3. Roscoe Jones, an IBM data processor.

4. Naydeen Coffey, a Delmar Photography employee.

5. James McAlister, a retired chemical salesman.

6. Gwendolyn Morrison, a machine operator from Charlotte.

7. Buddy Howell Dyer, who lived in the country and worked
   at a liquor store.

8. Catherine Boardman, who at twenty-three was the young-
   est juror.

9. Ray Love, an electrician from Monroe, North Carolina,
   who did not subscribe to the *Charlotte Observer*.

10. Vivian Ferguson, a retired domestic worker.

11. Thomas Teeples, a home builder.

12. Barbara Dalley, a mother who was home-schooling her five
    children.[6]

With the exception of two who wavered, the rest of the
jurors were keenly soured on Jim Bakker, his witnesses, and his
attorneys. Jurors told us that they thought Bakker's witnesses
were "strange"[7] and often "made no sense."[8] Catherine Boardman called them "fanatics."[9] They felt the government's witnesses, on the other hand, had been "sincere"[10] and
"believable."[11]

George Davis had angered several jurors during the trial and
they accused him of being overly dramatic and obstreperous in
the courtroom. Ms. Boardman commented she "didn't care for
them [the defense attorneys] at all . . . they made us feel like
idiots."[12] Rick Hill told *St. Louis Post-Dispatch* reporters, "we
kept looking for something from the defense and we never saw
it."[13] The prosecutors, however, got high marks. Barbara Dalley
said of Deborah Smith and Jerry Miller, "there was such a sense
of decency there." And she described Smith's closing argument as "so beautifully done I felt like standing up and
applauding."[14]

But it was Jim Bakker himself whom the jurors particularly disliked. They had eagerly awaited his testimony but were sorely disappointed with it. In their eyes, he really laid an egg on the witness stand. James McAlister characterized the evangelist as "pretty miserable"[15] as a witness. We are protecting the privacy of one juror we interviewed (Juror X) and he will not be named. Juror X thought Bakker was "a complete dummy, a pawn"[16] who was guilty as hell and deserved more than forty-five years. Juror X even complained to us that the whole trial had been a terrible waste of taxpayers' money because he was so obviously guilty. "Why he did not plead guilty and avoid a trial is beyond me,"[17] Juror X says today.

Boardman told the *Charlotte Observer:* "I don't think he'll realize, ever, how he's hurt people. I think he basically lives in his own world."[18]

And, the jury was pretty well fed up with Tammy Faye, too, by the time the trial ended. In addition to her brief but flamboyant courtroom appearances, her only involvement had been on the videotapes of *The PTL Club* programs which both the prosecutors and defense counsel made the jury watch. We have learned that one juror actually said, "If I have to listen to Tammy Faye sing again, I'm going to cause a mistrial!"[19] Every juror vividly recalls the videotapes.

Rick Hill was chosen to be foreman of the jury after two other men refused to do it. Hill told us he had "a lot of experience with handling meetings and work"[20] and found being foreman was comparable to directing a business meeting. He said he tried to make sure that "everybody could get a fair shake of being able to talk"[21] during the deliberations. "You had to keep people on the right track,"[22] he said. "We were looking at one indictment, and people wanted to look at another, and think about other things, so you had to keep them on track basically."[23]

Hill described their plan during deliberations in this way: "We first went through the ones [charges] we thought were guilty and got that out of the way first. And then we went through the ones we had trouble with."[24] Hill's own personal opinion, which he of course expressed to the others, was that

the evidence against Jim Bakker was "overwhelming."[25] Most
of the others agreed. "There was not hardly any doubt at all by
the time we went into the deliberations about the guilt,"[26] Hill
told us.

Barbara Dalley remembers that the jurors "who passionately
believed he was guilty"[27] turned their attention to convincing
the others, including the two who were wavering [whom
other jurors told us were Teeples and Jones]. Specifically, the
vacillators expressed doubt that Bakker actually intended to
defraud anyone.[28] Bakker's lawyers had argued to the jury at the
close of the case that their client's guilt or innocence would
hinge on that key question of intent. Jones and Teeples, apparently, had serious doubt about it. They were the only
ones.

The rest of the jury was against Bakker. Rick Hill told us,
"We basically agreed that he was guilty and that he knew that he
was taking the money and did not have enough time-shares, or
whatever."[29] Hill remembers that the only question in the
minds of most jurors was when exactly Bakker knew it. James
McAlister remembers that the jurors agreed that Bakker was
guilty of twenty-two of the twenty-four counts right away. He
recalls that what took the next four or five hours was "poring
through exhibits"[30] to find the exact dates and the amounts of
money in question on the remaining counts.

Eventually, it was the PTL bank statements and checking
account records that the jurors found proved Bakker knew the
partnerships were oversold.

Barbara Dalley and Catherine Boardman were two of the
most vocal jurors during deliberations and both were adamant
about Bakker's guilt. Boardman was only twenty-three years
old. She wrote in her diary, published in the *Charlotte Observer,*
"It was obvious he was guilty and most of us felt that way. . . .
At first I yelled and screamed a lot to make people see what I
saw."[31] Boardman told us that reluctance of the two holdouts
caused tempers to flare and that several jurors raised their voices
and shouted at each other.[32]

Other jurors remembered her emotion. Juror X, describing
the jury as a combination of "half talkers and half listeners,"[33]

chuckled that he was one of the listeners and that Boardman was definitely one of the talkers. "This one young lady [Board-man] was in tears . . . [because] she was so damn mad with this other fellow [one of the two who was wavering]."[34]

What frustrated Boardman was that some jurors at first did not see Bakker's guilt as clearly as she did. Convincing the doubters became the task and many jurors characterized the deliberations as unpleasant and strained. One in fact remembered it incorrectly when he told us, "Oh, it went on for several days' deliberation. Several days. Where it shouldn't have gone over a few hours except for that one little detail. . . ."[35] The detail was the obstinance of the two waverers on the question of intent. The juror told us that the first man refused to agree to convict Bakker "until we could prove to him figure-wise that it was a conspiracy. The amount of money for the first embezzlement charge is what it amounted to. And we had to send out for two or three days getting figures, and figure up figures, to show him the amount of . . . partnerships that were sold. . . ."[36]

Barbara Dalley recalls that the debate inside the jury room was definitely "heated" but that "I just had a commitment . . . to hear what everyone had to say. It's hard to listen when you've already made up your mind."[37] Still, she felt that most jurors were thoughtful and methodical in reaching their decision. Others, however, she did admit "wanted to get out of there."[38]

What eventually turned the tide irretrievably against Bakker in the jury room, and which with its undertow took down his two lone potential supporters, were a few smoking pieces of evidence. Barbara Dalley told us that "I remember a little statue [David slaying Goliath]. He [Bakker] had [on a videotape the government played] the original and said it was worth a lot of money. . . . It was obviously a piece of junk and he knew what it had cost . . . that showed intent."[39] Remember that one of the replicas of that statue had been passed to the jury during the trial and the sword fell off.

Secondly, it was the documents that the jury requested from the judge several hours into their deliberations that sank

Bakker. There, in black and white, were PTL's own computer records showing the number of partnerships that had been issued by month and year. The jurors compared those figures to the PTL bank records of the partnership accounts which they spread out on the jury table. Barbara Dalley remembers that everyone on the jury agreed that "if they could show a greater amount of money in [one of the hotel partnership accounts] by a certain date,"[40] it would show his guilty intent. After looking over the documents for several hours, she remembers that the jurors "determined a point [during his promotion of the hotel partnerships] where Bakker had to know he'd oversold and made the decision to offer more partnerships anyway."[41] As Dalley remembers it, "two people [jurors] were adding up [Bakker's PTL checks and computer runs introduced in evidence] by hand and when they reached one million, that meant he [Bakker] knew on this date he'd oversold."[42] Then it only took a few votes to confirm it.

Foreman Hill agrees that is how it happened:

We finally figured out [from] . . . the bank statements. . . . [And] that the money was coming in and he was getting the reports of how much money was coming in . . . and how many rooms he had, and that he would not be able to have more people than he had rooms. And that he knew this and kept on selling. So we thought that . . . he was knowledgeable of all of this.[43]

James McAlister remembered it too:

It took us four or five hours of poring through the . . . exhibits . . . to find that date [when sales exceeded capacity] and the amount of money, and once we found it and they [the holdouts] read it, they were satisfied and that was it.[44]

Rick Hill remains critical of Bakker:

Probably the key was he just oversold so badly. I mean, he just didn't oversell by just a few, but . . . he just kept getting money and overselling and overselling and overselling. I mean, his intent was that he was just going to oversell. . . .[45]

NOTES

1. Wright, McClain, and Shepard, "Jurors Jolt Court with Hint of Verdict, Then Go Home," *Charlotte Observer,* October 5, 1989 at 1-A (Westlaw printout).

2. Wall, "A Bakker Believer: Devoted Winston-Salem Woman Has Moved to Charlotte for Trial," *Charlotte Observer,* October 5, 1989 at 29-A (Westlaw printout).

3. Wright, McClain, and Shepard, *supra,* n. 1.

4. Jim Bakker, interview by author, in Rochester, Minnesota, June 26, 1993. *See also* trial transcript, *United States of America v. James O. Bakker,* Docket No. C-CR-88-205-1, U.S.D.C. (W.D., N.C.), October 2–5, 1989, vol. 10 at 2247–49.

5. McClain, "Ending on a High Note Tammy Bakker Says the Ministry Will Continue," *Charlotte Observer,* October 6, 1989 at 14-A (Westlaw printout).

6. Trial transcript, *United States of America v. James O. Bakker,* Docket No. C-CR-88-205-1, U.S.D.C. (W.D., N.C.), October 2–5, 1989, vol. 10 at 2224–26.

7. Barbara Dalley, telephone interview by Suzan Brooks, June 21, 1993.

8. Juror X, telephone interview by Suzan Brooks, September 20, 1993.

9. Catherine Boardman, telephone interview by Suzan Brooks, October 3, 1993.

10. *Id.*

11. *Id.*

12. *Id.*

13. "Bakker Convicted on Fraud Charges," *St. Louis Post-Dispatch,* October 6, 1989 at 1-A (Nexis printout).

14. Barbara Dalley, telephone interview by Suzan Brooks, *supra,* n. 7.

15. James McAlister, telephone interview by Suzan Brooks, May 31, 1994.

16. Juror X, telephone interview by Suzan Brooks, *supra,* n. 8.

17. *Id.*

18. Vaughan, "Diary Shows Bakker Trial as Juror Saw It," *Charlotte Observer,* October 28, 1989 at 27-A (*Observer* computer printout).

19. Barbara Dalley, telephone interview by Suzan Brooks, *supra,* n. 7.

20. Rick Hill, telephone interview by Suzan Brooks, November 24, 1993.

21. *Id.*

22. *Id.*

23. *Id.*

24. *Id.*

25. *Id.*

26. *Id.*

27. Barbara Dalley, telephone interview by Suzan Brooks, *supra,* n. 7.

28. *Id.*

29. Rick Hill, telephone interview by Suzan Brooks, *supra,* n. 20.

30. James McAlister, telephone interview by Suzan Brooks, *supra,* n. 15.
31. Vaughan, *supra,* n. 18.
32. Catherine Boardman, telephone interview by Suzan Brooks, *supra,* n. 9.
33. Juror X, telephone interview by Suzan Brooks, *supra,* n. 8.
34. *Id.*
35. *Id.*
36. *Id.*
37. Barbara Dalley, telephone interview by Suzan Brooks, *supra,* n. 7.
38. *Id.*
39. *Id.*
40. *Id.*
41. *Id.*
42. *Id.*
43. Rick Hill, telephone interview by Suzan Brooks, *supra,* n. 20.
44. James McAlister, telephone interview by Suzan Brooks, *supra,* n. 15.
45. Rick Hill, telephone interview by Suzan Brooks, *supra,* n. 20.

Chapter 22

The Verdict

Moment of Truth

At 11:30 A.M., on Thursday, October 5, 1989, the jury sent Judge Potter its final note—it had reached a verdict and was ready to return to the courtroom. Marshals were immediately dispatched to summon the attorneys, retrieve Jim and Tammy from the second floor, and alert the media. The courthouse erupted in a frenzy as spectators and reporters jostled for seats and the principals positioned themselves. When the dust settled, Judge Potter noticed a large number of Bakker supporters crammed into the benches behind the defense table. He addressed them sternly:

> **Judge Potter:** When the verdict comes in, no matter which way it goes, there had better not be any demonstration of any kind on this side of the room [behind Bakker]. If there is, I'm going to order the marshals to clear the courtroom.[1]

With the courtroom hushed and the emotion of the five-week trial welling in the faces of everyone present, the judge ordered that the jury be brought in. Single file, all twelve took their seats in the jury box. Judge Potter would be the one who would read the verdict.

> **Judge Potter:** Has the jury reached a verdict?
> **The foreperson:** Yes.
> **Judge Potter:** Would you give that to the marshal, please. ***
> **Judge Potter:** In the matter of James O. Bakker, as to counts 1

through 24, the jury finds the defendant guilty. Is that your verdict, so say you all?

([t]he jury indicates in the affirmative.)[2]

Bakker tightly grabbed the table where he was sitting, as one might tense their muscles before a doctor gives them a shot. Otherwise, he remained composed and showed no other outward signs of emotion. Even Tammy Faye, sitting behind him, remained calm.

Harold Bender was the first to speak and he demanded that the judge poll the jury, asking each of them individually whether they agreed with the verdict. Potter did that and, sure enough, it was unanimous.

The judge then thanked the jury for their service.

> **Judge Potter:** You've been through an unusual ordeal. We've had everything in the world happen, I think. Even up to Hugo coming through. *** You certainly have diligently performed your duties. *** I'm sorry it was so long. ***
>
> I don't think we could have had a more attentive, more diligent jury than we did have in this case and we do thank you and appreciate it. *** I'll ask the marshals to escort you out. *** Thank you so much for the time served. I'd like to shake each of you's hand.[3]

The judge then bounded back to the dais to turn to the question of whether he would allow Jim Bakker to remain free for the next three weeks until the date of his sentencing. Jerry Miller argued that Bakker should be jailed during that time because otherwise he would flee, his partners would hide him, and nobody would ever see him again.

Harold Bender called Donna Puckett, Jim Bakker's sister, to the stand in an attempt to convince the judge that Bakker wouldn't try to escape. She was crying and barely able to answer questions.

> **Mr. Bender:** Do you think that there is any possibility that your brother . . . would flee this jurisdiction . . . and not come back and face up to whatever sentence he is facing?
>
> **Ms. Puckett:** No way, no way.

Mr. Bender: If he did, do you think he'd be recognized almost immediately?
Ms. Puckett: I think so, I know so.[4]

Jerry Miller pressed hard to have Bakker jailed immediately.

Mr. Miller: And those people [Bakker's supporters] are sufficiently loyal to him to where they would be motivated to provide him safe houses or hiding houses all over—
Ms. Puckett: No.
Mr. Miller: —All over this country, wouldn't they?
Ms. Puckett: No, no way.[5]

Potter, not surprisingly, was a hard sell.

Judge Potter: The only thing that sticks in my mind, quite honestly, is I saw some thirty-five of these people you called up here, his supporters, and they were so zealous in their defense of Mr. Bakker. They really have what I would call the Jim Jones mentality. I mean, anything he does is all right.
George Davis: Your honor, may I interrupt you, please.
Judge Potter: Yes. You interrupted all along. Go ahead and do it again, Mr. Davis. Go ahead, sir.
Mr. Davis: Well, I hope it doesn't offend you, Judge, for me to represent my client.[6]

At that, George Davis attempted to call Tammy Faye Bakker, still noticeably gasping at Potter's comparison of her husband to Jim Jones, to the stand to testify on Jim's behalf. But the judge disagreed. "I don't need to hear from her because I know she's his wife and she naturally is going to be supportive of Mr. Bakker. I don't think that would serve any purpose at all,"[7] snapped Potter.

But Harold Bender went toe to toe with the judge and kept banging away.

Mr. Bender: [H]e'll be here, he will face up to it. He has a deep faith in the Lord that is going to get him through this no matter what, and he's willing to face up to it. We've talked about it. This is no great shock and surprise to he and his family. . . .[8]

Potter finally caved in, albeit reluctantly. He set Bakker's bond at a quarter of a million dollars, and ordered that the evangelist be taken to a holding cell in the courthouse until his attorneys could return with ten percent of that as surety. Potter then set October 24 as Bakker's sentencing date.

> **Judge Potter:** I'm going to let him go. I don't think that—I'm not so sure that you've submitted clear and convincing evidence, but you're pretty convincing, I guess, Mr. Bender. *** I'm going to require that he do report in person to the probation office in Orlando once a day. . . . [and that he telephone the probation officer on both Saturday and Sunday.] *** I hope Mr. Bakker understands if he does flee, it's going to be even worse for him than it would be otherwise. I still have some doubts.[9]

Bender and Davis spoke briefly with their client and then rushed downtown to raise $25,000 in cash to free him. It would take them three hours to do it.

Tammy Faye went with them out the door of the courthouse and stopped in front of a bank of microphones to offer her reaction to the 400 journalists and spectators who had overtaken the lawn. Without a single tear, she broke into song and warbled, "On Christ the solid rock I stand/All other ground is sinking sand/All other ground is sinking sand."[10] Then she winced and said, "It's not over 'til it's over, I have a strong faith in God and He will not let us down."[11]

As she and the two attorneys pushed their way toward their car, Bakker supporters shouted "God loves you, Tammy," "keep smiling," and "praise Jesus."[12]

A reporter yelled out a question about whether she was going to continue the ministry, and she replied, "Of course, that's what we do."[13]

The Bakker loyalists on the courthouse lawn were horrified. Many held hands and prayed. Others wept openly. "I can't believe all this,"[14] said Florence Tinker of Chester, South Carolina. Her husband, George, was defiant: "Come what may, heaven, hell or high water, Jim Bakker will always be our pastor."[15]

Marjory Grey of Richlands, North Carolina, who herself had thirty-two lifetime partnerships, protested that Potter was biased against Bakker: "The Judge just showed his caliber when he called us all Jim Jones mentalities."[16] Bea Martin, the Bakkers' loyal nanny and housekeeper, was crushed and told everyone, "I know he's not guilty. If Jim has to go to jail, every one of those who gave $1,000 ought to go, because he did it all for us."[17]

Helen Gordon, who had been in the spectators' gallery throughout the trial, was angry: "He didn't get a fair trial. This is not the end. Just the beginning. God's not through yet."[18]

There were a few dissenting voices in the huge crowd. One woman demanded to see the defeated. "I want to see Jim Bakker," she said, "he's the one who stole the money . . . She [Tammy Faye] spent it."[19]

Bakker's brother Norman and sister Donna walked out the front door of the courthouse shaken and overcome with emotion. When they got to their red Taurus parked on the street, they embraced. Norm took his suit jacket off, put both arms on the top of his car, and buried his head. A few minutes later, he went back inside the courthouse to wait with his brother while Tammy and the attorneys found bail money.

The gaggle of reporters was still waiting when Bakker emerged a free man three hours later. He managed a trademark smile for those watching on television and spoke calmly, "I went into the courtroom innocent of the charges against me, and I come out today still innocent."[20] Before turning away to get a grip on what had just happened to him, he quoted a verse from the Bible for the press, "Romans 8:28 says that all things work together for good to those that love God, for those called according to His purpose."[21]

The Reaction across the Country

The jury's verdict was colossal, electrifying news. The television networks interrupted regular programming with bulletins reporting Bakker's guilt. Major newspapers around the nation ran the story on front pages. TV programs such as *Nightline* and *Larry King Live* quickly offered analysis. Everybody was talking about it.

- **Rick Hill, jury foreman:** He was called by God. But eventually the money became too much for him. He got corrupt, and I feel sorry for the man.[22]

- **Deborah Smith, prosecutor:** The message is that you can't lie to people and you can't use the telephone and the mail to lie to people to get them to send you money. It doesn't matter who you are or how well known you are.[23]

- **Tom Ashcroft, United States attorney for North Carolina** who originally indicted Bakker: With today's verdict, reality has finally dawned for Jim Bakker. He refused to behave responsibly of his own accord at PTL, so a jury of his peers imposed responsibility on him in a court of law.[24]

- **Arthur Borden, executive director of the Evangelical Council on Financial Accountability:** All Christian organizations have been hurt by this in some way.[25]

- **Jerry Falwell, Bakker's accuser:** While I am personally sorry for Mr. Bakker, his family and the thousands who have been hurt by the PTL saga, I am pleased that this dark chapter of religious history has concluded.[26]

- **Billy Graham, evangelist:** I am saddened by the Bakkers' personal tragedy, but at the same time, I feel sorry for the many sincere supporters who have also been hurt by this situation. Christians need to get away from the celebrity syndrome and get their eyes off personalities. The only star we should focus on is the bright and morning star, which the Bible says is Christ.[27]

- **Reverend Sam Johnson, Bakker's successor at PTL:** When they announced the verdict, I just became uncontrollable. I wept profusely because of my long tenure and friendship with the parties involved. . . . But I was reminded of the prophet who said, "If you sow the wind, you reap the whirlwind."[28]

- **Rufus Reynolds, retired U.S. bankruptcy judge who presided at the PTL bankruptcy proceedings:** The verdict was no surprise to me or anybody else who knew anything about the situation. . . . You can see what I had to put up with for a year and a half.[29]

- **Roy Grutman, attorney at law:** I hope it closes a wound and people realize this was a guilt personal to Jim Bakker. It reflects on his excesses, his perversities, his badness.[30]

- **Jim Lufts, founder of Fundamentalists Anonymous:** I think the television evangelist industry as it existed three years ago is going to be history at this point.[31]

- **The *Charlotte Observer*, in an editorial:** In soliciting donations from its flock, a preacher may promise eternal life in a celestial city whose streets are paved with gold, and that's none of the law's business. But if he promises an annual free stay in a luxury hotel on Earth, he'd better have the rooms available. *** Jim Bakker will proclaim his innocence 'till Heritage USA's water slide freezes over. Twelve ordinary citizens heard all the facts and decided otherwise. His lawyers will no doubt appeal, but the jury was right.[32]

- **Bea Martin, Bakker nanny and housekeeper:** If he didn't have Jesus, he could not make it. He hasn't lost his Christianity. He's closer to the Lord than he's ever been. Jim is very compassionate. He even loves the prosecutors. He's praying for them.[33]

- **Samuel Cook, Charlotte area resident:** I am a 70-year-old Christian who is appalled . . . by the Jim Bakker hangers-on who still publicly praise him . . . [and] keep yelling about Bakker's innocence. *** Are these people nuts?[34]

- **Jessica Hahn, retired church secretary:** I'm sorry I don't have a song to sing like Tammy, but I know this is God's amazing grace. . . . If nothing else, this proves the little guy can beat the big guy. I'm going to Disneyland.[35]

- **George Davis, who came in second at the trial:** We will appeal this. There is a court in this land we can go to where we'll get justice.[36]

NOTES

1. Trial transcript, *United States of America v. James O. Bakker,* Docket No. C-CR-88-205-1, U.S.D.C. (W.D., N.C.), October 2–5, 1989, vol. 10 at 2223.
    2. *Id.* at 2223–24.
    3. *Id.* at 2226–27.
    4. *Id.* at 2239.
    5. *Id.* at 2241.
    6. *Id.* at 2245–46.
    7. *Id.* at 2246.
    8. *Id.* at 2249.
    9. *Id.* at 2250–51.

10. McClain, "Ending on a High Note Tammy Bakker Says the Ministry Will Continue," *Charlotte Observer,* October 6, 1989 at 14-A (Westlaw printout).

11. *Id.*

12. *Id.*

13. *Id.*

14. Garloch, "Faithful: God's Not Through,'" *Charlotte Observer,* October 6, 1989 at 15-A (Westlaw printout).

15. *Id.*

16. *Id.*

17. *Id.*

18. *Id.*

19. McClain, *supra,* n. 10.

20. Applebome, "Bakker Is Convicted on All Counts; First Felon among TV Evangelists," *New York Times,* October 6, 1989 at 1-A, col. 4.

21. *Id.*

22. "Bakker Convicted on Fraud Charges," *St. Louis Post-Dispatch,* October 6, 1989 at 1-A (Nexis printout).

23. Applebome, *supra,* n. 20.

24. *Id.*

25. *Id.*

26. McClain, "Words of Sadness, Relief," *Charlotte Observer,* October 6, 1989 at 14-A (Westlaw printout).

27. *Id.*

28. *Id.*

29. *Id.*

30. *Id.*

31. *Id.*

32. "Justice for Jim Bakker Fraud, Not Religion, Was the Issue before the Jury," *Charlotte Observer,* October 6, 1989, at ED-A (Westlaw printout).

33. Applebome, *supra,* n. 20.

34. "Letters to the Editor," *Charlotte Observer,* October 13, 1989, at ED-A (Westlaw printout).

35. McClain, *supra,* n. 26.

36. May, "Bakker Guilty of Fleecing His TV Flock of Millions," *Los Angeles Times,* October 6, 1989 at 1-A, col. 5.

Part Three

After the Trial

Chapter 23

Bakker Is Sent to Prison

Jim spent the three weeks leading up to his sentencing planning his return to daytime television. The idea was for him and Tammy to spend their time paying bills and "then we'll go back on television, no matter what."[1] The government calculated they were still bringing in $100,000 a month in contributions to their flagging ministry.[2]

On Sundays, he delivered sermons to nearly a hundred followers at his storefront church in Orlando. From the pulpit, he insisted he was innocent despite the jury's verdict. "God has forgiven me for my sins—I'm not guilty,"[3] he declared. He told parishioners that he was not worried about Judge Potter sentencing him because, "I'm going to keep my faith in God."[4]

Jerry Miller, preparing for the sentencing hearing, saw Bakker as remorseless and unrepentant. "He's going to have to stop running the con at some point and I think this may be the time," he grumbled. "It's time to pay the piper."[5]

At 2:00 P.M. on Tuesday, October 24, 1989, Judge Potter gaveled to order the hearing to determine the punishment he would mete out for Bakker's crimes. The scene in his crowded courtroom was déjà vu, as it had been on the last day of the trial three weeks before. Bakker was there, of course, with his daughter sitting behind him. The attorneys sat erect in their chairs poised to make their last pleas to the court. Reporters, spectators, and the Bakker faithful jammed the gallery. Agents from the FBI, IRS, and Postal Inspection Service who had worked on the government's case watched in silence. Tammy Faye was a no-show, remaining in Orlando with son Jamie.

Potter wasted no time. He listened unengagingly as both sides presented brief arguments. He then made a lengthy speech of his own and threw the book at Bakker. The whole hearing lasted just one hundred minutes and they would be the last one hundred minutes of freedom Jim Bakker would see for a long, long time.

Harold Bender was given the chance to speak first and he startled those in the courtroom by suggesting that the judge should sentence Bakker to five years at Heritage USA to finish building "his vision, his dream and his promise to his partners. Who gets hurt? No one. The partners, the victims are made whole,"[6] he argued. It was an alluring idea. If Bakker's fraud was in diverting partners' money and denying them vacation benefits, wasn't this the only way those people would ever have a chance to see anything for their contributions?

Of course, sentencing Bakker to five years in the presidential suite at the Grand was surely not Potter's idea of punishment, and Bender's offer of such a creative alternative was quickly spurned.

Bender then brandished a stack of letters from Bakker supporters, all of which asked for compassion in the judge's sentencing. "Consider the whole man—James O. Bakker," Bender implored, "consider what he has done for these people. Consider the love and the compassion and the vision he has had. These people are not the followers of Jim Jones," he persisted. "They are good, decent people who found something in this man and his ministry that touched their lives . . . [and Bakker] has touched them with his life, his love and his care for people."[7]

Bender concluded, "allow this defendant the benefit of the court's compassion and mercy."[8] Fat chance.

Jerry Miller didn't share the same view of Bakker, and was seething at Bender's attempt to sugarcoat his client and dust him off for sentencing day. He spoke passionately. Pointing to

Bakker, Miller told Judge Potter, "This man is a common criminal. The only thing uncommon about him was the method he chose and the vehicle he used to perpetrate his fraud. He was motivated by greed, selfishness and a lust for power."[9]

"This was a crime that was not spontaneous," the prosecutor argued, "Jim Bakker—minute by minute, hour by hour, day by day, year by year—consciously made the decision to defraud people."[10] Strong words.

Miller described Bakker as "the most brazen con man who has ever touched the western district of North Carolina" and "the man who would be God at PTL." Don't let him go, said Miller, or "he's going to be right back at it as soon as he gets the chance."[11]

Judge Potter then gave Bakker a chance to speak on his own behalf, and Bakker solemnly responded: "I am deeply sorry for the people that have been hurt, the partners, the people that have worked at Heritage USA. And I have sinned and I have made mistakes. But never in my life did I ever intend to defraud anyone."[12]

Potter disagreed. It seems that he had been receiving mail from some of those who sent Bakker money over the years, and he read one aloud that he thought best summarized the crime. It was from a seventy-six-year-old woman in New Jersey who was living on Social Security. Her donations had been squandered, and she wrote the judge that "It would be a great injustice if he got off scot free. He shows, nor has, no humility. All that money has changed Jim and Tammy. They should be off the air for good."[13] The judge was willing to do more than that.

Potter set Harold Bender and Jim Bakker straight, by rejecting their spin on the case and lecturing them that this really was a "massive fraud"[14] that had to be severely punished. The judge then highlighted the evidence in the case of the millions of dollars in bonuses that the Bakkers had received from PTL over the years and the luxurious homes they had purchased from one end of the country to the other. As the judge saw it, Bakker had been a greedy, self-indulgent man-child on a never ending shopping spree financed by the offerings of innocent people who thought they were building Christian hotels. For that, he would go to prison.

Potter, his voice strong, said Bakker wouldn't change. The jury's verdict had not changed him. In fact, he was still sending out fund-raising appeals from his new church in Orlando. The judge pulled out a letter Jim and Tammy had recently mailed out which begged for money with the words: "We never seem to have enough [money] . . . in fact we are getting further and further behind."[15] As the judge saw it, Bakker just didn't get it. His lack of remorse proved he just didn't understand that it was wrong to keep soliciting money from his flock after he had been caught with both hands in the cookie jar.

Potter was going to take care of it. He hadn't earned the nickname "Maximum Bob" for nothing. When he got to the point of announcing the sentence, his words concealed nothing: "Those of us who do have a religion are sick of being saps for money-grubbing preachers. . . ."[16]

And with that, he sentenced Bakker to forty-five years in prison and slapped on a $500,000 fine.

Instead of allowing the forty-nine-year-old Bakker to remain free long enough to get his personal affairs in order before reporting to prison, the judge ordered federal marshals to immediately seize him and take him into custody. He was quickly handcuffed. Leg irons were placed on his feet. Potter ordered that he be transported at once to the medium security federal prison in Talladega, Alabama, where he would await a decision from the Department of Justice as to permanent placement.

Bakker showed no outward emotion, but his nineteen-year-old daughter immediately burst into tears. Within the hour, at exactly 4:22 P.M., federal marshals led Bakker through the back parking lot of the courthouse as hundreds of spectators watched, many crying in disbelief. He was placed in the back seat of a brown Chevrolet Impala with bars to cage him for the seven-hour drive to Talladega. He arrived there late that night.

As Bakker drove off, Bender told reporters: "I have just spent a few minutes with Reverend Bakker. He is in as good a spirits as he can be under the circumstances. He is, of course, concerned about the length of sentence as we all are. But he still has a strong faith, and he will come through."[17]

Jerry Miller was satisfied that Potter's stiff sentence "sends a message"[18] that evangelists can't use TV to defraud people. Jessica Hahn said from her home in Hollywood that she thought the judge had been too lenient "but at least it's a start."[19]

Some chortled in delight that Bakker had been bent in half by the judge. Comedians had a field day.

But many of Bakker's supporters weren't so sure. On the courthouse lawn, Mervell Mullen scoffed, "They don't treat murderers like they've treated him."[20]

An op-ed piece authored by Clarence Page in the *Chicago Tribune* expressed dismay.

> What did Bakker do wrong? A jury convicted him of fraud and conspiracy counts essentially for selling more vacations at his Heritage USA Christian resort than he could provide. In other words, Bakker is going to jail for overbooking. If that's a felony, every airline employee who ever bumped someone with a reservation or cancelled a flight without warning should go to jail.
>
> Bakker was "motivated by greed, by selfishness, by lust for power," said prosecutor Jerry Miller. Well, so are quite a few Washington politicians; yet they get elected again and again. It is sad to see the poor and elderly (viewers over age 50 make up the bulk of the televangelists' audiences) bilked of their savings. But by whose standards are they being "bilked"? No one holds a gun to their heads and forces them to pay up.
>
> The government can do only so much to protect people from themselves before it has stepped over the thin line separating the church and the state. *** People are entitled to waste their own money the way they see fit.
>
> I am certain we're coming down on Bakker too hard. When Jim Bakker was sentenced to 45 years in prison, I actually felt sorry for him.[21]

Regardless, the reaction was swift in Orlando. Taped to the back door of the Bakkers' makeshift strip mall studio was this sign:

THE TELEVISION MINISTRY IS ON HOLD UNTIL FURTHER NOTICE.

They got that right.

NOTES

1. Banks, "Bakker Resumes Orlando Pulpit, Says TV Soon," *Charlotte Observer,* October 17, 1989 at 16-B (Westlaw printout).

2. Shepard and Wright, "Bakker Gets 45 Years, Ex-PTL Leader Fined $500,000, Taken to Alabama Prison," *Charlotte Observer,* October 25, 1989 at 1-A (Westlaw printout).

3. Banks, *supra,* n. 1.

4. Preston, "Bakker to Be Sentenced Tuesday," UPI [wire story], October 21, 1989, BC Cycle.

5. *Id.*

6. Shepard and Wright, *supra,* n. 2.

7. *Id.*

8. Defendant's Motion to Be Sentenced under the Guidelines of the Sentencing Commission, filed October 20, 1989, *United States of America v. James O. Bakker,* Docket No. C-CR-88-205-1, U.S.D.C. (W.D., N.C.).

9. Shepard and Wright, *supra,* n. 2.

10. "Bakker Begins Prison Term," UPI [wire story], October 25, 1989, BC Cycle.

11. Shepard and Wright, *supra,* n. 2.

12. *Id.*

13. *Id.*

14. *Id.*

15. *Id.*

16. *Id.*

17. Applebome, "Bakker Sentenced to 45 Years for Fraud in His TV Ministry," *New York Times,* October 25, 1989 at 1-A, col. 4.

18. May, "Bakker Gets 45 Years in Prison," *Los Angeles Times,* October 25, 1989 at 1-A, col. 5.

19. Schmich, "Bakker Gets 45 Years and Fine of $500,000," *Chicago Tribune,* October 25, 1989 at 1-A (Nexis printout).

20. Applebome, *supra,* n. 17.

21. Page, "Jim Bakker's Sentence Is too Harsh," *Chicago Tribune,* October 29, 1989 at 3-P (Nexis printout).

Chapter 24

The Appeal

A Long Ride in a Brown Impala

Jim Bakker, wearing a bright orange jumpsuit, began his sentence at the federal prison in Talladega, Alabama. Within a few days, he was transferred to the sprawling federal correctional institution in Rochester, Minnesota, to serve his forty-five years. A medium security facility, the Rochester prison is one of three within the federal system operated as a major medical center. Of the nearly 800 inmates, half receive psychiatric or medical care. Bakker was placed in the general population—not the psychiatric unit despite the mental collapse he had suffered during his trial. He was there to do serious time.

It was his darkest hour. At the bankrupt Heritage USA, now a ghost town, vandals threw cinnamon buns on the sidewalks and defaced buildings with graffiti. His eighty-three-year-old mother, Furnia Bakker, told reporters in a telephone interview from her home that the forty-five-year sentence broke her heart. "I've cried so much. I didn't know it was possible for a person to cry this much. I probably won't be alive by the time he comes out,"[1] she said. And echoing the anger of many of Bakker's supporters, his mother expressed frustration with Judge Potter: "The Judge is so mean. He's just unfair. He was so prejudiced against Jim."[2]

The firm belief among Bakker loyalists who had observed the trial from the courtroom gallery was that Bakker had not received a fair trial.[3] But Potter's shocking sentence was the final straw. Enraged, they vowed to appeal and prove to a higher court that Jim had been wronged by the judge.

With her husband behind bars, Tammy became the field general in the charismatics' battle against Potter. The loyal partners rallied around her and quickly contributed $15,000 to purchase copies of the mammoth 4,000-page trial transcript so that the appeal process could begin.

Since Bakker was convicted in the federal district trial court in North Carolina, there were only two courts higher that could overturn the decision—the United States Court of Appeals for the Fourth Judicial Circuit and the U.S. Supreme Court. There are eleven Circuit Courts of Appeals, located geographically throughout the country. Sitting in Richmond, Virginia, the Fourth Circuit heard cases from states along the eastern seaboard. It was to Richmond that the Bakker brigades would march.

Preparing the Appeal

Bakker had surely shown no instinct for self-survival or legal intuition before or during his trial. The question was whether that would change now.

George Davis did not remain on the team. Jim retained Harold Bender, however, because of the Charlotte attorney's continuing presence in that city. Bakker had been convicted there and it would always be judges in that courthouse who would have continuing jurisdiction over his case. He needed a Charlotte player and one the judges knew. But Bakker also realized he needed to bring in additional legal muscle, and from his prison cell he tried to enlist some major heat.

He struck out with his first choice, Miami attorney Milton Grusmark, who burst onto the scene with a flurry. Grusmark demanded an early, preliminary hearing before the Court of Appeals in which he argued passionately that Bakker should be released on bond during the full appeal cycle. He told the judges that Bakker's trial was "a circus" and that "there was no excuse" for Judge Potter not sequestering the jury during the trial to make sure they didn't see any news coverage that might have influenced them.[4]

But Grusmark's flamboyance caught the attention of the media and, in checking his background, the *Miami Herald* and the *Charlotte Observer* found that his license to practice law had been suspended in Florida. He had received three reprimands from the Florida Supreme Court prior to that. The suspension was because the seventy-year-old Grusmark had overcharged a client, and the earlier suspensions were imposed because he failed to return money to clients. The irony of it and the contrast to Bakker's own crimes was too much for even Bakker to endure. Not only was Grusmark history, the Court of Appeals denied his request to allow Bakker out during the year that it would take for the case to be perfected on appeal.[5]

Despite that shaky start, Bakker then recruited Houston attorneys Donald Ervin and Brian Wice. Their job would be to draft the fifty-five-page appellate brief setting out the reasons that Bakker's conviction should be overturned.

To argue on Bakker's behalf at the Court of Appeals, the televangelist finally found a legal heavyweight to fight for him—Professor Alan Dershowitz of Harvard who had master-minded Claus von Bulow's stunning appeal overturning his conviction for murder a few years before. Dershowitz, the attorney of last resort and appellate god, who has also repre-sented such celebrity clients as Leona Helmsley, Mike Tyson, and O.J. Simpson, would bring some much needed fire to Bakker's sagging cause. Bakker was lucky to have him.

And he was proud of it, too. "Alan has agreed to be the voice on my appeal. He will make the presentation of our case,"[6] said Bakker from prison. Jim's supporters had made it possible by contributing the $20,000 fee Dershowitz reportedly charged.

The hearing before the court in Richmond was scheduled for October 30, 1990. Dershowitz, Ervin, and Wice would have almost a year to prepare.

The three lawyers briefed Jim and Tammy on their strategy for the appeal. First, they would argue that Bakker's constitu-tional right to a fair trial was violated when Potter refused to grant the request for a change of venue and move the proceed-ings outside Charlotte. What they found troubling was the years of publicity negative to Bakker which had permeated the city. They doubted that a truly impartial jury could ever be impaneled. On top of that, Ervin emphasized that "really and truly it was just a circus"[7] and the atmosphere inside and outside the courtroom was prejudicial to Bakker. They said he never enjoyed a presumption of innocence.

The attorneys also believed that Potter had watered down his instructions to the jury on the pivotal question of criminal intent to make it easier to convict. And, that several of Potter's evidentiary rulings had wrongly deprived Bakker of the chance to introduce evidence on his own behalf, including the charts that he made showing the number of rooms at Heritage.

Beyond that, the severity of the shocking forty-five-year sentence would be hit hard by the three as an example of the harshness with which Judge Potter handled Bakker throughout the trial.

They were convinced they had a good shot. "It's a case that should be reversed,"[8] Ervin said repeatedly. Brimming, Tammy told a churchfull in Florida that "our lawyer felt we have a 77% chance, praise the Lord."[9] The congregation burst into applause and shouting. In his cell, Jim waited anxiously: "I pray God will speak to the judges."[10]

The Oral Arguments in Richmond— Dershowitz for the Defense

The hearing was held on Tuesday, October 30, 1990 in the ornate federal courthouse in Richmond. Three seasoned federal appellate judges presided, and alone they would decide the case. They were Circuit Judge James Harvie Wilkinson of Charlottesville, Virginia, 46, appointed to the federal bench by President Ronald Reagan in 1984; Circuit Judge James Dickson Phillips, Jr., of Durham, North Carolina, 67, appointed in 1978 by President Jimmy Carter; and Senior Circuit Judge John D. Butzner, Jr., of Richmond, Virginia, 72, named to the court in 1967 by President Lyndon B. Johnson.

In the parlance of entertainers who perform in nightclubs, this was not an easy room. Those judges were tough, and Dershowitz had his work cut out for him.

Dershowitz went straight for Judge Potter's jugular, strategizing that the lengthy sentence and Potter's apparent hostility toward Bakker were weak links in the evangelist's conviction. "This is a judge who doesn't understand the difference between a year and a decade, who always adds a zero to the sentence other judges would impose,"[11] Dershowitz argued. He calculated Bakker's sentence was, incredibly, longer than the average sentence for rape or murder. Beyond that, what particularly ignited the professor's wrath was what he saw as Potter's injection of his own religious beliefs into the case. That, he told the panel with unmistakably strong feeling, was as wrong as it could possibly be.

And, in terms of Bakker's guilt or innocence, Dershowitz faulted Potter for instructing the jury in such a way that they could not find the evangelist innocent even though he had acted in good faith, not intending to defraud anyone.

It was impossible to read the reaction of the judges as Dershowitz spoke, but his co-counsel were impressed by the oratory. Ervin said it was "like watching a terrific maestro in front of an orchestra."[12] Wice called him "mesmerizing," adding: "He looks like a schlep, wearing suits he could have bought in Filene's Basement, woolen socks, and shoes—I don't know if they still call them Earth shoes. But the judges hung on every word he had to say and bought what he was selling."[13]

The Court Issues Its Opinion— A Mixed Blessing for Bakker

On February 11, 1991, more than three months after hearing oral argument in the case, the three-judge Fourth Circuit panel reached its final decision. The court affirmed Bakker's conviction for fraud and conspiracy, but threw out his forty-five-year sentence. The result was that Bakker would remain in prison but that the case would be sent back to a new federal judge in North Carolina to review all the evidence and decide what sentence would be fair.

The good news for Bakker was that the appellate court judges found that his constitutional right to due process was violated by Judge Potter at the sentencing hearing. Specifically, it was Potter's lecture to Bakker on the day he sentenced the evangelist that drew the foul. "He had no thought whatever about his victims and those of us who do have a religion are ridiculed as being saps from money-grubbing preachers or priests,"[14] is what Potter had said.

That was wrong, the appellate judges held, because it created an impression "of the bench as a pulpit from which judges announce their personal sense of religiosity and simultaneously punish defendants for offending it."[15] Characterizing Potter's comments as "too intemperate to be ignored,"[16] the judges concluded "that the imposition of a lengthy prison term here may have reflected the fact that the court's own sense of religious propriety had somehow been betrayed."[17] That kind of unconscionable judicial behavior would not be tolerated. So Bakker would be given a chance for a lighter sentence when a different judge would look at the case in a few months.

But the bad news for Bakker was that the Court of Appeals upheld his conviction on all twenty-four counts of fraud and conspiracy. In ten detailed pages, the court rejected each of the four major arguments Dershowitz had made on Bakker's behalf. It had been the amalgam of all four that Dershowitz argued deprived Bakker of a fair trial, but the appellate court found just the opposite after reviewing the case. "We conclude, therefore, that Bakker's trial was free of reversible error,"[18] the judges wrote.

The judges rejected Dershowitz's argument that Bakker was deprived of an impartial jury because of the venomous publicity that had swirled around him in Charlotte between his 1987 resignation from PTL and his 1989 trial. The court reasoned that the "sheer volume of publicity alone does not deny a defendant a fair trial,"[19] and that most of the news coverage about Bakker during that time was simply straightforward factual reporting on events that were occurring. Noting Bakker's appearances on *Nightline, Sally Jessie Raphael,* and his own new TV show, the court observed "the source of much of the publicity in this case was Bakker himself who . . . engaged in a calculated media campaign to deny any wrongdoing and regain control of the PTL. . . ."[20] They didn't think he should be allowed to do that and later claim that he couldn't get a fair trial because of all the publicity.

In addition, the court was convinced that Judge Potter sufficiently questioned prospective jurors during the formal voir dire process to make sure that anyone unalterably prejudiced against Bakker would not sit on the jury. The jury that Bakker eventually got was an impartial one, the court found, despite the fact that Judge Potter had refused to ask potential jurors some questions Bakker wanted put to them. [Bakker wanted the jurors to be asked: Do you believe in miracles? And, would you be offended by someone blaming the Devil?]

The court also tersely rejected the argument that Bakker was deprived of his right to effective assistance of counsel when Potter refused to grant his attorneys a continuance on the day that he returned to Charlotte from Butner. At that time, Harold Bender had asked for a five-day continuance in order to "reestablish the attorney-client relationship."[21] The reason was that Bakker had been locked up in Butner for a week and unable to assist his attorneys in the case. The judges thought that argument was absurd because Bakker was coherent during his stay at Butner and his attorneys could have driven over and spent all the time they wanted with him. Beyond that, not lost on the court was the fact that "the defense had nine months prior to trial to prepare"[22] and they should have been fully trial ready on the first day of the trial.

Third, the court dismissed criticism about two pieces of evidence in the trial. It found that Potter was right in allowing the government to show videotapes of excerpts from Bakker television programs rather than the shows in their entirety. The eight hours of government tapes had been culled from 200 hours of actual broadcasts, and the court said that it wasn't necessary for the jury to sit through 200 solid hours of *PTL Club* tapes in order to get the gist of what Bakker was saying about lifetime partnerships.

And, as far as Potter refusing to let Bakker use his own charts during his testimony, the appellate judges saw nothing wrong in that, either. They found the charts misleading in that they showed partners accepting campsites instead of hotel rooms when, in fact, "Bakker admitted that he did not so notify prospective partners."[23] Because of that, he should not have been allowed to use those charts and Potter had correctly called him on it.

The fourth contention urged on the court by Dershowitz was that Judge Potter had not correctly instructed the jury on the law to apply in the case. But the appellate court reviewed what Potter had said and found that he had not strayed from the instructions that are commonly given in criminal trials. The court noted that Potter had told the jury that "the government must establish beyond a reasonable doubt that the defendant acted with a specific intent to defraud."[24] And, that "one who expresses an opinion honestly held by him is not chargeable with fraudulent intent even though his opinion is erroneous or his belief mistaken."[25] The judges found those instructions had given Bakker every chance with the jury, and that it was not because of their wording that the jury had found him guilty. He was doomed by the evidence that was piled up against him during five weeks of hammering by the prosecutors and their witnesses.

So, Bakker's conviction would stand but not his forty-five-year sentence. Even a mixed bag like that looked better than what Bakker had been handed by Judge Potter, and his supporters rejoiced.

Reaction to the Appellate Court's Ruling

- **Alan Dershowitz, law professor and lead attorney:** A gigantic victory. Bakker is entitled to be sentenced before a judge free of that kind of bigotry. *** I hope this sends a message to judges about religious tolerance. This was an outrageous sentence. He [Bakker] was really being punished because he had a different religious perspective.

  Jim is thrilled. Tammy says this is a great victory for Christians. I told her it was a Jew that did it, so let's call it a great victory for religious freedom in America. She agreed.[26]

- **Tammy Faye Bakker, prison widow:** I'm just delighted. Needless to say, our family is grateful and excited. *** I talked to my husband, and the whole prison was excited for him. He was in his non-smoking class, and they broke in and said, "Jim, Jim, you've won your appeal!"[27]

• **George Davis, former Bakker counsel:** I never doubted from the moment he was sentenced that it would be reversed.[28]

• **The *Chicago Tribune*, editorializing:** It was a commendable decision. Every criminal is probably also a sinner. But it is the business of the courts to sentence criminals, not punish sinners. And judges must not be allowed to forget that.[29]

• **Jerry Nims, former Moral Majority president and Falwell ally who took over Heritage USA after Bakker's resignation:** [To let Jim Bakker go] would be like turning Caligula loose in Disney World. He stole millions from people who trusted him . . . and he should have the same sentence as a bank robber.[30]

• **Don Hardister, whom Bakker employed for twelve years as his bodyguard:** If he gets out soon, that is scary. Jim will hit the ground running. Once they get back on TV, the Bakkers will have a record following, far bigger than before. It will be awesome for Orlando—Jim Bakker and Mickey Mouse as lifetime partners![31]

A Second Bite at the Apple—
Bakker's Resentencing Hearing

Undoubtedly the most amazing reaction of all to the appellate court's decision was that of the principal in the case, Jim Bakker himself. Bakker told me that it was only after reading the opinion that he understood for the first time "what I have been convicted of."[32]

That realization prompted him to pen a desperate letter to Alan Dershowitz on May 21, 1991 from his prison cell in Rochester. His purpose in writing was to arm Dershowitz with arguments for the resentencing hearing, and to offer his own more studied reaction to the evidence that convicted him in the first place. "Until then, I never really understood what the crime was or how they claimed I committed it,"[33] explained Bakker. But as he carefully took apart the appellate court decision, his focus sharpened for the first time in years and he engaged himself in developing a defense strategy.

This is what he wrote Dershowitz:

I am so frustrated at not being able to get people to look at the facts. If all the Grand lifetime partners came to Heritage USA in one year, we could have housed them! The PTL members knew and were informed often everyone could not come to Heritage USA at the same time. Reservations were based on room availability. How could the government say that partners could not get rooms at Heritage USA when, from January 1985 to July 1987, Heritage USA had 125,091 vacant rooms at the Grand Hotel and Heritage Inn alone!

Those working so hard to destroy me had tried to say our lifetime partner program was time-share. [But I said on television on] September 25, 1984, 'this is not time-share. You don't have a guaranteed time of the year. You come when you can book it in. . . .'

To my knowledge, every brochure about lifetime partners said, 'this gift is for the ministry' or 'worldwide ministry of PTL.' Every receipt said PTL had the right to use the gift where needed.

I know if we had full access to the PTL library, we could prove our innocence of all government charges.

The government has accused us of stealing $3.7 million dollars over a five-year period. What they don't say is that this was our salary, bonuses and benefits over that five-year period. Tammy and I paid fifty percent to sixty percent of our income to taxes. Another fact that is not well-known is that Tammy and I donated almost one hundred percent of our royalties from our books, records, tapes, etc. For a three-year period, our donated royalties amounted to $8 million. How could we have stolen $3.7 million . . . when we gave PTL . . . $8 million in royalties that we chose not to receive?

In one year alone (1986), our daughter's recording of her music made $1.6 million for the ministry of PTL. The income to the ministry that our daughter generated in 1986 more than paid for all remuneration for our entire family.

I know it sounds like I am trying to justify what the Board paid me, but I feel that I earned my income. I would have worked for nothing as I was doing what I thought was the will of God.

Someday, I know the truth will set me free.[34]

Bakker's Resentencing

The two-day resentencing hearing was scheduled for the end of August 1991. The case was assigned to newly appointed federal district court judge Graham Mullen, who occupied a court-room one floor above that of Maximum Bob Potter in the

Charlotte federal courthouse. Mullen, 51, who had practiced corporate and real estate law in Gastonia, North Carolina, for twenty-one years before being appointed to the bench by President Bush in 1990, had a reputation as a smart and meticulous judge.

Since the hearing was so many months away, Harold Bender attempted to obtain Bakker's release from prison pending the hearing. Government prosecutors resisted, claiming that Bakker might very easily jump bail and never be seen or heard from again. On March 6, Judge Mullen decided that Bakker should stay in Rochester. He wrote, "Combined with Mr. Bakker's previously demonstrated susceptibility to aberrant behavior in stressful situations, prevents this court from concluding that the defendant is clearly and convincingly not a flight risk. . . ."[35] The government had argued that if Bakker were freed from prison, extremist followers could hide him in an underground railroad from one state to the next to elude the FBI and that Jim would end up essentially as chaplain for the A-Team in Los Angeles.

Right. And you are going to be able to keep two people like Jim and Tammy Bakker under wraps or in disguises for the rest of their lives. Like those two would want to live a life on the lam, as fugitives.

So, Bakker went back to his prison routine cleaning toilets and making ceramic mugs for the next few months. He was permitted to return to Charlotte for the August hearing so that he could personally plead with the judge.

What transpired in that hearing August 22 and 23, 1991, in the Charlotte courthouse that held such bad memories for Bakker, surprised many observers. It surprised Bakker himself. For Dershowitz took a tack with the judge different from that his client had urged from prison. Rather than portray Bakker as a choirboy who had done nothing wrong at all at Heritage USA, Dershowitz offered a less flattering perspective.

The courtroom scene was different in two major respects from twenty-two months before when Bakker was convicted. Much was also the same, including the presence of the energetic and well-prepared prosecution team of Deborah Smith and

Jerry Miller. They would take five hours presenting their case that Bakker deserved every inch of the forty-five-year sentence he was originally handed. Harold Bender, for the defense, was there again. Jim Bakker, brought into the courtroom in hand-cuffs and leg irons, sat passively at the defense table. His father, Raleigh, sat behind him. The gallery was filled with reporters and Bakker supporters. Glaringly, however, Bakker's case this time was argued by one of the nation's experts in defending celebrities charged with crimes—Dershowitz. And, there was a new sheriff in town—Potter was out, Mullen was in, and the hand on that gavel was a much gentler one.

The hearing got off to a dramatic start on Thursday when Professor Dershowitz made the surprising statement that he would guarantee that if Bakker were paroled, he would never raise money on television again. Dershowitz described Bakker that day as contrite, fully accepting responsibility for what happened. He told Mullen that Bakker "made serious mistakes, but they were not calculated."[36]

Dershowitz also offered a harsh assessment of the government's case, beginning with what he characterized as the wildly inflated contention that Bakker had committed a $158 million fraud. He emphasized that, except for the small fraction spent on Bakker's salary and bonuses, the millions raised were spent legitimately at Heritage. He saw Bakker as having "a tiger by the tail"[37] that could not be stopped. Forced to raise so many millions of dollars each month to keep the PTL television programs on the air and Heritage USA up and running, the whole fund-raising operation spun "out of control"[38] during the offering of the lifetime partnerships.

Dershowitz characterized Bakker as "unsophisticated"[39] in finance and business, and a person who on television "talked too much, too often."[40] Because of that, things at Heritage eventually imploded and the whole bubble burst under the financial pressure that drove the fund-raising cycle. Dershowitz acknowledged that people were hurt and that Bakker should pay. But his sentence should be no more than from three years to twelve years.

The stunning Dershowitz approach left many Bakker loyalists startled and uneasy. In prayer sessions on the courthouse lawn during breaks in the proceedings, they worried about how the prosecutors would respond. One group of partners formed a circle, held hands, and prayed for God to invoke a "spirit of confusion for the prosecuting attorneys, that they will not be able to tell the lies they told [at the trial two years before]."[41] Helen Reeves of Charleston, South Carolina, told reporters outside the courthouse that "the majority of partners believe it was the bankruptcy court, not Mr. Bakker, that defrauded us."[42]

The prosecutors, however, were armed to the teeth and ready to fight to keep Bakker behind bars. They wanted Mullen to reimpose the forty-five-year sentence Potter socked him with. In five full hours of argument, they showed Mullen the same graphs and copies of letters and memos that they had introduced into evidence at Jim's 1989 trial showing how the money was raised and spent at Heritage. They played an hour-long video of excerpts of Bakker's fund-raising showing him crying on the air in pleading with viewers to send him whatever they could. They emphasized how Bakker had spent millions on himself, languishing in the lap of luxury. Smith described him as a "successful con man"[43] who "used his talents to feather his own nest (while) destroying nest eggs across the country."[44]

She told Judge Mullen: "This is the largest single mail fraud prosecution in the history of the nation. It's very important that this court's sentence reflect that."[45] They portrayed Bakker as a master white collar criminal who to that day was unrepentant about his crimes and who must be given "significant jail time . . . to deter others."[46] Their idea of a fair and appropriate sentence was between thirty and seventy years.

But Bakker himself had the last word and he stood to speak directly to Judge Mullen. Noticeably, his appearance had changed from two years before. He had lost weight, appeared gaunt, and didn't have the chance to shave the night before. He had spent the night in the Mecklenburg County Jail where, ironically, the only bar of soap in the place was one that had been taken from the Heritage Grand Hotel and still had the PTL imprint on it. The path that bar of soap had traveled paralleled that of its creator. But now he was before yet another federal judge pouring out his heart in search of some compassion.

This was his chance. After shaking his head in disbelief while the government played its videotape, he would now be able to speak for himself. With wife Tammy Faye, daughter Tammy Sue, and the rest of his family sitting behind him he spoke emotionally for six minutes, bringing tears to the eyes of his supporters in the courtroom.

He did not admit that he was guilty of the crimes for which he was convicted, but he tried to bite the bullet. "I chose to accept full responsibility for the actions for which I am now being sentenced," he said. "I do not blame anyone else or minimize my responsibility as pastor and president of Heritage USA."[47]

> I failed so many people that trusted me, my own church congregation, this community, my partners, the church world as a whole, myself and my God and my dear family.
>
> Your honor, I am deeply and seriously remorseful for my moral failures and for the hurt I have caused so many people.
>
> Prison is a sad world. It's the land of the living dead for me. It's not just strip searches. It's separation from family and loved ones.[48]

He spoke emotionally about his family. He thanked Tammy Faye for sticking with him through good times and bad including "a fifteen minute affair a decade ago."[49] He explained how much he missed his fifteen-year-old son, Jamie, "who needs a father."[50] And his grandson, Jonathan, whom "I've never held."[51] He concluded with these words, "I ask all that I have hurt, please forgive me."[52]

Judge Mullen was ready to decide the case. Within just a few minutes he announced that, given all the evidence in the case upon which the jury found Bakker guilty, he should be sentenced to a prison term of eighteen years. While that was far less lenient than Bakker's attorneys were hoping for, the judge did give Bakker a break by nullifying the $500,000 fine that Potter had imposed two years before. But still, it was a shock as federal marshals again placed handcuffs and leg irons on Bakker there in the courtroom for his return trip to Minnesota. Bakker quickly turned around and reached over the railing to hug his wife, kiss his daughter, and shake hands with his father. After that, he was quickly led away.

The reaction, to be expected, varied. Walking out of the courthouse, Tammy Faye told reporters: "I am understandably very sad today. I was hopeful Jim could come home sooner."[53] Billy Graham, who visited Bakker in prison in Rochester, thought eighteen years was too much. "I thought that was an awfully heavy sentence for that when you see people like Milken and Boesky . . . getting lighter sentences,"[54] he said.

Eighteen years was harsh. Sentencing statistics gathered by the *New York Times* showed that prison terms exceeding ten years are mostly reserved for second-degree murder, possession with intent to distribute one hundred pounds or more of cocaine, and aggravated rape of a child under twelve years old.[55]

Jessica Hahn, still dependable for a sound bite on Bakker, took a different view: "[If he had been freed] the first thing he's going to do is get out his mailing list. He's a genius in marketing. And most geniuses are crazy."[56]

The *Atlanta Journal and Constitution,* editorializing, took a middle ground: "An 18-year prison sentence is still one hard kick in the pants, but it is more closely proportioned to convicted televangelist Jim Bakker's crime than the original 45-year doom pronounced for him."[57]

That newspaper offered further analysis which would prove food for thought over the next twelve months as Bakker's supporters cast about for anything they could use in keeping the legal fires burning.

> Bakker's swindle, though notorious because it was carried out on television, is nothing next to the predations of assorted Wall Street sharpies who have been bundled off to lesser prison terms, and the preacher, caught in a momentum of excesses, seems to have conned himself almost as much as others.
>
> The original sentencing judge . . . appeared to be sending Bakker off for 45 years as much because Bakker is kind of a jerk as because he is a crook.[58]

NOTES

1. "Bakker Begins Prison Term," UPI [wire story], October 25, 1989, BC Cycle.

2. *Id.*

3. Complaint of Judicial Conduct filed by Joe E. Haviland, *United States of America v. James O. Bakker,* Docket 89-5687, U.S. Court of Appeals for the Fourth Circuit, filed December 15, 1989.

4. "Bakker's Release Sought, Attorney Cites Flaws in Trial," *Charlotte Observer,* AP, November 2, 1989 at 1-B (Westlaw printout).

5. *Id.*

6. Preston, "Dershowitz Joins Bakker Defense," UPI [wire story], June 20, 1990, BC Cycle.

7. Banks, "Lawyer Optimistic He Can Get Bakker Out of Prison," *Orlando Sentinel Tribune,* September 13, 1990 at 1-B (Nexis printout).

8. *Id.*

9. "Tammy Bakker Hires Appeals Lawyer," *Washington Times,* December 22, 1989 at 6-B (Nexis printout).

10. "Bakker Lawyers File Appeal of Conviction," UPI [wire story], June 18, 1990, BC Cycle.

11. Margolick, "At the Bar; Dershowitz Wows 'em Again! (Is there no escaping this guy?)," *New York Times,* February 15, 1991 at 6-B, col. 1.

12. *Id.*

13. *Id.*

14. *U.S. v. Bakker,* 925 F.2d 728, 740 (4th Cir. 1991).

15. *Id.*

16. *Id.* at 741.

17. *Id.*

18. *Id.* at 738.

19. *Id.* at 732.

20. *Id.* at 733.

21. *Id.* at 735.

22. *Id.*

23. *Id.* at 737.

24. *Id.* at 738.

25. *Id.*

26. Marx, "Jim and Tammy Faye Bakker Cry Hallelujah at the Chance His Prison Term Will Be Cut," *People,* March 4, 1991 at 40; Marshall, "Bakker's Sentence Overturned, but Conviction Upheld," UPI [wire story], February 12, 1991, BC Cycle; Savage, "Bakker 45-Year Term Is Upset; Verdict Upheld," *Los Angeles Times,* February 13, 1991 at 1-A, col. 3.

27. Marx, *id;* James, "Bakker's 45-Year Prison Term Set Aside," *New York Times,* February 13, 1991 at 6-B, col. 1.

28. Savage, *supra,* n. 26.

29. "Jim Bakker's Sins and Sentence," *Chicago Tribune,* February 18, 1991 at 8-E (Nexis printout).

30. Marx, *supra,* n. 26.

31. *Id.*

32. Jim Bakker, interview by author, in Rochester, Minnesota, October 31, 1992.

33. *Id.*

34. Jim Bakker, letter to Alan Dershowitz, May 21, 1991.

35. "Judge Refuses to Release Bakker Pending Resentencing," UPI [wire story], March 6, 1991, BC Cycle.

36. Zelenko, "Bakker Renouncing TV Fund-Raising If Jail Term Cut: Lawyer," Reuters [wire story], August 22, 1991, AM Cycle.

37. "Former PTL Leader Looks for Lighter Sentence," UPI [wire story], August 22, 1991, BC Cycle.

38. *Id.*

39. Drape, "Repentent Bakker's Sentence Is Reduced; He Cites His Own Moral Failure as He Asks Judge to Show Mercy," *Atlantic Constitution and Journal,* August 24, 1991 at 3-A (Nexis printout).

40. *Id.*

41. "Former PTL Leader Looks for Lighter Sentence," *supra,* n. 37.

42. *Id.*

43. *Id.*

44. *Id.*

45. Zelenko, *supra,* n. 36.

46. "Former PTL Leader Looks for Lighter Sentence," *supra,* n. 37.

47. Drape, *supra,* n. 39.

48. Applebome, "Judge Cuts Bakker's Prison Term, Making Parole Possible in 4 Years," *New York Times,* August 24, 1991, at 10-A, col. 1.

49. Drape, *supra,* n. 39.

50. *Id.*

51. *Id.*

52. Zelenko, "Repentent Preacher Jim Bakker Sentenced to 18 Years Prison," Reuters [wire story], August 23, 1991, AM Cycle.

53. *Id.*

54. Garfield, "Graham's New Journey: Reflecting on His Past, Globe-Trotting Evangelist Works on Memoirs," *Charlotte Observer,* August 16, 1992 at 1-A (Westlaw printout).

55. "Jim Bakker's Startling Sentence," *New York Times,* October 29, 1989 at 22–4, col. 1.

56. Nichols, "Jim Bakker's Back, Televangelist in Court for Resentencing," *USA Today,* August 22, 1991 at 9-A (Nexis printout).

57. "Jim Bakker, Reduced," *Atlanta Journal and Constitution,* August 27, 1991 at 8-A (Nexis printout).

58. *Id.*

Chapter 25

The Prison Years

Rochester, Minnesota

While his appeal was being waged back in Charlotte and Richmond, Jim was stuck inside prison walls in Rochester, Minnesota. It was no Cancun. Close enough to Canada to notice it every day, Rochester has one of the most inhospitable climates in the country. The long frigid winters in this outpost are also light years from the sun's warmth that greeted the Bakkers in their Palm Springs homes in the middle of the California desert.

The prison itself is not a pleasant place, either. Razor-sharp barbed wire encircles the four main buildings, and the chilling setting resembles an old tuberculosis sanitarium where TB patients would be quarantined. Two three-story brick dormitory-like buildings fan out from an administration center and there is a small exercise yard with a walking and jogging track around it. The whole place had been a state mental hospital until 1985 when the U.S. Bureau of Prisons took it over.

No one could ever confuse this rough place with a country club prison. This was hell. After hearing a lecture from prison counselors on how to adjust to confinement, Bakker was placed in a small cell with three other men. There he began the life of a caged man.

I've been so broken by the humanity I've seen here. The ultimate sadness is to die in prison.[1]

He could have visitors five days each month, but only in the prison's sterile lounge. He and his guest would sit on cheap plastic chairs around a low coffee table while guards hovered like hawks. All inmates have to see their visitors at the same time. For many, it's a chance to spend a few hours with their wives and children who often must travel long distances from other states. It's one of the few contacts they have with the outside world, and nothing is bigger in a prisoner's week than visiting day.

> Being in prison is sort of like dying and being able to stay alive to see who your friends really are. I've decided to trust God. Some people write every single day. Billy Graham came to see me and wants to help. The local Assembly of God pastor, Reverend Phil Shaw, will do anything for me. This has been the most unbelievable nightmare in the world.[2]

The visiting room resembles a Greyhound bus terminal at the busiest time of the day. It's noisy, cramped, and smelly. Like all inmates, Bakker was strip-searched before and after each visit. But at least seeing someone in the visiting room was a chance to get out of his cell for a while.

The first time I visited Bakker there, we were making our way to the vending machines for lunch and he was stopped by a young man in his late twenties or early thirties. Handsome with soft features and blond hair, he was being visited by his seven- or eight-year-old son. The young man, doing time on a drug charge, introduced his son to Bakker. Without a second's hesitation, Bakker clasped the hand of the little boy and told him that he should know that his father was a leader in the prison, in Jaycees and other organizations, and that he could be very proud of his dad. What struck me about that was the instinctive kindness that it showed. Bakker was the celebrity, of course, but rather than take any attention for himself his first thought was to try to make that boy feel good and bolster his dad's standing in the little child's eyes.

Outside those vending machines during this visit and the others that followed, as we ate Star Kist Tuna Lunch Kits, Jim opened up.

> Today, I am a news junkie in prison. I subscribe to the *New York Times* and three major magazines and read all the time. My favorite radio program is Garrison Keillor for two hours each Saturday night. I escape from prison by crawling in my bunk with my headset and closing my eyes. That show was built for imagination and I grew up with radio and you can use your imagination so much with it. I listen to the Christian stations and Christian programs as well. I listen to lots of public radio. My other favorite show is *Car Talk*. They're fantastic—Click and Clack, the Tappert Brothers. [Bakker laughs heartily]
>
> I belong to every club in here. I am a member of the book club and have recently read *For Whom the Bell Tolls*. Some days, I read a book a day, maybe two. I've studied the Bible forward and backward here and never tire of that. I've made a total, exhaustive study of the teachings of Christ. I've spent every day in prison interpreting the Bible and reading every word of Christ.
>
> During the Christmas holidays, I get one to two thousand letters a week. I read every letter. I read all the time.
>
> I watch CNN. My next door neighbor is Lyndon LaRouche and he has a network that keeps him informed, and so he keeps me up to speed on things that are happening outside the prison.[3]

I was surprised by Bakker's sense of humor, and how good natured he is. He asked me if I wanted to hear the current jokes going around the prison.

> What do you have with 500 lawyers at the bottom of the ocean? A good start.
>
> What do you do if 200 lawyers are up to their necks in concrete? Get more concrete.[4]

But, realizing he had just told two lawyer jokes to a lawyer, so that I wouldn't feel uncomfortable he told a joke about Billy Graham and Jim Bakker in Hell. Billy started converting everyone, and Bakker raised enough money to be just $10,000 short of air conditioning for the whole place. And he had a good laugh at his own expense.

Yet prison is a sad place, and it was particularly difficult for Bakker.

> You've got to keep your mind alive in prison.
>
> I have sinned, but I never conspired to defraud anyone. I know I failed God. I am in prison for a moral failure. People were shocked and disappointed at the Hahn episode and my salary. I'm guilty of moral failure, but not guilty of the crimes I am accused of. If I were guilty, I'd want to confess and get it behind me. But I can never confess to conspiring to defraud or to defrauding the people. Dortch knows I didn't defraud anyone.[5]

For a time, he tried his hand at the prison craft room in Rochester, making pottery. In 1990, he gave his eighty-three-year-old father a vase with a drawing of Jim's childhood home in Muskegon, Michigan. He made Tammy a ceramic mug and filled it with ceramic hot chocolate for her kitchen.

But while visiting days are special for every inmate, the routine the rest of the time is spartan and regimented. In Rochester, Bakker woke up at 6:30 A.M., read the Bible, and dressed. He had to be at work at 7:30 A.M., cleaning toilets for 11¢ an hour. "I'm a porcelain expert,"[6] he told me. He did most of the janitorial work for the entire west wing of his building—from mopping and waxing the halls to scrubbing the shower room floors.

Lunch was at 11:30, and the afternoon was his to use as he saw fit. Jim spent his time studying the Bible, doing homework for the college classes he was taking, and reading. After supper, at 5:00 P.M., his evenings were filled with activities. He took evening college classes in sociology and computer science. After that, he worked on his correspondence course in Bible study and counseling from the North Central Bible College in Minneapolis and became a fully licensed counselor. Then, he read and answered his mail. The warden's office read all of his letters, those he received and those he sent, but he still received thousands a year from stalwart supporters. At 10:00 P.M. he turned again to reading scripture and praying before going to sleep at midnight.

In time, Bakker was moved to a 10-foot by 10-foot cell, which he shared with one other inmate. It had bunk beds, a small desk, and a locker. There wasn't much room, but at least he was assigned a fellow Christian as a cellmate and the two of them would pray and read the Bible together every day.

Each day, Bakker spent an hour working out or walking. And he shed several pounds. Today, he looks very fit and trim. He was a hospice worker at the prison hospital, and an officer in the prison Jaycees. He volunteered to run the United Way campaign and organize Christmas dinner for inmates and their families. He was asked by the Vietnam vets to be their chaplain. Basically, he took one day at a time and clung to the belief that God still had a plan for his life. He's proud of what he was able to do for other inmates: "I taught a quit smoking clinic here and got four times better results than the Mayo Clinic. I did it by teaching self-worth first. One inmate told me that was the first time in his life that anybody had told him he was worth anything."[7]

The Ministry Continues

In many respects, Jim and Tammy's actions after Jim was taken to prison paralleled what they did during the months before his trial.

Astonishingly, rather than banging their coffee cups across the bars of Jim's cell until his attorneys got him out of there, the Bakkers spent Jim's first few years behind bars jump starting what was left of their old PTL ministry. If it had been me in that cell, and like Bakker I was permitted to call my attorneys whenever I wished, I would have called them every single week and made sure that they were working hard on my case. After all, it was on their watch that the roof fell in on Jim, and it was now their job to dedicate every day to undoing the damage as quickly as possible. I wouldn't have let them have a moment's peace. I would have been a tough taskmaster and asked them pointed questions about what they were doing. I would have demanded results and if none were obtained, I would have replaced them.

In addition, I would have made my release my own first priority. I would have worked on it every day and dedicated my life to doing whatever it took to win my freedom.

But Jim and Tammy spent much of their time the first full year that Jim was incarcerated trying to raise enough money from their old PTL partners so that Tammy could continue what was left of the television program. In their defense, it is clear enough that the reason they were so determined to continue the ministry was because they saw it as God's will. God had called them to the television ministry. He had spoken to them. He wanted them to do that with their lives. And, by God, whether Jim was in prison or not, that's what they would do.

Some would scoff at that as being patently unrealistic. Psychologists might see it as textbook avoidance of reality by the Bakkers who were reverting to what they'd been doing all their lives when faced with a disaster with which they could not cope. But it could also be viewed as the innocence of two people who truly were subverting their own personal interests to God's will. Jim's supporters saw in it their man forsaking himself in order to continue to minister to others.

The ministry took several distinct forms during Bakker's years in confinement. Until 1992, when she bailed out, Tammy Faye led it. Two buildings in Orlando served as meeting places for Sunday services which Tammy would conduct. Each was also a makeshift television studio for the program she was able to broadcast for a few months until funds dried up. Starting out in somewhat meager surroundings in a strip mall on Oak Ridge Road in southwest Orlando, by April of 1990 Tammy felt the spirit move her to actually buy the old Tupperware warehouse on Orlando's Central Florida Parkway between Sea World and Universal Studios.

When the two of them were together on the old show, it really never fell to Tammy to carry the Biblical weight. So it was no surprise that her Orlando sermons were somewhat unorthodox and thin once she was on her own.[8] Her solo TV program foundered for a few months after Jim left for prison, and was then discontinued when the partners failed to contribute enough money to buy the air time on the twelve stations that were carrying her show.

In lieu of speaking to the partners by television each day, Jim and Tammy and their New Covenant Ministries reverted to the U.S. mails and sent a monthly letter to their circle of former partners. Until 1992, virtually all of the letters were from Tammy alone who penned them at her kitchen table. On rare occasions, Jim would handwrite a letter from his cell in prison and it would be typed at the ministry's headquarters and included in the mailing. But primarily it was Tammy's messages to followers that were sent out each month. Highlights of those letters reveal two major themes: first, fund-raising to continue the ministry and get back on television; second, suffering years of false hope as "a miracle" was sought from God to free Jim from prison while Tammy tackled the whole legal system.

This is what Jim and Tammy wrote their partners during the years after Jim's September, 1989 incarceration:

- **Jim, October, 1989:** I know that I am totally innocent of the 24 charges against me. *** I regret having to do so, but I have asked Tammy to discontinue television for the present time. I just could not allow the television bills to continue to grow . . . they are now in excess of $400,000. With your help we can quickly eliminate this debt and as your gifts continue to come in and we can see ourselves financially strong, I want to see our ministry back on the air![9]

- **Tammy Faye, November, 1989:** People are calling me daily, everyone telling me a different story about what I must do, saying that they are the only one with the right plan that I should follow! You know what that does? It puts me into total confusion! My mind starts to just shut down. *** Our financial needs are great. Without you understanding that need and responding with the very best gift that you can, there will be no way to get caught up on our huge debt to our TV affiliates. There will be no way to go back on television.[10]

- **Tammy Faye, December 15, 1989:** Jamie and I got to spend five days [in prison] with Jim. We had Thanksgiving dinner together from the quarter vending machines. Sandwiches, candy bars, and cakes. Ha! But that didn't matter. At least we were together! *** Sometimes it so totally overwhelms me that I can hardly breathe. *** I remembered saying, "Jim, what are Jamie and I going to do without you to take care of us?" Jim answered saying, "Tam, the partners will take care of you . . . they won't let you down."[11]

- **Tammy Faye, January 15, 1990:** I caught a glimpse of Jim and Tammy Sue on the front of the *Enquirer* magazine. It turned out to be an article about Tammy Sue posing for *Playboy Magazine* saying that she had agreed to do this in order to help Jim financially. *** Just like all the other articles including the one about me divorcing Jim they are nothing but lies from Satan! I just cannot believe that there are so many Christians purchasing and reading these filthy magazines. People, this is putting millions and millions of dollars into the pockets of these merchants of trash. *** Jim cries knowing that, due to the back TV bills, I haven't been able to continue our television program and to daily reach out and minister to each of you the Gospel of Jesus Christ.[12]

- **Tammy Faye, January, 1990:** Jim and I both feel the urgency to get back on television. We know that there are people who will never in their lifetime walk through the doors of a church but they will turn on their television sets! We want to be there for them.[13]

- **Tammy Faye, February, 1990:** Jim wrote me the other day. He said, "Tam, prison is the place of the living dead." *** I believe with all of my heart that we are on the brink of a miracle.[14]

- **Tammy Faye, April, 1990:** Our ministry has finally found a home [the old Tupperware building in Orlando]. *** We have wanted a place that you can come and visit us. A place where our partners can meet together and fellowship with one another. *** Jim has a dream for ten such places of refuge for the Christians. I believe that his dream is going to become a reality as we see God do a miracle! I am needing to make the down payment immediately and I need ten people to give $10,000 each so that we can make that possible. *** We need another 800 people to give $1,000 each and we could be in our new building debt free! Jim would be so pleased to know that we own our new building and that no one can take it from us ever again! *** Please remember to continue sending in your regular monthly support so that we can also stay current with our everyday overhead.[15]

- **Tammy Faye, April 15, 1990:** Jim was never allowed to present the facts that would have set him free. *** I understand an appeal can take anywhere from six months to two years. People, we need to pray![16]

- **Tammy Faye, June 1, 1990:** Please pray that God will provide the lawyer that He wants to take on the appeal. This is such an important step and we so need your prayers. God has been speaking to Jim lately about the importance of each individual's prayers. *** It's the Devil who would tell you that your prayers don't count. . . . Don't let the Devil get by with that lie! *** We can change Jim's circumstances through the power of prayer! *** Don't give up! We are on the brink of a miracle![17]

- **Tammy Faye, July, 1990:** You have been asking about Jim's appeal. . . . The lawyers are filing at this time what is known as a brief and appendix. *** Pray that God will give us a miracle and that the three judges in Richmond, VA will see the real truth concerning Jim and Heritage USA. Pray that it will be declared a mistrial and be thrown out! *** God is a big God! Let's expect big things from a big God![18]

- **Tammy Faye, August, 1990:** Jamie and I and Tammy Sue and baby James have just spent five days with Jim. On the 4th of July, the prison had a picnic for all the families that were visiting inmates. *** If we could all do just a little extra for the next couple of months, we should have our television stations totally paid in full by the end of summer. By early fall we could be starting our television program once again.[19]

- **Tammy Faye, September, 1990:** I was sitting in our living room talking to Jim on the phone when all of a sudden the spirit of the Lord came upon me. *** Jim and I were crying and praising the Lord over that phone. *** This is what God spoke to us: Man cannot stop what God is going to do! Mortal man is nothing but a puny, weak vessel in comparison to God's mighty power. *** God spoke to me that he is getting ready to send a spiritual flood . . . across this nation. . . . There is not a man alive that is going to be able to stop it![20]

- **Tammy Faye, October, 1990:** As you know, we are now in our church [the Tupperware building]. I am preaching again and singing. Our Sunday service starts at 10:30 A.M. each Sunday. *** We have been told that our building is not up to code and in order to bring it up to code we must put in a fire wall. *** We need $20,000 up front to even get started building the fire wall and we do not have it. *** If 200 of you would send in a gift of $100 this month that would do it! *** We have just received news that the date for Jim's appeal has finally been set. *** [What went wrong in his case was that] they would allow no Christians on the jury, or if you had ever watched Christian TV you could not be a part of the jury.[21]

- **Tammy Faye, October, 1990:** I would like to ask you one more time to do something in Jim's behalf. Would you please write the President, even if you have already done so? *** I believe we are going to see a miracle! *** Sometimes I want to give up so bad! *** The only reason I don't give up is that I know that is just exactly what the Devil wants me to do and I refuse to do anything that will make the Devil happy![22]

- **Tammy Faye, November, 1990:** I had never been alone before [like I was all year this year] ever! I married Jim when I was 18 years old. *** [This year] at times I have held on lying in bed crying . . . at times I have held on walking the floors at night screaming . . . but, I held on![23]

- **Tammy Faye, January 31, 1991:** God has been speaking to me about this new year and I believe that it is going to be a year filled with answered prayers![24]

- **Tammy Faye, March 25, 1991:** I no sooner hung up than the lawyer called confirming the information we had received [that the Court of Appeals in Richmond had overturned Judge Potter's 45-year sentence]. He told us that a hearing would be held immediately and that we could expect Jim home soon, as he saw no reason that the judge would deny bond. *** Please continue to pray with me about television. I long so to be back in your home again, every day. . . . *** Of course, finances are the biggest obstacle. Television air time is so terribly expensive. I need for God to speak to hearts that are financially able to help.[25]

- **Tammy Faye, June 21, 1991:** Please pray for Jim. He is getting so lonely and weary.[26]

- **Tammy Faye, October 17, 1991:** Jim called yesterday feeling better for the first time since the resentencing. *** Please continue to pray for Jim and please write him. *** Your cards and letters keep him alive![27]

- **Jim, November 23, 1991:** After my resentencing, . . . a deep depression came over me. Even though I was thankful for the reduction in my sentence from 45 years to 18 years, I realized at the earliest possible parole date I will have spent ten percent of my life in prison. *** [My daughter Tammy Sue visited me recently with her young children.] She was holding our one-year-old grandson, Jonathan Douglas, whom I had never seen. *** Tammy Sue and I hugged and I could not hold back the tears. . . . Their limited income had prevented them from making the long trip here to Minnesota for over a year. For four days, I held and got acquainted with my grandson, Jonathan. Each day, he would fall asleep in my arms. *** His mother had put my picture on the refrigerator and every day she would tell him, "this is your Grandpa," so we were not strangers.[28]

- **Tammy Faye, February 11, 1992:** Today, I feel like a wounded soldier that has been shot too many times and, as a result, is bleeding to death. *** The tabloids are once again running Jim and Tammy stories. *** You would think that, by now, Jim and Tammy would be tough enough to take anything, but you never get used to it . . . it always hurts! *** [Do not] believe the lies they print.[29]

But Tammy saved her most intimate reflections for her last letter, March 11, 1992, in which she announced to the ministry's supporters that she couldn't take it anymore. She was divorcing Jim.

> I am experiencing many emotions as I write to you today. Great sadness, fear of your rejection, and relief that I am able to be totally honest with you. I do not expect your understanding, but please try not to react cruelly. Jim and I are getting a divorce.
>
> For years I have been pretending everything is all right. I cannot pretend any more. Pretending becomes too hard on the physical body. I have been suffering with high blood pressure, anemia, asthma, hyperventilation . . . all, the doctors tell me . . . related to stress and severe nervous strain.
>
> I am lonely . . . and I am hurting.
>
> I can almost hear you gasping, saying, "It's not possible! How is this going to affect the Christian world?"[30]

It was a death blow to Jim. After all, through the good years and bad years, they had ridden life's roller coaster together since they were teen-agers. What life had taught them, they learned together. What God sent them to do first in the backwoods and later on national television, they did together. The thrill of being television stars and living very well, they embraced together.

Jim called it "the deepest pain of my life."[31] He said at the time:

> I felt as if my soul was crying from its depth as a primal scream of pain that I cannot describe, but no sound came out, just pain. How could I have lost the love of my life?
>
> For the next four weeks, I did not eat but three meals, the pain was unbearable. I had ministered to others that divorce was something more painful than death and now I was living that pain. You only live because you don't die.[32]

Compounding his pain was the news that Tammy already had a new beau—Jim's former best friend, Roe Messner, whom Jim had asked to watch out for Tammy while he was away in prison.

Richard Dortch, fresh from his own term in prison, jumped to Jim's defense at the reports that Messner was dating Tammy Faye: "He [Messner] should hide his face in shame and put on a sackcloth and ashes," he told *People* magazine. "Roe told us he would take care of Jim's family while he was in prison. But he didn't confide he intended to steal them,"[33] declared Dortch, who had known Messner for thirty-five years in church work.

Yet Tammy, yearning for a new life, packed up her belongings from the house she was renting in Orlando and headed West—to Palm Springs, California.

The Former "Jim and Tammy Ministry" without Jim or Tammy

Stepping in to fill the void left by her mother's abrupt departure, twenty-two-year-old Tammy Sue Bakker Chapman quickly assumed the presidency of New Covenant Ministries. Somewhat shy but very much down to earth, the dark-haired Bakker daughter is sharp, articulate, and far less mercurial than her mother. In her own way at only eighteen years old, she had sought her independence by leaving sumptuous Tega Cay and eloping with Doug Chapman, her sweetheart and former Heritage USA lifeguard. Since that time, the young couple had been living in a mobile home in northern South Carolina. Tammy Sue had given birth to sons James in 1990 and Jonathan in 1991 and was spending most of her time caring for them in her home.

Fiercely loyal to her father and next-in-line in family succession, "Sue" was asked by her father to assume the leadership of the ministry that boasted millions of adherents when she was in high school a few short years before. It was an unusual move in that Tammy Sue was not a minister, had not gone to Bible School, and was not ordained by the Assemblies of God or any other church. But she was legitimately credentialed as an experienced gospel singer with at least one top-selling album to her credit. So, she would speak for her father and sing, too.

Sue delivered her first sermon just four days after her mother dropped the divorce bombshell. To a handful of ministry followers in Orlando, she tried to sound upbeat but soon broke down in tears. "I love my mom and dad so much. The devil has tried to hurt us in so many ways. [But] we are not going to give up."[34]

The ministry began changing from one that offered traditional Sunday church services to more of an outreach ministry with Tammy Sue traveling to different cities in the country periodically to sing in Pentecostal churches and spread "the Word" through her music. She continued to reside in South Carolina with her husband and two small children. The day-to-day operation of the ministry was placed in the hands of a small staff in Orlando lead by long-time Bakker executive assistant Shirley Fulbright, who had been Jim's right arm for fourteen years and knew the territory well. Fulbright had the intelligence and competence to head up any business or corporation herself. She would be the one to whom Jim would turn now.

With Tammy Faye out of the picture, the goal of returning to television was abandoned. The Tupperware Building was vacated, and the office was moved to smaller facilities in the Gulf Coast town of Largo, Florida, near St. Petersburg. There, in a suite of offices in a small professional office park, Jim's personal library, his desk, and his belongings would be placed in a large office waiting for his return. The behemoth bank of computers and word processors that had been printing and personalizing hundreds of thousands of letters to former partners for so many years over Tammy's signature were reprogrammed and the new monthly letters were signed by Tammy Sue.

Although she would speak from her heart and often tap the same emotionalism that had characterized her parents' appeals for years, Tammy Sue's letters to the stalwarts were a couple of octaves lower. The most revealing part of the change in this important ministry lifeline was that Jim himself rolled up his sleeves in prison and picked up some of the slack by frequently writing letters of his own to include in the monthly reports and solicitations to partners. The division of labor typically was that Tammy Sue would brief followers on her singing tours, the efforts at any particular time to get her dad released from prison, and other family news.

Jim would write often lengthy, several-page letters interpreting different sections of the Bible. Some of his letters, in fact, ranged to twelve and sixteen pages in length as he would spend several hours each day studying and analyzing Biblical passages. His letters really became sermons which he would write out in longhand and mail to the ministry's offices for typing. And over the course of the three years that he wrote those letters, a steady evolution in his own personal religious faith could be seen. Never regarded as judgmental or hate-filled, Bakker clearly began growing into a much more liberal theologian. In the process, he put significant distance between himself and the pillars of the Religious Right, including Jerry Falwell and Pat Robertson.

Of course, some would quickly note that anyone in prison would view traditional, establishment thinking with gnawing skepticism and contempt. But the change in Bakker's religious views appeared to reflect new revelations he was receiving after hundreds of hours in his cell thinking and reading the Bible. Many of those changes were phenomenal, including his ultimate rejection of the very prosperity gospel that he had preached for years as a Pentecostal article of faith.

Again, the family's letters tell the tale.

- **Tammy Sue, July 11, 1992:** After seeing my dad again, Jamie and I are more determined than ever to see our dad released from prison. We sometimes feel so helpless! But, with God's help, I know we can see a miracle. *** To do that will require thousands of dollars in attorneys' fees. *** Please give a special offering this month so that we can get the people who can help my dad. [Contrary to what the tabloids are reporting] let me assure you, he is not suicidal in any way and he is doing very well under the circumstances.[35]

- **Jim, July 20, 1992:** It still surprises me how many people write to me and encourage me to fight my enemies. *** If you really trust God, you can pray God's blessings on your enemies and leave the results with Him.[36]

- **Tammy Sue, October 17, 1992:** Sometimes I don't know what to do next. I have done all I know to do to help my father be released from prison. *** Dad wants me to close the ministry if it gets to be too much for me.[37]

- **Jim, October 17, 1992:** If they have their way, there are those that would have me die in prison. *** My life is in God's hands, my reputation is destroyed, so I really have nothing to lose. *** The one I have the hardest time forgiving is myself. *** Many have written and chastised me for not fighting my adversaries, but . . . [above my bunk I have written this scripture] "In everything give thanks—for this is the will of God in Christ Jesus concerning you." *** We are not to be in love with this world and material things. *** If, by some miracle, I was transported back seven years ago to PTL, I would plead with the people to get, and keep, their eyes off the physical plant, the physical Heritage, and on to Jesus Christ and things eternal. *** Today, I beg you and all the PTL partners and friends, if you are in love with my dream, please stop! There's nothing eternal about my vision. It is only a group of buildings.[38]

- **Tammy Sue, December 23, 1992:** Praise God!!! Just before this letter was to be sealed, we got word from Judge Graham C. Mullen that Dad's sentence had been reduced. *** Dad is eligible for parole right now.[39]

- **Tammy Sue, January, 1993:** I think the best Christmas gift any of us got was the call I received from our lawyer, Jim Toms, saying there was a light at the end of the tunnel for my family at last. I laughed and I cried and stood in awe when he said that Dad could be home for next Christmas.[40]

- **Jim, March, 1993:** One of the greatest tragedies that has brought about catastrophic consequences is the church's involvement in the political system. *** When churches and church leaders started endorsing candidates and political parties, it has brought about division and the greatest polarization of our society. . . . *** The church must get back to preaching the Word of God. . . . *** The church is in a state of panic over the massiveness of abortion in this country, and rightly so. But marching and shouting and even new laws are not going to solve this problem. . . . *** How did God's message through his son, Jesus Christ, of love, forgiveness, and mercy become so twisted that millions now equate the Christian message with hate, bigotry, and cruelty? *** Throughout his life, Jesus was reaching out to sinners with compassion. *** Jesus had no political agenda. *** If I could say one thing to our church leaders today, I would plead with them to get out and stay out of politics. . . .[41]

- **Tammy Sue, April 27, 1993:** There's a new song I sing called "When Jesus Passes By." No matter what you are going through . . . it's not too big for Jesus. *** If you have faith even as small as a mustard seed, God will see you through your trials.[42]

- **Tammy Sue, August 3, 1993:** I am so excited about my new record. I believe it is inspired by God. Only God could have helped me to cut this record in the midst of my family's storm. [At the bottom of this letter she adds as a P.S.] Word has just come that my Dad's parole from prison has been turned down in Washington, D.C., by the Parole Commission. We are all deeply hurt and saddened.[43]

- **Tammy Sue, August 28, 1993:** Our New Covenant Prison Ministry is growing by leaps and bounds and has expanded to several more prisons. We are sending Bibles, books, study aids, and courses to prisoners free of charge. It is costing thousands of dollars to do this, but, as long as God supplies the need, we will not stop. *** I don't like to raise money and Dad feels I should close our little ministry before I have to beg for funds like he had to do in the past. *** My new tape and CD's are being sent out every day.[44]

- **Jim, September, 1993:** A whole doctrine of material prosperity and wealth has been built on the foundation of this verse . . . a doctrine totally opposite of the teaching of our Lord Jesus Christ. *** I preached material prosperity for years, but I must admit I was wrong; it is simply not what Jesus taught. *** Please prayerfully read what the Holy Spirit is speaking to me. *** My greatest mistake was that Jesus Christ was not Lord of my life. *** How many are still following Jesus for the loaves and fishes, the miracles and the blessings? Oh, that the church would fall in love with Jesus! *** If Jesus wanted us to "above all things" to prosper and to have wealth and all the material things our hearts desire, why did he say . . . "Woe unto you that are rich!"[45]

- **Tammy Sue, October 23, 1993:** New Covenant Ministries is almost totally out of funds.[46]

- **Tammy Sue, November 20, 1993:** Many of the inmates, along with Dad . . . had a picture taken to send to you to thank you for sending them books and Bibles. If you would like to see some of the people you are sending these materials to and some of the men Dad is incarcerated with, just ask for the . . . picture and I will send you a copy right away.[47]

- **Tammy Sue, January 23, 1994:** [My dad] worked on this message day and night for one month, spending up to 15 hours a day in the Word. *** [His study of the life of Samson] this letter could save many from great future heartache and disaster if they read it and heed it. Lust, pride, and disobedience brought Samson down and they are doing the same to millions today. *** Dad has taken time to write out all the scriptures so you wouldn't have to look them up as you read along. *** Ask for the "Samson Letter" and I'll send it right out. *** Several people have written me and said they just could not afford to send any money! Please don't think you have to send us money. We are a ministry . . . we want to minister to the world and tell people about Jesus. God will meet our needs. He has so far.[48]

- **Tammy Sue, February 17, 1994:** I want to share something so wonderful with you that I can hardly believe it myself! God has opened a door for me to go to Russia next month to sing and minister. We have the unbelievable opportunity of conducting rallies and going into high schools and colleges to witness the love of Jesus. *** I need a few people to help me with my expenses, but I don't want anyone to feel pressured to do anything. Most of all, I need and desire your prayers. If just a few of my friends could help and be one of my sponsors for a gift of $100 we could make it. I promise, we are keeping expenses to a bare minimum. Anyone who will be one of my sponsors, I am going to send a videotape of my trip plus a set of snapshots.[49]

- **Tammy Sue, March 23, 1994:** Dad's 16-page letter on Samson is helping so many people. If you know someone who is struggling and needs victory over temptation and sin, please write and ask for a copy of this detailed study to give to them. *** I'll write you as soon as I get back from Russia![50]

Jim was delighted his daughter would have the chance to travel abroad, but he still ached every day to be on the other side of the prison walls that were penning him in. He began a fevered search for options.

NOTES

1. Jim Bakker, interview by author, in Rochester, Minnesota, September 25, 1992.

2. *Id.*

3. Jim Bakker, interview by author, in Rochester, Minnesota, April 4, 1993.

4. Jim Bakker, interview by author, in Rochester, Minnesota, October 31, 1992.

5. Jim Bakker, *supra,* n. 1.

6. Jim Bakker, written answers to questions from the author, September 1992.

7. Jim Bakker, *supra,* n. 4.

8. Banks, "Orlando Is the Place For Me, Says Bakker after Year's Stay," *Orlando Sentinel Tribune,* May 10, 1990 at 1-B (Nexis printout).

9. Jim Bakker, letter to New Covenant Partners, October 1989.

10. Tammy Faye Bakker, letter to New Covenant Partners, November 1989.

11. Tammy Faye Bakker, letter to New Covenant Partners, December 15, 1989.

12. Tammy Faye Bakker, letter to New Covenant Partners, January 15, 1989 [sic]. [Mailed in January 1990].

13. Tammy Faye Bakker, letter to New Covenant Partners, January 1990.

14. Tammy Faye Bakker, letter to New Covenant Partners, February 1990.

15. Tammy Faye Bakker, letter to New Covenant Partners, April 1990.

16. Tammy Faye Bakker, letter to New Covenant Partners, April 15, 1990.

17. Tammy Faye Bakker, letter to New Covenant Partners, June 1, 1990.

18. Tammy Faye Bakker, letter to New Covenant Partners, July 1990.

19. Tammy Faye Bakker, letter to New Covenant Partners, August 1990.

20. Tammy Faye Bakker, letter to New Covenant Partners, September 1990.

21. Tammy Faye Bakker, letter to New Covenant Partners, October 1990.

22. Tammy Faye Bakker, letter to New Covenant Partners, October 15, 1990.

23. Tammy Faye Bakker, letter to New Covenant Partners, November 1990.

24. Tammy Faye Bakker, letter to New Covenant Partners, January 31, 1991.

25. Tammy Faye Bakker, letter to New Covenant Partners, March 25, 1991.

26. Tammy Faye Bakker, letter to New Covenant Partners, June 21, 1991.

27. Tammy Faye Bakker, letter to New Covenant Partners, October 17, 1991.

28. Jim Bakker, letter to New Covenant Partners, November 23, 1991.

29. Tammy Faye Bakker, letter to New Covenant Partners, February 11, 1992.

30. "Tammy's Troubled Waters," *People,* April 6, 1992 at 77; Marshall, " 'Hurting' Tammy Seeks Divorce," *USA Today,* March 13, 1992 at 1-A, col. 3; Blowen, "Bakkers divorce," *Boston Globe,* March 14, 1992 at 13-L (Nexis printout).

31. Jim Bakker, letter to New Covenant Partners, April 1992.

32. *Id.*

33. "Tammy's Troubled Waters," *supra,* n. 30 at 78.

34. *Id.*

35. Tammy Sue Chapman, letter to New Covenant Partners, July 11, 1992.

36. Jim Bakker, letter to New Covenant Partners, July 20, 1992.

37. Tammy Sue Chapman, letter to New Covenant Partners, October 17, 1992.

38. Jim Bakker, letter to New Covenant Partners, October 17, 1992.

39. Tammy Sue Chapman, letter to New Covenant Partners, December 23, 1992.

40. Tammy Sue Chapman, letter to New Covenant Partners, January 1993.

41. Jim Bakker, letter to New Covenant Partners, March 1993.

42. Tammy Sue Chapman, letter to New Covenant Partners, April 27, 1993.

43. Tammy Sue Chapman, letter to New Covenant Partners, August 3, 1993.

44. Tammy Sue Chapman, letter to New Covenant Partners, August 28, 1993.

45. Jim Bakker, letter to New Covenant Partners, September 1993.

46. Tammy Sue Chapman, letter to New Covenant Partners, October 23, 1993.

47. Tammy Sue Chapman, letter to New Covenant Partners, November 20, 1993.

48. Tammy Sue Chapman, letter to New Covenant Partners, January 23, 1994.

49. Tammy Sue Chapman, letter to New Covenant Partners, February 17, 1994.

50. Tammy Sue Chapman, letter to New Covenant Partners, March 23, 1994.

Chapter 26

Looking for Mercy

Once you find yourself in prison, there are only three ways out short of serving your time—ask the sentencing judge to reduce your sentence, obtain a parole, or dig a tunnel under the fence with your spoon. Bakker tried two out of the three.

Federal prisoners are permitted to seek reductions in their prison terms by pleading for mercy from the judges who sentence them. The procedure is to file what is known as a Rule 35(b) motion with the judge. Then, argue that the court's compassion is warranted and the sentence should be cut. In his 1992 plea for mercy, Bakker actually presented a compelling case. It almost worked.

The November 16, 1992 Hearing

Judge Graham Mullen scheduled a two-hour hearing on November 16, 1992 to hear whatever evidence Bakker had to support his plea. Bakker himself remained in Rochester and did not attend, but Harold Bender read a letter to the judge from his client.

> I beg for your forgiveness and for your mercy. *** I made many mistakes but I never conspired or intended to defraud anyone. *** [M]y moral failure which took place before Heritage USA was built was a sin which I am deeply sorry for and take full responsibility for. ***
>
> It has been a long six-year nightmare for me and my

family. . . . Shortly after the collapse of PTL, my young teenage daughter ran away and married. She is the apple of my eye and how much I wanted to give her a church wedding. . . . My sixteen-year-old son, who was ten at the time, . . . has quit school and has serious emotional problems. *** I love my son more than life itself. He has begged not to have to live with a man who has taken my place in his mother's life. ***

My wife of 31 years has divorced me since I came to prison. *** I have lost my ministry, my home, car, life savings and retirement. *** I am in my fourth year of imprisonment and I don't know what more the government can do to punish me except to see what is left of my family deteriorate and be destroyed. *** Prison is a place of living death. . . . *** Since 1989, I have served as an orderly, cleaning floors, sinks, toilets, showers, etc. *** Before God, I realize material things are not important and that one's family is what really counts.[1]

With the exception of Jim's own absence and that of ex-wife Tammy, the rest of the cast assembled for this hearing wasn't that much different from past episodes of the Bakker saga which had been played out in the same Charlotte courthouse. Judge Mullen presided, soft-spoken and sharp. From the comments he made during the hearing, it seemed that he was inclined toward Bakker's position. He appeared outwardly frustrated with the prosecutors' harshness toward the televangelist, and increasingly uncomfortable with the eighteen-year sentence that he had himself imposed only fifteen months before.

The government's counsel table was occupied by Deborah Smith and Jerry Miller. For the defense, Harold Bender. Attorney Jim Toms from Hendersonville, North Carolina, accompanied him. Daughter Tammy Sue and Jim's parents attended along with several Bakker supporters. Bender called three witnesses.

Dr. Daniel V. Foster, the chief of psychology services and associate warden at the Rochester prison, testified on Bakker's behalf that the evangelist had hit rock bottom while incarcerated but had remained a model prisoner. He was a broken man when he arrived in Rochester, having lost "nearly everything that he held important,"[2] Foster explained. And prison had been tough on him. There was "considerable grief."[3] He was assigned the job of cleaning the prison bathrooms for all the other inmates for three years and "he's taken the task seriously in the sense of he receives outstanding work reports and with a lot of humility."[4] Bakker never asked for any special treatment in prison.

Foster provided some behind-the-scenes insight into Bakker's years behind bars. "He was quite naive as to certainly what you might call a prison culture and the street culture broadly,"[5] the psychiatrist testified. "He wasn't accustomed to the kind of language that many Americans speak in a normal course of their day. *** He wasn't accustomed to the various cultural and ethnic styles that are represented within a prison. . . . I think he was a bit shell shocked. . . ."[6] All in all, it was "a pretty tough and lonely road for him. *** At first, he was at a loss of who to trust, of what to do, of who was safe to even talk to."[7]

But, Bakker pulled himself up by his bootstraps and "started lifting weights and learning to play . . . drums . . . in an effort, I think, to be somewhat closer to his son Jamie, and playing softball and doing other forms of recreation that he'd never done in his life,"[8] Foster reported.

Beyond that, Foster pointed out, "he's done similar kinds of activities within our hospice program with—we have men that come to FMC Rochester to receive the best care we can afford them as they anticipate their death from terminal illnesses, and Mr. Bakker has worked with those gentlemen in a quiet and humane way and has learned a lot, I think, about accepting his own losses as he works . . . in a relatively friendless environment where family, friends . . . aren't available to you."[9]

While Foster thought that Bakker had suffered enough and that his current family situation merited a reduction in his sentence, Jerry Miller was not as forgiving in his cross-examination.

Mr. Miller: Well, Dr. Foster, Mr. Bakker isn't the only inmate there whose wife has divorced him during his incarceration, is he?
Dr. Foster: That's the norm, not the exception, divorce while someone's incarcerated.
Mr. Miller: And Mr. Bakker is not the only one who has children

who find it difficult adjusting to the fact that their parents are
divorced and their father is in prison?
Dr. Foster: He is not.[10]

But to drive home the point to the judge that Jim Bakker's
family situation merited some compassion, Bender next called
Bakker's son to the stand. Jamie Charles, who at sixteen years
old had his dad's facial features and Luke Perry's haircut, was
the best witness who had testified for Jim Bakker in five years.
And he was scared to death. The boy was on the stand only a
few minutes, but his heartbreaking words cast a shadow over
the proceedings that the government prosecutors were never
able to erase. He spoke from the heart.

Mr. Bender: How old were you when your father went to prison?
Jamie: I was 13.
Mr. Bender: Approximately how often do you see your father?
Jamie: Maybe once every three months.
Mr. Bender: Do you talk to him?
Jamie: Yeah. He calls me. Once a week, twice a week.
Mr. Bender: Do you miss your father? Tell us about that.
Jamie: Well, it's the hardest thing that's ever happened to me. I
feel lonely, something's been missing in my life for the past three
years, very angered. I don't know how to explain this hurt, but
I've never hurt so bad before.
Mr. Bender: Now, Jamie, you—I believe you're dyslexic?
Jamie: Yes, I am. Correct.
Mr. Bender: And are you able to correspond with your father?
Jamie: Well, he writes me a letter about every day, but my
handwriting and my spelling is not too great so I'm kind of
embarrassed to write him, so I'm not able to. I just talk to him on
the phone.
Mr. Bender: Before your father went to prison, did he actually
help you as well with your writing and your work, your school
work?
Jamie: Yeah. He was—he always liked to make sure that my
cursive was good, you know . . . he would help me.
Mr. Bender: Where do you live?
Jamie: I live in St. Petersburg, Florida.
Mr. Bender: You don't live with your mother, do you?
Jamie: No, I don't.
Mr. Bender: And I believe you live with some family friends?

Jamie: Yes.

Mr. Bender: And have you thought about or talked to your dad about where you all [you and your dad] would live whenever he gets out of this situation?

Jamie: Yes, I have.

Mr. Bender: And do you need him?

Jamie: More than anything I've ever needed in my whole entire life.

Mr. Bender: Do you love your father?

Jamie: More than anybody in the whole world. He's my best friend.

Mr. Bender: Okay. Thank you. That's all.[11]

Jerry Miller was smart enough not to touch Bakker's son with even one question. He wanted him off the witness stand and the sting of his comments unemphasized. "No questions, your honor"[12] is all that Miller said.

Bender's third witness was Benjamin J. Malcolm of New York City, the distinguished former member and vice chairman of the United States Parole Commission who served under both Presidents Carter and Reagan. Since leaving that agency in 1984, Malcolm had operated a private consulting business offering assistance to federal inmates who sought to understand and access the federal parole system. It was in that capacity that Malcolm had been contacted by Jim Bakker. The bottom line of his testimony was that if Judge Mullen really wanted Bakker out of jail before the expiration of his sentence, he should reduce that sentence himself rather than expect that Bakker would win parole from the U.S. Parole Commission.

The government prosecutors attempted to dissuade Mullen from acting on Bakker's plea for mercy. Their argument was that the Parole Commission could be relied upon instead to consider the case, exercise compassion, and release Bakker early if he deserved it. Malcolm hotly contested that theory and told the judge point blank that because Bakker was such a high profile inmate, the Parole Commission would never reach out to give him a break. Instead, in Malcolm's view, the commission would let Bakker sit in jail for twelve full years and never release him early.

The other important part of Malcolm's testimony was that, in his view, the eighteen-year sentence that Mullen had imposed the year before was simply too harsh. Malcolm presented the judge with extensive research compiled by thirty Drake University Law School students who had volunteered their time in the effort to secure Bakker's release. Working literally night and day, those students spent hundreds of hours in the law school library locating and researching more than 400 federal white collar fraud cases in which the defendants were found guilty and sentenced to prison. What those students were able to prove was that, by comparison with virtually all other cases, Jim Bakker's sentence was extreme.[13]

The students summarized each of the 400 cases in detailed memoranda which were forwarded to Ben Malcolm. Relying on that research while on the witness stand, Malcolm offered numerous examples of those cases involving similar fraud offenses but where defendants received prison terms far lighter than Bakker.

> **Mr. Malcolm:** I am asking this court on the basis of other cases that the court modify its finding of 18 years with a sanction that I think is more in keeping with some of the cases that I've mentioned in the reports that I've submitted.[14]

But the prosecutors were unpersuaded.

> **Ms. Smith:** None of these cases that you've cited involve a man presenting himself as a religious and spiritual leader making misrepresentations to the people to get them to send them money and doing that on a daily basis, do they, sir?
> **Mr. Malcolm:** No.
> **Ms. Smith:** None of them involve misrepresentations made on national television that were beamed into people's homes on a daily basis for a 3-year period, do they?
> **Mr. Malcolm:** I don't recall so. *** I could have cited numerous cases of where public trust was violated. . . .[15]

After his three witnesses had concluded testifying, Harold Bender rose to offer oral argument on Bakker's behalf.

Judge, we're here to ask for compassion and mercy. . . . You have heard of an exemplary prison record and prison conduct. I know of no person who has fallen as far as Jim Bakker, a person who was probably recognized world-wide, not just in this country, but world-wide because of television. . . . And one day, he is on top of the world and the next day, he is scrubbing toilets. What a demeaning prospect that is to have to scrub toilets for a bunch of men in a common facility. But he did it with dignity, grace and humility and continues to do it to this day. Has never asked for a favor. Never asked to be shifted from that assignment. . . .[16]

Then, Bender read from a stack of letters that had been sent to the judge by people who believed that Bakker had already paid his debt to society and should be released from prison.

His friends have come forward with letters, Judge, which I submitted to you. Some of them are prominent people. Some of them are not so prominent people. Pat Boone wrote a letter to Your Honor. Oral Roberts wrote a letter to Your Honor. Chuck Colson wrote a letter to Your Honor. The Rev. Billy Graham said, "I thought it was an awful heavy sentence for that when you see people like Milken and Boesky and people in that area are getting lighter sentences." He said that with regard to the 18-year sentence that Jim Bakker is presently serving.[17]

Bender's final plea to the judge was a simple one:

But we're asking . . . you to show some compassion and mercy on Jim Bakker and his family and allow him to see the light at the end of the tunnel and get out of prison and go about doing good, because he's capable of doing good and he will do good.[18]

Jerry Miller wasn't buying any of it. In his arguments he complained that the only people who hadn't been heard that day were Bakker's victims. They were the ones who would never receive restitution "and will not get a dime back from Mr. Bakker."[19] And, as far as the son's testimony?

Your Honor, the fact that Jamie Charles Bakker was brought before this Court and the heart-rendering testimony that was presented to the court with that testimony, Your Honor, I submit to you that that is an effort to play upon the sympathy of the Court, that the Court needs to be very careful of that. It's become to be known at sentencing hearings as a "pinch the baby defense," where it actually happened in front of Judge Woodrow Jones one time up in Asheville where a bank robber was about to be sentenced. He literally brought a baby into the courtroom and had someone pinch the baby just moments before Judge Jones was to impose sentence. Judge Jones's response to that was, in addressing the defendant, "Sir, I'm about to sentence you to a period of incarceration. If you don't want your family to witness this unpleasant experience, I would suggest that you have them step out of the courtroom because that play on the sympathy of the Court is not going to work."[20]

Deborah Smith's position was that Bakker didn't deserve to be freed from prison until he admitted his guilt in defrauding his followers. Because of that, she was unwilling to let the judge be swayed by the lighter sentences given other high profile white collar fraud defendants like Michael Milken.

Judge Mullen: How about differentiating Mr. Bakker from Mr. Milken, who appears to have invented or at least utilized an economic device that undoubtedly hurt as many people or more [than did Bakker]?

Ms. Smith: In Mr. Milken's case, he pled guilty, Your Honor. He acknowledged his guilt; he admitted his guilt. The government's position, this is something Mr. Bakker has never done. He provides these carefully crafted statements accepting moral responsibility, and yet he and his defense counsel have successfully waged a campaign to convince large numbers of the public that he, in fact, was merely naive. *** We think before any reduction of sentence is provided, Your Honor, it's really vital that Mr. Bakker admit that he knowingly lied to people to get them to send him money. That's one very large difference between he and Mr. Milken that I think is almost insurmountable in this case.

Judge Mullen: But Mr. Bakker didn't have a brother to be held hostage by the government either, did he?

Ms. Smith: Well, he had a number of very close associates, Your Honor.

Judge Mullen: His brother was—his brother's case was dismissed.

Ms. Smith: I'm not familiar with his brother's case, Your Honor.
Judge Mullen: Well, it was dismissed.[21]

During this hearing, nothing was more obvious than the passion of the prosecutors for keeping Jim Bakker behind bars. But two flaws in their reasoning made their position seem unreasonable by 1992. It wasn't lost on the judge.

The first problem was that the prosecutors initially told Mullen that he didn't have the discretion to consider Bakker's plea for mercy but that he had to leave it to the Parole Commission to decide. They were apparently wrong on that.

Judge Mullen: Now, which is it? Is it the government's position that I have no discretion or not?
Ms. Smith: Your Honor, I believe the Court always has discretion in these matters.
Judge Mullen: That's absolutely not true under the new Rule 35 and you know it. Now, answer my question. Is it your argument that I do or I don't have discretion? ***
Ms. Smith: *** I think it's somewhat difficult to give the Court a very firm answer. We would ask that the Court elect not to exercise discretion in this case. . . .[22]

Smith must have missed Judge Potter most profusely at that very minute. The prosecuting attorneys had rarely been called to task or barked at during the original five week trial over which Potter presided.

The second problem was more subtle, but lethal. When Bakker was originally sentenced by Judge Potter three years before, Bakker's attorney begged to have the evangelist sentenced under the new U.S. government sentencing guidelines which had been adopted by the Congress in order to assure some uniformity of sentencing across the country. Attorneys Miller and Smith fought to persuade Potter not to use the guidelines because that would have only required a prison term of from forty to fifty-two months. Instead, they wanted Bakker sentenced under the old law which would permit Potter to put him away for up to 120 years. They won that debate, Potter bought their argument, and Bakker bought forty-five years on the farm.

Now, the same prosecutors were telling Judge Mullen that the reason he didn't have the discretion to reduce Bakker's sentence was because the federal government was now using uniform sentencing guidelines so that all sentences would be comparable and presumptively fair. Under the new guidelines, no judge has the power to reduce a sentence.

Of course, the fact that the prosecutors were attempting to have it both ways in Bakker's case was not very well concealed. The illogic of it would work against them.

As well, the unyielding position the prosecutors took over the years to keep Bakker behind bars gives some credence to Bakker's belief that the government was zealously driven to convict him and put him far away.

Mullen concluded the hearing and told the attorneys that they had two more weeks to submit any additional evidence in writing. He would reach a decision by Christmas.

Speaking Up for Bakker

In an effort to persuade Judge Mullen to show some mercy on Bakker, several prominent evangelicals and many ordinary people from around the country wrote letters to the judge urging him to reduce Jim's sentence. Excerpts from the more interesting ones include:

- **Chuck Colson, chairman of Prison Fellowship and former aide to President Richard Nixon who served time for a Watergate offense:** I believe in punishment, but I think it is tragic that we incarcerate non-dangerous, non-violent offenders in prison where they have very little meaningful work to do. That is more barbaric than the chain gangs of the thirties. I know from my own experience how hollow and empty life can be in a prison lived out hour by hour, day by day, with nothing meaningful to do. People are literally driven insane that way. *** That is why I write on behalf of Jim Bakker, who has already spent two years in prison. *** If he needs continued punishment, couldn't justice be better served if he were required to complete his sentence working in the inner city or through some other form of community service?[23]

- **James Watt, Secretary of the Interior under President Ronald Reagan:** When I served in President Reagan's first

Cabinet I learned first hand about the sting of the anti-Christian bias in America. The hostility against those of us who claim, or admit, to be practicing Christians in some instances is subtle and in other instances is blatant. *** This letter is written to urge you to show mercy as you review the sentence that has been given Jim Bakker. He is a man that has done wrong. But the good he has done, as measured by those of us who have known him for a long period of time, is massive. *** Jim Bakker has suffered unmeasurable humiliation, disgrace and personal pain and suffering. From my vantage point it seems enough.[24]

- **Pat Boone, entertainer:** I just know how he and his family have suffered, far more than any material or economic or even public punishment; the interior torture of feeling you have "blown" a mission from God Himself, and somehow forfeited the respect and cooperation of a formerly extremely supportive public—the pain of this is incalculable. *** I myself have heard countless people, even those who were always critical of Jim and PTL, talk about the fact that murderers and rapists in today's criminal justice system often get off completely, or spend less time in prison than Jim Bakker has, or may.[25]

- **Oral Roberts, evangelist:** After reflecting on what happened, I sincerely believe that we have a case of a young man coming from a small background whose ministry exploded on him and he quite literally did not know how to handle it. At no time did I ever feel he had a crooked bone in his body. I did feel at times that he was naive in dealing with the large number of employees, the multiplied thousands of visitors, and the finances which became complex. I believe he has paid the price for that naiveté . . . a very dear price.[26]

- **George Otis, former CEO of the Lear Jet Corporation and now head of a Christian television network:** It was my privilege to minister at PTL and visit their services numerous times. Lives changed for the better numbered near the 100,000 level. There isn't a month which goes by that I don't encounter people who bear testimony about Jim Bakker's life and ministry. I strongly encourage you to commute the remainder of his sentence.[27]

- **David A. Lewis, frequent PTL guest and Jim and Tammy's occasional traveling companion:** I know a Jim Bakker that never appeared in the descriptions of him in the newspapers. I saw in him a kind and compassionate man. He was always giving, giving, giving. *** Jim Bakker had weaknesses. I told Jim over and over that he was trusting the wrong people. He told me that I was paranoid. *** He made mistakes of judgment but I do not think his errors arose from criminal intent.[28]

- **Dr. James McKeever, president of Omega Ministries of Medford, Oregon:** It is true he is guilty of mishandling ministry funds which is a terrible thing. On the other hand, he did a lot of good. Many peoples' lives changed for the better through Mr. Bakker's ministry. It is possible that the number of people positively touched by his ministry would be in the millions. I do not condone his actions, either morally or in the fiscal realm. I do believe that he has paid his debt to society. I am encouraging you to exhibit mercy on this fallen brother.[29]

- **Melvin Belli, famed San Francisco trial attorney:** This is just a short and simple note but from the bottom of my heart asking for your compassion and mercy on another sinner who has appeared before you, Jim Bakker. *** I do think he is deserving of compassion and mercy. *** I love the man and his family and I think he has a lot of spirit left in him that can help all of us if he is put on the right track for the rest of his life.[30]

- **James Robison, evangelist:** As a matter of information, in case you are not familiar with our ministry, I speak daily to 65 million households throughout the U.S. and Canada. *** I believe I know the pulse and the heartfelt sentiment of much of the Christian community and even the general public. Over and over I've heard Christians and non-Christians say how horrible it was for Jim Bakker to have been sentenced so severely. *** There are murderers, rapists and kidnappers who are walking free after a matter of a few years. God have mercy on us! Please, please, Judge, do consider shortening this sentence and giving this man an opportunity to redeem himself in the eyes of the public and the people he has loved and, yes, those he has hurt.[31]

- **Rev. Jim Ammerman, retired Army chaplain and Dallas evangelist:** As I visit conferences of the more than 40,000 churches and pastors we represent . . . *** the voiced opinion of thousands of Christians is that the disproportionate sentence [given Bakker], by today's standards, borders on persecution of a Christian.[32]

- **Jamie Buckingham, author:** I have known Jim Bakker since I wrote Pat Robertson's autobiography back in the early seventies. For several years, after he moved to Charlotte and his TV ministry was growing, I flew up every month to host the PTL

Club. When the ministry started into the real estate business I backed off—and refused from that time on to participate in what was happening at PTL. After Jim resigned I stepped back into the picture, trying to minister to Jim and Tammy. However, events were happening so quickly and Jim was so devastated by the mistakes he had made, that there was little I could do. *** I talk to hundreds of Christian leaders across the nation each year. Not a single one feels Jim deserved even the 18 year sentence—especially in the light of the sentences handed out to violent criminals.[33]

Judge Mullen Decides

On December 22, 1992, three days before Christmas, Judge Mullen reached his decision. He decided "that indeed on further reflection the [eighteen-year] sentence seems unduly harsh,"[34] and cut ten more years from it. The bottom line appeared to be that Mullen was persuaded that Bakker's sentence should be more in line with those of other high-profile defendants convicted of fraud like Michael Milken and Ivan Boesky. And a bit less like the sentence a murderer would get.

Back in Rochester, Bakker was elated. He scribbled out a written statement in his cell saying that he was "deeply overwhelmed and thankful to God and thankful for the compassion and mercy of Judge Mullen. This is the greatest Christmas present aside from the birth of my son, that I have ever had. I am very, very happy."[35]

> **Jim Bakker in prison:** I'd like to be on TV again and my message would be: God loves you. He loves people going through pain and loneliness and rejection. He is there to help people who are near suicide, whose spouses have left them, and who are at the end of their rope in life.
>
> I'm a whole different person today. My theology is different. I feel our flamboyancy was wrong and that I preached materialistic too much. The problem with that was that, and I understand it now, that if people lose their material things, then they lose faith in God.[36]

His attorneys spiked his euphoria. Jim Toms told the Associated Press that Bakker was eligible for parole immediately and would be out at the latest by the following Christmas.[37]

The anticipation began building within the Bakker camp. When his attorneys calculated the good time that he should receive for being a model prisoner, they were sure the Parole Commission would release him soon—perhaps within a month. Bakker was brimming and in a telephone call to United Press International reporters from prison said, "I was in the warden's office and he calculated my release date at April 29, 1992. So I have been eligible for parole for eight months."[38] Bakker said that news accounts he heard on his prison radio that he would be eligible for release the following Christmas were simply wrong, and that he would be out long before then.

But the evangelist's joy was shattered by the news that his eighty-six-year-old father had been in a car crash at noon on Christmas Day. Tammy Sue told her dad, "Grandpa Bakker has been in a wreck and he is in serious condition. His pelvic bone is broken and he is bleeding internally and he has been transferred from one hospital to another, one with a trauma center that could care for him better. His car was broadsided on his side and was totaled."[39] It was like a knife through the heart for Bakker, who lived each day with the fear that his parents would not live to see him freed from prison. Immediately, Bakker asked the warden for permission to fly to North Carolina to be at his father's bedside. Inasmuch as Judge Mullen had just reduced his sentence and Bakker was already presumptively eligible for parole, the warden approved the trip and sent Bakker and a guard by commercial airline to Charlotte. Those would be Bakker's first breaths outside prison walls in years.

When he arrived in the hospital's intensive care unit, he was told by the doctors that his father's condition had been stabilized and the bleeding stopped. He was out of immediate danger. Bakker was allowed a six-hour visit and spent the time commiserating with all the members of his family arrayed around the hospital bed. His eighty-five-year-old mother was there, his brother, his sister, Tammy Sue and her young husband and infant sons, and Jamie. Jamie went out for food and brought back Kentucky Fried Chicken and Pizza Hut pizza. It was the first nonprison food Bakker had eaten in years. His daughter said later that Bakker looked like a starving man with a chicken leg in one hand and a piece of pizza in the other as he wolfed them down.[40]

The warden had let him out for the day on the condition that he be back in the prison before midnight, through the connecting flight from Charlotte to Minneapolis. As Bakker rushed out of the hospital room to make his plane, everyone in the family was in tears, hugging tightly the lost eagle. But at least it appeared that Grandpa Bakker was going to make it. Arriving at the Charlotte airport for the return flight, Bakker got another shock—severe winter weather had delayed the flight. His guard made the decision to rent a car and drive to the nearest federal prison to spend the night. Ironically that prison, three hours away, was the infamous Butner.

But the way Bakker was able to deal with spending the night in solitary confinement at Butner this time showed how much he had changed in three years. When his guard, Officer Brendle, marched him into the prison, Bakker quipped to the duty officers who escorted him to his cell, "I've heard the accommodations were so good I wanted to stay here tonight."[41]

Jim Bakker in prison: After all I've been through since that trial, and all the horror that Butner had been for me, in the end I conquered it.[42]

The following morning the weather cleared, they flew back to Minnesota, and the gates once again closed behind Bakker. His Christmas had been a tumultuous one, and ended in the next several days with his supporters around the country adopting "Set Free in '93" as their motto for the year based on what Bakkers' attorneys were saying. Bakker himself got the fever. He wrote his followers this note:

I celebrated my 53rd birthday, January 2. Pastor Shaw came to spend the day with me. We had a cupcake with a make-believe candle made out of a piece of paper plate. He said he hoped this would be my last birthday in prison. I have much to be thankful for even in prison.

I am so thankful today for you and all of my friends who never gave up, for every card and letter and for every prayer. At this moment, it looks like I will go to the parole board in April. By then, I will have been eligible for parole for a year. Please pray that God will give me favor with the parole board and that I will be home with my family soon.[43]

But that hope proved false, too.

NOTES

1. Jim Bakker, letter to Judge Graham C. Mullen, November 4, 1992.

2. Transcript of Rule 35 Hearing, *United States of America v. James O. Bakker,* Docket No. C-CR-88-205-1, U.S.D.C. (W.D., N.C.), November 16, 1992 at 6.

3. *Id.* at 11.

4. *Id.* at 7.

5. *Id.* at 7–8.

6. *Id.* at 8.

7. *Id.* at 8–9.

8. *Id.* at 9.

9. *Id.* at 9–10.

10. *Id.* at 12.

11. *Id.* at 16–18.

12. *Id.* at 18.

13. Led by upper class members Debra Scorpiniti, Briget Biernat, and James Moody, the law students who served on the Bakker task force were Eric Carlson, Paul Carter, Lisa Castellano, Robert Cataldo, Elizabeth Ciesla, Edward J. Cord, Steven T. Durick, Zenaida Falcon, Elizabeth Flansburg, Kara Gibney, Bradley Grothe, David Herd, Jeff Ireland, Michael D. Jackelen, Wendy Jones, Lori Kitterman, Jack Lammers, Julie Lierly, Brian Lohse, Craig Oppel, Joseph Partain, Chip Pritchard, Jeffrey B. Redick, Scott E. Schroeder, Robert F. Tappa, Matthew Tarbox, Glenn Tornillo, Patrick Waldron, and Pamela Weidler.

14. Transcript of Rule 35 Hearing, *supra,* n. 2 at 35.

15. *Id.* at 38.

16. *Id.* at 49–50.

17. *Id.* at 49.

18. *Id.* at 53.

19. *Id.* at 54.

20. *Id.* at 55–56.

21. *Id.* at 63, 65.

22. *Id.* at 59.

23. Charles W. Colson, letter to Judge Graham C. Mullen, December 18, 1991.

24. James G. Watt, letter to Judge Graham C. Mullen, December 16, 1991.

25. Pat Boone, letter to Judge Graham C. Mullen, December 6, 1991.

26. Oral Roberts, letter to Judge Graham C. Mullen, December 12, 1991.

27. George Otis, letter to Judge Graham C. Mullen, Decmeber 2, 1991.

28. David A. Lewis, letter to Judge Graham C. Mullen, December 20, 1991.

29. Dr. James McKeever, letter to Judge Graham C. Mullen, December 6, 1991.

30. Melvin M. Belli, letter to Judge Graham C. Mullen, December 5, 1991.

31. James Robison, letter to Judge Graham C. Mullen, December 6, 1991.

32. Col. E. H. Jim Ammerman, letter to Judge Graham C. Mullen, December 16, 1991.

33. Jamie Buckingham, letter to Judge Graham C. Mullen undated.

34. Order of Judge Graham C. Mullen, *United States of America v. James O. Bakker,* Docket No. C-CR-88-205-1, U.S.D.C. (W.D., N.C.), December 22, 1992.

35. "Jim Bakker Could Be Paroled in a Year," *Chicago Tribune,* December 23, 1992 at 3-A (Nexis printout).

36. Jim Bakker, interview by author, in Rochester, Minnesota, September 25, 1992.

37. "Jim Bakker Could Be Paroled in a Year," *supra,* n. 35.

38. "Bakker Looks Forward to Quick Release," UPI [wire story], December 23, 1992, BC Cycle.

39. Jim Bakker, letter to New Covenant Partners, January 22, 1993.

40. *Id.*

41. Jim Bakker, interview by author, in Rochester, Minnesota, April 4, 1993.

42. *Id.*

43. Jim Bakker, letter to New Covenant Partners, *supra,* n. 39.

Chapter 27

Fighting for Parole with Nose Hair Clippers

Jim Bakker would never have had to run the Parole Commission gauntlet if Judge Mullen in December, 1992, had reduced his sentence to time served. He would have walked that day. Still, Mullen's sharp reduction in Bakker's sentence to eight years immediately altered the math affecting Bakker's eligibility for parole.

Parole is the release of a prisoner from incarceration before the end of that person's sentence. Requests from prisoners seeking early release are heard by the nine-member U.S. Parole Commission in Washington, D.C., which releases prisoners all the time who satisfy them that they deserve it. Parole is never automatic. A prisoner must make a case for early release that is convincing to the commission. And it is a venue that is quite different from the federal judges before whom Bakker had been pleading his case for so many years, because the parole commissioners are presidentially appointed agency members and not judges.

The parole apparatus is political and a part of the correctional system. It is not a court whose judges are insulated with lifetime appointments. The significance of that to Bakker was that Parole Commission members were, in the final analysis, reluctant to release such a high profile prisoner. Their fear may have been for the political embarrassment that could be caused if the public saw the Parole Board or the Clinton administration being soft on crime and giving Bakker special treatment. Would

Jay Leno begin his next monologue with some crack comparing Jessica Hahn to Gennifer Flowers?

Questions abounded that may have impacted the parole dynamics. Had press reporting on Jim Bakker the last several years so seared public opinion that letting him out of prison early would cause a public backlash? Did board members see him as a Public Enemy whose crime alone disqualified him from early release? The Parole Commission operates within the Justice Department. Would Bakker find any support from Attorney General Janet Reno or other top administration officials? What would board members look for in making their decision?

It was into those unfamiliar waters that Bakker waded in an attempt to win parole.

April 8, 1993 Parole Hearing

A hearing on Bakker's parole was held in the Rochester prison on April 8, 1993. Presiding were two examiners from the Kansas City regional Parole Commission office—Ronald Bartee and Gerald Mills. In some respects, it was a moveable feast with Harold Bender again by his client's side and Ben Malcolm on hand to testify on Bakker's behalf.

Bakker was given the chance to tell his side of the story and explain why he believed he should be released on parole. The examiners asked him questions about the details of his offenses, his prison record, and his plans for the future. They even got into the details of the Jessica Hahn scandal. Bakker was ready to talk.

He had spent weeks in his prison cell collecting old photographs of all the buildings he constructed at Heritage USA with contributions from his television viewers. He showed the examiners photographs of the Heritage Grand Hotel, the World Outreach Center, the broadcast studios, the Heritage Inn Motel, the Water Park, and dozens of other structures. He emphasized that he was getting a bad rap for stealing money from his contributors. The money was spent right there at Heritage, he told them. He built buildings with that money, he bought television time, he paid the salaries of thousands of employees. All of the media hype about him stealing $150 million was just not true, he argued.[1]

He told them that if he had known that PTL was really in financial difficulty, he never would have accepted the bonuses or salary that he was paid. He said he was not in charge of the books. He left those things to the accountants. He was the visionary, the dreamer, and the fund-raiser. He wasn't the treasurer. And his system of accounting and financial management couldn't be found in the pages of the *Wall Street Journal*. He ran that place's finances on the faith that whatever money was needed would be provided by God. God would move enough contributors to send whatever money was needed for Heritage.

Call me unrealistic, Bakker said, for those beliefs but don't call me a thief. And don't punish me like a thief.

He answered questions about Jessica Hahn and admitted his moral failure and the terrible mistake that had been. He blamed only himself.

He spoke with passion and in the end accepted full responsibility for all that had happened at Heritage. He spoke of his three and a half years in prison and how he had been brought to his knees. Nothing would ever be the same again in his life, and all he could hope for was being released so that he could go quietly back to St. Petersburg, Florida to live with his son in peace. When asked if he had a job to return to, a stock question asked of every parolee, Bakker was ready: He had been offered a job in Largo, Florida working for D'Andrea Electrical Contractors.[2]

It was then Ben Malcolm's turn and he argued that Bakker's intentions were always honorable when he was raising money at PTL. This was no Milken. This was no Boesky. There were no hidden bank accounts under assumed names and nothing was concealed from the public. Bakker never purposely set out to defraud anyone. The worst that you could say about him was that of the $172 million he raised from partnership proceeds, he spent $4 million on himself and Tammy, and Jessica Hahn was promised $257,000. And how could you say that all of that $4 million was undeserved? Wasn't he entitled to some salary as president of PTL? How about Tammy Faye? Should she have been appearing on television all year long for nothing? Malcolm urged the examiners to put all of the evidence in the case in broader perspective and not treat Jim Bakker like an ax murderer to be left rotting away in prison.[3]

The hearing was over in just fifty minutes and the examiners asked Bakker to leave the room while they deliberated. A few minutes later, they called him back and told him that they were recommending that he be released on parole that December, 1993—eight months from then. With six months in a halfway house, Bakker could be free by June. To him, the news was God-sent.

He immediately wrote a letter to his friends telling them of the examiners' decision. The first paragraph captured his reaction to the news:

> Hallelujah!!! Praise the Lord!!! Glory to Jesus!!! Bless the Lord, O my soul, and all that is within me, bless His Holy Name!!! Glory to God in the highest!!! My soul doth magnify the Lord, and my spirit rejoices in God, my Savior!!! Hallelujah!!! Hallelujah!!! Hallelujah and Amen!!![4]

Later in that same letter, he wrote: "remember, the last chapter has not been written yet. The best is yet to come!"[5]

Well, not exactly. It was the other way around. The worst was yet to come.

Bakker's Hopes Dashed

The higher-ups in the Parole Commission didn't like the idea one bit of releasing Jim Bakker early, and they reversed the decision of the examiners who had conducted the prison hearing. Parole Commission member Carol Pavilack Getty from Kansas City was the one leading the charge against Bakker and she argued that he should not be freed from prison because he had "grossly abused public/national trust."[6] She calculated that "the exact amount of [Bakker's] fraud is difficult to access [sic] but the minimum amount appears to be in the neighborhood of $130 million."[7] As Commissioner Getty saw it, Judge Mullen had already given Bakker "a most generous"[8] deal by reducing his sentence to eight years and he should be content with that. In persuading the other commissioners to vote with her against Bakker, Getty wrote the televangelist, "[y]ou abused the trust implied by your chosen profession and the fact that you were a highly respected public figure"[9] disqualifies you from early release from prison.

Getty only needed two other votes to block Bakker's parole, and she got them on May 11, 1993 from Commissioners Jasper R. Clay of Baltimore and John R. Simpson of Boston.

When he got the word back in Rochester, Bakker just couldn't believe it. He was stunned. "My children and I are devastated,"[10] he said at the time. Desperate at the thought of having to remain in prison until 1997, he hunkered down and decided to fight it. It was the first time since he was indicted more than five years before that he had stood up on his hind legs and engaged the enemy.

Bakker's All Out Battle for Parole

He had only one chance—to appeal the decision of the three commissioners who voted to block his parole to the full nine-member commission. They would be meeting in Washington, D.C. in late July 1993. At the outset, however, his efforts were dogged by missteps. Bakker told me his attorneys in North Carolina didn't get right at first one of the dates for the parole appeals process. Although he didn't confront them directly, he was angry. And he finally took charge of his own case from his prison cell in Rochester. He would quarterback it him-self.[11]

His nineteen-year old son Jamie moved to Rochester for the summer and lived with Assembly of God pastor Phillip Shaw and his wife. Jamie would be his dad's eyes and ears and be in charge of attempting to mobilize Christian leaders around the country. The goal would be to inundate the Parole Commission with letters urging Bakker's release. Jamie spent hours every day on the telephone calling figures from his past that he had met only as a child—Oral Roberts, Richard Roberts, Jimmy Swaggart, and other Christian leaders and celebrities who had appeared on his dad's TV programs. Pastor Shaw hit the phones also and called everyone he knew in the Evangelical community. The two of them kept Bakker posted daily and visited him several times a week on visiting days. There was urgency to their work and they really got down to business. They organized it like a campaign and worked night and day.

Quickly, Pastor Shaw drove Jamie to Des Moines, Iowa for a meeting with my research assistant, Suzan Brooks, and I. Jim sent them from Rochester for two purposes—for me to brief Jamie on all that I had learned about the case in two years of research, and to have the four of us brainstorm and develop some strategy for fighting the parole appeal. Des Moines is four hours south of Rochester by car.

Jamie had been so young when his father's PTL empire collapsed that he understood very little about the case. I gave him an overview and highlighted the evidence that had been used against his dad in the Charlotte trial. Most of it was news to him. Tammy Faye had kept him in school in Orlando throughout the ordeal to shield him from the trauma. But his dad felt that it was time that he know so that he would be better able to deal with the Christian leaders and Bakker supporters whom he would be telephoning.

In an intense six-hour meeting, the four of us developed a strategy which they took back to Jim in prison. One part of the plan was to have me contact former FCC colleagues in Washington, D.C. to see if they could recommend a politically connected Washington lawyer to speak on Bakker's behalf at the parole appeal hearing.

The thinking was that those parole commissioners were politically appointed and would better heed the arguments of an established Washington attorney with whom they had dealt before and with whom they would deal again, rather than two attorneys from North Carolina who were total strangers to them. It only made sense.

I immediately telephoned the person I trusted most in Washington, who was one of the capital's best known and most admired lawyers. He suggested that I call Richard Hauser, a savvy member of Washington's powerful Baker & Hostetler firm. I did so, explained the situation to him, and promised to immediately forward him the research that I had done on the case. He was willing to represent Bakker before the Parole Commission. As a former White House deputy counsel under Ronald Reagan, he knew how to do it.

Jamie's telephone calls started getting results. One of the biggest scores was Mark DeMoss, the former aide to Jerry Falwell who now advised other nationally prominent Christian leaders including Billy Graham's son, Franklin. DeMoss was extremely well connected nationally and knew several U.S. senators. He was a channel to Evangelicals and fundamentalists around the country who hadn't exactly cried themselves to sleep over Bakker's downfall and conviction, but who were beginning to believe that enough was enough and that Bakker should be set free. At Jim's urging, Jamie scheduled another meeting at the Drake University Law School in Des Moines on three days' notice between himself, Mark DeMoss, Pastor Shaw, Suzan Brooks, and me. At the meeting, a strategy was developed to encourage as many Bakker supporters as possible to write the Parole Commission on Jim's behalf.

The more phone calls that Jamie and Pastor Shaw made around the country, the clearer it became that there was strong sentiment among fundamentalists that Bakker had long since paid his debt to society and that any further incarceration amounted to nothing less than persecution of him. They were determined to let the Parole Commission know it.

The most surprising response Jamie received was from none other than Jimmy Swaggart, who had played such a prominent role in Bakker's downfall. By this time, Swaggart strongly believed that Jim had been punished far too severely and that he should be released. Swaggart went on the air and told his own national television audience on July 11, 1993, to write letters to the Parole Board on Jim's behalf. Said Swaggart on that broadcast:

I'm doing that [writing a letter] and I think the Lord would bless you for doing that as well. I believe that the touch of God is still in Jim's life. Would you write that letter?[12]

Mark DeMoss started working quietly behind the scenes to see if other prominent Christians would now stand up for Bakker. Nationally syndicated *Los Angeles Times* columnist Cal Thomas joined in, penning a scathing column:

The public interest is not served by continuing Jim Bakker's incarceration. He has been punished enough. He has cleaned toilets in prison, his wife divorced him, and he is a broken man. It borders on cruel and unusual punishment to attempt to extract additional pounds of flesh from a man who has no more to give.[13]

Backing up her brother, Tammy Sue sent an urgent memo to tens of thousands of Bakker supporters around the country: "Please, would you do me a favor and write the Parole Commission today and tell them why you feel my dad should be granted parole. Please ask every member of your family and others who care to write immediately, and be sure to remind them to be kind in their letters. *** I need your help so desperately. Thank you from the bottom of my heart."[14]

Letters started pouring in to the commission's Washington offices:

- **Oral Roberts, pioneer televangelist:** I do not attempt to speak for everybody but I do appeal in behalf of many thousands of sincere Christian people who believe he [Bakker] has paid the penalty by his imprisonment and by the open condemnation of his actions by the public in general.[15]

- **A. T. Lawing, former thirteen-year PTL board member from Huntersville, North Carolina:** I could go on and on . . . about the good acts performed by Jim Bakker during his time at PTL. [He] is capable of once again serving his fellow man when allowed to leave prison. Please reconsider your decision![16]

- **J. Don George, Dallas pastor and former PTL board member:** It is my observation that the entire Christian community of our country is saddened, disturbed and disappointed by the harsh sentence which was handed down to Jim Bakker following his conviction. I speak regularly at churches and conferences throughout the United States. *** Without exception, the many people who have spoken to me regarding Jim Bakker's prison sentence have expressed their sorrow for the length of the sentence which was imposed. I believe there are millions of Christians throughout the United States who are praying now that the recent decision of the parole board will be reversed.[17]

- **Dr. Don Argue, president of North Central College in Minneapolis and of the National Association of Evangelicals:** Although I cannot speak for the 50,000 churches and 70 denominations that the National Association of Evangelicals represents, I do speak as their president. The sentencing and lack of parole for Jim Bakker is unreasonable. *** The overwhelming opinion in Evangelical circles is that parole would be appropriate at this time.[18]

- **H. Edward Knox, former longtime PTL attorney and mayor of Charlotte:** In many instances prior to Dr. Dortch coming to that ministry, Jim Bakker not only heeded reasonable legal advice to bring the PTL ministry's house in order, but made some reductions. The ministry really turned around when Dr. Dortch came to PTL. Dr. Dortch placed himself beyond following legal advice. *** The grievance of my complaint is that Dr. Dortch received such a light sentence and Jim Bakker received such a tremendous sentence. It is my opinion Jim Bakker played a lesser role in the downfall of the ministry than did Dr. Dortch.[19]

- **Rev. Rex Humbard, televangelist:** I believe with all my heart that his debt has been paid to society and if released, Jim will be a productive part of any community. *** The scripture tells us to pray for those who are in a position of authority. We are praying for you.[20]

- **Robert R. D'Andrea, president, D'Andrea Electric, Inc.:** We are willing to hire James O. Bakker as a full-time employee, 40 hours per week. In the past, we have hired several other home confinement, half-way house, and parolees with good results.[21]

While his son, daughter, and Pastor Shaw were scrambling, Jim himself was hard at work in his cell doing something that he should have done six years before—accumulating the evidence that could help him. For sixteen hours a day, he pored over thousands of pages of PTL audits and all of the magazines and newspapers that he had mailed from Heritage describing the lifetime partnership program. Page by page and line by line, Bakker went through boxes of documents looking for proof that he had told his contributors that he was going to use their donations for things at Heritage other than just building the two hotels. He was also searching for photographs of the several buildings that he had erected which appeared earlier in PTL magazines. His plan was to do something he had not done before—defend himself on the charges against him.

The prison didn't allow inmates to have scissors, so Bakker used a pair of nose hair clippers to cut pictures out of the old PTL brochures. Night after night, he taped pieces of evidence together onto sheets of notebook paper and mailed them across town to Pastor Shaw who in turn put them into binders. When they finished after several weeks of work, Bakker and Shaw had three full notebooks of evidence which Bakker mailed to the Parole Commission in Washington. It was some of the best lawyering that had been done on his case in years.

The Evidence Bakker Sent to the Parole Commission

Two of Jim's loyal supporters, Mr. and Mrs. Andrew D. Schuessler of Marietta, Georgia, had saved their fund-raising letter from Jim offering them a $1,000 lifetime partnership in the Towers Hotel. It was the actual letter, all right, with their home address printed on it and even a computer-generated key number identifying the run. At the bottom of the letter, these statements appeared: "Your gifts are used to support PTL and all its programs."[22] And, "Reservations are based upon completion of the Heritage Grand Towers and availability of lodging."[23] That was what he had been trying to tell everyone for years, and he placed that letter prominently in the notebook.

Jim included the Towers receipt received by Karl Garmager of Walled Lake, Michigan, which read: "Your $1,000 gift has been received for the world wide outreach of PTL."[24] Not for construction of the hotel only, of course, but for all of the activities at PTL which constituted its worldwide outreach including its television broadcasts, overseas missions, orphanages, and other programs.

Bakker then found the actual brochure that was mailed out announcing the Towers partnerships. Under an artist's drawing of the hotel itself, these words appeared: "Yes, when you send your Towers membership gift of $1,000 for the work of PTL, . . ."[25] It couldn't have been more clear that the Towers contribution was going to be used for any PTL work and not just the construction of the hotel.

Bakker located a receipt received by partners Mr. and Mrs. Roland Hadley of Ypsilanti, Michigan, for their Eleven Hundred Club lifetime membership which contained this language: "Thank you PTL partner. Your gifts are used to support PTL and all its programs."[26] The partnership monies raised, plain enough from this preprinted receipt, were going to be spent to support PTL and all of the programs it was involved in. The money was not only for the construction of lodging facilities. It was there in black and white.

And, from a videotape that the government had used against him in his trial, this statement he made on the air September 28, 1984 in discussing the Grand Hotel partnerships: "We'll just stop at 25,000, and then it will kind of trickle over and, because we can't go over 30,000 in the Grand, and, you know what, it's not only trickled over the 30,000, it's avalanched over the 30,000. . . ."[27] During the trial, Bakker and his attorneys hadn't realized the significance of those words, but the more he thought about it in his cell the clearer it was that with those words he in fact was telling his viewers that the 25,000 member limit in the Grand Hotel was being exceeded and the lodging program enlarged.[28]

Then, Bakker calculated for the Parole Commission the lodging that was already available for Grand Hotel lifetime partners. Remember that he had sold 66,683 memberships in the Grand. He added up the 500 rooms in the Grand, the 96 rooms in the Heritage Inn, the 21 rooms in the Lakeside Lodges, the 350 sites in the Wilderness Campgrounds, and the 396 berths in the Fort Heritage Campground for a total of 1,363 rooms and sites. All of those would have accommodated 62,414 partners over a year's time at three nights, four nights, or even ten nights each. On that same page, Bakker then cut out small pictures of each of those lodging facilities and taped them to the margins to make the point that this was not proposed construction but buildings already in the ground and being used.[29]

In the second volume of his evidence binders, Bakker cut out pictures of every building at Heritage—hotels, motel, broadcast studio, television satellite center, bunkhouse, Kevin's House, Fort Hope, the girls' home, amphitheater, restaurants, and shopping mall. Then, he attached pictures of different PTL activities that had appeared in magazines and newspapers over the years—all-night prayer sessions in the Upper Room, church services, miracle healings, prayer in the campgrounds, baptisms, fellowship, and gospel singing.[30]

In forty-five additional pages, he argued that the government was wrong to say that the amount of his fraud was $170 million. What he told the commissioners was that the money was spent at Heritage on those buildings and those activities. It didn't end up in any Swiss bank account. In page after page, he put a price tag on each building based on actual certified PTL audits done by the Big Eight accounting firms that had overseen the expenditure of PTL contributions during those years. The audits showed these outlays: $171 million to build and equip Heritage USA from 1984 through 1987, $35 million for general operating expenses, $13 million to build the Heritage Island Water Park and slide, $22 million for food and lodging, $91 million to pay for television and satellite broadcasting, $101 million for wages and salaries, $17 million for Bibles and books, $15 million for printing and postage, $21 million for new real estate development, $15 million for maintenance and utilities, and $17 million to pay interest and fees for CPAs and lawyers.[31]

Then, in his third binder, Bakker ripped the covers off all of the books that he had written, including the popular PTL Parallel Bible, and all of the records and cassettes that Tammy had recorded over the years and taped them to the pages. There were fifteen pages in all, many with four or five books or albums on each. He emphasized that he and Tammy gave every penny of the $8 million in personal royalties those books and records made right back to PTL. And he asked the commissioners how they could say that he ever stole $4 million from PTL when he gave $8 million in royalties back to it?[32]

As an exhibit, Bakker attached actual copies of the certified audits for 1984, 1985, and 1986 prepared by Deloitte Haskins & Sells and Laventhol & Horwath.[33]

When he was done, Bakker put plastic covers on each of the 144 pages of evidence that he organized into those three binders, and asked a fellow inmate who did calligraphy to help him with a cover. The finished product was entitled "Appeal to the United States Parole Commission by Jim Bakker 07407–058" and the covers contained pictures of the Heritage Grand and Grand Towers hotels, and an aerial map of Heritage USA. It was impressive work.

The only question remaining was how his materials would be delivered to the parole commissioners. At a meeting in Rochester in June 1993, Bakker asked me to do whatever was necessary to enlist the help of Washington, D.C. attorney Hauser to present the materials and make whatever presentation he could to the parole commissioners on Bakker's behalf. It never happened.

In a telephone conversation with Bakker's executive assistant, Shirley Fulbright, a short time later, she leveled with me that if another attorney were brought in, the North Carolina attorneys might perceive it as a slap in the face. There was concern that they would be so offended that they might withdraw from the case. That simply could not be risked because they apparently held the key to Judge Graham Mullen. They were the ones who knew the judge and practiced before him.

The North Carolina attorneys indicated to Shirley Fulbright that they were going to ask Judge Mullen for a letter addressed to the Parole Commission urging that Bakker be released that summer. Of all that anybody could possibly do to help get Bakker paroled, a letter from the sentencing judge would be the best. Without question, that letter was needed. So, it was decided not to ask Richard Hauser to deliver the materials to the Parole Commission or speak on Bakker's behalf. I called

Hauser in Washington later that day and explained the situation, and he understood completely.

So, everything was left in the hands of the North Carolina attorneys and Bakker's notebooks were mailed to the Parole Commission in Washington. The commission met on Thursday, July 29, 1993, and turned Bakker down flat. My research assistant spoke by telephone with Commissioner Clay and he said he read the three volumes from Bakker, and that the other members did also. They weren't persuaded. No Washington, D.C. attorney appeared before them to speak on Bakker's behalf.

Mark Sakaley, a spokesman for the Parole Commission, announced that Bakker would not be paroled. "This was his last available remedy, so at this point in time, he will be serving his sentence to expiration,"[34] Sakaley said from Washington.

With time reduced from his eight-year sentence for good time and even extra good time, Bakker would be automatically paroled in October 1994. That would include more than two years of good time taken off his sentence. He would still be monitored and supervised by the Parole Commission until 1997, the exact date on which his eight year sentence would expire.

And, that was that. From the euphoria surrounding the promise of parole, the mobilization of people all over the country, and in the end to a hollow thud. A big buildup, and another letdown. From Hallelujah to being hit in the face again with a two-by-four.

One mystery remains from the entire parole odyssey. No one is saying whether Judge Mullen ever considered writing that letter to the Parole Commission. What is known is that no such letter was ever received.[35]

The Move to Georgia

The only good news that Bakker got from the government in 1993 was that he was going to be transferred.

In July 1993, after serving nearly four years in Rochester, Bakker was moved to a minimum security prison camp in

Jesup, Georgia. He remained there until being released to a halfway house in June 1994.

Jesup, a new prison housing 500 inmates, looked more like a small community college anchored on red Georgia clay. Silhouetted with tall pine trees in a forest-like setting, it didn't have prison walls and fences with razor wire like the Rochester facility. The buildings were clean, and trees and flowers could be seen from the common areas. But, Bakker remained locked up tight as a drum. It's just that the view was better and the other inmates decidedly more white collar and, fortuitously, religious. "There is a large Christian fellowship here that made me feel welcome and accepted,"[36] Jim said. "There is a really beautiful Spirit of God moving in this prison."[37]

There were Bible studies or church services of some kind most nights of the week. The chapel was often filled nightly with prayer services. On Sundays, there were so many inmates wanting to attend church services that they were offered on a rotation basis because there was not enough room for everyone and their families to attend at the same time. Some inmates actually got up at 3:00 A.M. for private prayer time.

Jim's own daily routine was not that much different than it was in Rochester. He still got up most mornings at 5:30 A.M. to study the Bible with several other inmates including a former lay preacher, Larry Wright of Jacksonville, Florida. Jim's job description remained about the same and he continued to mop floors and scour toilets. "I'm a bathroom orderly,"[38] he said, being responsible for all the sinks, showers, and toilets used by sixty inmates.

But there were major changes in his life, including being able to see his two children most weekends. Jesup, with a population of 9,300, is only an hour and a half north of Jacksonville, Florida, and four hours by car from Tammy Sue's home in South Carolina. Sue would bring the two grandsons for visits and Bakker delighted in sending friends photographs of his clan spending time with him on visiting days.

Son Jamie, who had spent the summer of 1993 living with Pastor Shaw in Rochester, moved to Atlanta to attend a private high school and be closer to his dad. With Jim so close, his children saw him frequently and that gave him a real boost. Bakker is very much a nurturing, hands on parent and always was. Despite his own celebrity, he took his parental responsibilities seriously from the time those children were babies. They are very close and tightly bonded, and being able to see them each weekend gave Jim the strength to grind out the last of his sentence.

As well, a stream of nationally known evangelists and gospel singers added that backwoods federal outpost to their itineraries because of Bakker's presence there and that of so many other Christians anxious for their religious messages. The prison mess hall was used for those concerts and services, and Jim reported that most of them were jammed to the walls.

But of all the emissaries to visit Jesup, not one could top the November 1993 stopover by none other than Jerry Falwell himself, the prince of much of the darkness which had engulfed Bakker's life. Falwell swooped down in his own private jet after a breast-thumping evangelical blitz at the First Assembly of God Church in Jacksonville. Falwell aides described the Jesup meeting as "a pastoral visit"[39] in which the two men embraced, then prayed and "had almost no discussion about the past."[40]

Bakker reported details of the curious rendezvous in a letter to his PTL and New Covenant partners, many of whom still loathed Falwell and blamed him for Jim being in prison and Heritage being in bankruptcy:

> I can almost hear you say, "How did you feel?" There was no pain or stress, no hate, just peace and forgiveness. At that moment, I knew God had done a complete work in my life.
>
> The Prison Chaplain took us to his office where Jerry and I shared and prayed. I had no desire to talk about the past. *** We asked each other's forgiveness . . . we embraced and said our "goodbyes."[41]

Talk about turning the other cheek. Reunited with the man who accused him on national television of moral depravity, who refused to let him return to PTL, and who turned the

Justice Department loose with his files, and after four years in prison Bakker hugs him.

The transfer to Georgia truly was a good one for Bakker. More than anything, it became clear that he was taking the first steps toward moving forward with his life. He was coping better with the cards that had been dealt him. He began speaking, although guardedly rather than with the effervescent enthusiasm of the past, about what he wanted to do next and about life as a free man. One idea was for Bakker to join Billy Graham's son, Franklin, in the worldwide ministry that the young Graham headed, Samaritan's Purse. Bakker would help build hospitals and orphanages around the world, and would take his son Jamie with him to do it. They would move back to North Carolina and live near the Graham family. Jim considers that state home, and he has tens of thousands of supporters there.[42]

Another sign of his transition as he counted down his own months in Jesup was his work on other inmates' cases and their appeals. Not his own. During my February 1994 visit with him, one of the top priorities he wanted to discuss with me at length was the case of fellow inmate Larry Wright. Bakker asked me to help Mr. Wright and offered me a detailed analysis of Wright's case and the reasons he thought his friend should be released. Bakker looked good and his mind was razor-sharp. His heart still bled for others who had hit bottom.

Free at Last

On Friday, July 1, 1994, the U.S. Department of Justice opened the gate at the Jesup prison and allowed Bakker to walk slowly into the scorching Georgia sunlight. After four and three quarters years in prison, he was free. He earned his own release by serving the required two-thirds of his eight-year sentence. Good time he had accumulated from years as a model prisoner cut his time even more.

Met at the door by his son, Jim was driven to Asheville, North Carolina, a few short hours away. There, he would have to live in a halfway house operated by the Salvation Army until

December 1 when he would be granted his unconditional release.

Before leaving prison, he wrote out a statement for the press:

Statement to the press by Jim Bakker

It is with great joy and thanksgiving to God that I walk from prison today.

I look forward to a time of rebonding with my son, Jamie Charles, and daughter, Tammy Sue, and my two delightful grandsons, James, my namesake, and Jonathan, who was born while I was in prison.

Also, I am anxious to spend time with my other family members, especially my mother and father who both will celebrate their 88th birthdays in a few weeks and who have faithfully stood by me.

There are no words to express my gratitude to my friends and family who have fulfilled the great Proverb, "A friend loveth at all times and a brother is born for adversity."

Most of all, I want to thank my Lord and Savior Jesus Christ who walked with me through this valley of despair and loneliness and turned it into a time of healing solitude with Him, for truly in this valley "He restored my soul."

Once again, I want to humbly ask for forgiveness to those I have offended or hurt in any way by my sin and arrogant lifestyle.

I also humbly ask the Family of God to forgive me for the pain and shame I brought on them, and most of all on the Name of our Lord.

After Halfway House, I will make my home with my son, Jamie Charles.

I leave you with the words of the Apostle Paul, written from his prison cell ". . . The Lord stood with me and strengthened me."[43]

Media Coverage of Bakker's Imprisonment

Newspaper and magazine articles chronicling Bakker's years behind bars were infrequent, largely because Bakker refused to grant any press interviews. But the absence of hard facts or serious sources, while typically an impediment to the mainstream press, didn't slow the tabloids which followed his Rochester and Jesup tours with a steady stream of vacuous and often totally fabricated prattle. Bakker told me, "I do see the rag mags here."[44] He showed me a current issue of the *Examiner* which used the old picture of him, bloated, crying, and in shackles en route to Butner during his trial. "Why do they still use that terrible picture? But I can't do anything about it, so I just let it roll off my back."[45]

Some of the articles were so vicious that Bakker's Rochester cellmate, David Miskavige, wrote a scathing letter to the press accusing them of assassinating Jim's character. What set his roommate off were stories that Bakker had become a raving lunatic behind bars, and that he was hallucinating and preaching to imaginary congregations. "He is . . . in full control of his faculties," Miskavige seethed. "All reports to the contrary are sheer fantasy."[46]

There was a lot for Bakker to ignore during those years.

- *National Enquirer,* **March 31, 1992:** That Tammy Faye was giving up the ministry in order to make millions as a guest on TV game shows and sitcoms. The article went on to quote Jim Bakker's eighty-five-year-old father, Raleigh, as saying, "It's clear the devil got into her."[47]

- *Examiner,* **May 26, 1992:** That since Tammy divorced him, "everyone has been afraid Jim will either try to take his own life or die in prison of a broken heart." And that the couples' best friends are sure Tammy will never marry Roe Messner, but instead will get back together with Jim.[48]

- *Examiner,* **June 8, 1993:** Their hearts afire, the *Examiner* headline reads "Jim and Tammy plan to remarry in prison!"[49]

- *Examiner,* **August 17, 1993:** The story lead with the news that "Jim Bakker has finally escaped from the prison hell that nearly drove him insane." Later in the article, readers learned that he hadn't really escaped but had been transferred to Jesup, Georgia.[50]

- *Examiner,* **September 28, 1993:** The headline read that Bakker was "wasting away" in prison, "now a thin, ravaged shadow of his former self." In what was certainly an insult to Jim after two years in the Rochester weight room working out, the story continued that his prison clothes hang "limply from his bony neck and gaunt chest."[51]

It had all been such a turbulent odyssey—the trial, the four and three fourths years spent trying to free him, the unending tabloid frenzy, and in the end some nagging doubts about his guilt. No wonder Tammy Faye couldn't take it any more.

NOTES

1. Initial Hearing Summary, April 29, 1993, Reg. No. 07407–058, U.S. Department of Justice, U.S. Parole Commission; Bakker, *Appeal to the U.S. Parole Commission,* June 1, 1993, vol. II; Jim Bakker, interview by author, in Rochester, Minnesota, May 29, 1993.

2. Robert R. D'Andrea, letter to U.S. Parole Commission, February 8, 1993.

3. Initial Hearing Summary, *supra,* n. 1.

4. Jim Bakker, letter to New Covenant Partners, May 1993.

5. *Id.*

6. Memorandum to National Commissioners, U.S. Parole Commission, from Carol Pavilack Getty, May 3, 1993, Reg. No. 07407–058.

7. *Id.*

8. Referral to Regional Commissioner, April 29, 1993, Reg. No. 07407–058, U.S. Department of Justice, U.S. Parole Commission [comments by Commissioner Getty].

9. Memorandum to National Commissioners, *supra,* n. 6.

10. Sneed, "News," *Chicago Sun-Times,* May 18, 1993, at 2-A (Nexis printout).

11. Jim Bakker, interview by author, in Rochester, Minnesota, May 29, 1993.

12. Videotape of *Jimmy Swaggart Hour* broadcast, July 11, 1993.

13. Thomas, "Jim Bakker Deserves Parole," *Los Angeles Times,* nationally syndicated column, July 28, 1993.

14. Tammy Sue Chapman, letter to New Covenant Partners, June 1993.

15. Oral Roberts, letter to U.S. Parole Commission, May 19, 1993.

16. A.T. Lawing, letter to U.S. Parole Commission, June 18, 1993.

17. J. Don George, letter to U.S. Parole Commission, May 17, 1993.

18. Don Argue, letter to U.S. Parole Commission, June 4, 1993.

19. H. Edward Knox, letter to U.S. Parole Commission, June 24, 1993.

20. Rev. Rex Humbard, letter to U.S. Parole Commission, June 15, 1993.

21. Robert R. D'Andrea, letter to U.S. Parole Commission, February 8, 1993.

22. Bakker, *Appeal to U.S. Parole Commission,* June 1, 1993, vol. I at 6.

23. *Id.*

24. *Id.* at 3.

25. *Id.* at 9.

26. *Id.* at 14.

27. *Id.* at 22.

28. Jim Bakker, interview by author, in Rochester, Minnesota, April 4, 1993.

29. Bakker, *supra*, n. 22 at 40–41.

30. Bakker, *Appeal to U.S. Parole Commission*, June 1, 1993, vol. II at 49–91.

31. *Id.* at 50–95.

32. Bakker, *Appeal to U.S. Parole Commission*, June 1, 1993, vol. III at 113, 141.

33. Bakker, *Appeal to U.S. Parole Commission*, June 1, 1993, Exhibit 2.

34. "Bakker to Serve Out Time," *Houston Chronicle*, July 30, 1993, at 2-A (Nexis printout).

35. Michael A. Stover, General Counsel, U.S. Parole Commission letter to the author, November 14, 1994.

36. Jim Bakker, letter to the author, August 19, 1993.

37. Tammy Sue Chapman, letter to the author, August 28, 1993.

38. Jim Bakker, letter to the author, January 2, 1994.

39. "Feuding TV Evangelists Embrace, Pray Together," *Orlando Sentinel*, November 27, 1993 at 13-D (Nexis printout).

40. *Id.*

41. Jim Bakker, letter to New Covenant Partners [undated] (mailed November, 1993).

42. Jim Bakker, interview by author, in Jesup, Georgia, February 12, 1994.

43. Jim Bakker, statement to the press, Jesup, Georgia, July 1, 1994.

44. Jim Bakker, interview by author, in Rochester, Minnesota, September 25, 1992.

45. *Id.*

46. "Bakker Cellmate Denies Evangelist Is 'Raving Lunatic,'" UPI, *Los Angeles Times*, June 4, 1990 at 2-P, col. 6.

47. "Tammy Faye Dumps Church for Shot at Show Biz," *National Enquirer*, March 31, 1992, at 44.

48. "Jim and Tammy Plan to Rewed," *Examiner*, May 26, 1992 at 17.

49. "Jim and Tammy Plan to Remarry in Prison!" *Examiner*, June 8, 1993 at 27.

50. "Bakker's Escape!" *Examiner*, August 17, 1993 at 20–21.

51. "Jim Bakker Is Wasting Away," *Examiner*, September 28, 1993 at 9.

Chapter 28

The Problems with Bakker's Case

Jim Bakker in prison: I went into my . . . trial unprepared. . . .[1]

My own interviews with jurors, spectators, and, of course, Jim Bakker himself prompt this chapter's inquiry: could anything have been done in that courtroom to win an acquittal?

A Mountain Too High

1. He didn't have a strategy that worked.

If part of the defense strategy at trial was to destroy the government's witnesses on cross-examination, as Bakker remembers it, it dislodged little testimony. It certainly got off to an inauspicious and surreal start when Steve Nelson collapsed of what people thought was a heart attack under Harold Bender's forceful cross-examination on the third day of the trial. After that, the remaining government witnesses, including the big guns like Pastor Dortch and the FBI agents, offered testimony that was simply too powerful to erode on cross-examination.

The key defense arguments and theories that were advanced just didn't play with the jury. Day in and day out throughout the trial, George Davis kept interrupting and objecting whenever the prosecutors would use the word "sell" when referring to the lifetime partnerships. He was even successful in obtaining an order from Judge Potter prohibiting any reference to "sales" in describing the partnerships. Davis's argument was that they were donations, not sales. Therefore, since no one had actually bought anything, Bakker couldn't be guilty of fraud.

Dozens of partners in fact testified that they didn't think they were buying anything and that they were only making free-will contributions to Bakker's ministry. Sam Gasaway, Bakker's witness from Atlanta, testified, "I did not expect a [real estate] title or anything of this nature."[2] Bryan Hiser from Houston told the jury that he considered his four lifetime partnerships flat out gifts to Bakker's ministry.[3] Dorothy Taylor, of Jacksonville, Florida, took the stand for Bakker, too, and explained that she had always considered her several partnerships as free-will donations to PTL rather than payments for lodging.[4] Several other Bakker witnesses said the same thing.

But all of those attempts to put that spin on the facts struck the jury as hollow. To some, it was a trumped up technicality to contend that lifetime partners weren't buying lodging with their $1,000 donations. After all, through eight hours of edited tapes of *PTL Club* programs, Jim and Tammy had repeatedly promised contributors that they would receive hotel or campsite benefits in return for their $1,000 pledges. And most of those who claimed that their partnerships were only donations also testified that they looked forward to staying at Heritage each year to share in its unique Christian fellowship. Dorothy Taylor, for instance, admitted on the witness stand that she couldn't wait to visit Heritage. "It was the most wonderful place in the world,"[5] she said. So, to argue that they weren't purchasing lodging at Heritage with their donations didn't ring true.

A better approach would have been to argue that there were always rooms available at some point during the year at the Grand, and therefore Bakker had not broken his promise to contributors that they would have a place to stay at Heritage for their $1,000.

2. Nobody found the videotapes that might have cleared him.

Bakker maintained all along, and said it again on the witness stand during his own testimony, that he had emphasized two points on several of his television programs. First, that partnership income could be spent on any PTL activity, not just the hotels. And second, that he was changing the plan and would be going over the originally announced limits on the hotels. Obviously, that would be evidence the jury might have found sufficient to clear him. Two or three minutes of videotape with Bakker saying those things on his TV program, and this trial could have changed dramatically.

What we know today is that a tape was made of every *PTL Club* broadcast ever aired. By the time of Bakker's trial, those thousands of tapes reposed in one of only two places—either in the PTL library at Heritage USA under the control of the Federal Bankruptcy Court, or with reference to the tapes the government had chosen to preview and excerpt, in a special evidence room in an office building across from the Charlotte courthouse.

Why weren't those tapes found? Was it because they really didn't exist and Bakker in fact never said those exculpatory things on his show? Or was it because no one looked hard enough to find them?

Why wasn't it understood that this was a trial about what Bakker said on television? And that the most relevant defense evidence was what Bakker did say on TV that undercut the government's case?

One wouldn't even need to have an attorney sit there and watch every one of those thousands of tapes. All it would take would be a college student, high school student, or even partner loyal to Jim wanting to do something to help him in his case, and there were thousands of those people in the Charlotte area. Their job would be to spend as many days as it took over the several months before trial to keep watching those tapes until they hit pay dirt. They could even have put a composite tape together like the prosecutors did. One could have recruited hundreds of Bakker followers to do that. It would have been a snap and they could have gone through those thousands of tapes in a matter of weeks. It wouldn't have cost a dime. But it wasn't done.

The fact that it was not done left Bakker wide open to this attack by Deborah Smith on cross-examination:

Deborah Smith: You never told the public that, did you?
Jim Bakker: I'm sure I discussed that with the partners.
Deborah Smith: Again, can you give me a date?
Jim Bakker: No. There are so many tapes, I couldn't. I don't know what day I did anything.[6]

3. The defense was decidedly low-tech.

The prosecution's case was high-tech, visual, and understandable. The government built a methodical case with hundreds of PTL documents, the important ones being shown to the jury on a huge overhead projector. They played several hours of highlighted *PTL Club* broadcasts in which Bakker made claims and promises about the lifetime partnership program which, in the end, were exaggerated and not kept. Watching those programs on the courtroom monitors, the jury was a part of the action and they were watching television rather than listening to the attorneys orate.

For major evidence, government artists prepared huge charts and diagrams showing such things as Bakker's salary and bonuses over the years. Damaging memos sent to Bakker by his former attorneys and finance directors were enlarged and mounted on posterboard for the jury to see. The prosecutors actually had a government cameraman walk through Bakker's presidential suite at the Heritage Grand Hotel and shoot footage for the jury showing them how elegant the place really was.

And what juror could forget the Yacov Heller statue that fell apart when it was passed to the jury? The prosecutors' case was a strong one because they used technology to make their evidence come alive and facilitate the jury's understanding of it.

Not Bakker's team. One of the ironies of their whole case was that they were representing a television star with visual techniques from the radio age. When they wanted the jury to see something, they would pass around photographs. Why didn't somebody take a camcorder out to Heritage and put some sharp video together for Bakker that would have made the point that the tens of millions of dollars he raised was all sunk in those buildings?

Bakker to this day says that he knew he was done when the judge wouldn't let him use his own charts and show them to the jury. But, the real question should be—why did Bakker have to prepare his own charts to begin with? Why didn't his attorneys prepare or supervise the preparation of charts that would correctly summarize evidence in the case? Why didn't they have an artist prepare some charts? Why was it left up to Bakker to scratch out some charts on the eve of trial?

In addition to failing to prepare high-tech graphics for the jury's benefit during trial, Bakker's attorneys also didn't employ other new technologies before trial. Amazingly, they largely stayed away from video technology. Many trial attorneys today routinely have camcorders in their offices and use them to videotape clients and witnesses during the preparation of their testimonies. It is extremely effective as the client is videotaped in the lawyer's office responding to the questions that lawyer will be asking him later at the trial. Then, the attorney and the client review the tape and the attorney offers suggestions to the client on how he might strengthen his responses and his testimony when he takes the stand for real at trial. It's not only a great dress rehearsal that makes witnesses better than they would be without such preparation, it gives witnesses some experience responding to both easy and hard questions before they have to do it in front of the jury.

But, no videotape preparation of Jim Bakker was undertaken by his attorneys. And, of course, his own testimony later at trial was one of the classic examples of someone being pounded on the witness stand by a vigorous cross-examination. He would have been a much better witness if somebody with a camcorder in hand had spent time with him before trial. It would have been so easy. And Bakker was a natural in seeing from such a tape how he was appearing to his audience. As a TV star, he had the eye for it and would have been such a quick study in making the necessary adjustments in, for instance, answering cross-examination questions with authority.

The same can be said of all the other major witnesses that Bakker's attorneys called to the stand. All of those partners who were ambushed on cross-examination and those who sounded odd to jurors could have been equipped to deflect the prosecutors' questions with some video preparation. They could have acquired the experience answering questions necessary to make them decent witnesses.

Another technique used today by some trial attorneys is to pay six or twelve people to come into the office for an evening before trial to sit as a jury in a mock mini-trial. The point is to allow defense attorneys to "try out" their arguments on a panel of ordinary people to see how they'll be received. It is done in major cases and it costs peanuts. Ordinary people love to do it, from college students to housewives to office workers. They think it's fun and it's like being on a jury, but with only a three- or four-hour commitment required of them. Employing such a mock jury in this case would have opened the eyes of Bakker's attorneys to the fact that some of their arguments simply would not fly with anybody other than Bakker loyalists. If Jim's attorneys had known that before trial, they could have retooled some of their case and developed arguments that were more viable.

Nor did Bakker's attorneys reach for any significant outside help as they put the case together. Other defense attorneys experienced in high profile cases would have asked the court for a professional media study at the same time they filed their motion for a change of venue. Such a study may have documented bias against Bakker that existed in Charlotte and which perhaps made it impossible for him to get a fair trial there after years of negative publicity in the *Charlotte Observer*. Those studies are often persuasive to judges, and even if this one hadn't moved Judge Potter it would have been some evidence on appeal to permit a reviewing court to order that the trial be held elsewhere.

Those studies are strong because they are typically done by impartial media experts or college communications professors, and they are credible and reliable. Such community bias against an individual can be scientifically established by professional polling and analysis of newspaper articles. It is media studies that judges can rely on when considering changes of venue.

Another modern technique used by trial attorneys in high voltage cases is to bring in a professional jury consultant to help choose jurors who will be fair and maybe even sympathetic to your client. There are several such consultants in the country today and they are used in many cases involving defendants whose beliefs or actions are outside of the mainstream. Jim Bakker is a perfect example of the type of person whose unorthodox ways subject him to real cynicism and skepticism on the part of others. It often takes a jury psychologist sitting in the back of the courtroom and consulting with the attorneys to spot the psychological manifestations of a jury panel member's reactions to such a defendant.

There is actually a science to it and such jury consultants have been used with success in defending William Kennedy Smith, Lorena Bobbitt, and the Menendez brothers. Leaving nothing to chance, William Kennedy Smith's lawyers employed three jury selection experts in his trial. Jo-Ellan Dimitrius, a nationally heralded jury consultant, actually sat with O.J. Simpson and his attorneys as they selected jurors in 1994 for his criminal trial. In fact, many observers credit Dimitrius's selection of Simpson's jury as one of the major reasons O.J. is a free man today. Undeniably, jury psychologists represent new thinking and savvy preparation. Why wasn't a nationally-known jury consultant with experience helping celebrity defendants brought in for Bakker?

Of course, the answer to some of these questions is that Bakker did not have the money. If that was true, he should have been using his well-known powers of persuasion with his wealthy partners and backers. He should have raised the funds for visual aids, videotape research, video highlights, mock juries, jury consultants, camcorders, and attorneys' fees. Not spent his time raising money to get back on television. It was his attorneys' responsibility to get him involved in raising a defense fund for these trial expenses.

On the other hand, what if money had already been contributed by Bakker supporters for the trial but none of it was spent on these preparations? Bakker loyalists tell me there was such a defense fund. What was it spent on—ham sandwiches?

4. George Davis angered the judge and jury.

It was readily apparent to anyone in the courtroom during the trial that George Davis grated on Judge Potter. Not concealing his anger, Potter at times even yelled at Davis in open court. In addition, our interviews with the jurors confirmed that many of them, too, were rubbed the wrong way by Davis. Virtually every one of them with whom we spoke cited Davis's behavior as one of the negatives plaguing Bakker's defense.[7]

One of the things jurors noticed was that Davis was unable to get along with Judge Potter. But wasn't it just as likely that it was Potter who couldn't get along with Davis? And if the judge had not been jumping all over him throughout the trial, wouldn't the jurors have liked Davis better?

Trial lawyers call what happened to Davis "home towning," when an out-of-town lawyer is treated severely by a local judge. But it went beyond that here. Potter was mean to Davis at trial's end, actually threatening to have Davis ejected from the courtroom by the marshals. The jury saw all of it.

5. Jim Bakker went into his own cross-examination unarmed.

Deborah Smith's cross-examination of Jim Bakker was a turning point of the trial and extinguished the last remaining hope he had with the jury. In contrast to his strong testimony during several hours of direct examination, Bakker came apart when confronted with Smith's tenacious questioning. It was a blowout.

Not only was Bakker unprepared to respond to the prosecutor's questions with answers that would put the best possible face on the facts that dogged him, he was unable to even answer basic questions. It made him appear evasive to the jury. Several times, in response to pointed questions from Smith, Bakker could only say "I don't remember" or "I don't know." Much of what he didn't remember involved the compensation he was paid at PTL and the details of lifetime partner memos that had circulated among the top brass there. He didn't remember receiving a $500,000 bonus in 1986. He didn't remember receiving an additional $100,000 Christmas bonus that same year. He didn't remember $600,000 in bonuses within a six week period.[8]

That's a lot to forget, obviously, and it's a good deal of evidentiary landscape in the case with which to be totally unfamiliar particularly if you are the one involved in it. It was no news to Bakker's attorneys, or any one of thirty million people who were even casually following the allegations in the case through the press and the tabloids, that Bakker was accused of receiving $600,000 in bonuses in late 1986. It was even in the indictment. But when asked about it by Deborah Smith, Bakker couldn't remember. He acted as though he were blind-sided by the question.

I asked about it and he told me that going into his cross-examination he didn't know what to expect.[9] Careful preparation for cross-examination, of course, is essential. The extent to which Bakker was prepared or unprepared by his attorneys, or whether he had been prepared but just had trouble answering the questions once he was in the witness chair are the questions.

Often, an attorney will spend time asking tough questions of their clients, simulating what they will face in the courtroom on cross-examination, and then help their clients frame adequate and helpful responses. An attorney helps arm witnesses with such answers.

For two years before the trial, it was known that one of the most damaging allegations against Bakker was that he accepted large bonuses at times his ministry didn't have enough money in the bank to pay its bills. And so, during the trial, would it really come as a big surprise that Deborah Smith would ask such a question of Bakker? It did to him.

6. *Bakker needed different witnesses.*
Few of Bakker's witnesses had any persuasive testimony relevant

to the charges against the evangelist. Instead, they spoke of things wholly unrelated to whether Bakker sold more space in the hotels than there were rooms available. They didn't speak to the question of whether Bakker misspent lifetime partnership income. They did not talk about Bakker changing the hotel partnership programs after a few weeks to sell more than the original 25,000 limit.

Even worse than missing the mark with their testimony, some struck jurors as odd and extreme.[10] The jury would have been much more receptive to accountants and auditors.

If PTL's former accountants had agreed, the case could have been artfully defended as commercial litigation—with accountants and expert witnesses. With facts and figures. With the Big Eight CPA firms' annual certified audits of Heritage. With testimony from the accountants who prepared those audits each year which showed the financial vitality of the place and the propriety of its spending practices. Those outside accountants never uncovered any fraud and their certified audits could have been used to defend Bakker against these charges of fraud. After all, wouldn't a professionally trained CPA know more about fraud than some partner who didn't know anything about PTL's finances?

The accountants could show with facts, figures, and worksheets that all of the contributions other than salaries and bonuses were legitimately spent on actual business expenses. That testimony would leave for another argument the issue of whether someone who runs a $160 million a year business and works eighteen hours a day including several hours a day as a major national television star, is entitled to $1 million a year in compensation.

Sadly for Bakker, the going was tough for most of the five weeks he sat in that courtroom. Some of his followers will always believe that the result would have been different had Roy Black, Johnnie Cochran, or F. Lee Bailey been sitting next to him. But the friends of Harold Bender and George Davis may swear that the result would have been different had someone other than Jim Bakker been sitting next to them.

The fact is that most cases that go to trial have problems of one kind or another. In this case, from the defense perspective, the problems simply could not be overcome. Perhaps they never could have been surmounted. But then again, might there have been a way for Bakker to win? Those intriguing questions about this case will always remain.

NOTES

1. Jim Bakker, written answers to questions from the author, September 1992.

2. Trial transcript, *United States of America v. James O. Bakker,* Docket No. C-CR-88-205-1, U.S.D.C. (W.D., N.C.), vol. 7, September 19–25, 1989, at 701.

3. *Id.,* vol. 8, September 26–27, 1989, at 1311.

4. *Id.,* vol. 9, September 28–29, 1989, at 1466.

5. *Id.*

6. *Id.* at 1793.

7. See Suzan Brooks's interviews with Bakker jurors in chapter 30, *infra.*

8. Trial transcript, *supra,* n. 2, vol. 10, October 2–5, 1989, at 1869–70, 1872–73, 1878–79, 1881.

9. Jim Bakker, interview by author, in Rochester, Minnesota, April 4, 1993.

10. See Suzan Brooks's interviews with Bakker jurors in chapter 30, *infra.*

Chapter 29

Prison Q. & A: Bakker Looks Back at the Trial

When Jim Bakker received my invitation to be interviewed about his trial, he was ready to talk. It was in 1991 that I wrote to him in the federal prison in Rochester, Minnesota, expressing an interest in unraveling the mysteries surrounding his trial. My curiosity had been piqued by a reporter's comment in a story on the Bakker trial that prosecutors had asked questions about the religious beliefs of Arnold Santjer on the witness stand.

As a law professor and trial attorney, that allegation was a bright red flag, and I wanted to research the true facts and get to the bottom of it. Was Bakker's trial flawed?

One of the most celebrated trials in recent history, Bakker's case was uniquely fascinating and interesting. Since its spectacular conclusion with Bakker being sent to prison for forty-five years, the public had assumed the legitimacy of the process and the correctness of the jury's findings. Yet suddenly, a crack in the veneer appeared and I wanted to probe deeper. The place to start was with the most important figure in that Dixie courthouse, the defendant himself.

My interviews with Bakker spanned his last two and a half years in confinement. I visited him in Rochester several times for day-long discussions, and in Jesup, Georgia, before he was released.

One reason he opened up to me was because at that very

time, he was beginning to emerge from the trauma of it all and was looking for answers, too.

Q: How could this happen?

A: For six years, I have tried to grasp what I did that was criminal. I am still not sure what I have gone to prison for. Only in the last year have I come out of the state of shock enough to see what happened in my case. It wasn't until I read the appellate court's decision that anybody had explained to me what I was supposed to have done wrong. And that opinion [pulling out his copy] contains several factual errors, including the statement that "of the proposed Heritage Village facilities, only the Grand Hotel and one bunkhouse were actually completed." That is absolutely not true—a whole city had been built.[1]

Q: Please tell me about the trial itself from your perspective. What do you remember most?

A: During the trial, I was in a state of shock. I was so blurry. I would compare my experience at Butner to the old days of Communism in Russia under Stalin. I felt like I had been dragged from my bed in the middle of the night.[2]

Q: What was it like sitting at that counsel table as your whole life was examined with the jury a few feet away, and the national press reporting every word?

A: I was at the end of my rope, emotionally. By the time the trial started, I had gone through a terrible hell for two years. On a scale of 1 to 10, I was a 1 throughout the trial. I was embarrassed, bewildered, and out of my element—like a beaten dog. It was the most painful experience of my life and I just wanted out of there.[3]

Q: What were you doing each day at the counsel table?

A: I took notes on a legal pad, but I wished I were anywhere else in the world but there.[4]

Each day's interview would range freely for up to seven hours. Bakker was very articulate, and it was obvious he had spent months and years thinking about and analyzing the things we talked about. I saw early on the mental power that so many people over the years who worked with him described as genius. He is definitely sharp. But there is substance behind the quickness and alertness, a depth to him that comes across after long hours in a small room. And I was surprised at how genuine and even self-effacing he was.

I have a lot of faults. I mean . . . here I am in prison, right? But before God, I didn't know about the fraud. I have sinned, but I never conspired to defraud anyone. I never hid anything from the partners. When we were in California, we had a camera crew come into our Palm Springs home and give viewers a complete tour—even the bedrooms. I mounted a camera on the old Rolls Royce I got and took viewers for a ride in the desert. And they were told everything about the lodging programs, the expansion of them, and that the money they contributed went to the whole PTL ministry.[5]

We met most days in a small, eight-by-ten-foot room adjoining the prison's visiting room. This smaller room was reserved for inmate attorney visits and it was furnished with two plastic chairs and a small plastic table. Windows along one wall faced the noisy visitors' room which was always crowded with other prisoners and their wives, children, and parents.

Bakker looked pensively out into the visiting area one day and said quietly that some of the inmates were there because prosecutors wanted to win for the sake of wining, often to advance their careers, rather than search for the truth.

Look at some of those kids there [pointing] who were convicted as drug kingpins. But when you talk to them, you can tell they are not. They were just kids [when they were arrested].[6]

During our first marathon interview, we left our small room to go out to the nearby vending machines for lunch. Bakker pointed out Lyndon LaRouche to me as we made our way through the crowd. Bakker wanted a frozen cheeseburger and said that it was really good. There was a microwave by the vending machines. I told him some tuna that I'd spotted at the bottom of the vending machine looked a lot better to me. I said that he should go ahead and get his cheeseburger. Extremely polite, he was determined to eat just what I ate and so he had tuna, too. We took our food back into the small room and continued our conversation. From then on, in all later interviews, we continued to eat out of those twenty-five-cent vending machines.

Bakker was strip-searched by the guards before and after each of our meetings, but he was allowed to bring a tattered legal file with him from his cell. Stuffed in that file were all the papers and documents he had saved from his trial. As we talked, he would spread those papers on the floor of our room as he showed each one to me. There were several surprises.

Evidence Jim Was Not Guilty

Q: What evidence could have proved your innocence?
A: Tons of corporate documents that would have exonerated me were either burned or buried in a dump on the Heritage grounds along with tons of mail all buried under the PTL water tower.[7]

Also, the certified audits of PTL prepared by DeLoitte, Haskins & Sells and Laventhol & Horwath. Those auditors should have been called to testify on my behalf but were not.[8]

The videotapes of my TV programs would have established the fact that we fully discussed that the Lifetime Partnership program was enlarged; that the partnerships were not time-share— contributors were not buying property; and that they were donating the $1,000 gift to the work of the ministry.[9]

The facts in the lodging reports at Heritage USA would prove that in the last three-year period there were 125,000 vacant rooms in the Grand Hotel and Heritage Inn. This would establish that there was room for more lifetime partners at Heritage USA.[10]

And there were several articles in the PTL monthly magazines and Heritage USA newspapers about the lodging plans and fund-raising that support what I'm saying about the full disclosure we always made.[11]

Q: Did your attorney present those facts to the jury in a way that they could understand?
A: Absolutely not.[12]

Q: How could the CPAs have helped you if they had been called as witnesses?
A: Full-time, all year around, one of the so-called Big Eight national auditing firms was at PTL.[13]

I told them that, "if there is ever any doubt, pay taxes for me on everything." I remember saying, "I want this [PTL] so clean, it squeaks." I personally assured them, "it's all yours, you've got full access; no one will hamper you."[14]

Sometimes, the auditors would tell me to write personal checks to PTL for $40,000 or even $75,000 to reimburse the ministry for anything that personally benefitted me. I always followed their orders. The auditors know I'm not guilty.[15]

Q: You've argued that to your knowledge every one of your brochures contained a reference to the fact that money donated would be considered a gift to the ministry.

A: Yes, the donors understood very well that money donated to PTL was considered a gift. Every receipt stated that funds could be used for the total work of the ministry at the discretion of the ministry. Almost every single program where I raised funds, I said over and over again that they were not buying anything, that they were giving to the total support of the ministry. To my knowledge, every single fund-raising program had reference to that fact.[16]

Q: Did you make that point in your testimony on the witness stand?

A: No.[17]

Q: Did Judge Potter's refusal to allow the jury to visit Heritage hurt your case?

A: Paul Harvey said that I got forty-five years for overbooking a hotel. If that was the crime, the jury should have been allowed to see Heritage. The water park alone cost $13 million. I was putting the money into the place.[18]

The *PTL Club* Videotapes

Q: You have told me that if you had full access to the PTL library, you could have proved your innocence. Why weren't you able to gain access to that library? Did the government seize it?

A: The library was at Heritage USA. To this day, I have not had access to it. I was locked out of Heritage. Otherwise, I could have defended myself. Falwell had hired Pinkerton guards. After that, the Bankruptcy Court was in control.[19]

The few tapes we used were from the tapes the government picked. We only had access to the tapes that the government was using and wanted us to have access to. Those tapes were placed in the so-called discovery room [located in a building across from the courthouse].[20]

Q: Did you visit the discovery room?

A: I went over to try to help and I couldn't believe how selective the government had been. I couldn't believe all the files and videotapes that had been left behind at Heritage. I saw my old rolodexes in the room. It was like my ministry had been raped, sacked. They'd destroyed what took me a lifetime to build.[21]

Q: What would those tapes have proved?

A: The tapes would prove that I explained the growth of the Lifetime Partnership program in detail hundreds of times. The main point the government tried to make was that the people were not aware that, after the original 500 rooms, there was not any growth of the program. If anyone would view the videos of our programs, they would be shocked that the government could put me in prison with their blatant misrepresentation of the truth.[22]

Q: [At this point, Bakker reaches into the pocket of his khaki pants and pulls out a crumpled, torn page of paper. It was about 3 inches by 3 inches, and was wrinkled and colored from age.] What is that?

A: During the trial, I wrote these notes down from two of the tapes that the government chose to excerpt. From the September 24, 1984 program: "It not only trickled over the 30,000 now, it's avalanched over the 30,000." So, I did inform viewers that it went over 25,000. From the February 28, 1984 program, this is what I said about what the $1,000 was for: "Gift to God in Jesus' name to go to all the world and preach the gospel to every creature."[23]

Q: So, even from the government's own edited, excerpted tapes, there was evidence to support your contentions?

A: Exactly.[24]

Q: Did your attorneys call that to the jury's attention or make a point of it at all?

A: No.[25]

Q: What else would the tapes still in the PTL tape library at Heritage have proved?

A: The partners were informed of changes and enlargements in the Lifetime Partnership programs via letters and partner updates. On telethons and programs, too, I'd use my marker, I can remember it today, and show on a photo mural all of the buildings and activities at Heritage. I had a floor-to-ceiling mural that we used on the set with huge enlargements of photos of the Girls' Home, etc., and I told viewers, "This is what your money will go for." And when I said that, I was pointing to all of those buildings and all of those activities. I went over it, hour by hour during the telethons. There could have been no mistake that the money was going for everything at Heritage.[26]

Q: Were other videotapes used in your defense to counter the edited tapes that the government used?

A: We did not have the funds to hire editors to edit programs for us and my defense team was not organized. . . . So we just ran a few whole programs to try to demonstrate how the government had edited hundreds of pieces of videotapes to paint a distorted picture of our program and ministry.[27]

Q: What was unfair about the government's edited tapes?
A: I know broadcasting. I was a pioneer in it. I know it from the black and white days—we were the first Christian broadcasters to go color. I know editing and all of the technical end. It was simply wrong for them to have edited hundreds of hours of my programs, excerpting, without any explanation for it. It was all out of context, never showing the "in between" parts. The fraud, the misrepresentations charged, and the way PTL was portrayed were all based on an unrepresentative sampling of the thousands of hours of PTL programs.[28]
Q: Are the tapes the hidden key to this case? The missing proof?
A: If the jury could have seen two or three hours unedited from even one telethon, they wouldn't have found me guilty. I could have put a tape together in two days that would have won the case! The tapes are still in that library, with classics like my interview with Colonel Sanders. The proof of my innocence is in that room. That's why my partners stay with me—they saw it every day on television. They know I told them what the government claims I concealed.[29]

Copies of PTL fund-raising letters and partnership promotional brochures confirm much of what Bakker told me.

- The September/October, 1986 *Together Update* Bakker sent to potential Bunkhouse lifetime partners which contained this explanation: "For a gift of $500 to the PTL ministry, you and your family can enjoy two nights and three days in the Bunkhouse Hotel every year for the rest of your life. As with all other lifetime membership lodging facilities . . . reservations are based upon room availability."[30]

- The standard lifetime partner application form which contained this legend: "Your gifts are used to support PTL and all its programs."[31]

- The Towers Lifetime Partner solicitation brochure which contained this language on its cover: "Yes, when you send your Towers Membership gift of $1,000 for the work of PTL. . . ."[32]

The other independent fact that supports Bakker's argument is that Judge William Thurmond Bishop, sitting without a jury in the subsequent PTL bankruptcy hearing, after considering the same evidence, ruled in Bakker's favor and held: "[The testimony] demonstrates that Lifetime Partnership benefits were, in fact, delivered and provided"[33] by Bakker. Same facts, different judge, no jury, and the exact opposite result. Which judge was right about Bakker? What if it was Bishop?

The Prosecutors

Q: What's your evaluation of Deborah Smith and Jerry Miller?

A: The government wanted me so bad. I can't understand why. There was a fervor there. I've lost everything—my family, my ministry, every dime I had. I have spent four years in prison. I can't understand what more . . . [they] want of me other than for me to die in prison.[34]

Q: Are there specific examples . . . which stand out in your mind?

A: The trial was a show. Nobody said I stole any money. The Taggarts and Dortch never said I conspired to defraud contributors. Robinson, the first bankruptcy court trustee, said that there was no money missing there—it was all in the ground.[35]

Q: As you were sitting in that courtroom, what . . . [else] struck you as unfair?

A: They [the government's charts] misconstrued the facts and figures so much it would have taken a Philadelphia lawyer to untangle the horrible lies. For instance, one floor-to-ceiling chart represented cars over a five- or ten-year period. They had twenty-five cars on that enormous chart, but they never explained that many had been traded in for other cars. I never owned all of them at the same time. In fact, I didn't even own all of them—some were loaned to us.[36]

They also made a big point about the condominium in Florida, but it was purchased before the 1984 to 1987 window that this case was limited to. An Assembly of God pastor who had a nervous breakdown stayed in it far longer than I did. He was there for months. It was no improper inurement to me.[37]

Q: Was the government overreaching in any other way in your case?

A: The IRS was unbelievable. The corporate minutes very elaborately detailed the money part of the ministry. But the IRS decided we weren't a church, retroactively revoked our charitable tax exemption, and I now owe $2 million plus in back taxes. I'll never be able to pay it as long as I live. On top of paying 60 percent of my income in taxes, which I always did, the IRS has now charged me personally with hundreds of thousands of dollars in PTL business expenses—including guests, travel expenses for the TV show, hundreds of hotel rooms all right there in Charlotte, and clothes for my band and singers. They had ten to twenty outfits that Tammy and I bought wholesale. What in the world would I be doing with twenty suits all in the same color in twenty different sizes? Those weren't for me. Those were for the cast. But the IRS charged all of that back to me personally, and that's how they got my individual tax liability so high.[38]

I worked day and night, twenty-four hours a day, to finish that hotel lobby. I moved into the presidential suite for a year with my family so that I could do that. But the government went back and decided that it was not a business expense since I had a house fifteen minutes away, and they charged me tens of thousands of dollars for the suite for a year.[39]

Q: Did you feel at any time during the trial that your religious beliefs were being ridiculed by the prosecutors?

A: Yes, absolutely, the whole thing. I believe in miracles and did not build Heritage USA with massive loans or on money in the bank or on facts, but I built Heritage USA by faith in God. I believe it is going to be almost impossible to practice this faith in God and believe in miracles. You will be required by the government to bring a Madison Avenue type in to run the church as a business, not as a work of faith.[40]

Behind the Scenes at the Trial

Q: What was your own assessment as the trial moved from day to day based on your own observations?

A: The first few days, we seemed to be winning until Steve Nelson fell from the witness stand on his head, many thinking he was dead. When he collapsed, I went into a side room and, to the best of my recollection, I cried for the first time since I lost PTL. It was like the pain of the last few years all fell in on me at that moment.[41]

My doctor gave me some medicine, Xanax, that he assured me would not hurt me. I don't think he comprehended how highly sensitive I was to tranquilizers.[42]

Instead of relaxing me, it greatly accelerated my stress and panic. It caused the most frightening experience a human being could ever have. I had had a panic attack before, while at CBN. So, when I was to go back into court, I was totally disoriented. My lawyers tried to tell the judge, on the advice of the physicians, that I was in no shape to continue the hearings.[43]

To my understanding, the judge was so angry that he had me seized and placed in leg irons, chains, and handcuffs. I was then thrust into the back seat of a police car in a compartment resembling a cage. I was driven across the state in chains to a prison. They wouldn't stop to let me go to the bathroom and my kidneys were almost exploding.[44]

There I was stripped naked in front of many people. I was in a stupor, in a state of shock. I had never been in prison in my life. Never been in jail. Never had a speeding ticket. They searched every inch of my body and took my money and credit cards from my wallet. It was a nightmare that will never leave me.[45]

I kept asking, "What are you doing to me?"[46]

I put on prison clothes and was moved to another area where I was told to strip naked again, and every cavity of my body was examined and I was given a complete physical. I was then led through the compound where I could hear the voices of prisoners shouting out to me, "Jim, don't let them break you." I was led into another room where I was told to strip down naked for photos. I heard a voice from one of the men saying, "Let him leave his underpants on." Then they took pictures of me in my shorts. I was then placed in the mental division of the prison where I was with deranged people, many of whom were screaming and very obviously hallucinating.[47]

The cell I was placed in had a metal slab for a bed and an open shower and a toilet in the center of the room. I was not allowed to even have a pillow. There was a window in my cell where I was observed twenty-four hours a day. They ran tests on me, drew blood at 5:00 A.M. By that time, I was living in absolute terror. I think if it had not been for a Godly guard who told me I was going to be okay, I would have lost my mind. I would have died.[48]

Some day, I would like to see the full reports from that incarceration.[49]

I was taken from this government mental institution right back into the courtroom in a few days and my trial began again. By then, what little will I had to fight for my own rights was totally gone. From then on, it felt as if we totally lost the trial.[50]

The Bankruptcy of PTL

Q: Any thoughts about Jerry Falwell forcing PTL into bankruptcy?

A: PTL should never have been put into bankruptcy. It was not bankrupt. It was up and going, and the land and buildings were worth far more than any money that was owed to creditors.[51]

Q: U.S. Bankruptcy Judge Rufus Reynolds attacked you in the press.

A: He referred to me as "a sawed-off little runt." He just loved the publicity my case gave him, and he granted interviews.[52]

The Press

Q: How do you react to all the tabloid articles?

A: I have to live with those, we call them "ragmags," running pictures of me at the lowest point of my life when I was in chains like a dog. There has been so much of it. It hurts, but I can't stop it. I've got to let it fall like water off a duck. Last week there was an article about my son having trouble in school—that's tough to take. It really upset him.[53]

Q: Was the local newspaper fair to you in their reporting over the years?

A: No. The *Charlotte Observer* took an adverse position over fifteen years ago. I made the mistake of fighting back and winning in every situation that they threw against me. The old adage of "Don't get in a fight with those who buy ink by the barrel" surely holds true.[54]

Q: Given all of that negative publicity about you over the years in Charlotte, do you think it would ever have been possible to impanel a jury of open-minded people to sit in judgment of you?

A: Absolutely not.[55]

Regrets

Q: What's been the hardest part of all of this on you?

A: I'm trying to raise my son from prison. He wouldn't move with Tammy to California because of the man she moved with. [Messner][56]

Q: And your adversaries?

A: I have prayed and I have studied. I have been putting God first, and even if I die in prison I haven't touched my enemies and they haven't prospered. Even Swaggart. When the press would ask me for a comment about Swaggart's troubles, I never said anything against him. I take no joy in what happened to him. He had a great talent to win souls.[57]

Q: And Judge Potter?

A: I can forgive him for sending me to Butner in shackles. It was a miracle of God that I didn't break down and never come out of it. But it would be unforgivable for him to do it again—to anyone.[58]

NOTES

1. Jim Bakker, interviews by author, in Rochester, Minnesota, October 31, 1992 and June 26, 1993.

2. Jim Bakker, interview by author, in Rochester, Minnesota, April 4, 1993.

3. Jim Bakker, interviews by author, in Rochester, Minnesota, October 31, 1992, April 4, 1993, and June 26, 1993.

4. Jim Bakker, interview by author, in Rochester, Minnesota, June 26, 1993.

5. Jim Bakker, interviews by author, in Rochester, Minnesota, September 25, 1992, October 31, 1992, and April 4, 1993.

6. Jim Bakker, interview by author, in Rochester, Minnesota, October 31, 1992.

7. Jim Bakker, interview by author, in Rochester, Minnesota, September 25, 1992.

8. Jim Bakker, written answers to questions from the author, September 1992.

9. *Id.*

10. *Id.*

11. *Id.;* Jim Bakker, interview by author, in Rochester, Minnesota, September 25, 1992.

12. Jim Bakker, written answers to questions from the author, September, 1992.

13. Jim Bakker, interview by author, in Rochester, Minnesota, September 25, 1992.

14. Jim Bakker, interview by author, in Rochester, Minnesota, October 31, 1992.

15. Jim Bakker, interviews by author, in Rochester, Minnesota, October 31, 1992 and April 4, 1993; Jim Bakker, written answers to questions from the author, September, 1992.

16. Jim Bakker, written answers to questions from the author, September 1992.

17. *Id.*

18. Jim Bakker, interview by author, in Rochester, Minnesota, October 31, 1992.

19. Jim Bakker, interview by author, in Rochester, Minnesota, April 4, 1993; Jim Bakker, written answers to questions from the author, September, 1992.

20. Jim Bakker, interview by author, in Rochester, Minnesota, April 4, 1993.

21. *Id.*

22. Jim Bakker, written answers to questions from the author, September 1992.

23. Jim Bakker, interview by author, in Rochester, Minnesota, April 4, 1993.

24. *Id.*

25. *Id.;* Jim Bakker, written answers to questions from the author, September 1992.

26. Jim Bakker, interview by author, in Rochester, Minnesota, April 4, 1993.

27. Jim Bakker, written answers to questions from the author, September 1992.

28. Jim Bakker, interview by author, in Rochester, Minnesota, October 31, 1992.

29. Jim Bakker, interviews by author, in Rochester, Minnesota, October 31, 1992 and April 4, 1993.

30. Bakker, *Appeal to U.S. Parole Commission,* June 1, 1993, vol. I at 30.

31. *Id.* at 6.

32. *Id.* at 9.

33. Judgment, *In Re Heritage Village Church and Missionary Fellowship, Debtor,* U.S. Bankruptcy Court, D.S.C., Case No. 87–1956, Order of Judge William Thurmond Bishop, November 4, 1991.

34. Jim Bakker, interviews by author, in Rochester, Minnesota, October 31, 1992, April 4, 1993, and May 29, 1993.

35. Jim Bakker, interviews by author, in Rochester, Minnesota, September 25, 1992 and April 4, 1993; Jim Bakker, written answers to questions from the author, September 1992.

36. Jim Bakker, interview by author, in Rochester, Minnesota, April 4, 1993; Jim Bakker, written answers to questions from the author, September 1992.

37. Jim Bakker, interview by author, in Rochester, Minnesota, April 4, 1993.

38. Jim Bakker, interview by author, in Rochester, Minnesota, October 31, 1992.

39. *Id.*

40. Jim Bakker, written answers to questions from the author, September 1992.

41. *Id.*

42. *Id.*

43. *Id.;* Jim Bakker, interview by author, in Rochester, Minnesota, September 25, 1992.

44. *Id.*

45. *Id.*

46. Jim Bakker, interview by author, in Rochester, Minnesota, April 4, 1993.

47. Jim Bakker, written answers to questions from the author, September 1992.

48. *Id.;* Jim Bakker, interview by author, in Rochester, Minnesota, September 25, 1992.

49. Jim Bakker, interview by author, in Rochester, Minnesota, September 25, 1992.

50. Jim Bakker, written answers to questions from the author, September 1992.

51. Jim Bakker, interviews by author, in Rochester, Minnesota, September 25, 1992, October 31, 1992, and April 4, 1993.

52. Jim Bakker, interviews by author, in Rochester, Minnesota, September 25, 1992 and October 31, 1992.

53. Jim Bakker, interviews by author, in Rochester, Minnesota, September 25, 1992 and October 31, 1992.

54. Jim Bakker, written answers to questions from the author, September 1992.

55. *Id.*

56. Jim Bakker, interview by author, in Rochester, Minnesota, September 25, 1992.

57. *Id.*

58. Jim Bakker, interview by author, in Rochester, Minnesota, October 31, 1992.

Chapter 30

Jury Room Q & A: The View from the Jurors

As Jim Bakker's trial ended with the reading of the guilty verdict, Judge Potter dismissed the jury. Pointing to the door, he told them, "You are released from your obligation not to discuss the case and you can talk about it with anyone you wish. [B]ut you do not have to talk to anyone. Anybody approaches you and wants to talk . . . you can just tell them you don't want to . . . that's up to you."[1]

Reporters on the scene and even national network anchors in New York immediately scrambled for interviews with them. A few agreed. Gwendolyn Morrison appeared on the *CBS Morning News*. Rick Hill did *Larry King Live, Crossfire,* and *Prime Time* with Sam Donaldson and Diane Sawyer.

As I began researching the Bakker case for a law journal article, it was soon clear that some of the keys to the mysteries of the trial remained in the jurors' hands. I asked my trusted research assistant, law student Suzan Brooks, to attempt to locate those jurors and alternates who would be willing to help cast some light on the courtroom drama they had witnessed.

Suzan, a victims' rights advocate before coming to law school, didn't shrink from a tough assignment. Tracking them down at their jobs and homes, she was surprised by how friendly they were. Open and willing to talk, they were generous with their time and receptive to her questions.

Most indicated that they still followed news reports on

Bakker and his family. They knew, for instance, that he was still in prison and that Tammy had divorced him and married Roe Messner. In telephone interviews each often lasting more than an hour, they responded to a wide array of questions. Their memories were strikingly similar in some areas, and notably dissimilar in others. Altogether, Suzan found them to be an intelligent and articulate group of individuals who took their civic responsibilities as jurors very seriously.

Serving on the Jury

Each juror was asked whether they had wanted to be selected for the jury or if they hoped they wouldn't be.

- **Barbara Dalley:** I was horrified but I was consoled with the thought it would be absolutely fascinating. It was.

  One of the ways they [the defense attorneys] could have kept me off the jury . . . my [six] children were adopted. They [PTL at Heritage] ran an adoption agency . . . the way they handled adoption wasn't right. They had only used that [home for unwed mothers, adoption service] to get money.

  I really believe the only reason the defense left me in is . . . everyone was real tired . . . [they had been asking questions] all day long. They only needed one more juror. As I waited to use the phone to let my family know that I would be late, Bakker's daughter was waiting, too, and the way people looked at her. . . . it just seemed unnecessarily unkind. I smiled at her, thinking that all this wasn't her fault. When they went back, I saw her lean over and say something to her dad . . . who leaned into Mr. Bender. . . . [Dalley was the last juror chosen, at 7 P.M., after a long day of jury selection. She and Catherine Boardman later became the two members of the panel who most vigorously advocated a guilty verdict during deliberations.][2]

- **Catherine Boardman:** I can't say that I hoped I would be on it, but I thought it would be interesting. I'm not sure I realized how long . . . [it would last].

  . . . he was on trial and everyone had been to so much trouble and research, and you didn't want to let the system down. That's how I felt.[3]

- **Rick Hill:** [looked forward to serving because] I thought it was kind of an adventure.[4]

- **Juror X:** Well, it was a duty to do it. I mean, I was called upon to do it.[6]

The Unsequestered Jury

Unlike jurors in the O.J. Simpson trial, Bakker's jurors were not sequestered. They only had to be at the courthouse during the day. At noontime, they roamed to restaurants around the courthouse, each wearing a white button pinned to their lapel with the word JUROR in bold blue letters. At night, they returned to their homes. In their free time, they continued to do whatever they wanted. They were on the honor system not to watch the news, but other than that they could watch all the television they liked. Their responses to the situation were as varied as their personalities.

- **Barbara Dalley:** We'd come out [of the courthouse] and the cameras were on us . . . they'd be walking backward . . . it was horrifying.[7]

- **Catherine Boardman:** They only started that right at the end. [U.S. marshals escorting the jurors into the courthouse from the parking lot and out again at the end of the day.] We got a letter, as a matter of fact, from the judge that he was sorry he hadn't done it earlier. But we went in and out to our cars and to the courthouse unescorted for most of the trial. You had to walk right past them [reporters] right to the front of the courthouse and they were lined up and down the sidewalk. But I don't think it bothered anybody or influenced them. . . . Outside the court-house was a circus. But we were in our little room all day long and that wasn't a circus. It was nice. I mean, we made friends with each other and got to know each other.

  I'm not sure that I didn't listen to any news about the hurricane, and I didn't need to know a lot more since I was right in the middle of it. It wasn't that hard to stay away from the media, though. I mean, you were so tired when you came home at night that you didn't really feel like watching TV or any-thing.[8]

- **Rick Hill:** [Throughout the trial, all jurors were admonished not to watch TV or read the papers. That proved particularly difficult during the hurricane.] Basically we didn't watch the news type things. If anything came on we, you know, basically had our remote controls so I could switch it real quick and if we did see something, we were supposed to tell the judge the next morning. So, you know, that happened a few times.

Something would come on and I'd flip it quick, but I would go ahead and tell the judge what I had seen . . . He would have both lawyers from both sides come up and listen and hear what I had seen and see if that made any difference in the trial or on my judgments or anything.[9]

- **Professor Gary Tidwell, who worked as a CBS News analyst and consultant during the trial:** The jury was never sequestered. Every day, every lunch, the judge would ask, "have you read, seen or heard anything about the case? No. No. No." I had them [the local CBS affiliate] do a story where the jurors ate, right across the street [from the courthouse], and they would come out of there and every day [in newspaper racks outside] the *Charlotte Observer* had the headlines, "Bakker did whatever," putting their spin on it. And I just—it just didn't make a lot of—you couldn't help but see that.[10]

[Remember that juror Hill did admit to Judge Potter that he had been watching TV one night and heard it reported that Tammy Faye had blamed Hurricane Hugo on the trial, saying it was a warning from God. Hill told the judge, "I thought it was crazy."][11]

The Scene of the Crime

The Simpson jury was taken on a tour of O.J. Simpson's estate in Brentwood. Since Judge Potter refused to allow the Bakker jurors to view Heritage, it was left to those of them who had visited there to remember what they had seen.

- **Catherine Boardman:** I think I'm the only one who hadn't been there. Still haven't been.[12]

- **Shirley Wise [alternate juror]:** I never have gone. My husband wouldn't take me. That was a place everyone around here went to see at Christmas . . . oh, it was fabulous on TV. I wish I had been able to see it like it was then.[13]

- **James McAlister:** I thought all the time that he had the greatest thing in the world that could have really put Charlotte on the map and put himself in a place of great renown, because he was doing a good thing. But I don't know what happened. He might have got greedy, I don't know, but when it came to the point that he couldn't deliver what he had promised for all this money, then that's when he got in trouble.

Those who were able to come and have a vacation . . . and the place is beautiful. . . . I went a couple of times to see the Christmas lights. . . . I had the head of the McAllister clan from Scotland visiting me for a week and I took him out there and he was at one time a photographer by trade, a commercial photographer, and it just boggled his mind. He couldn't believe it.

He [Bakker] turned the lights on about the first of December and they stayed on until New Year's. They were spectacular. I don't hear anything about it any more.[14]

Jim Bakker on the Witness Stand

O.J. Simpson never took the stand in his murder trial. Jim Bakker did, and tried to explain his entire ministry, including the partnership lodging program at Heritage. Jurors were asked how they thought he was as a witness.

- **Barbara Dalley:** When he talked about his early ministry . . . he was very sincere . . . [but] he seemed somehow to have been corrupted along the way. When he'd talk about him and Tammy at first, his gestures and look were different. As he went along, it got worse. It was real obvious . . . the loss of eye contact, like when someone is lying to you. . . . Bakker would deny a letter was his . . . then they'd bring out the fingerprints.[15]

- **Catherine Boardman:** I think he basically got up there and told his whole story . . . how he got started and what happened, and I think that he really started out with good intentions. You could tell that in his voice. He looked at the jurors and made eye contact, and seemed to believe what he was saying. Then, when things started to go wrong [with his ministry] he really changed up there. He quit looking at us, there was no more eye contact, his voice changed. [Eventually] I think he knew he was asking for the money for wrong reasons. You know, just the point where it wasn't a ministry anymore.

  [This juror admitted she sometimes glanced over at Jim Bakker at the counsel table while others were testifying both for him and against him.] He didn't show it if he did [ever feel surprise]. He took a lot of notes. He didn't have a lot of expression, though.[16]

- **James McAlister:** [He was] pretty miserable. He stayed shook up all the time. He couldn't give good answers, and so forth.

  [About the ill-fated chart] I think he tried to give it orally without the chart and it wasn't very believable. It was a bunch of mathematics . . . how he was going to come out of it . . . it just didn't add up.[17]

- **Robert Thornberry [alternate juror]:** Probably the most disappointing witness was Mr. Bakker himself. I guess I think he was basically dishonest in a lot of the impression that he attempted to make by his responses and the way he responded. My feeling relative to him was that . . . he sincerely didn't really perceive it as being something wrong. That actually has since bothered me the most, that I felt that he did not see that [overselling the partnerships] as being something wrong.[18]

- **Juror X:** He should never have got on . . . he should never have got on. He didn't help himself at all . . . not at all. I mean he was up there just grinning and they should never have put him on the stand to my form of thinking, no. He would have been better off just not saying anything. Because he would not, could not remember anything when asked a question. . . .

  I don't know if I should say this. [But I thought he was] a complete dummy . . . I mean, a pawn. [I don't think he knew what was going on during the trial] I'm sure he didn't. He was like in a daze, like "how can this be happening to me?" He was surprised that anyone brought him to trial or anyone could bring him to trial. That he was above this. "I can do no wrong type of attitude."[19]

Bakker's Partners

Jurors were asked to describe how effective they thought the defense witnesses had been, particularly the PTL Partners.

- **Catherine Boardman:** I was so far away from their point of view that I could not really relate to them.[20]

- **Juror X:** There was no help from the witnesses. What they said was childish stuff, you might say. One fellow, I'd say he was sixty-five to seventy years old, and the reason he bought his partnership was because . . . of their health program. They had an exercise gym. And he wanted an exercise gym because he'd

married a young woman and he wanted to keep up with her. . . .
Why in the world they called any of them I'll never know.[21]

- **Rick Hill:** In general, they basically all had the same story where
  it felt like they were all spreading the story-type thing. It was just
  a repeat of the same story.[22]

- **James McAlister:** I felt they were almost as a cult member.
  They were for him [Bakker] and "I don't care what he had
  done."[23]

Pastor Dortch on the Stand

Jurors were asked to comment on the testimony of Pastor
Dortch.

- **Barbara Dalley:** Reverend Dortch . . . absolutely slimy. . . .
  Sold out his best friend . . . you could see on the tape, when
  Bakker was away he was squeezing Jim out. He was even more
  guilty than Bakker . . . really awful.[24]

- **Rick Hill:** He seemed very honest and straightforward and
  willing to take the guilt of, you know, overselling, and willing to
  say, "Yeah, we did make a mistake and we did oversell and I am
  willing to take my responsibility on this." I gotta feel that
  probably Dortch knew it before Bakker did.[25]

- **James McAlister:** . . . I think he was someone who wanted to
  make amends or atone, or something.[26]

- **Gwendolyn Morrison:** He got scared and did what he had to
  do . . . he told the truth.[27]

Roe Messner—Bakker's Best Friend

Jurors were asked how they responded to Roe Messner's
testimony.

- **Barbara Dalley:** When he first got up there I did believe some of
  what he said. Later, I began to say to myself, "Why in the world
  isn't HE being prosecuted?"[28]

- **Robert Thornberry [alternate juror]:** I had responded to him
  very positively. I thought his answers were very straightforward
  and I don't know if "relaxed" is quite the right word, but I was
  positive about his comments.[29]

- **Rick Hill:** It seemed like it was a scheme between him and Jim,
  you know, money scheme of him building or him getting

money, or him lending money to Jim. I'm not exactly sure, exactly, but it seemed like there was some kind of scheme between the two.[30]

Bakker's Attorneys

Unlike O.J. Simpson, who obviously took early charge of his own case and recruited what became known as a dream team of high-powered specialists to defend him, Bakker remained largely aloof from pretrial preparations and walked breezily into court with two seasoned trial attorneys to plead his case. Some jurors volunteered comments about the defense attorneys. Others were asked. They said several things about the kind of job they felt Harold Bender and George Davis did for their famous client.

- **Barbara Dalley:** Some of the defense seemed . . . personally degrading to the defense attorneys. [But] someone needed to defend him. . . .[31]

- **Catherine Boardman:** I didn't care for them at all. . . . I think they didn't think highly of the jurors. You know, they made us feel like idiots . . . [and] assumed we didn't know things that most people know. They didn't go about it very well at all . . . they weren't good at it at all. And they didn't fool anybody. No one on the jury cared for them . . . it was something you kind of pick up from the very beginning.[32]

- **Robert Thornberry [alternate juror]:** Mr. Bender, I thought that he was in general, for the most part, very good and professional. The other gentleman, as far as I was concerned, I felt a constant need to try to ignore his theatrics and not let that influence me negatively. [Davis was a] . . . very negative influence. A very definite minus in my opinion.[33]

- **Rick Hill:** I was very surprised that they didn't have a very—a better defense than what they did. . . . I was expecting some type of surprise of how they were going to defend themselves. [But all they basically did was say] that the people that gave the money were giving it as a gift and not as respecting [sic] anything in return. I thought he [George Davis] would be a better lawyer, a slicker lawyer than that.[34]

- **Juror X:** My first impression in the first three days of the trial, myself now, "what is Jim Bakker doing with these lawyers?"

They are not helping him. He better get him some other lawyers. As the trial went on I realized within myself it wasn't his lawyers' fault . . . they had nothing to work with.[35]

Jurors were questioned about the apparent tension between Judge Potter and George Davis.

- **Rick Hill:** [I recall Judge Potter] slapping the desk several times . . . with his hand. [Because] something Mr. Davis would say. Mr. Davis knew that he was supposed to not say certain things and he would say it and then he would push it a little further, and Judge Potter would get really upset with him. Davis pushed it through the whole trial. I think Davis was trying to . . . make points that he knew he shouldn't get away with to the jury, and I think it probably hurt him more than it helped him.[36]

- **Barbara Dalley:** But the histrionics used by the defense! They picked up on the fact that he [Judge Potter] was short tempered. [Davis tried to push Potter] so he'd look unkind. [The whole thing was] planned for effect. It got to where he [Judge Potter] got mad at everything they [defense] did. . . . Yet, he didn't allow a lot of the prosecutors' attempts, either.[37]

- **Juror X:** Well, it's hard to explain unless you've been there. Mr. Bender was a first class lawyer, yes. Mr. Davis went out . . . of his way to provoke Judge Potter. He definitely did. With petty stuff. He tried to provoke the judge. There is no doubt. [Davis tried] to bait the judge. He would nitpick, I guess would be the best word for it. It was obvious he was trying to provoke him. But, I mean, he [Judge Potter] sat down on that fellow . . . I don't know how many times. He told him one time, "Hey, either hush up or get out of the courtroom." He came down on him hard, he sure did.[38]

- **Robert Thornberry [alternate]:** The amazing thing to me was that Mr. Davis could get away with what he did get away with. I certainly thought the judge restrained himself enormously.[39]

The Prosecutors

Jurors responded more favorably to questions about the prosecutors, Deborah Smith and Jerry Miller.

- **Barbara Dalley:** I remember Deborah Smith's closing argument was so beautifully done. I felt like standing up and applauding.

She looked so young and we didn't know how she'd do. He [Miller] did a good job, too. There was such a sense of decency there. They didn't manufacture . . . didn't hem and haw.

[The videotapes] were really horrible . . . we watched them morning 'til night. Finally someone said [back in the jury room], "If I have to listen to Tammy sing again, I'm going to cause a mistrial."[40]

- **Catherine Boardman:** Yes, I did like them. Particularly Mr. Miller. You know, I've thought about it since and thought that maybe I was fooled, but I really liked him. I thought he was really honest and Deborah Smith was the same. She was a little more businesslike. He let more of his personality show. I mean, I had a feeling for a long time that he must be a real nice, honest person.[41]

- **Rick Hill:** They were very professional, very organized. It looked like they had everything ready to go.

    We got tired of watching [the prosecution's videos of Bakker's TV shows]. They [Jim and Tammy] seemed to be asking for money all the time where other televangelists just asked for a contribution, you know, maybe at the end of the show for a tape or something. They were always asking for money, they were always scheming for this or for that. For the building and different ways to raise funds.[42]

- **Juror X:** Miller and Ms. Smith were as sharp as any people I've ever listened to in my life. When they had something to say, they had it on paper. Here it is right here. They were very, very, very prepared. They had everything right there, right now together. They were very convincing. And very efficient and very professional. They were.[43]

Judge Potter

All jurors were asked what they thought of Judge Potter.

- **Barbara Dalley:** He was so much like Judge Wapner. You know, he was testy like him . . . he looks like him. The similarities were kind of funny.[44]

- **Catherine Boardman:** I had a lot of respect for him. I thought . . . [he] was really fair.[45]

- **James McAlister:** I thought he was extremely fair in everything he did. For both sides.[46]

- **Rick Hill:** The judge was very strict, very stern. I happened to think maybe that he was a little bit rough on the Bakker side. . . . It was just the way he was acting, you know—his demeanor. [He treated the prosecutors] not as rough—with a little bit more respect.[47]

- **Juror X:** [Potter was] very courteous. One day on recess I was walking outside the courthouse . . . and I was looking at a [Civil War] statue . . . and he stopped and looked at it and talked about how nice that statue was and everything. . . . And he'd ask each of us each morning if we had our power back on, because of the hurricane and everything.[48]

Hurricane Hugo

The hurricane hobbled Charlotte and delayed the trial. Jurors were asked what effect the storm had on them personally.

- **Barbara Dalley:** We weren't watching the news or reading the papers, so we weren't prepared when the hurricane came through. We didn't know how big it was. We live in a big old Victorian . . . four giant oaks dropped on our house. . . . There was no power, no phone, the driveway was blocked by huge old oaks that had fallen. I thought, "I've got to get to a phone; the marshals will be coming for me if I don't show up at court."

  After the hurricane, we had no power for two weeks. There weren't enough transformers available to replace all the ones that were destroyed. We had to practically forage for food. We didn't have fuel. We tried to cook what we could salvage from the freezer by burning green wood from the fallen trees. We had black smoke all over us. My bathroom doesn't have a window . . . there were no lights . . . I put on my makeup by candlelight. One day I had purple eyebrows . . . I'd grabbed the wrong stick instead of the brown one. People's clothes got steadily worse . . . there was no way to get them cleaned.[49]

- **Catherine Boardman:** We had a tree on our car and no power. Luckily we had hot water. We were about the only ones who did. . . . We lived right in the city so it wasn't that bad. I was only a mile from the courthouse. [Still, their power was out for about a week.][50]

- **Juror X:** No power at all . . . I live in the country and I am pretty well isolated. I'll say about—I'm thinking four weeks, I guess. It was very surprising to me [that every juror made it to the courthouse every day]. The storm happened on a Thursday night as I recall. Friday morning when I got up my driveway was blocked. No power, no phone, no nothing. And I sawed my way out to get into the road and my phone lines were down, of course. And I spliced the phone lines together. I could call out but no one could call in. When I called in finally on a Sunday, I guess, court as usual, which surprised me. . . . All the power out. The power was out in Charlotte, also. And I said, "how in the world can you get into Charlotte?" Charlotte is a pretty good sized . . . a big city. And how in the world can you get through Charlotte and be there 9:00 Monday morning? Which I did, but I was surprised that they had police officers at every intersection to pass traffic. They had the National Guard in town too.

And some of the jurors were without power longer than I was. In remote areas.[51]

- **Rick Hill:** Our power was off Friday till Tuesday . . . Friday we didn't go at all and we didn't know not to go. Then Monday we just showed up, so I reckon we just figured it out on ourselves.[52]

- **Robert Thornberry [alternate]:** Our power was out for two days. It wasn't really a significant problem, I don't think. The hurricane came through early Friday morning so we missed Friday of the trial and then by Sunday afternoon we had power back.[53]

- **James McAlister:** I was without electricity for two weeks. I lost numerous 300-year-old oak trees. My wife's car was demolished. It was a total ruin. I tried to get up and go that first day and I saw that it was physically impossible. It took chain saws a day and a half to saw our way out. We're in an extremely wooded area with only one entrance. . . . But I did go expecting not to see anyone, and everyone was there because we were warned that we would be charged five dollars a minute for any minute we were late. And eighteen jurors in the some six weeks of that trial, there was not a single person late. Essentially, everyone tried to get there about thirty minutes early.[54]

Laughing at Bakker's Witnesses

Some of the jurors commented on one of the trial's sensitive areas—allegations that prosecutors made fun of some of Bakker's witnesses and that it caused laughter in the courtroom.

- **Catherine Boardman:** There was some. I guess it came from the prosecution—them being kind of sarcastic toward the Jim Bakker fanatics. That was some of it.[55]

- **Rick Hill:** Yes, somewhat. I think Jerry Miller was more of that than the other lady . . . I think he was downplaying some of the witnesses.[56]

- **Robert Thornberry [alternate]:** Certainly they [prosecutors] attempted to make some of their [Bakker's witnesses'] thinking look foolish. Not extremely so. I wouldn't say that it was—well, the judge did once or twice have to warn the courtroom about being quiet, but it wasn't—I wouldn't have called it extensive.[57]

- **Barbara Dalley:** The man who'd been an alcoholic and they [PTL's Fort Hope] straightened him out. He was obviously brain damaged . . . didn't make sense. The prosecutors looked at each other and started laughing. That made me angry that they would laugh at someone damaged like that. I gave them a filthy look and it mattered to them.[58]

NOTES

1. Trial transcript, *United States of America v. James O. Bakker,* Docket No. C-CR-88-205-1, U.S.D.C. (W.D., N.C.), vol. 10, October 2–5, 1989, at 2227.

2. Barbara Dalley, telephone interview by Suzan Brooks, June 21, 1993.

3. Catherine Boardman, telephone interview by Suzan Brooks, October 3, 1993.

4. Rick Hill, telephone interview by Suzan Brooks, November 24, 1993.

5. Juror X, telephone interview by Suzan Brooks, September 20, 1993.

6. Barbara Dalley, telephone interview by Suzan Brooks, *supra,* n. 2.

7. Catherine Boardman, telephone interview by Suzan Brooks, *supra,* n. 3.

8. Rick Hill, telephone interview by Suzan Brooks, *supra,* n. 4.

9. Professor Gary Tidwell, telephone interview by Suzan Brooks, November 8, 1993.

10. Trial transcript, *supra,* n. 1, vol. 8, September 26–27, 1989, at 1180.

11. Catherine Boardman, telephone interview by Suzan Brooks, *supra,* n. 3.

12. Shirley Wise, telephone interview by Suzan Brooks, November 17, 1993.

13. James McAlister, telephone interview by Suzan Brooks, May 31, 1994.

14. Barbara Dalley, telephone interview by Suzan Brooks, *supra*, n. 2.

15. Catherine Boardman, telephone interview by Suzan Brooks, *supra*, n. 3.

16. James McAlister, telephone interview by Suzan Brooks, *supra*, n. 13.

17. Robert Thornberry, telephone interview by Suzan Brooks, January 3, 1994.

18. Juror X, telephone interview by Suzan Brooks, *supra*, n. 5.

19. Catherine Boardman, letter to the author March 9, 1997.

20. Juror X, telephone interview by Suzan Brooks, *supra*, n. 5.

21. Rick Hill, telephone interview by Suzan Brooks, *supra*, n. 4.

22. James McAlister, telephone interview by Suzan Brooks, *supra*, n. 13.

23. Barbara Dalley, telephone interview by Suzan Brooks, *supra*, n. 2.

24. Rick Hill, telephone interview by Suzan Brooks, *supra*, n. 4.

25. James McAlister, telephone interview by Suzan Brooks, *supra*, n. 14.

26. Barbara Dalley, telephone interview by Suzan Brooks, *supra*, n. 2.

27. Robert Thornberry, telephone interview by Suzan Brooks, *supra*, n. 17.

28. Rick Hill, telephone interview by Suzan Brooks, *supra*, n. 4.

29. Barbara Dalley, telephone interview by Suzan Brooks, *supra*, n. 2.

30. Catherine Boardman, telephone interview by Suzan Brooks, *supra*, n. 3.

31. Robert Thornberry, telephone interview by Suzan Brooks, *supra*, n. 17.

32. Rick Hill, telephone interview by Suzan Brooks, *supra*, n. 4.

33. Juror X, telephone interview by Suzan Brooks, *supra*, n. 5.

34. Rick Hill, telephone interview by Suzan Brooks, *supra*, n. 4.

35. Barbara Dalley, telephone interview by Suzan Brooks, *supra*, n. 2.

36. Juror X, telephone interview by Suzan Brooks, *supra*, n. 5.

37. Robert Thornberry, telephone interview by Suzan Brooks, *supra*, n. 17.

38. Barbara Dalley, telephone interview by Suzan Brooks, *supra*, n. 2.

39. Catherine Boardman, telephone interview by Suzan Brooks, *supra*, n. 3.

40. Rick Hill, telephone interview by Suzan Brooks, *supra*, n. 4.

41. Juror X, telephone interview by Suzan Brooks, *supra*, n. 5.

42. Barbara Dalley, telephone interview by Suzan Brooks, *supra*, n. 2.

43. Catherine Boardman, telephone interview by Suzan Brooks, *supra*, n. 3.

44. James McAlister, telephone interview by Suzan Brooks, *supra*, n. 13.

45. Rick Hill, telephone interview by Suzan Brooks, *supra*, n. 4.

46. Juror X, telephone interview by Suzan Brooks, *supra*, n. 5.

47. Barbara Dalley, telephone interview by Suzan Brooks, *supra*, n. 2.

48. Catherine Boardman, telephone interview by Suzan Brooks, *supra*, n. 3.

49. Juror X, telephone interview by Suzan Brooks, *supra*, n. 5.

50. Rick Hill, telephone interview by Suzan Brooks, *supra*, n. 4.

51. Robert Thornberry, telephone interview by Suzan Brooks, *supra*, n. 17.

52. James McAlister, telephone interview by Suzan Brooks, *supra*, n. 13.

53. Catherine Boardman, telephone interview by Suzan Brooks, *supra*, n. 3.

54. Rick Hill, telephone interview by Suzan Brooks, *supra*, n. 4.

55. Robert Thornberry, telephone interview by Suzan Brooks, *supra*, n. 17.

56. Barbara Dalley, telephone interview by Suzan Brooks, *supra*, n. 2.

Chapter 31

The One Juror Who Thought
Jim Bakker Might Be Innocent

Like all of the other jurors we interviewed, alternate juror
Shirley Wise took her role in the Bakker trial seriously.

Unlike other jurors, however, Ms. Wise was sharply critical
of Judge Potter's conduct and she questioned the ultimate
fairness of Bakker's trial. More than anything, she was saddened
by the way justice was dribbled out to Jim Bakker in that
courtroom.

Ms. Wise was unwilling to turn the other way when she saw
a fellow juror appear to be napping during the trial. She was
even more distressed by the reaction from the court attendant
and Judge Potter to her efforts to do something about it.

Most intriguing is the prospect that the outcome of the trial
could well have been remarkably different had Ms. Wise been
one of the twelve voting jurors. Instead, she was dismissed with
the other five alternates before the deliberations began.

But if Barbara Dalley, the last of the twelve jurors seated, had
not been accepted, and Ms. Wise had been moved up instead,
the final twelve person panel would have lost one of its two
most vocal members against Bakker and gained one who had
her doubts about the case. Bakker may never have been convicted.

Suzan Brooks spoke at length with Shirley Wise.[1]

Q: As one of the six alternate jurors, did you sit next to the twelve
regular jurors throughout the trial?

A: I was there every day. I heard it all. [Judge Potter] didn't excuse . . . [us] until he talked to the jurors before they went into the room to deliberate.

Q: How did the judge act toward Jim Bakker?

A: I did not go along with the way the judge treated Jim Bakker. He was intimidating to Jim Bakker. He wouldn't let him finish a sentence. You could tell there was animosity. He acted like he despised him when he walked into the courtroom. It was so apparent to me. . . .

Q: Was it that way for all five weeks of the trial?

A: Well . . . I got to the point I had to take a nerve pill every day because of the way the judge reacted to Mr. Bakker. If it was incriminating to Jim Bakker, naturally, he would listen to it and let it be said, but if it was anything in his behalf he closed his mind to it. It seemed so unfair. But I thought, if this is the way it goes [in criminal trials] people are—they are railroaded before they even go into the courtroom. And to me he was.

Q: Was there laughter in the courtroom? Were people sometimes laughing at Bakker's witnesses?

A: Oh yes. *** The federal lawyers . . . made remarks wanting to bring laughter.

Q: Did the judge join in?

A: No. Well, he had that little smirk on his face.

Q: How did Mr. Bakker strike you as a witness on his own behalf?

A: He never did get to finish a sentence. That's why—the man [Bakker] had some points to make. He even had a great big piece of cardboard. A chart. Apparently the judge saw it, but he wouldn't allow us to see it. And he wouldn't let him [Bakker] elaborate on it. He was going to explain how he came about setting up his lifetime memberships. But he [the judge] would not allow it to be presented. He told him to put it away.

Q: Did you notice anything else between the judge and Jim Bakker?

A: He [Judge Potter] purely despised him.

Q: Did Bakker's attorneys make an effort to protect him? Did they jump in when he wasn't allowed to finish sentences and things?

A: Weakly. That's what got to me. The judge would turn red in the face. He—it was so obvious. He really didn't want to hear anything in his [Bakker's] defense.

Q: What was your evaluation of Harold Bender?

A: . . . He just didn't seem to be doing what I thought he should be doing. He didn't—I don't think he stood up for Jim Bakker as much as he should have. *** It seemed like when Bender was put down by the judge, it didn't faze him. He was expecting it. He didn't fight for it. It seemed like he'd get a little belligerent after a while, but he never did.

Q: And George Davis?

A: Oh, that judge didn't like him one bit. He didn't like him. That was just like Jim Bakker being out there on the floor. He didn't like him.

Q: How did Bakker impress you?

A: He seemed meek and humble, and naturally you would feel sorry for someone like that who couldn't talk in his own defense. He just seemed like he was actually a man of God.

Q: Do you think he meant to cheat anybody?

A: No I don't. I totally do not.

Q: You told me that if you had been on the final jury, if one of the original twelve had not made it to the end and you had to re-place them, that it would have been a hung jury. What is your reason?

A: I couldn't have said he was purely guilty. I couldn't have because there were too many other people involved, and I couldn't have said he was the one that did it.

Q: Mr. Dortch?

A: That man should have served what Jim Bakker is doing right now. He's the man who did the bad stuff. And he was really carrying on after Jim Bakker got out of it in the manner that they accused Jim Bakker of.

Q: Are there any other reasons it would have been a hung jury if you had been on it?

A: Because it [the trial] was unfair. There were just a lot of things bad that I didn't think were fair, [or] right. There was a juror that sat beside me that slept through half the thing and that was part of my—why I wrote the judge. *** I don't remember her name. . . . I had to wake her up. That's what I said to the judge. Someone that was on trial for what Jim Bakker was, I knew he [the judge] was going to make it hard on him. But a juror should be able to. . . . *** If that's the way normal court procedure is, God forbid, I hope I never have to go to court.

I pointed out to the court attendant that a juror was sleeping. I wanted it relayed to the judge. The court attendant told me not to worry, that most people have made up their minds by this point in a trial. That's when I wrote this letter directly to the judge. He responded by saying he could not talk to me before the sentencing, after which he would be glad to go over my points.

[Later in the interview, Ms. Wise remembered the name of the juror and identified her. She also located her copy of the letter she sent to Judge Potter, which appears in this chapter.]

Ms. Wise was corroborated on this point by the jury foreman, Rick Hill:

> **Suzan Brooks:** Did you have the sense that some of the . . . jurors had a hard time paying attention?
> **Mr. Hill:** Yeah. The one older . . . lady. I can't remember her name, she had trouble staying awake a few times.
> **Suzan Brooks:** Would this be Miss ———?
> **Mr. Hill:** I think it was probably her.
> **Suzan Brooks:** Did the judge ever admonish you all to pay attention, wake up, or. . . .
> **Mr. Hill:** No, not one time.[2]

Ms. Wise made several other interesting comments during her interview with Suzan Brooks.

> **Q:** The judge seems to have made an effort to be humorous to the jury. And maybe they liked that.
> **A:** Oh, he did. He tried to be solicitous to us. Even sent our lunch in there one day and said it was from him.
> **Q:** What kind of slant did the *Charlotte Observer* take on all this over the years?
> **A:** Slamming Jim Bakker. Anything that they could slant against him. Never, it was always biased, nothing was ever in his favor. That's—in that letter, . . . I did say in there, Judge Potter, I don't think that trial should have been held in this area. Because to me, people were aware of it, heard too much. . . .
> **Q:** What are people in the Charlotte area saying about Bakker's forty-five-year sentence?
> **A:** Just generalizing what people say, everyone thinks it was too long. It was too much for the crime in comparison to what a murderer gets. It was just unheard of. I just couldn't understand—no one can understand why he got such a heavy sentence for what he did. And then I hear people say that he didn't hold a gun to anybody's head for them to send the money. They did it on their own.

NOTES

1. This chapter is based on Suzan Brooks's telephone interviews with Shirley Wise, November 16 and 17, 1993.

2. Rick Hill, telephone interview by Suzan Brooks, November 24, 1993.

October 17, 1980

Dear Judge Potter:

I want to thank you for the opportunity of allowing me to serve on the panel during the trial of Jim Bakker, even though only in the capacity of an alternate.

I wanted to have a moment of your time afterwards and relayed it to Sammie but I do understand you were pressured for time and duties and could not allow me that, after much thought I decided to write since I could not put "finis" to the matter until my mind was relieved. Maybe your position will not allow you to answer my questions but try I must.

I drew the fact to the attention of Sammie but she assured me at the time that there was nothing for me worry about—that the lady had already formed an opinion. Ms.   who sat beside me, went to sleep at least twice a day and continually made noises that indicated that she was in a sleep-state. I woke her once because her head was on her chest but decided that was not my responsibility so did not do it anymore. How can a person doing this assume such an enormous responsibility not being fully aware of all going on in a court-room? It offended me and I certainly would not have wanted her weighing my future.

In my opinion, considering the notoriety of the case, it should not have been allowed to trial in this area. Other parts of the country were not as aware of and concerned as in this section. I know that as factual.

Next—why were you allowed to hear the cases of Dortch and the Taggerts prior to Mr. Bakker when, by human nature, it would have you highly opinioned and prejudicial toward him when his time came. I'm sure you were sick of the mess when he did have his day in court. Is it normal for a judge to be so obviously intimidating to the defense as you appeared to be in this incident and so lenient, so it seemed, to the prosecution? The obvious feelings for the defendant were beginning to really get to me. I don't think I could have lasted another week. I'm not saying Mr. Bakker should not have been convicted of the charges against him—that sort of soliciting cannot go on forever in TV ministries—but he did deserve the respect of the court—which I did not think was allowed him and his counsel.

* * *

This may not set well with you but I respect your position and, as I intimated, you are a mortal and human nature isn't applicable only to me.

Respectfully yours,
Shirley Wise

A copy of Shirley Wise's letter to the judge. A name and a passage which might embarrass named individuals have been omitted.

Chapter 32

Plenty of Blame to Go Around

It would be unfair to lay all of the blame for Bakker's conviction at any one person's doorstep. The fact of the matter is that an incredible combination of forces collided during his trial which made it impossible for him to win. It would be interesting to go back and see what Bakker's horoscope had to say about his planets and moons that bizarre month in Charlotte because absolutely everything went wrong for him. He didn't get one break.

1. Judge Robert Potter

It would have been difficult for Jim Bakker to have drawn a tougher judge. "Maximum Bob" openly treated Bakker and his attorneys icily and frequently flashed his disgust at them. The UPI reporter covering the trial described Potter as "mean-spirited."[1] In a later dispatch, that reporter wrote that while the defense played a videotape of *The PTL Club,* "a scowling U.S. District Judge Robert Potter stuck his index fingers in his ears and the jurors sat expressionless."[2]

"They don't treat murderers like they've treated him [Bakker],"[3] insisted Bakker supporter Mervell Mullen in an interview with reporters outside the Charlotte courthouse.

Jim Bakker in prison: The judge glared down at me throughout the trial and shouted at my attorney—he hated his guts. As the judge would yell at my attorney, I sat there in that courtroom like

a beaten dog—embarrassed, bewildered and out of my element. It
was the most painful experience of my life.[4]

Time and again in key rulings at critical junctures during the
trial, Potter stung Bakker. In the most important ruling in the
case, he denied Bakker's motion for a change of venue which
would have relocated the trial not only out of Charlotte and the
cesspool of anti-Bakker sentiment that had existed there for
years, but may have meant that a different judge would be
presiding in another part of the state.

Another ruling of enormous significance was Potter's refusal
to allow the jurors to board a bus and drive out to Heritage to
view the body. Defense attorneys asked for the trip so that the
jurors could see all of the buildings that had been erected with
the money Bakker was raising, but the judge said it would be a
waste of time. Heritage is an impressive place with dozens of
buildings erected with lifetime partners' dollars. Permitting the
jury to see all of the construction would have been a real break
for Bakker.

Certainly the speed and manner in which Potter selected the
jury was pivotal and thwarted Bakker from the beginning.

The judge also kept Bakker and his attorneys off balance.
Davis and Bender were frequently interrupted and hurried
along by Potter. The judge had sat patiently for nearly four
weeks while the prosecutors called more than ninety witnesses
against Bakker. But after only a day and a half of defense
witnesses, the judge became impatient and rode Bakker's
attorneys for two or three days threatening not to let them call
anyone else to the stand. Potter said that the defense, after only
a few hours, had become "ridiculous."[5] Three weeks for the
government's case, one day for Bakker's case, and then it's the
two-minute warning.

Another vivid example of Potter's effect in this regard had to
be scaring the daylights out of Bakker during his panic attack by
ordering federal marshals to rope and tie him and force him
into a prison psychiatric ward until he dried out. The law
required that a psychiatric evaluation be done since Bakker was

suddenly claiming he couldn't go on with the trial. But the force that was used on him, including the handcuffs and leg irons, seemed unnecessarily harsh to many observers.

Potter's conduct was blasted by critics. To Alan Dershowitz, Potter was the "harshest sentencing judge in the nation"[6] whose punishment of Bakker exceeded that typically given murderers or rapists. To the judges on the Court of Appeals in Richmond, Potter's statements at Bakker's sentencing were "too intemperate to be ignored"[7] and the judge abused his discretion in sentencing the evangelist. To George Davis, whom he had bludgeoned for weeks, Potter had perpetrated "the most outrageous abuse of due process I had encountered in my law practice."[8] To the political writer for the *Washington Times,* he was a judge with "a private score to settle."[9]

A devout Roman Catholic, Potter was born in 1923 and graduated from Duke University Law School in 1950. In the private practice of law most of his life, Potter served as a member of the Mecklenburg Board of County Commissioners in the late 1960s and made a name for himself as a hard-nosed conservative. In 1968, he accused other politicians of supporting the federal government's anti-poverty programs to "buy off the militants,"[10] and complained those programs would "bring about a completely socialistic government if it is not stopped."[11]

Potter was active in the successful 1972 U.S. senatorial campaign of arch-conservative Jesse Helms. It was Helms who nominated him to the federal bench in 1981 and recommended that President Reagan appoint him. Attorneys practicing before him rate him as pro-prosecution and government-oriented. He is described as crusty, demanding, and strict. Others characterize him as tough but fair.[12] To this day and even in the wake of all of the criticism Potter has received as a result of the Bakker trial, Jesse Helms is unwavering in his affection. I sought Helms's reaction and this was his response:

Mr. Potter is indeed a treasured friend whom I admire because of his courage and integrity—and his refusal to be intimidated by criticism. He is a capable lawyer. He did indeed support me in my 1972 campaign, but once a federal judge, he quite properly did not participate in any public way. His daughter, a fine lawyer, once served as my chief legislative assistant and I've never had a better one. She tormented the Senate's left wing Democrats.[13]

In 1990, Judge Potter was asked by students at Belmont Abbey College about the AIDS crisis. He replied: "I've got a solution. Ship 'em all to Australia. Not the AIDS patients, just the people who cause this thing. Ship 'em to Australia and put a fence around them."[14] The reaction in Sydney was fierce, with the *Sydney Daily Mirror* calling him a "stinking hide."[15] Another editorial referred to him as one of a small number of "rednecked political illiterates."[16] One cartoon showed him with his foot in his mouth and the caption, "ugly idea from ugly American."[17] Back in the states, the *Asheville Citizen* editorialized that his biting comment "was thoughtless, shallow, insensitive and completely inappropriate for any public or private figure, much less a United States judge."[18]

A question does arise. Isn't exiling Jim Bakker to the frozen reaches of Minnesota for forty-five years about the same as sending someone to Australia and putting a fence around them? Is Potter as tough as leather, or what?

Stunned by the judge's trial and sentencing antics, the *Washington Times* snapped that Potter "may be the judge that Mencken had in mind when he suggested that a fixed percentage of our federal judges ought to be shot annually, to make the survivors pay attention to their oaths of office."[19]

2. An Immovable Jury

Another time, another place, another jury, and sympathy for the defendant may have swelled within the jury box, perhaps even enough to steel at least one or two jurors to hold out for acquittal. Such a mistrial scenario at the hands of a holdout or even outright acquittal were legitimate possibilities but both required at least one juror with guts to refuse to buckle under to pressure from the other jurors.

Given the juggernaut of the prosecutors' case, the mass of

evidence against Bakker, and certainly the way the jury turned against Bakker during the trial, it would have been unrealistic to expect any juror here to go to the wall for Bakker. If the televangelist's case had been stronger and had equipped a Bakker-leaning juror with more potent ammunition to use in the jury room, that may have been different. But, absent that, the two jurors who wavered at the outset of deliberations simply did not have the conviction or fortitude to hold out for long. And they didn't have the horses to persuade other jurors to their way of thinking.

One of the most intriguing things about this jury was that not one of the final twelve developed any lasting sympathy for Bakker.[20] Often, a backlash will be created and jurors will embrace a defendant when it is clear to them that the judge, who in all fairness should remain neutral during the trial, becomes hostile to the defendant or his attorneys. It did not happen here.

After a five-week trial, Jim Bakker didn't get to first base with this jury. But the twelve people in that jury box weren't the only ones in North Carolina who viewed Bakker uncharitably.

3. *The Scene Was Charlotte*

The Michigan-born and Minnesota-educated preacher had always been regarded as an outsider in Charlotte. To some, he was a carpetbagging Pentecostal evangelist who fit neither Charlotte's deep antebellum tradition nor its new cosmopolitan ways. Jim and Tammy Bakker, waltzing down the Heritage USA's Main Street promenade by Goosebumps Collectibles or speaking in tongues in the Upper Room, were as far as they could get from being accepted in Charlotte.

With a population of 400,000 in 1989, and with banking one of its growth industries, Charlotte prides itself on being the third largest financial center in the nation. It is buttoned-down and conservative. By car, it is two and a half hours due west of the Atlantic Ocean. Atlanta, Georgia, is five hours away.

This was hostile territory for the evangelist.

4. *The* Charlotte Observer *and the Media in General*

As the largest newspaper in that part of the state, the *Observer* was read by hundreds of thousands of Carolinians and was their major source for news. The paper had been on Bakker's back for years, dogging him from the 1970s when he first burst on the scene in Charlotte.

Not showing much respect or tolerance for the Evangelical beliefs of the millions who visited PTL each year, *Observer* reporters portrayed Bakker as a real-life Elmer Gantry, a holy roller out to fleece his flock. It was the role of protector, exposing Bakker, that the young Turks on the staff of the *Observer* seemed to relish throughout the 1970s and 1980s.

There was an unmistakable paternalistic arrogance to the *Observer's* Bakker-watch over the years. It was the perfect liberal angst, really, as staffers patronized the born-again Christians who watched Bakker on TV and vacationed at his resort.

The *Observer's* own humor columnist, Doug Robarchek, was having a field day. When local Pentecostal churches held prayer vigils for the Second Coming of Christ, called the Rapture, Robarchek could not contain his howls. Wrote the columnist, "Jim Bakker claimed he was Raptured early, while picking up Tammy Faye's makeup bag. But doctors later determined this was not the Rapture but merely the Rupture."[21]

In fact, Pentecostals are one of the few groups anyone can degrade today and still be politically correct.

In a 1993 column on politically correct public nags, *Chicago Tribune* columnist Mike Royko wrote that they "believe they were put on Earth to save us helpless dummies from ourselves."[22] That is a very good description of several reporters who hounded Bakker for years, but it wasn't the only time Royko's impish wit had pierced the Bakker case. In a 1987 *Tribune* column, the Chicago humorist offered another slant. Wrote Royko about Bakker's congregation, "[S]ince it's their money that's been squandered, embezzled or whatever, it seems only fair that they be preached to by the squanderer or embezzler of their choosing."[23] Even though it was with the back of his hand, Royko pinpointed the essential overreaching of all paternalists.

That Bakker was an irresistible target of liberals in the press can be demonstrated. Liberals in this country could not control their anger and contempt when the U.S. Supreme Court shut George Carlin's potty mouth in a landmark 1978 decision. "The Seven Dirty Words" case, as it was known, involved an FCC ruling that Carlin's X-rated monologue containing seven words describing sex and excrement could not be broadcast on radio or TV during the day. The Supreme Court upheld the FCC, expressly rejecting the argument of press and media liberals who supported Carlin's free speech right to say whatever he pleased on radio. In Carlin's behalf, they insisted that listeners could turn him off with a flick of the wrist and never be harmed by hearing his profanity.[24]

Liberal Supreme Court Justices William Brennan and Thurgood Marshall wrote a blistering dissenting opinion, arguing that "unlike other intrusive modes of communication, such as sound tracks, '[t]he radio can be turned off,' [citing case law] and with a minimum of effort."[25] They went on to emphasize that a listener ". . . can simply extend his arm and switch stations or flick the 'off' button. . . ."[26]

That argument from Carlin's apologists and other leading liberals has validity, it appears, only if the substance of what is being broadcast is to the liberal's liking. If it is the conservative, Christian, Pentecostal PTL program, the government has every right to move in and punish it even though each one of Bakker's millions of viewers could also turn him off with a flip of the remote. No one was forcing anyone to watch him.

But to the press, Jim Bakker was no George Carlin and Bakker's viewers were not Carlin's listeners. The medium was the same—broadcasting—but the message was not. Carlin's message simply did not offend the liberal press. All seven words of it. Bakker's message did, and they kicked him around in the media for years.

A 1986 memo from the *Observer*'s perplexed publisher to his staff, reported by Charles Shepard in his book, addressed the hundreds of stories of waste and sloth at PTL which had appeared in that newspaper. It ended with the observation that all of the bad press had not deterred Bakker's supporters.

> PTL's givers—the people our coverage is primarily intended to enlighten—have not shown us in any substantial way that they appreciate our revelations. Rather, they seem to endorse the show biz life-styles of the Bakkers and to admire the creation of Heritage USA.[27]

Such revealing in-house grousing speaks volumes about the mission the newspaper envisioned for itself in its rapacious Bakker reporting over the years—to straighten out PTL's gullible supporters.

Yet for the short term, the more negative press Bakker got in the *Observer,* the more his followers were energized. It must have galled the paper that Bakker turned their attacks into bloody flags on his television programs. Brandishing scathing articles, Bakker would ask his viewers to stand with him and be counted against the media attacks on their religion and way of life. It worked. The more the paper chased him, the more money Bakker's followers gave to build their Pentecostal oasis right under the *Observer*'s nose.

However, as attacks in the *Observer* accelerated in 1985, Richard Dortch sent a letter to the newspaper pleading for more balance in the reporting on PTL.

> Why are your people so bitter and mean? Are we upsetting to your people because we worship differently? *** Don't we fit the preppy establishment mentality of the editorial and management staff of the *Observer*? It does make us wonder if there is an element of bigotry or just plain meanness toward this ministry.[28]

As the months wore on, the paper was increasingly faulted for its anti-Bakker bias. Critical letters to the editor appeared in its own pages with greater frequency, most of which took the tack of the succinct missive from Mrs. George Conklin of Locust, North Carolina: "The news media are like maggots; they keep after someone until they destroy them."[29]

In a 1989 interview, the *Observer*'s Charles Shepard offered this response:

> The liberal press tends to come down harder on conservatives than it does on liberals, and I think if the press did not tend to be dominated by atheists and agnostics it would probably treat religious leaders and their institutions with more seriousness and respect.[30]

The *Observer* was after him, all right. But of course there were some skeletons in those huge fifty-foot Bakker closets along with all of Tammy's shoes. You can't blame the media for that. But having the local newspaper with all of its resources on his tail every day, driving and digging and rooting out any negative thing, was another very bad break for Bakker. If he had been sitting on the top of a water slide in the middle of Louisiana or Oklahoma, venues where Jimmy Swaggart and Oral Roberts have for decades been treated with kinder gloves, it might well have turned out differently for Bakker.

In the mid-1980s, the *Observer* reporters following Bakker began to smell the scent of the biggest PTL story of all. Tips and rumors about Bakker's tryst with Jessica Hahn, other sexual indiscretions, and proof that Jim and Tammy were spending enormous sums riveted the news staff. It was something local reporters live for—their own Watergate, and they ran with the story. In fact, it was the *Observer*'s exposés of Bakker's mismanagement, deception, and greed that toppled him. The paper won a coveted Pulitzer Prize for public service in 1988 for doing it.

So the *Observer* kept beating Bakker over the head, casting him as a crook and a clown, and apparently suffering some indignity that he was polluting the national television airwaves from a studio within a newspaper boy's toss of the *Observer* itself. Right up to the end, the paper was firing shots against Bakker. Remember that on the Sunday before the jury was selected, it ran its full-page "Down the Tubes" game presaging his trial, implying his guilt, and getting in a few final jabs.

In all, it was simply too much for Bakker to overcome.

5. *The Palace Guard Left the Emperor Naked*

At the end of one of the exhausting days I spent with Bakker, he wistfully offered an afterthought telling me, "[y]ou know, I could have made it if we had all stuck together."[31]

Intriguingly, that analysis was shared by Efrem Zimbalist, Jr. who testified at the trial that if Bakker had only been allowed to continue on for a few more months at Heritage all the lodging would have been completed and there never would have been a problem. This particular take on Bakker's unraveling requires that one reject the premise that at least until all the hotels were up, Bakker's representations on the air were fraudulent. But there is some truth to it. Specifically, it would have been extremely difficult if not impossible for the government to have convicted Jim Bakker of anything without the active help of two people closest to Bakker—Richard Dortch and Jerry Falwell.

It was Falwell, just after being named the new PTL president, who uncovered the memos and records which documented serious financial trouble at PTL at the time the Bakkers were spending millions of dollars on themselves. Enraged, the fundamentalist allowed FBI and IRS investigators full access to Bakker's private PTL files where, of course, they found evidence harmful to Bakker.[32]

But of all the things that could have gone wrong for Bakker as he faced trial, nothing was more significant than Richard Dortch's decision to plead guilty and testify in Bakker's case. While Dortch never admitted on the witness stand that he and Bakker conspired to defraud anyone, the most harmful thing he said was that Bakker knew that more lifetime partnerships were being sold than could be accommodated. That kind of testimony coming from Bakker's Number Two in command at Heritage sunk him.

6. *The Eighties Backlash*

Bakker's timing could not have been worse, or the government's better, to haul him before a jury. Two separate societal undercurrents in 1989 contributed to the jury's lack of sympathy for Bakker. First, 1989 was no time to be a televangelist.

Nine years earlier was the time to be one when the Religious Right was beginning to flex its political muscle in this country, as fundamentalists and Evangelicals by the millions united and organized. Their goal was to force a midair course correction in what they perceived as the country's precipitous lunge toward the left. They were fighting mad about the red hot social issues of the day, with their vehement opposition to abortion at the top of the list.

Encouraged by local fundamentalist preachers in their hometowns and by such national televangelists as Falwell and Robertson, hundreds of thousands of Evangelicals abandoned the sidelines and thrust themselves into the vortex of several wrenching and divisive issues. They picketed, they paraded, they campaigned door to door, and they called radio talk shows. They boycotted the sponsors of television programs that featured too much sex, and brought them to their knees. And, they targeted five liberal Democratic United States senators in the 1978 election for their pro-choice beliefs and other liberal agendas, and defeated every one of them.

Ask former Senators Dick Clark, Floyd Haskell, William Hathaway, Thomas McIntyre, and Wendell Anderson. Suddenly the Evangelicals were in your face. And on the news. And in grocery store parking lots. They were everywhere and particularly they were at the polls when it counted.

It was precisely at that time that Jerry Falwell emerged as a national figure to be reckoned with as one of the New Right's leaders. The Evangelicals stayed involved, too, and were a significant factor in Ronald Reagan's 1980 White House victory, rolling up huge margins for him in the Bible belt and among fundamentalists nationally. It was certainly not by accident that Reagan appeared with Jerry Falwell frequently in public and that Reagan even stood with Jim Bakker on *The PTL Club*. Throughout the late 1970s and well into the 1980s, the Religious Right was riding high in America.

But, by the end of the 1980s the public began to turn against fundamentalist activists. After a few years, they began to seem too strident, too militant, and too shrill. Their unforgiving stance on abortion began to seem harsh to many people. And, like most political phenomena, the New Right began to cycle out.

Society's pendulum swung, knocking many Evangelicals on their backsides. Not that Bakker was ever a subscriber to the most militant of the Religious Right's agenda items or that he could ever be characterized as militant or political, but the differences between nationally known fundamentalist evangelists were simply too subtle for most people to grasp. Falwell, Robertson, Swaggart, and Bakker all seemed the same to the unsophisticated eye.

The majority of people in the country simply came to reject the New Right's politics by the end of the '80s decade. The proof of that political equation would be seen in the 1992 presidential election in which attempts by George Bush to steep himself in the New Right's agenda from the Houston convention all the way to the end of the campaign were soundly rejected by a majority of voters who didn't want anything to do with it. Falwell sure didn't give any prayers in Washington during the inaugural festivities the following January, either. That was the difference between 1980 and 1992. Things just changed for the worse for Evangelicals.

Even graver for Jim Bakker, the *New Yorker* took a wide view of several other societal phenomena aligned by the end of the decade and concluded pejoratively that Jim and Tammy were "exemplars of the 1980's. . . ."[33] As that magazine saw it, "[t]he Bakkers on stage had a good deal in common with Ronald Reagan. On stage, they were sweet, tolerant, hugely optimistic people who wished no one any ill. Like the President, too, they were stars and believers in salvation by popularity."[34]

Many people in this country were of the opinion that the 1980s had been stained by the greed of several successful and highly visible public figures. For Bakker, being a wealthy exemplar of that greed was not at all helpful. Undeniably, some who had profited so enormously in the 1980s found themselves the subjects of hatred and derision. Public opinion polls showed that many people thought the go-go eighties had gone too far, and that the rich had gotten richer at the expense of the middle class and the poor. It was no time to be a fat cat.

Leona Helmsley learned that accusations of greed are tough for a rich person to shake when she faced an unsympathetic jury in New York two and a half years after Bakker was brought down in North Carolina.[35] The evidence of high living, million dollar salaries, and a lifestyle of inordinate luxury was red meat in the Bakker case for his jury, too. From the half million dollar bonuses paid him when the ministry didn't have enough money to buy stamps, to the Palm Springs villas paid for with PTL contributions, the evidence spoke powerfully and played perfectly into the eighties stereotype.

Another time, another decade, another place. A different horoscope. And Jim Bakker might have survived.

NOTES

1. Preston, "Judge Threatens to Jail Bakker during Trial," UPI [wire story], September 12, 1989, BC Cycle.

2. Preston, "PTL," UPI [wire story], September 26, 1989, BC Cycle.

3. Applebome, "Bakker Sentenced to 45 Years for Fraud in His TV Ministry," *New York Times,* October 25, 1989 at 1-A, col. 4.

4. Jim Bakker, interviews by author, in Rochester, Minnesota, October 31, 1992 and April 4, 1993.

5. Trial transcript, *United States of America v. James O. Bakker,* Docket No. C-CR-88-205-1, U.S.D.C. (W.D., N.C.), vol. 8, September 26–27, 1989, at 1119.

6. Drape, "Ex PTL Chief Bakker Makes Plea to Reduce 45-year Prison Term," *Atlanta Journal and Constitution,* August 23, 1991 at 1-A (Nexis printout).

7. *U.S. v. Bakker,* 925 F.2d 728, 741 (4th Cir. 1991).

8. Pruden, "A Little Spankie for the Judge," *Washington Times,* February 13, 1991 at 4-A (Nexis printout).

9. *Id.*

10. Nichols, "Bakker's Fate Rests with Tough Judge," Gannett News Service [wire story], October 23, 1989.

11. *Id.*

12. Chase, ed., *Almanac of the Federal Judiciary,* vol. 1 (Aspen Law & Business, Englewood Cliffs, N.J.: 1996) at 25.

13. Senator Jesse Helms, letter to the author, February 23, 1994.

14. Preston, "Federal Judge Shuts Up about AIDS," UPI [wire story], April 24, 1990, BC Cycle.

15. *Id.*

16. *Id.*

17. "Australians Blast 'Ugly American' Judge for AIDS Remark," UPI [wire story], April 23, 1990, BC Cycle.

18. *Miami Herald,* UPI [wire story], May 2, 1990, BC Cycle.

19. Pruden, *supra,* n. 8.

20. *See* generally chapter 30, *supra.*

21. Preston, UPI [wire story], September 13, 1988, AM Cycle.

22. Royko, "It's Beef for Dinner, not Veggie or Tofu Burgers," *Des Moines Register,* April 28, 1993 at 11-A, col. 1.

23. Royko, "Jim and Tammy's Recovery Should Be an Inspiration to the Unfaithful," *Des Moines Register,* October 13, 1987 at 7-A, col. 6.

24. *FCC v. Pacifica Foundation,* 438 U.S. 726 (1978).

25. *Id.* at 765.

26. *Id.* at 766.

27. Shepard, *Forgiven* (Atlantic Monthly Press, New York, 1989) at 403.

28. Romine, "The Man Who Exposed the PTL Scandal—Reporter's Book Delves into Mind of Jim Bakker," *Charlotte Observer,* September 24, 1989, at 1-E (Westlaw printout).

29. "The Observer Forum: Our Readers' Views," *Charlotte Observer,* September 8, 1989, at 1-ED (Westlaw printout).

30. Romine, *supra,* n. 28.

31. Jim Bakker, interview by author, in Rochester, Minnesota, June 26, 1993.

32. Harris, "$$$ and Sins: Jim Bakker's Case Hits Court; In Charlotte, a Sordid Saga Nears Its Spicy Conclusion," *Washington Post,* August 22, 1989, at 1-E (Nexis printout).

33. FitzGerald, "Reflections (The Bakkers)," *New Yorker,* April 23, 1990 at 87.

34. *Id.* at 86.

35. "Helmsley Surrenders at Prison," *New York Times,* April 16, 1992 at 3-B, col. 1.

Chapter 33

How David Letterman Might Critique the Bakker Trial— The Top Ten Reasons Jim Bakker Didn't Win

10. He Is Not a Fighter

As his trial approached in 1989, Bakker was not fighting. When Ted Koppel asked him on *Nightline* when he was going to fight back, Bakker responded curiously that Scripture forbade "returning evil for evil."[1] But more than that "turn the other cheek" mentality, he does not have the temperament or personality to counterpunch. Bakker is unlikely to even confront someone if they hurt him. He is simply too mild-mannered and forgiving for it, and even jabbing at him evokes no measurable meanness in kind. He does not fight with people. "He can't face anybody,"[2] is the way former PTL missions director Robert Manzano once explained it to the FCC.

There are plenty of people in the world like that and Jim happens to be one of them. That's why some things went wrong over the years.

I found Jim Bakker to be a gentle, kind, and nice person. He is very pleasant and likeable. But those are not the characteristics you want in Marines who are being dropped by helicopter to rescue you from your foxhole in the face of hostile fire. You want people who are mean, fighting mad, and anxious to shove their bayonet through the throat of anybody who stands in their way. You want a fighter.

Even on cross-examination, being beaten about the face and head with all kinds of accusatory questions by Deborah Smith,

Bakker did not fight back. He let her push him back to the ring rope time and time again without throwing any significant punches of his own. It was that weak performance on cross that so many jurors remembered when they retired to decide his fate. He needed a bayonet and a bad attitude.

9. He Didn't Bark Loudly Enough at His Former Associates

As a Pentecostal preacher, Jim Bakker certainly did not deal with underlings in the coarse, threatening way a toughened corporate CEO might who wanted to light a punishing fire under his staff. But there are times when only the most impolite abrasiveness can communicate to others how important something is to you. In a crisis, sometimes you have to yell at others to get their attention and get them moving. But Bakker did not do that. He did not rain verbal thunder on key former associates to sound a deafening alarm before the trial to save him by finding some evidence to win the case.

8. He Was Too Mannerly in Dealing with the Prosecutors

Bakker had obviously been reading too much Miss Manners and not enough Jimmy Hoffa. Particularly, Hoffa found a way for a criminal defendant to do a little bit for his case even while sitting solemnly by his attorney in the courtroom during trial. Bakker told me that, "I gave up in my heart when the judge was so mean to me and my attorney. I just wanted out."[3] That was not the Hoffa way.

A great story is told by Nashville attorney James Neal, who during the Kennedy administration was the assistant attorney general who successfully prosecuted Teamsters leader Jimmy Hoffa. The charge against Hoffa was jury tampering and the trial was held in the federal courthouse in Chattanooga.

When he arrived in the courtroom each morning, Neal would look over at the defense table a few feet away where Hoffa was already sitting. And every morning, Hoffa would acknowledge Neal's arrival by briskly extending his middle finger under the table at the prosecutor. Neal told the *ABA Journal*, "I can still remember him shooting me the finger. He was a tough old bird. [And] he would invite me to go to the gym every day at noon and settle the matter in the gym, just between us."[4]

Hoffa had it right. You don't give up in the middle of a trial when things look bleak. Even when you are sitting, unable to speak, between two attorneys with a judge scowling at you, you fly the colors.

7. He Left a Video Trail

Paper trails in fraud cases are often difficult for jurors to follow. In this case, though, the government played several hours of videotape of edited PTL programs in which Bakker appeared to make several promises concerning the lifetime partnerships which were later changed. In his exuberance in talking about Heritage USA on television, the edited tapes made it appear that he got caught up in exaggerating and embellishing the partnerships and the facilities. It was all on tape for the jury to see and readily understand.

Like Richard Nixon, Bakker was done in by his own tapes. Without them, he might have had a chance.

6. He Was Obsessed with Building Heritage USA

At the very root of all of Bakker's problems was the need for millions of dollars a week to bankroll Heritage. To millions, the place was a tabernacle for born-again Christians and an oasis in a world where Satan lurked. But it was also a money pit. If Bakker's dream for Heritage had not been so gargantuan, financing for the place would never have forced the economic stress that eventually ate into his ministry like a cancer.

5. Jim and Tammy's Spending was Spinning Out of Control

Nobody should have laughed when Tammy repeatedly said on television that she had "a shopping demon."[5] By God, she did and somebody should have exorcised it; the reason Jim and Tammy needed bonuses in the hundreds of thousands of dollars was because they were spending that much money on themselves. The list is familiar, from Palm Springs homes to Rolex watches, but the specter of two evangelists spending money like that should have set off a smoke alarm in their own heads or in somebody else's. An alarm should have sounded, "Slow down! Do you see what you are doing?"

4. He Resisted Criticism

In his haste to build Heritage, Bakker was not about to be slowed down by any attorney. And, like the rest of us, he didn't much like having his dream criticized, either. He believed he was on a mission from God to build that place, and when his lawyers shot some of his ideas down, he shut them off. When they tried to dissuade him from spending so much money on himself for fear the IRS would consider it private inurement, he ignored them. When they told him to change the plan for raising and spending partnership money for building construction, he didn't listen. He simply was not willing to hear any negativism from PTL lawyers about his baby.

His decision to ignore the advice of counsel came back to haunt him in two ways. They were right in most instances, and had Jim followed their advice he could well have avoided indictment. And their letters to him were among the most potent of the government's exhibits in his trial. Because at that point the jury had the chance to see how uncautious Bakker had been in charging off on his own, even after being warned of the danger in what he was doing.

3. He Was Killed on Cross-Examination

Bakker had one chance to eke out an acquittal in this case—with his own testimony. If the jury believed it, he would have gone free. They didn't. Jury foreman Rick Hill said, "[t]he only thing I believed about his testimony was that when he started out, he was earnest."[6] Of course, it was Deborah Smith's cross-examination that exposed Jim to the jury's ignominy. She pelted him with so many questions which drove hard at his own representations on the air that he was repeatedly forced to plaintively answer, "I don't remember." In fact, that was one of the things that the jury remembered most—Bakker not remembering.

2. He and Tammy Cashed Their Bonus Checks

In his defense, Bakker said that allegations of his greed were unfair because he never took a dime in salary or bonuses that the PTL board of directors didn't vote him. His attorneys argued it repeatedly to the jury. But the prosecutors made one quick point with four short words which destroyed that argument and made Bakker look even more suspicious for advancing it: he cashed the checks.

Worse, it appeared that he cashed them at times when PTL was on the rocks financially, when it could barely meet payroll or pay long-standing debts.

1. No Miracles Today

After fifteen years of living on the edge and living by faith, this time there was no miracle. No ninth inning home run in the last at bat. No Hail Mary pass into the end zone by the team five points down with one second left on the clock.

Bakker had been banking on the power of prayer to perform a miracle that would somehow shield him when the chips were down. Hundreds of thousands of prayer clocks had been mailed out by Tammy just before the trial. He actually did believe that prayer would bring him through, that God would again hold him in His hand. After all, he'd had his biscuits saved a thousand times before from imminent disaster, times just like this one when he didn't have anything going for him—not a dime in the bank to make the next day's mortgage payment on his church, not a dollar in his pocket to buy tonight's dinner, not a chance in the world that he could really persuade hundreds of thousands of people to contribute $3 million a week to build a city for Pentecostals in the North Carolina pines. But God always provided for him by coming through in a clutch.

But this time, there was no divine intervention. No miracles this day. And Bakker fell to the ground.

NOTES

1. Stern, Kelley, and Johnson, Gannett News Service, May 28, 1987.

2. "Understanding Jim Bakker," *Charlotte Observer,* January 27, 1986 at 4-A, col. 1.

3. Jim Bakker, interview by author, in Rochester, Minnesota, June 26, 1993.

4. Curriden, "From Elvis to Exxon," *ABA Journal,* November, 1990 (Nexis printout).

5. Harris and Isikoff, "Limos, Minks, Gucci Give 'Dynasty' Glitter to PTL's TV Empire," *Des Moines Register,* May 25, 1987 at 1-A, col. 1.

6. Applebome, "Bakker Is Convicted on All Counts; First Felon Among TV Evangelists," *New York Times,* October 6, 1989 at 1-A, col. 4.

Chapter 34

How Bakker Could Have Been Successfully Defended

Although a long shot, this case might have been won. Undeniably, it was leaking water and the defendant was carrying some heavy baggage; but several defense strategies existed which may have salvaged the case for Bakker.

Set the Record Straight— Whatever He Did, It Wasn't Fraud

A major defense could have been that, sure, some of what he did may have been wrong. But it was not fraud.

Bakker was charged with violating the federal wire fraud statute, which provides:

> Whoever, having devised or intending to devise any scheme or artifice to defraud . . . [or to obtain money by false representations] by means of wire, radio or television . . . shall be fined . . . or imprisoned. . . .[1]

His attorneys could have enlarged that statute the size of a window and positioned it on an easel for the jury to carefully examine. Then, each phrase and element of it should have been defiantly scrutinized.

The jurors may have doubted that the prosecutors proved that Bakker intended to defraud or falsely obtain money. Rather, his intent may well have been to carry out the mission that he believed God had given him: to build Heritage as fast as possible with money from his viewers. The argument would be that there was no evidence at all that his intent was to dupe people or to concoct some phony scheme to get people to send him money.

He wasn't sitting with slick confederates figuring out ways to get people from the Midwest to invest in a nonexistent gold mine they would never see. That would be a true fraud, a criminal enterprise. The Grand Hotel was built and Bakker was on national television five days a week urging people to come to South Carolina to stay in it. When they got there, viewers found a majestic hotel with elegantly furnished rooms and all the resort amenities Bakker promised.

And if Bakker really were perpetrating a fraud with his appeals to PTL's viewers, why in the world would he not only save a videotape of every program but also have every word he spoke on the air catalogued and indexed by topic? To make the prosecutors' jobs easier? No—he did it because he was proud of what he was doing on the air and wanted an archive made of it. He never dreamed anything he was saying was wrong, let alone criminal.

This wasn't a Michael Milken who premeditated a scheme to sell $400 million in bogus junk bonds to unsuspecting investors.[2] Nor was this an Ivan Boesky who was one of Wall Street's most brilliant and successful megaminds. Boesky became one of the richest men in the world with his stock market acuity, but lost everything and had to pay $100 million in fines when he pleaded guilty to insider trading in 1986.[3] Those men were frauds.

There is a difference, of course, between misspending a small fraction of the money raised from others, which Bakker did, and hatching a plot to trick people into giving him money, of which Bakker was convicted.

Jim Bakker did not sit down one day, lean over to Richard Dortch, and say, "How can I defraud these poor suckers out of $158 million?"

He did not fleece anyone of $158 million. He ended up with income of $3.7 million for three years and the rest of it was spent on Heritage and PTL. If accepting that salary and bonuses was the fraud here, it was only 2.4 percent of a fraud—the rest of the money was spent lawfully.

It is ludicrous to argue that Bakker's motive in soliciting $158 million from his followers was to pocket 2.4 percent of it for himself. That makes no sense and the jury should not have been allowed to buy into it. His motive, without any doubt, was to sustain the building frenzy at Heritage and keep pumping money into air time for *The PTL Club.*

It should have been argued to the jury that spending lifetime partnership money for those purposes may well have been wrong in some peoples' eyes, but it sure as the world wasn't fraud.

And the jury should have been told to answer one question in their own minds about whether Bakker's intent in all of this was to defraud people of their money: If that is true, why did he refund every dime to any lifetime partner who asked for their money back, for any reason, including their inability to make a room reservation exactly when they wanted it?

At the very end of his trial, under relentless cross-examination, an exhausted Bakker somehow found the words to capture his own confusion. What he simply did not understand was how he could be charged with intending to cheat anyone out of their hard-earned money if he was always willing to give them their money back.

He was asked about the emotional testimony of Lila Angel, the ninety-year-old partner on Social Security who bought Grand and Towers partnerships with her daughter. The Angels had testified against Bakker, complaining that they tried to stay at the Grand before it was completed but were turned away. Bakker had an answer.

Jim Bakker on the witness stand: [I]f she had been unhappy for any reason with her lifetime membership, I would have given her a refund. If . . . she didn't like that the trees had turned too soon in the year . . . my policy was . . . to return anyone's gift who wanted it returned. *** [Even] . . . if somebody had given 15 years before, I've returned people's contributions if their grandchildren would come and say, our grandmother gave to you and we want our money back, we would refund that.[4]

This is what a con man does to defraud unsuspecting people of their money?

Put the Fraud Allegation in the
Context of Religious Fund-Raising

The jurors should have been told that the reason the government had spent much of its time during the trial emphasizing Jim's homes, his dogs' homes, Tammy's clothes, and their vacations was because the proof of fraudulent intent was so thin.

One could direct the jury's attention to the elements of fraud on that easel, too, and walk them through a few analogies to be sure they get the point.

For instance, explain that it was not a violation of that statute for Oral Roberts to tell TV viewers in 1983 that a miracle cure for cancer would be found if his followers each contributed $240 for medical research and the construction of a sixty-story hospital. Even when no cancer progress was made and the hospital ended up with 600 less beds than was first represented.[5] It was not fraud because he didn't intend to defraud anyone. He honestly believed they could find the cure for cancer and operate that medical center.

Nor was it a violation of the fraud statute when Roberts warned viewers in 1987 that if he didn't receive $8 million within a month he was going to die. He honestly believed that God was going to "call him home" if he couldn't raise the money.[6] He wasn't trying to deceive anyone.

Pat Robertson doesn't violate that statute when he pleads for donations so that he can continue healing the sick over television, and performing other miracles.[7] There is no intent to defraud anybody of anything—he honestly believes he has that supernatural power.

Reverend Jesse Jackson's written promise to contributors to his Rainbow Coalition that "we will form a new majority"[8] through their political efforts does not violate the fraud statute, either. Although his donors were never taken to that plane and his majority never materialized, his intent was not to defraud them. He honestly believed their contributions would permit the realization of that goal.

Nor was it fraud for Bakker to raise $158 million by promising lodging for life. He sincerely believed there would be sufficient accommodations by the time they were needed, and that his construction of the Towers and other facilities would more than meet demand.

Tackle the Money Issue Head-On

Overlooked during Bakker's own two days on the witness stand was an off-hand comment he made in exasperation when trying to field a question from Deborah Smith about the deficit financing that PTL had used for years in building Heritage. "I did not understand finances,"[9] Bakker muttered. Nobody particularly noticed it, but that was one of the most intriguing quotes of the trial and within it lies a strong defense. Everything fits to support it, including the government's own evidence.

I firmly believe that the stratosphere to which Heritage USA had risen in terms of financial complexity, long-term debt, short-term debt, interest on the debt, and all of those other details of high finance that the Donald Trumps of the business world have perfected were largely foreign to Bakker. He was living in a world of faith and miracles, and never worried about the things that keep accountants and financiers awake at night.

Bakker was an evangelical exuberant who really didn't have a hard-nosed sense for business. He was a visionary and a dreamer. He could raise money by the millions of dollars, but he didn't have a businessperson's conservatism when it came to carefully spending it and shepherding assets. He didn't sit down each day with staffers from accounting to steer the finances of his $160 million a year business. He got together every day with hundreds of worshippers and prayed for the Lord to show them the way and provide tomorrow's donations.

He was the farthest thing you could get from a Wall Street financier or a conservative small town Main Street banker, but that doesn't necessarily prove that he intended to defraud his followers of their money. It might prove that he was careless in trying to construct so many buildings at Heritage at breakneck speed, but that's not a federal crime.

Even Dortch has frequently described Bakker as more of the idea man at PTL than the type of CEO who would take care of the financial side of the business. And Assistant U.S. Attorney David Brown, who successfully prosecuted James and David Taggart for tax fraud and embezzling PTL money, spoke directly to the point at the conclusion of the Taggarts' 1989 trial. Brown said that the evidence showed that David Taggart—not Jim Bakker—ran the ministry's executive offices and helped himself to PTL contributions. Brown told UPI reporters, "I think the testimony in this trial [Taggarts' trial] showed Jim Bakker was somewhat removed from the day-to-day operations of PTL. I think he was the idea man and often with idea people, they aren't concerned with the details."[10] Bingo, from a federal prosecutor who knew how PTL was run.

The fact was that Bakker spent his time each day after his television program roaming the grounds of Heritage making sure everything was immaculate and solving problems for visitors. He was preoccupied with the physical aspects of the place and spent much of his time out on the grounds. He saw that as his God-given responsibility. He wasn't back in the office scouring over profit and loss statements to try to figure out how he could steal or misuse contributions that were being received each day.

Educate the Jury and Enlarge Their Perspective on Televangelists

Undeniably, the subtext of a part of the government's case against Jim Bakker was that it was wrong for a minister to be paid millions and live like a king. Before Bakker's defense even got off the ground, prosecutors were hitting the evangelist's first witnesses with shots that would be fired time and again

before the trial was over. They reiterated the same theme—
what do you think the pastor of a church should make a year? A
million dollars? How many homes should a minister have?
Don't you think Jim Bakker could have done a lot more to help
needy people if he had not accepted $4 million in salary and
bonuses over the years?

That strategy may well have invited jurors to compare
Bakker's compensation and lifestyle to that of their own
hometown ministers. It was an unfair comparison because it is
not a crime for a minister to make that kind of money. But it
looks bad. When we asked jurors about it later, one admitted to
us flat out that ministers just don't live like that.[11]

To blunt that, the jury should have been told about the
compensation other national television ministers actually receive. By comparison, Bakker would not have appeared so
selfish and grasping. *Observer* reporter Shepard calculated, for
instance, that Jerry Falwell's 1986 income was $435,000,
which included a $100,000 base salary plus royalties on his
books and fees for speaking.[12] That is the same self-righteous,
humble man of the cloth who accused Bakker of immoral greed
on national television for the salaries Jim and Tammy were
pulling down at PTL.

Pat Robertson, who wrote a letter berating Bakker for
spinning out of control, was reported by *Newsweek* magazine
to have received with his son, Tim, $1.1 million in salaries
and bonuses in 1993 from the Family Channel's holding
company.[13]

Jim and Tammy's own tax returns, introduced into evidence
by the prosecutors, showed that their combined income from
all sources, including bonuses and salaries, averaged
$1,080,374 each year from 1984 until 1987.[14] The Bakkers'
own records also confirm that approximately 60 percent of
Jim's taxable income was paid back to the government in
income tax.[15] The closer you look at it, the less Bakker's income
seems out of line.

Bakker and Falwell had national ministries. They traveled in
jets and rode in luxury automobiles.

And the same with Jimmy Swaggart, Oral Roberts, and the rest. They live in mansions, earn staggering incomes, and vacation in luxury. They are, after all, television stars and nationally famous figures. They do well. Had the jury been permitted to compare Bakker's income and lifestyle to those of his peers, they may well have been more sympathetic toward him.

The Whole Case against Bakker Was Pure Speculation

One overarching fact should have been emphasized to the jury until every one of them understood it like their own middle name—there was not one shred of evidence during the whole trial that you couldn't get a room at the Heritage Grand Hotel. To the contrary, the evidence from the impartial Brock Company manager of the hotel was that there were rooms available during several months of the year right up to the end.[16] Undeniably, it was filled to capacity during peak vacation months, but written lifetime partner membership materials specifically alerted donors that rooms were subject to availability.

And there were *always* rooms available during nonpeak months. Even one of the government's key witnesses, former PTL finance chief Peter Bailey, told the jury that Bakker gave away 6,000 free hotel rooms in the Grand during one year alone as part of PTL's outreach ministry to people who wouldn't otherwise be able to stay on the grounds.[17]

Despite the sale of 66,000 lifetime partnerships in the Grand, all of those people never attempted to stay there during a year's time. That is evidence that the government's case was based on the speculation that at some time in the future every one of those people would try to make reservations during the same year and there wouldn't be enough room. The defense argument should have been that if the government had a case at all it would be then, not now. It should have been drilled into the jurors' heads that if, as the government contended all along, this was nothing but a real estate scam, that the government's entire real estate case was wholly theoretical.

More Than Another Fish Story

The problem is that Bakker's trial lies like a trout on the shore, both stinking and shining in the moonlight. The more one learns about the case, the more unsettling the verdict becomes. Gnawing doubts persist about the rightness of the result.

Different strategies for defending Jim Bakker did exist and may have coalesced to get him acquitted. But that is not to say that George Davis and Harold Bender didn't represent him well. They worked their hearts out and scored points for Bakker during the trial. In fact, their defense of him was determined and proficient even in the face of the most adverse of circumstances with a difficult judge and harmful facts. Many of their cross-examinations were superlative. Davis's direct examination of Bakker was one of the highlights of the trial for the defense and the only time Jim Bakker looked good to the jury in five weeks. Bender's closing argument was excellent. They made some of the points in this chapter. But the jury wasn't buying much the defense had to offer.

What remains is the question whether any of the defense strategies suggested in this chapter or used by Bakker's attorneys would have worked anywhere—with any jury and in any courtroom in the land. It may well not have been salvable. Maybe Bakker's only chance would have been to move the whole trial to Australia. Judge Potter, after all, is known there.

NOTES

1. Title 18, United States Code, Section 1343.
2. "Milkin's Plea Bargain," *Christian Science Monitor,* April 30, 1990 at 20 (Westlaw printout).
3. "Battlin' Boeskys," *People,* May 31, 1993 at 79–80.
4. Trial transcript, *United States of America v. James O. Bakker,* Docket No. C-CR-88-205-1, U.S.D.C. (W.D., N.C.), vol. 10, October 2–5, 1989 at 1908.
5. Maraniss, "Reaping Faith's Rewards?; For Roberts, Wealth Is a Spiritual Measure," *Washington Post,* February 15, 1987 at 1-A (Nexis printout).
6. *Id.*
7. *Id.*

8. Rev. Jesse L. Jackson, letter to the author [membership solicitation form letter], June 30, 1995.

9. Trial transcript, *supra,* n. 4, vol. 9, September 28–29, 1989 at 1801.

10. Preston, "PTL," UPI [wire story], July 26, 1989, BC Cycle.

11. Suzan Brooks's telephone interviews with jurors. See chapter 30, *supra.*

12. Shepard, *Forgiven* (Atlantic Monthly Press, New York, 1989) at 533.

13. Isikoff and Hosenball, "With God There's No Cap," *Newsweek,* October 3, 1994, at 43.

14. Trial transcript, *supra,* n. 4, vol. 6, September 14–18, 1989 at 428–29.

15. Benjamin J. Malcolm, Parole Services of America letter to Hon. Carol Pavilack Getty, U.S. Parole Commission, March 29, 1993 at 5.

16. Trial transcript, *supra,* n. 4, vol. 3, August 28, 1989 at 840.

17. *Id.,* vol. 5, September 13–14, 1989 at 1780.

Chapter 35

Where Are They Now?

Tammy Faye Bakker Messner

While her thick makeup, spidery eyelashes, and born-to-shop persona made her the butt of many jokes, Tammy Faye showed the strength of steel when the floor fell out from under her at PTL. Throughout all the humiliating disclosures in the national press which kept driving the sex and money scandals that toppled them, throughout her husband's tumultuous trial, and for two and a half years after Jim was sentenced to prison, Tammy stood by her man.

When Jim was taken away to prison, Tammy stayed in Florida and tried to keep the ministry going. She set up the folding chairs in the Tupperware warehouse and she delivered the sermons. She not only wrote Jim every day, she would hand-write up to fifty letters a day to PTL stalwarts across the country urging them to keep the faith and stand behind Jim during his darkest hour. "I write sometimes until my fake fingernail hurts,"[1] she once told reporters in Orlando. She was Jim's biggest cheerleader, fanning the faint embers of what had once been the world's largest television ministry.

That is not to say she didn't sound like a ditz from time to time. One of her sermons was about the poor. "Love has no nose," preached Tammy Faye, explaining that street people and poor people "sometimes don't smell too good, so love can have no nose."[2]

When Jim asked best friend Roe Messner to help Tammy

cope while he was in prison, he was turning to a true confidant. Messner believed in Jim, in PTL, and was the obvious choice when Jim faced the gravest personal tragedy of his life—being separated from his family by 12-foot prison walls. So, the fox began guarding the chicken yard and things rolled along.

In time, as the days turned into weeks and the weeks into months, the weight of Jim's absence was too much for Tammy. For the first two years of Jim's incarceration, she had faith that Alan Dershowitz would work a miracle and earn Jim's freedom. But when Judge Mullen, at Bakker's resentencing in 1991, ordered that the evangelist remain in prison for eighteen years or until paroled, Tammy couldn't hold on any longer. She filed for divorce.

Jim was devastated, but he didn't contest it. A Tallahassee, Florida judge needed only a few minutes to sign the order dissolving the union of the most famous televangelists in the country. Circuit Court Judge Hal S. McClamma did what even years of nonpayment for television time had never been able to do—he cancelled the Jim and Tammy show.

The Bakkers' followers, who for so many years had been captivated by the chemistry of the two and who really were their extended family, expressed sadness and shock. Few could forget Tammy's childlike penchant for surprises, like the time she brought two giraffes on the PTL set for Jim's birthday. (The giraffe was Jim's favorite animal.)

But this time, two years after divorcing Jim, Tammy brought Roe Messner on the set of the *Sally Jessie Raphael Show* as her new husband. Sure enough, the two were married in the fall of 1993 at a country club in Palm Springs. She was 51, he was 58, and the two were having a blast as they launched their second childhoods together. It wasn't exactly low-key, the couple having sold the television rights to their wedding to *A Current Affair* for a reported $100,000. They also charged the tabloid, *Globe*, $75,000 for the privilege of taking still photographs of the nuptials.[3] Jim, sitting in prison, was fit to be tied.

Reveling in her new life in California, Tammy soon struck a deal with the Fox Television Network for a new TV show. Billed as an alternative to all the sleazy daytime talk shows, the new *Jim J. and Tammy Faye Show* debuted at Christmas in 1995 and featured an openly gay co-host, Jim J. Bullock, formerly a star of *Too Close For Comfort*. Tammy was back, for an hour a day of interviews and bantering in her high-pitched little girl voice. Foxlab, which produced the show, advertised it to local affiliates around the country with this description: "Ever notice how some ideas are so crazy they work?"[4] With that, Tammy's positive alternative talk show was on the air.

Two months later, Tammy abruptly quit the show, complaining that the workload was too great. "The rigorous tape schedule [three shows a day, three days a week] and stress . . . is more than I can handle at this personally difficult time in my life,"[5] Tammy said in a statement. Ann Abernethy immediately replaced her. But job stress alone was not behind Tammy's departure. It was much more dire.

Trouble with the law again rocked her life. Roe was indicted and convicted of bankruptcy fraud, after federal prosecutors insisted that "[T]he penalty for hiding assets [during a bankruptcy] and lying [about it] is jail."[6] Roe vehemently maintained his innocence, but a jury in Wichita saw it differently.

On March 20, 1996, three weeks after Tammy quit her TV show, Judge Wesley Brown sentenced Messner to twenty-seven months in prison. The judge did allow Messner to remain free at his Rancho Mirage home on $25,000 bond while the case was appealed.[7] His appeal was unsuccessful and he is in prison now.

There was even worse news for the Messners. Tammy Faye was suddenly diagnosed with colon cancer in early 1996 and had surgery. Roe's doctors found he had developed cancer, also, of the prostate.[8] Few in the country were laughing any more.

Appearing on *Larry King Live* in June 1996, Tammy spoke openly of her cancer and her continuing religious faith. She also stood up for Jim, disputing the government's claim that PTL was a fraud for their personal gain. She said Jim was always devoutly Christian—every hour, every day he was trying to do God's work. None of PTL or Jim's TV shows were an act—he was not a phony or a fake. "Jim was probably one of the most honest men I've ever known,"[9] she told Larry.

Heritage USA

Shuttered during bankruptcy, Heritage USA was a virtual ghost town for three years. The Grand was closed, the shopping mall stores went out of business. The only signs of life came from the few hundred families who continued to live on the grounds in homes that they themselves owned. Jim Bakker's elderly parents and uncle Henry Harrison were among those souls left isolated on the expansive grounds. Henry kept the Christmas tree up year-around in his living room while Jim was in prison, his way of keeping the fires of Heritage burning for its founder. One resident, Jean Lyons, explained that "God told us to come. He hasn't told us to leave."[10] Many outsiders shared her enthusiasm for Heritage and the place claimed powerful suitors during the post-Bakker years.

All 2,200 acres and nearly everything on it were on the auction block during PTL's lengthy and tumultuous bankruptcy proceedings. Oral Roberts offered $6 million for the defunct PTL satellite network.[11] Pat Robertson was interested in not only the network but also the whole theme park and he made two separate bids to the court.[12] In the end, though, San Diego–based Charismatic faith healer Morris Cerullo and his business partners from Malaysia made an offer the bankruptcy court could not refuse—$52 million for all of Bakker's empire.[13]

Cerullo is an electric, stadium-packing evangelist best known in Africa and Latin America for his hugely successful crusades. His daily television program, *Victory with Morris Cerullo,* is seen by millions throughout the world and features heavy doses of fundamentalist theology, faith healing, and fund-raising.[14]

Cerullo was ebullient when his bid was accepted by the judge, reportedly telling friends that the real value of Heritage was closer to $250 million. He promised to spend $15 million sprucing up the grounds, then named William Lund of Disney World fame to manage the place, and conducted a full month-long telethon which raised $11 million from his own viewers to be applied toward the purchase.[15]

The California evangelist even extended the olive branch to Jim and Tammy, telling reporters that "I want them [Jim and Tammy] to know we love them and we forgive them and we want the world to forgive them. When you sin, God is in the business of forgiveness."[16]

Cerullo could have used a little of that himself because within a few months his Malaysian partners, Malayan United Industries, which owned fifty-one percent of everything, filed a lawsuit against him for fraud claiming that he had sold $300 and $1,000 Heritage passes without sharing the proceeds. Miffed and unable to patch up their differences with their junior partner, the Malaysians quickly bought Cerullo out and he was history.[17] They run the place now, promising in their brochures that they "will never, ever solicit nor accept contributions, donations, offerings or tithes."[18]

They bill the "New Heritage USA" as "America's premier Christian resort" and are beginning to attract conventions and conferences of fundamentalist and Evangelical Christians as well as individual families to the refurbished resort. They do a big business in the booking of church retreats and other events which the owners describe as a "mix of fun and faith." Travel brochures beckon, "[c]ome invigorate and revitalize your soul. Recharge physical and spiritual batteries with wholesome, good clean fun."[19]

The grand reopening of New Heritage USA in 1992 featured a rip-roaring speech by Pat Robertson and gospel music performed by the former *PTL Club* singers. The mission of the new place is noticeably narrower—there is no more Fort Hope, home for unwed mothers, or People That Love Centers. It's not a ministry today, it's a Christian theme park and resort community. Millions of dollars are being spent to revive it. A new golf course has been added, and there are a few signs of life again throughout the village. Even the Heritage Grand is now attempting to regain strength as a Radisson Hotel franchise.[20]

But while there have been many changes, some things have stayed the same. Melanie Anne Fornum from Memphis told reporters that she was looking forward to returning to Heritage after it had been hobbled for so many years. "It is a much more spiritual environment than Disney World. God is what is important, even on vacation. But I hope they keep the old jewelry store and dress shops. Tammy Faye did see to it that you could have a shopping adventure, and that's important, too, when you are on vacation,"[21] she said.

And that was really a point that was lost on many of Bakker's detractors over the years. Jim Bakker struck a responsive chord in millions of Evangelicals by inviting them to love the Lord, and, at the same time, have a good time. Millions flocked to Bakker's Heritage to connect with fellow Christians and exercise their gold cards. And who is to say that's wrong?

So, New Heritage USA goes forward today, downscaled but not down. The old PTL cable network is now The Inspirational Network. And while all symbols of Jim and Tammy Bakker have been removed, no one walking through the lobby of the Radisson Grand or careening down the water slide can forget them. For good and for bad, they and their dream are inseparable. Heritage USA was everything to Jim Bakker. He was driven by it and he was destroyed by it. It stands today as a 2,200 acre monument to both.

Jerry Falwell

In the years since Falwell railed against Bakker on national television, he has found other objects to deride.

Falwell's broadcasting venue is his weekly *Old Time Gospel Hour* which appears on about 150 television stations around the country. Lately, his targets have been gays, lesbians, public school curricula, abortion clinics, video stores, topless bars, and President Clinton. It seems as if an issue has anything to do with sex, Falwell is all over it.

On his program, he sells an attack video on homosexuals and Bill Clinton which contains footage from the 1993 Gay Inaugural Ball. "There is no such thing as a good fairy,"[22] Falwell has said and his video denigrates the gay political agenda. Falwell explains that this particular video can be purchased for what he calls a $35 love offering.[23]

Another *Old Time Gospel Hour* video features Paula Jones describing in lurid, uncensored detail Bill Clinton's alleged sexual advances in a Little Rock hotel room in 1991.[24] Falwell offers the tape for $43.[25] But somehow, the story of a president dropping his pants seems particularly out of place in a religious video sold by the same people who complain there is too much sex and violence on TV.

Falwell takes his television seriously, too. He went ballistic when Ellen DeGeneres came out on her TV show in April 1997. Protesting loudly the glorification of gays in the media, Falwell pressured several major national advertisers, including General Motors and Chrysler, to withdraw their sponsorship from the show. "It's important for us to do our part during the upcoming 'Ellen' broadcast,"[26] he warned.

But Falwell has lost much of his political clout. He disbanded the Moral Majority in 1989. He was blamed by many Republicans for George Bush's defeat in 1992. He's been frozen out of the White House and is not as welcome on Capitol Hill. He was stung by an embarrassing tiff with the IRS in 1993 which ordered his ministry to pay $50,000 in back taxes for wrongly engaging, as a tax-exempt organization, in political campaigns in 1986 and 1987. The charge was that his *Old Time Gospel Hour* ministry helped raise money for a political action committee that had ties to his Moral Majority. The *Old Time Gospel Hour* agreed to pay the back taxes and accept the punishment.[27]

He has been beset by other money woes as well, including a marked downturn in contributions from his television flock after the Bakker scandal. "He is tired,"[28] said spokesman Mark DeMoss of Falwell, describing in 1992 how the big man was surviving his recent battles. The evangelist is now sixty-three years old and as large as a lanai. Falwell says confidently, "I plan to live to 115 and give hernias to the ACLU, Planned Parenthood and all the liberals."[29]

Falwell has been concentrating recently on Liberty University, the Baptist college he founded several years ago in Lynchburg. Twelve thousand students attend Liberty. Falwell is the chancellor. His closest friends say that the college will be his legacy, and he has taken a very active and hands-on approach in enlarging the campus, adding buildings and facilities, and shaping the school. It is a very strict environment which Falwell has described as a "spiritual boot camp."[30] There is a dress code which requires men to wear ties to class and women to wear dresses. Students are permitted to wear jeans only during the evenings and on weekends. A curfew is imposed six nights a week and students aren't allowed outside their dorms after midnight. No drinking or swearing is allowed on the campus, and students are forced to submit to random drug testing. Kissing is not allowed on college property and there are no coed dorms.[31]

In describing his vision for the school, Falwell has repeatedly compared Liberty to Notre Dame and insisted his goal is to develop some athletic prowess on his campus and through it begin to achieve national recognition. "Football is the quickest ticket to the top,"[32] he reminds his students and coaches, but it was the Liberty Flame's basketball team that in 1994 stunned everyone by taking an early lead over the nationally ranked North Carolina Tarheels in the NCAA East Regional Championship Finals. The Flames were eventually extinguished in that game, but Falwell was encouraged. "We should go into the turn of the century competitive with anybody in any sport,"[33] he boasted. The Liberty Flames?

Not everybody cheers for Falwell today. Former Presidents Jimmy Carter and Gerald Ford both accused Falwell of lying about them.[34] Conservative icon Barry Goldwater suggested that "Falwell and the Moral Majority should both be kicked square in the ass."[35] And, in one of the biggest jolts of all, Mel White of Dallas, the person who ghost-wrote Falwell's autobiography, *Strength for the Journey,* announced in 1993 that he was gay but had concealed it from Falwell.[36]

Falwell does have his admirers, however, including Senator Jesse Helms who literally dotes on him as a symbol of morality in this country. Falwell returns the compliment, calling Helms "a national treasure."[37]

In one of the most unbelievable ironies of the entire PTL

saga, Jim Bakker today is speaking rather charitably about Falwell. After their reconciliation in prison in 1993, Bakker wrote: "Forgiveness is so key to our salvation and victory on life's road to our eternal reward. [Quoting Scripture] 'Let us love one another.'"[38]

Jimmy Swaggart

Irony chased Swaggart, and caught him in all the wrong places. His hell-fire and damnation oratory against Jim Bakker and Marvin Gormann for sexual misconduct collapsed both their ministries. Swaggart, of course, had been the driving force behind Bakker's resignation from PTL as Jim feared Swaggart would blow the lid off the Jessica Hahn story. A short time before, Swaggart's accusations of adultery against New Orleans televangelist Gormann persuaded the Assemblies of God to defrock Gormann, too.[39]

But Swaggart wasn't spending all of his time as the Chief Detective and Enforcer for Religious Virtue. It seems he was making inexplicable nocturnal pastoral visits to the seediest part of New Orleans. His Lincoln Towncar would roll along Airline Highway, a haven for prostitutes and by-the-hour motels, and park behind the Texas Motel. One night in October 1987, gumshoes reportedly photographed Swaggart meeting with a prostitute in that steamy precinct.[40] The news rocked Evangelicals and gave David Letterman and Jay Leno some of their best material in years.

With Bakker bounced from PTL, Swaggart was the nation's number one Assemblies of God preacher and the most watched televangelist in the country. His fall from grace would be loud. Hobbled, Swaggart spent more than eight hours before a church tribunal in February 1988, and apparently admitted to them that he had a lifetime obsession with pornography and had paid the prostitute in New Orleans to perform pornographic acts while he watched.[41] The elders were satisfied that his confession to "moral failure"[42] showed "humility and repentance"[43] on his part, a prerequisite to remaining in the faith. They wouldn't pull his ordination, but ordered him to undergo two years of rehabilitation and to stop preaching for up to one year. "We'll be merciful, and he'll be restored,"[44] said the Reverend Robert King of the church's front office. "Something got hold of him and he just couldn't shake it,"[45] added Reverend Glen Cole of the Assemblies national board.

At Sunday worship services later in February 1988, the then fifty-two-year-old Swaggart, his voice breaking, begged for forgiveness from his wife Frances, his congregation, and from God.[46] Three months later, he returned to his television pulpit explaining that God had forgiven him for his sins.[47] Marvin Gormann was not so charitable. He sued Swaggart for defamation in Louisiana state court over Swaggart's allegations that Gormann had committed adultery. In 1991, a jury heard the case and awarded Gormann $10 million in damages.[48] It soon got worse.

On October 11, 1991, three years after the New Orleans motel shocker, Swaggart was pulled over for a traffic violation in the red light district of Indio, California. With him inside his flashy Jaguar was another known prostitute.[49] Reeling, the evangelist returned to Baton Rouge amid a national drumfire of ridicule. He went before his congregation once again, but this time only 1,000 of the 7,000 seats were filled. It would be a tough sell. For more than half an hour, he sat in a leather wing chair on stage and spilled his guts.[50] With tears streaming down, he riveted parishioners by telling them that he had considered committing suicide over the latest scandal but that God had wanted him to go on. From now on, he vowed, he would consort only with "Godly men"[51] and would "fight Satan"[52] wherever he could be found. When asked for more specifics by reporters, Swaggart replied tartly, "The Lord told me it's flat none of your business."[53]

Although Swaggart dropped a million and a half viewers short term from his two million TV congregation, he showed surprising resilience. Today, he can be seen on numerous television stations and cable systems in the United States.[54] He conducts television crusades all over the world and still packs hundreds into his family worship center outside Baton Rouge.

Outwardly, nothing has changed. He's the same fire-breathing, Bible-banging tiger he was before. But there are indications he has at least moderated his feelings toward Jim Bakker. In response to a plea by Bakker's son, Jamie, Swaggart made a personal appeal during his July 4, 1993 television program urging his viewers to write letters to the U.S. Parole Commission on Jim Bakker's behalf.

> Request that . . . Jim be allowed to get out of prison. I'm doing that and I think the Lord would bless you for doing that as well. I believe that the touch of God is still in Jim's life. Would you write that letter? Thank you.[55]

But no matter how you cut it, Swaggart is the hands-down winner of the "What goes around, comes around" award among all the players in the Bakker drama.

Richard Dortch

After Dortch testified against Bakker, Judge Potter reduced the former Number Two man's sentence from eight years down to thirty months. Bakker's sister, Donna Puckett, was flabbergasted: "They reduced his sentence? Why is that? Was he a good boy? He still has to answer to God for what he has done and he may not be able to plea bargain that."[56]

Dortch was confined for sixteen months in the federal prison camp at Elgin Air Force Base in Pensacola, Florida.[57] One of the original "Club Feds," Elgin is a minimum security detention center located on twenty-eight acres in the middle of an Air Force base. No prison walls surround it. No barbed wire fences. The guards don't carry guns. The inmates are virtually all nonviolent, white collar criminals. But while they are allowed to bring their tennis rackets to prison with them, they are definitely denied their freedom while they are there.

After release from Elgin in June 1991, Dortch spent five months in a halfway house in Tampa before returning home to his wife and children in Clearwater.[58] He continues to reside there today, where he is the president of Life Challenge, Inc., a ministry he founded to provide help to professionals facing major crises in their lives. Now sixty-five years old, he has survived several health problems in the last few years, including being diagnosed with cancer, having a cancerous kidney removed, and battling Crohn's Disease.

In November 1991, the Assemblies of God was satisfied that Dortch had demonstrated sufficient remorse and rehabilitation after his misdeeds at PTL to warrant reinstating him as a minister of the church. He earned that vindication, in large part, by speaking out publicly and confessing his sins since being released from prison. He authored a book in 1991 entitled *Integrity* in which he wrote candidly about the PTL odyssey. He explained that he had lost his integrity "by not speaking up when I knew things were going wrong at PTL. I compromised and reaped the painful results."[59] He confessed to being ashamed, embarrassed, and guilty for all that happened there.[60]

To this day, he gives Jim Bakker balanced and somewhat mixed reviews. He has said that he realizes that Bakker is without question, "a genius."[61] Dortch confirms the accuracy of Bakker's version of the Falwell takeover of PTL and faults Falwell.[62] Attorney Norman Grutman has come in for strong censure from Dortch for representing both the Bakker/Dortch administration at PTL and Jerry Falwell.[63] Dortch has also placed in some perspective all the good that Jim Bakker did at PTL during the fourteen years of that ministry. As he saw it, PTL had been phenomenally successful and touched the lives of millions of people for the better.[64]

At the same time, Dortch has acknowledged that he should have protested the Bakkers' spending hurricane. "I should have screamed and confronted Jim Bakker more than I did," Dortch has told reporters, "but at the heart, I wanted to be a good guy, so I did nothing."[65] As for his role in responding to Jessica Hahn's threat to go public with her allegations against Bakker unless she received an out of court payment, Dortch admitted that "we should have gone to the FBI, but we didn't because we were trying to protect Jim."[66]

Dortch and Bakker have spoken and begun a reconciliation, with Dortch traveling from Florida to the Rochester prison to spend the day with his former confidant and blood brother. He came down strongly on Jim's side later when it was announced that Roe Messner and Tammy Faye were going to be married. "He should hide his face in shame and put on a sackcloth and ashes,"[67] Dortch bristled. "Roe told us he would take care of Jim's family while he was in prison. But he didn't confide he intended to steal them,"[68] he told *People* magazine.

Pat Robertson

Marion G. "Pat" Robertson, at sixty-seven, devotes his energies today to a successful broadcasting empire. He has transformed his brainchild Christian Broadcasting Network into the country's tenth largest cable channel, and renamed it. It's now the "Family Channel" and Robertson uses it to offer alternative programming around the clock on cable.[69]

During the day, the Family Channel airs harmless comedies and game shows, including *Shop 'til You Drop* and *TV's Bloopers & Practical Jokes,* for hours opposite the steamy soaps served up by the three major broadcast networks. In the after-school hours, the nonviolent *Carson's Comedy Classics* and *Carol Burnett and Friends* are offered for children. At night, Robertson slates *Highway to Heaven* and *The Waltons* reruns to air opposite the network liberal issue-laced programs like *Murphy Brown* and the *Baywatch* genre of suggestive programming.

The Family Channel's mainstay, however, remains *The 700 Club,* hosted by Robertson, which is broadcast three times a day. The show leads with a half-hour of news, reported by little-known correspondents and Pat himself in the studio in Virginia Beach. There is a very obvious conservative slant to Robertson's news stories. Frequent in-depth reports present the conservative, pro-life, antigovernment take on many breaking stories that the mainstream press, in Robertson's view, too often taints with liberal spin.

The remainder of *The 700 Club* is devoted to interviewing Christian authors, introducing gospel singers, discussing the

Bible, and praying on the air. Robertson, every inch still a Pentecostal, is a firm believer in faith healing and miracles, and he often heals viewers and congregants with serious illnesses. In one 1981 Philadelphia meeting, he shouted to those in the hall: "God is healing people all over this place. An inguinal hernia has been healed. You—you wearing a truss, you can take it off—it's gone!"[70]

Robertson can raise money with the best of them, and on regular *700 Club* telethons, he aggressively solicits donations to keep his broadcasts on the air. Many of his telethons are actually frantic with a big clock ticking away the seconds before the latest challenge pledge lapses. In fact, watching Robertson plead for donations today on TV would remind anyone of Jim Bakker in his heyday.

Oral Roberts

Oral Roberts, now seventy-nine, is still a commanding force in religion and the second most famous evangelist in the country. Only Billy Graham is better known. Roberts, the barnstorming tent revivalist and emotional faith healer who presaged modern televangelism when he first rolled a TV camera into one of his noisy tent services in Oklahoma in the 1950s, continues to preach on television. His new show, *Miracles Now,* is co-hosted by his son and heir apparent, Richard, and is carried on more than forty stations in the U.S. and Canada.

Robert "Maximum Bob" Potter

Potter's stiff sentences and reputation for toughness proved to be a delightful recipe for fiction in 1991. Author Elmore Leonard's twenty-ninth novel, entitled *Maximum Bob,* featured as its main character a trial judge reportedly named after the real and original Maximum Bob Potter of Charlotte.[71] In Leonard's novel, it's Maximum Bob Gibbs, a judge in Palm Beach County, Florida, whom the author describes as an established redneck who sentences everybody he can to heavy prison terms because he believes that "hard time in prison makes the boy a man."[72]

Since being pulled off the Bakker case in 1990 by the Circuit Court of Appeals, Judge Potter has not had any further opportunity to lay a hand, or a handcuff, on Jim Bakker.

Deborah Smith

Smith has remained as a respected trial attorney with the U.S. Department of Justice. After she concluded her work on the Bakker case, she was named head of a federal task force to investigate and prosecute bank fraud in Boston. She has continued to confine her comments on Jim Bakker to the courtroom and her written pleadings.

Jerry Miller

Miller remains with the U.S. Attorney's Office in North Carolina and continues to ably prosecute federal criminal defendants in the same Charlotte courtroom that was the scene of the Bakker shootout.

Miller did offer some interesting opinions on the Bakker trial to reporters for the *Business Journal* in Charlotte:

> How [Harold Bender] maintained his composure with the theatrics of his co-counsel [George Davis] is a real tribute to his abilities.
>
> He [Bender] was doing a very effective job of building the theory that Bakker was surrounded by people who were in it for themselves, that these people were perpetrating fraud without his knowledge. [But all that work came undone when Bakker said on the witness stand that there had not been any wrongdoing at all at PTL.] I suspect it wasn't Harold's idea to let Bakker testify.[73]

Harold Bender

Bender, who is still one of Charlotte's top trial attorneys, has his own take on Bakker's trial. He told the *Charlotte Business Journal* that if he had been lead counsel rather than George Davis he would have done things differently:

> The first thing I would have done is I would have associated a young, bright lawyer to assist. I would have insisted that the client become more involved in the investigative stage. [Jim Bakker] was,

during that period of time, trying to reestablish his television ministry.[74]

Bender himself doesn't have much time for watching TV. He spends most weekends during the fall refereeing college football games all over the South, duties which took him to Lynchburg, Virginia, one Saturday to officiate a game played by Jerry Falwell's Liberty University Flames. They won, and nobody knew the man under the white hat was Jim Bakker's attorney.[75]

Alan Dershowitz

After getting Bakker's sentence reduced from forty-five to eighteen years, Dershowitz's role in Jim's case ended. Bakker is very grateful for what Dershowitz was able to accomplish because the wheels were put in motion which eventually led to Bakker's release in 1994. And, of course, if Potter's original sentence had not been struck down, Bakker would probably not have lived long enough to ever see freedom again.

Dershowitz, as the country knows, went on to other high profile cases, including attempting to overturn Mike Tyson's 1992 Indiana rape conviction and serving on O.J. Simpson's 1995 criminal defense dream team.

George Davis

Davis, now eighty-nine years old, is in vigorous health and living on his cattle ranch in Waimea, Hawaii. He still maintains an office and he looks and sounds twenty or thirty years younger than his age. He rides his horse often and he swims in the ocean. His mind is razor-sharp and he is articulate and extremely well-spoken.

Not surprisingly, he is a celebrity on the islands and accepts speaking engagements routinely. During the O.J. Simpson trial, for instance, civic groups asked him to speak about its contrasts to the Bakker trial. He remains as well known for his hundreds of other major cases litigated throughout his career.

Davis speaks very warmly of Bakker: "I don't think he's a

criminal. I think he was overwhelmed by the immensity of the work that he was doing."[76] But Davis didn't mince words when asked by a local paper, *West Hawaii Today,* for his evaluation of Judge Potter:

> After all, any person who is charged with a crime is presumed to be innocent . . . and is entitled to a fair trial. Bakker did not get that kind of a trial. [When you look at the Court of Appeals' reversal of Potter's forty-five-year sentence because of his comments to Bakker at the sentencing] . . . if the trial judge were so biased and prejudiced that he couldn't even render a legal sentence, how would he have been able to handle and conduct that trial without the same bias and prejudice?[77]

Jessica Hahn

Hahn, now thirty-seven, definitely is not the shy church secretary she claims she was in 1980 when she and Jim Bakker met at the Sheraton Sand Key in Clearwater. She's shown a lot of skin since Bakker's trial. Posing semi-nude for *Playboy* in 1987 for nearly a million dollars "brought me closer to God,"[78] she explains. And since those saucy shots, she has had her breasts enlarged, teeth straightened, and nose coifed.[79] In 1990, she launched a 900 number where people from around the country could call in and hear a recording of her reminiscences of the tryst with Bakker. Among other insights, she tells callers, "I did not seduce Jim Bakker; I was seduced."[80]

Shock jock Howard Stern, an admirer, encouraged her to take a job as the host of a Phoenix radio talk show, and she has also acted in her own "love phone" infomercial. Her most notable achievement recently, however, has been her one-hour strip video for *Playboy, Jessica Hahn Bares It All,* which in 1993 sold more copies than any video except *Beauty and the Beast.*[81]

She has dabbled in television, to mixed reviews. In a 1992 guest appearance on *Married with Children,* she was a customer in Al's shoe store who was sexually attracted to him. Trying on a pair of high heels with four-inch stilettos, she told the panting Bundy that she "loved to see a man on all fours."[82]

Jessica remains a controversial figure in many quarters today.

Some view her sympathetically; others do not. Appearing on a November 1992 *Joan Rivers* program, Hahn shocked the audience by demanding an apology from Rivers at the top of the show for jokes that the comedienne had done at Hahn's expense. Sparks flew.

Hahn: My little brother heard it [Rivers' jokes].
Rivers: Your brother should worry about who you slept your way to the middle with.
Hahn: You are a dried-up old prune.
Rivers: I may be old but I'm not a tramp.[83]

Jim Bakker

Jim Bakker's every move from 1989 until the summer of 1994 was under the watchful eyes of federal marshals and prison guards. But until recently, he has been the least visible of all the major figures in his case. Living alone in a mountaintop farmhouse, Bakker's new life has been relatively quiet.

What Jim has been doing is cutting a path out of the briars—in his own way.

On July 2, 1994, he was finally released from prison in Jesup, Georgia. He was immediately driven six hours to Asheville, North Carolina, where he reported to a halfway house operated by the Salvation Army. He lived at the halfway house and worked there as part of the typical spending down of the last few months of most convicts' sentences. Rather than release someone right into the street after several years of incarceration, the way it's done is to have them serve the last four or five months of their time in transition at a halfway house.

After two months of exemplary work and adjustment at the halfway house, the U.S. Bureau of Prisons reduced its grip on Bakker one more notch. He was placed under house arrest and allowed to move to a small acreage twenty miles away with his nineteen-year-old son. He wore an electromagnetic ankle bracelet at all times so the authorities could trace his movements, and he had to report in at least once a night.[84]

Finally, on December 1, 1994, after having served exactly five years for his crimes, Bakker, at fifty-four years old, was officially released from custody and became a free man for the first time since Judge Potter had him taken away in leg irons in 1989.

Reporters and photographers gathered outside Bakker's home expecting him to make an announcement and talk to the media on his first day of freedom, but Jim surprised all of them by not even opening his door. Demanding an explanation for the unexpected snub, reporters were told by Chris Nichols, a local Bakker attorney, that "[h]e's been sitting in jail for five years, so a few more days by himself doesn't matter."[85] Nichols raised some eyebrows with the comment that Bakker was "adamant" about protecting his privacy.[86] "To him, things are much different today,"[87] explained Bakker's attorney.

Bakker's freedom, however, was somewhat limited. He remained on probation and was supervised by a local probation officer until April 18, 1997.

He lives in a rented farmhouse near Hendersonville, North Carolina, a quaint small town nestled in the Blue Ridge Mountains. Jim and Tammy used to travel directly through Hendersonville when driving from Heritage USA to their get-away chalet in Tennessee during better times.

While Bakker does venture out almost daily to shop for groceries, run errands, and keep his house and farm maintained, mostly he stays at home working. He is somewhat reclusive, certainly compared to his glory days. Generally, he is using his time in the mountains to think, to heal, and to plan for the future.

Harold Bender offered the view that, after being demeaned by prison, "you've got to rebuild, and probably have to rebuld from the inside out."[88] After that, Bender predicted, his former client would become a roving preacher for a church denomination and "share a message of hope and redemption."[89] Bakker's attorney in Hendersonville, Jim Toms, said, "Jim looks forward to rebuilding his life, and being of useful service to others."[90] Daughter Tammy Sue wrote to New Covenant Ministry supporters, "I just can't wait to minister alongside my Dad in some of our future crusades."[91] Reporter Charles Shepard, who won the Pulitzer Prize for breaking the PTL scandal, admitted "[t]he man has extraordinary talent in front of the television camera."[92] Jim's former PTL sidekick, Uncle Henry Harrison, also saw television in Bakker's future. After speaking with Jim, Uncle Henry told reporters that Bakker had joked with him, "I have crammed so much of the Word in the last five years that I feel I will explode if I don't have the opportunity to share some of it."[93] A few weeks later, another twist of fate in Bakker's life gave him just that chance—at Uncle Henry's funeral.

Harrison, who had left the Christmas tree up in his living room all the years his friend Bakker was in prison, died unexpectedly at Heritage USA on February 5, 1995, at age sixty-seven. Henry had told his wife Susan, when once discussing their own funerals, that he wanted Jim Bakker giving the eulogy when he passed away. Bakker, Henry's closest friend, had been the best man at Henry's wedding twenty-four years before (Pat Robertson officiated), so Susan made an emotional phone call to Jim for comfort in her darkest hour.[94]

Quickly agreeing to her request to eulogize his old friend, the irony could not have been more startling. The memorial service for Henry was scheduled to be held in Jim's former broadcast center—the Grand Assembly Hall once known as the Barn Auditorium right in the heart of New Heritage USA. A week later, 2,000 friends of Henry Harrison and of Jim Bakker and the old *PTL Club* TV show gathered in that studio theater to hear Bakker speak for the first time in more than five years.

Tammy Sue joined the singers and musicians from the *PTL Club* broadcast, opening the service with several of Harrison's favorite gospel songs. Then, shyly, Bakker stood up and walked toward the microphone. He was wearing a navy blue double-breasted suit and carrying a black Bible. The audience erupted and gave him an enthusiastic standing ovation. "I'm scared to death," he began. "It's the first time I've been back . . . [and] only Uncle Henry could've gotten me off the farm."[95] During his eighty-minute speech, he talked both about Henry and his own spiritual rebirth in prison. He said that Henry was a true Christian and had shown it by standing with Bakker and helping him walk "through the valley of the shadow of death [the years of his downfall and those spent in prison]."[96]

"True Christians are valley-walkers," Bakker said, "a lot of people want to be mountaintop Christians . . . but I'll take a valley-walker."[97] In describing his triumph over imprisonment, Bakker commented, "I almost wore my prison khakis here because I'm much more comfortable in them. My best friends are felons—criminals you would call them—but Jesus sat with the criminals, with the sinners."[98]

The response was overwhelming. "We love you, Jim!" were shouts heard from several in the audience. "Welcome back!" and "Welcome home!" yelled others from the huge auditorium.[99] A second standing ovation followed. "Don't ever feel sorry for me,"[100] he warned. "Prison was God's best for me. Nobody put me in prison—God did."[101] At one point he exclaimed, "Oh God! I'm not worthy to stand behind this sacred desk."[102]

Even area reporters, long suspicious and skeptical, thought Bakker sounded like a changed man. But a few couldn't resist having more fun at his expense with lines in their stories like, "[i]t's not often that an ex-convict can return to the scene of his crime and receive a standing ovation from his victims."[103] But the 2,000 PTL stalwarts who filed out of the auditorium left singing Bakker's praises anew.

In fact, many then and there started talking about Jim returning to Heritage on a permanent basis, convinced that only he could attract the hundreds of thousands of visitors the park needed to snap out of its Malaysian malaise. Languishing in anemic visitor numbers, the park today is a shell of its former self. Some nights, only a dozen visitors can be counted walking by the stores in the enclosed Main Street shopping mall adjacent to the Grand Hotel. Bobbie Woodle, who runs two of those stores, summarized the feelings of many: "[y]ou've got to hand it to Jim and Tammy. They drew millions, because people loved them, and they still do."[104] Former PTL partner Paul Parsons, a salesman from Johnson City, Tennessee, surveying the ghost town that was once the nation's third most popular destination park, seconded the motion: "Yes, Jim done wrong . . . [but he paid the penalty]. [H]is charisma [today] would be a gift."[105]

Is it really possible that Bakker would return to Heritage? Many people believe so, positive that its Malaysian owners can't keep the place afloat without the draw Bakker alone could provide. Another scenario, advanced by the tabloids in 1996, is that two of Bakker's multimillionaire supporters, still convinced he was framed, are going to buy back Heritage outright from the Malaysians and return Bakker to where he was eight years ago.[106]

The speculation is rampant, but the only point on which there is agreement is that one way or another Jim Bakker will stage a comeback. Attorney Toms admitted as much: Jim's "considering opportunities . . . offers concerning the ministry . . . appearances on TV shows."[107] Returning to televangelism has not been ruled out.[108]

Some are predicting that Jim will eschew the limelight and move to Africa and run an orphanage for Billy Graham's son, Franklin.[109]

Others think he'll continue where he left off at Uncle Henry's funeral by giving similar speeches to church meetings across the country. And, Jim has shown a willingness to move in this direction already, making a handful of appearances in 1995 and 1996 in different places, such as one sermon to 8,000 at Oral Roberts University and another one before 14,000 pastors and church members in Phoenix.[110] Whenever he speaks, he receives extremely supportive, emotional receptions and loud standing ovations.

But most of the time, Bakker is back on the farm and appears content to be there away from the fishbowl that public figures must bathe in. He has written a book on the evolution of his religious beliefs while he was in prison, entitled *I Was Wrong*. Jamie has moved to Atlanta to co-pastor a youth church. Jim is alone in the house, living only with his fluffy cat and a large white sheepdog. Tammy Sue visits on the weekends and brings her two young sons to play with their grandpa in the elaborate tree house Jim built for them in a huge, old tree overhanging the yard.

Major figures in Bakker's downfall have their own opinions about his future. "My opinion is he's a sincere and earnest man [who] . . . has learned from his mistakes,"[111] says Jerry Falwell. Jessica Hahn isn't as charitable: "He'll be passing those collection plates real soon, believe me. [He's a] master manipulator who's far from done."[112] On his *Late Show,* David Letterman joked, "[S]houldn't this guy have some kind of lifetime suspension from God?"[113]

As much as the future seems to be tugging at Jim Bakker, shades of his past trouble with the law and with lawyers cast a shadow over his life. In September 1995, Bakker attorney Jim Toms surrendered his license to practice law, admitting to the North Carolina Supreme Court that he had "misappropriated" $150,000 from a client trust account he managed and that he also "misappropriated" nearly $1.4 million from estate funds he controlled.[114] It was Toms who had been advising Bakker so extensively the last few years. One reason Bakker moved to Hendersonville after being released from prison was to live in the same town as Toms and have easy access to him.

And there remained the threat that Bakker himself would be back in a North Carolina courtroom, sitting as the defendant in a pending class action lawsuit brought by several former PTL Grand and Towers lifetime partners who claim he owes them millions for securities fraud in selling the partnerships.[115]

Little wonder that Jim's parents, both still active at ninety years old and adamant that their son was innocent in 1989, worry about their son. But his mother, Furnia, looks on the bright side. "He has not lost his smile through all of this,"[116] she says. "That is a miracle."[117]

Bakker's Tega Cay Parsonage

Jerry Falwell auctioned off Jim and Tammy's cherished home on Tega Cay for $675,000 to Robert Rubino, the owner of a chain of North Carolina pizza restaurants.[118] It was a stunning five-story showplace, complete with a fish-shaped swimming pool, two dozen closets, and three kitchens. The Bakkers spent their rarified PTL years there and raised their children in that place. They loved it. It symbolized all that they had fought for in their lives from the earliest days in dusty campgrounds and downscale trailers.

In March 1990 the home burned to the ground. Fire investigators poking through the charred ruins said that arson could not be ruled out. An official with the South Carolina arson unit told reporters at the scene that "we're looking at all possibilities and talking with everyone who knows anything, but one thing's for sure—[Jim] Bakker's alibi is solid."[119]

From his prison cell in Rochester, Bakker wrote out a statement: "I am very sad that a house that was such a good friend to our family and children is now gone, but our hope is in God and his wonderful, eternal, heavenly home."[120]

The next day, a single red rose was laid in the doorway of the home that still smoldered. The small card attached to it read simply, "Jim Bakker."[121]

NOTES

1. Banks, "Orlando Is the Place for Me, Says Bakker After Year's Stay," *Orlando Sentinel Tribune,* May 10, 1990 at 1-B (Nexis printout).

2. *Id.*

3. "For Richer," *People,* October 18, 1993 at 64.

4. *Broadcasting & Cable,* December 11, 1995 at 60–61.

5. "She's Still Afloat," *People,* March 11, 1996 at 61.

6. Dauner, "Bakker Builder Indicted," *Kansas City Star,* February 10, 1995 at 1-C, col. 6.

7. Laviana, "Messner Gets Jail Term for Hiding Assets," *Wichita Eagle,* March 21, 1996 at 1-A (Westlaw printout).

8. *Id.*

9. Cable News Network, *Larry King Live* [transcript of television broadcast #1768], June 7, 1996.

10. Garfield, "Isolation Settles in at Heritage USA," *Charlotte Observer,* October 29, 1989 at 1-A (Westlaw printout).

11. "Trustee Accepts Oral Roberts University's Bid to Buy PTL," *St. Petersburg Times,* May 19, 1990, at 6-E (Nexis printout).

12. Franklin, "Robertson Bids for PTL network," *Boston Globe,* October 28, 1989 at 40-P (Nexis printout).

13. Preston, "PTL Sold to California Evangelist," UPI [wire story], July 26, 1990, BC Cycle.

14. Forest, "You Can't Say Morris Cerullo Has No Faith," *Business Week*, December 31, 1990 at 59.

15. *Id.*; "Dr. Morris Cerullo Reveals Plans for the 'New Heritage USA' Family-Oriented Christian Destination to Reopen Summer of 1991," *Business Wire* [wire story], August 6, 1990.

16. Preston, "New PTL Chief Urges World to Forgive Jim Bakker," UPI [wire story], August 7, 1990, BC Cycle.

17. "The South in Brief," *Atlanta Journal and Constitution*, April 17, 1991 at 3-D (Nexis printout).

18. "New Heritage USA—America's Premier Christian Resort" [brochure], published by New Heritage USA, Fort Mill, S.C., 1993.

19. *Id.*

20. Shepard, "Jim Bakker's Out, but He's Not Back," *Washington Post National Weekly Edition*, December 19, 1994 at 29.

21. Schwartz, "The New, Improved Heritage USA," *Dallas Morning News*, May 31, 1992, at 1-F (Westlaw printout).

22. Bouchier, "No More Mr. Good Guy," *Humanist*, July/August, 1990 at 22.

23. Raasch, "Religious Right Feels Snubbed by Clinton," Gannett News Service [wire story], April 25, 1993.

24. Van Deerlin, "Religious Right Gloms onto the Perils of Paula," *San Diego Union-Tribune*, May 20, 1994 at 5-B (Nexis printout).

25. Reuters, "Falwell's Clinton Tape Criticized," *Chicago Tribune*, May 20, 1994 at 9-CH (Nexis printout).

26. Pitts, "Ellen only TV; Gays Fuss Will Fade," *Des Moines Register*, April 10, 1997 at 17-A, col. 1.

27. "Falwell Fined," *National Journal*, April 10, 1993 at 883.

28. Sylvester, "Rev. Falwell Criticizes Clinton's Plans," *San Francisco Chronicle*, November 14, 1992 at 19-A (Westlaw printout).

29. Lambert, "NRB '91: Preparing for New World," *Broadcasting & Cable*, February 4, 1991 at 44.

30. Scarton (Scripps Howard News Service), "Falwell Fans Flames with 'Champions for Christ,'" *St. Louis Post-Dispatch*, September 29, 1991 at 12-E (Nexis printout).

31. *Id.*

32. *Id.*

33. *Id.*

34. Van Deerlin, *supra*, n. 24.

35. *Id.*

36. Colker (*Los Angeles Times*), "In the Fold, Out of the Closet: Gay Minister Finds Peace," *Tulsa World*, December 12, 1993 at 10-L (Westlaw printout).

37. "Senate's One-Man Juggernaut," *U.S. News & World Report*, November 19, 1984 at 17.

38. Jim Bakker, letter to New Covenant Partners, December, 1993.

39. Hutcheson, "Swaggart Admits Sinning Just Like Others He Attacked," Reuter Library Report [wire story], February 22, 1988, PM Cycle.

40. *Id.;* Brightbill, "Swaggart Punished for 'Moral Failure,'" UPI [wire story], February 23, 1988, PM Cycle.

41. Brightbill, *id.*

42. *Id.*

43. *Id.*

44. *Id.*

45. *Id.*

46. *Id.*

47. "Repent, Ye Sinners—and I'll Be Right Back!" *TV Guide,* January 7, 1989, at 8.

48. "Free Falling," *People,* November 4, 1991, at 58.

49. *Id.*

50. *Id.*

51. *Id.*

52. *Id.*

53. "Rate-A-Wreck Index," *People,* December 30, 1991 at 100.

54. "Free Falling," *supra,* n. 48.

55. Videotape of *Jimmy Swaggart Ministries* broadcast (July 4 and 11, 1993).

56. Preston, "Bakker Supporters Urge His Sentence Also Be Cut," UPI [wire story], April 26, 1990, BC Cycle.

57. *Id.*

58. "PTL Official Refuses Parole," *St. Petersburg Times,* July 10, 1991 at 3-B (Nexis printout).

59. Dortch, *Integrity* (New Leaf Press, Green Forest, Ark., 1991) at 9–10.

60. *Id.* at 10.

61. Bosworth, "Divorce: Tammy Bakker Plans to Remarry, Associate Says," *St Louis Post-Dispatch,* March 23, 1992 at 1-Ill. (Nexis printout).

62. Dortch, *supra,* n. 58 at 212–18.

63. *Id.* at 151–55, 188.

64. *Id.* at 55–56, 65–68.

65. Bosworth, *supra,* n. 61.

66. *Id.*

67. "Tammy's Troubled Waters," *People,* April 6, 1992, at 78.

68. *Id.*

69. Isikoff and Hosenball, "With God There's No Cap," *Newsweek,* October 3, 1994, at 42.

70. Weisman, "The Ex-TV Preacher Aims to Convert Voters to His Cause," *TV Guide,* January 30, 1988 at 27, 29.

71. Holt, "Justice for a Redneck Judge" [book review], *San Francisco Chronicle,* July 28, 1991 at 1-SR (Nexis printout).

72. *Id.*

73. Boudrow, "Bender for the Defense," *[Charlotte] Business Journal,* November 11, 1991 at 12-A (Nexis printout).

74. *Id.*

75. *Id.*

76. Weigard, "Bakker's Flock Fleecing Trial Starts Today," *Sacramento Bee,* August 28, 1989 (Westlaw printout).

77. Stephl, "Man Who Defended Bakker Is Delighted with Decision," *West Hawaii Today,* February 15, 1991 at 4-A, col. 1.

78. "The Jessica Hahn Story," *Playboy,* December, 1987 at 122.

79. "Jessica Hahn: 'Someday I'll Learn to Act,'" *People,* March 7, 1994, at 273.

80. "The Dial M for Monotony Medal," *Time,* July 23, 1990 at 21.

81. Nohlgren, "The Story, in a Word, is Buttafuoco," *St. Petersburg Times,* March 24, 1994 at 1-A (Nexis printout).

82. Rosenthal, "The Nutley Viewer; More of What You Could Be Missing," *Mediaweek,* February 10, 1992 at 32.

83. Talbot, "The Joan Rivers Showdown," *Newsweek,* November 30, 1992, at 87.

84. "Former Televangelist Bakker to Be Released," Reuters [wire story], November 28, 1994, BC Cycle; Jim Bakker, telephone interview by author, October 15, 1994.

85. "Jim Bakker Freed after Almost Five Years in Jail," AP, *[Memphis] Commercial Appeal,* December 2, 1994 at 4-A (Nexis printout).

86. Nowell, "Bakker Is Free Man, in Seclusion for Now," AP, *[Durham, N.C.] Herald-Sun,* December 2, 1994 at 1-A (Nexis printout).

87. *Id.*

88. Shepard, *supra,* n. 20.

89. Garfield (*Charlotte Observer*), "Bakker's Revival; Curiosity Stalks Release of Fallen Evangelist," *The Phoenix Gazette,* November 30, 1994 at 1-A (Nexis printout).

90. Wrenn, "No More Public Appearances from Jim Bakker? Praise the Lord!" *Chapel Hill [N.C.] Herald,* December 11, 1994 at 5-ED (Nexis printout).

91. Tammy Sue Chapman, letter to New Covenant Partners, November 9, 1994.

92. Garfield, *supra,* n. 89.

93. Shepard, *supra,* n. 20.

94. Religion News Service, "Bakker to Be in Pulpit to Eulogize Old Friend," *Orlando Sentinel,* February 11, 1995, at 5-D (Nexis printout).

95. "Field Says She's a Shy One," *Palm Beach Post,* February 13, 1995 at 2-A (Nexis printout); Frazier, "Bakker Back in PTL Pulpit to Give Eulogy," *[Charleston, S.C.] Post and Courier,* February 13, 1995 at 1-A (Nexis printout).

96. Frazier, *id.*

97. *Id.*

98. *Id.*

99. *Id.*

100. *Id.*

101. *Id.*

102. Frazier, "Will Jim Bakker's Words Match His Actions?" *[Charleston, S.C.] Post and Courier,* February 19, 1995 at 7-B (Nexis printout).

103. *Id.*

104. Shepard, "A Testament to Unfinished Business: As New Owners Attempt to Resurrect Heritage USA, Jim Bakker Begins Life after Prison," *Washington Post,* December 11, 1994, at 3-A (Nexis printout).

105. *Id.*

106. "The Secret Plan to Bring Jim Bakker Back as TV Preacher," *National Enquirer,* December 20, 1994, at 29.

107. Smith, "Jim Bakker—What's a Convict to Do after a Prison Term?" *San Francisco Chronicle,* November 30, 1994 at 3-E (Nexis printout).

108. *Id.*

109. *Id.*

110. Tammy Sue Chapman, letters to New Covenant Partners, May 10 and July 25, 1995; Garfield, "Religious Leaders Speak Out," *Charlotte Observer,* June 10, 1995 at 6-C, col. 2.

111. Ritter, "Jim Bakker a Free Man Today/Ex-PTL Head May Return to the Pulpit," *USA Today,* December 1, 1994 at 3-A (Nexis printout).

112. *Id.*

113. Kelleher, "Punchlines," *Newsday,* December 9, 1994 at 54-A (Nexis printout).

114. "Bakker Lawyer Admits Misappropriating Funds; Attorney Says He Will Surrender License," AP, *Charlotte Observer,* September 9, 1995 at 1-C (Westlaw printout).

115. "Securities Fraud Claims against Bakker Triable," *National Law Journal,* October 10, 1994 at 2-B.

116. Burritt, "Around the South, Jim Bakker Truest Believers; Parents Hope He'll Pastor Large Church after Release Today," *Atlanta Journal and Constitution,* December 1, 1994 at 3-A (Nexis printout).

117. *Id.*

118. Preston, "Investigator: 'One Thing's for Sure—Bakker's Alibi Is Solid,'" UPI [wire story], March 10, 1990, BC Cycle.

119. *Id.*

120. *Id.*

121. *Id.*

Afterword

Striking Oil

Like the earth suddenly erupting an 80-foot geyser after crude oil broods beneath it for centuries, Heritage USA, from deep within locked vaults in 1996, disgorged the hard evidence that could actually have cleared Jim Bakker of the fraud of diverting partnership proceeds.

Diverting much of the $158 million raised through the lifetime partnerships to pay for other PTL expenses and a few luxuries for the Bakkers was at the heart of the government's case against the evangelist. He was convicted, in large part, for not using enough of the partnership funds on the Towers hotel and remaining bunkhouses.

But what happened at Heritage USA in 1996 was that the rest of the *PTL Club* video tapes were found and transcribed verbatim by a former Miami police detective. These were the 200 hours of tapes that Bakker insisted in my prison interviews with him existed, which would prove he never diverted lifetime partnership funds. The tapes he protested no one looked for before his criminal trial, but which he said established his innocence. The tapes which so frustrated him on the witness stand when he kept begging the jury to believe that the prosecutors' edited *PTL Club* tapes painted an incomplete and untrue picture of his fund-raising. The tapes that emphatically punctuate the overarching question this book asks.

Ronald Heacock is the one who struck oil in 1996. After 14 years on the Metro Dade Police Department where his detective work ranged from investigating narcotics to homicides, Heacock retired in 1984 and moved to North Carolina. In 1992, he opened a private investigative service in Asheville, N.C., a few miles from Bakker's Hendersonville farmhouse. Since going into business, Heacock has offered his investigative expertise to area attorneys. He can still solve the toughest mystery, and even Melvin Belli called for Heacock to come from Asheville to California to investigate one of Belli's cases in Los Angeles.

It was Asheville attorney Lamar Gudger, a highly respected former U.S. Congressman and retired state superior court judge, who in 1996 asked Heacock to help in the latest Bakker litigation. By 1996, Bakker's legal troubles had not yet run their course even though he had served five years in prison and had finally been released from custody.

What remained for Bakker to face was one last civil trial.

The Civil Trial

It began in 1987, even before Bakker's criminal trial convened in Charlotte. A handful of purchasers of PTL lifetime partnerships from around the country filed a civil suit against him demanding money damages for themselves and nearly 160,000 other PTL lifetime partners. They claimed to have been damaged because they were unable to stay in the hotels that Bakker promised they would be able to enjoy for the rest of their lives. They argued that Bakker had defrauded them, essentially in the same way that the criminal jury was convinced he had committed criminal fraud by overselling partnerships in the Grand and Towers hotels.

The remedy available to plaintiffs who are injured in civil actions is money damages. The punishment if someone is found guilty of a crime, of course, is typically imprisonment or a fine. In this case, it was money that the plaintiffs sought and in order to improve their chances of recovering some money they added Deloitte, Haskins and Sells, the national CPA firm that prepared PTL's annual audits, as a defendant along with Bakker. With Bakker sitting in prison and facing a forty-five-year sentence, the prospects of recovering money from him personally must have appeared bleak to the plaintiffs, which in all likelihood explains their efforts in 1990 and the years that followed to find a responsible party, to find another defendant who would have the money to compensate them.

To bolster their case, the plaintiffs also included allegations of common law fraud, federal and state securities fraud, state time share fraud, federal and state racketerring violations and negligence. Their contention was that Bakker committed all of those wrongs in his oversale of the lifetime partnerships.

But the road on the civil side quickly turned rocky. It was not at all the near slam dunk of Bakker that had been the criminal trial. And in the final analysis, after more than five years of litigation and two jury trials, one in 1990 and the second in 1996, the plaintiffs ended up with nothing.

In the 1990 civil trial, the jury found Jim Bakker guilty of only common law fraud. It assessed damages against him of $129 million in compensatory damages and another $129 million in punitive damages. The CPA firm was absolved of all liability. But even though the plaintiffs had been successful in obtaining common law fraud damages against Bakker, they appealed the decision of the trial court judge which did not allow them to argue securities fraud to the jury. While the plaintiffs' precise strategy is a secret known only to them, a good assumption is that the $260 million in damages against Bakker on paper seemed worthless to the plaintiffs. What they no doubt wanted was a liable party who could cover damages of that kind, and their principal target quickly became PTL's old insurance carrier.

Sure enough, PTL during Bakker's heyday had a sizable errors and omissions insurance policy. Coverage like that protects officers and directors of corporations, and if an officer acts negligently in the conduct of the corporation's business, damages caused by that negligence can be recovered from the corporation's insurance carrier. But since the 1990 verdict against Jim Bakker was based on the jury's finding of common law fraud, that particular category of wrongdoing was apparently not covered by PTL's insurance.

The plaintiffs wanted one more trial and one more bite at the apple to somehow tap the reserves of PTL's insurance company. And they were successful in persuading the Fourth Circuit Court of Appeals that the trial judge had been wrong in not allowing them to argue securities fraud and negligence to the jury. They got their chance for a second trial in July of 1996.

The narrow issues to be decided by the jury were whether the PTL lifetime partnerships were securities and whether Bakker violated federal and state securities fraud laws in his promotion and sale of those partnerships.

Just before trial in 1996, the plaintiffs suddenly stipulated that they were no longer seeking any money from Jim Bakker personally. In essence they were forfeiting the $260 million verdict they had won six years before. No one could doubt that it was PTL's insurance company that was the new target.

While there probably did exist a legal question whether that insurance company in fact was liable for anything that happened in connection with the lifetime partnership promotions, the company didn't take any chances and assembled the legal talent necessary to defend itself and to defend Jim Bakker. In addition to Lamar Gudger, Michael Quiat from Hackensack, New Jersey was brought in as lead counsel, and Nelson Casstevens, Jr., of Charlotte was added to the team. With paralegal John McKenna, private investigator Ron Heacock, and others, they were ready to fight. It was Gudger who urged the defense to commit the necessary resources to finding the *PTL Club* tapes. That, and their other strategies, worked. Their task was to persuade the jury that the PTL lifetime partnerships were not securities, and that Jim Bakker did not commit securities fraud or negligence. One of their strategies, once they had the old PTL videotapes, was to let the tapes speak for themselves and let the jury see what Bakker had to say on those tapes rather than having Bakker testify in person at the trial.

The trial really became a battle of tapes, with the plaintiffs using the prosecution's edited tapes from the 1989 criminal trial and Bakker's new lawyers using the PTL tapes that Ron Heacock had found and highlighted.

Jim Bakker personally assisted his attorneys throughout their preparation of the trial and was kept closely apprised of all the work in the case by Mr. Gudger, in whom he had great confidence.

The facts upon which the plaintiffs were relying in this new trial were the same facts that the 1989 criminal jury had convicted Bakker on, and for which he was sent to prison. They were the same facts upon which Bakker was found guilty of common law fraud in 1990 by the first civil trial jury. But there were also differences.

The Tapes Bakker Claimed Cleared Him

The most significant difference between the approaches taken by Bakker's civil attorneys in 1996 from those taken before the 1989 criminal trial was that Bakker's new team of lawyers listened to a client who was engaged. When Bakker told them that videotapes of the old TV shows would prove his innocence, they hired Ron Heacock to pursue it and bring back the evidence. He did.

The new Malaysian owners of Heritage USA were willing to cooperate. They showed Heacock the secured warehouse on the grounds where the old *PTL Club* tapes were stored. They allowed him to bring a video technician with him to dub as many of the tapes as were needed. And they let the two of them stay in the warehouse on and off for two solid months. For nine hours a day in two- and three-week marathon viewing sessions, Heacock and the technician spent the spring of 1996 holed up in that warehouse.

Under the watchful eyes of Heritage security guards who were assigned to the project, the two investigators watched 200 hours of *PTL Club* telecasts. They dubbed virtually all that they saw.

Confining their research to the 1984–1987 window during which Bakker promoted the lifetime partnership programs on his show, they were helped by Bakker himself who gave Heacock a list from memory of the approximate dates the programs had aired when he had announced and explained each new lifetime partnership package. Bakker also vividly remem-

bered the *PTL Club* telethons, those special fund-raising programs where he would spend the most time talking about the
partnerships. Bakker gave Heacock the telethon dates and told
him he was sure there would be helpful evidence on those
telethons because he remembered what he told viewers about
the partnership plans and how their money would be spent. He
even remembered the telethon sets and where he was standing
when he said it. It was that clear in his mind.

With a good idea of what to look for, Heacock dove in. The
tapes were actually in a huge vault inside the warehouse, on
shelves organized by date just as they had been left when Jim
Bakker was still in charge. Surprisingly, the tapes were in
pristine, mint condition, owing to Bakker's fastidiousness
about keeping a permanent record of every *PTL Club* broadcast, doing it on the highest quality videotape, and putting all
of the tapes in the best airtight containers he could buy. When
Heacock put the tapes in his VCR, the programs looked just as
if they were brand new and first run, even though some were
ten or twelve years old.

Some people might question whether a true con man would
go to such lengths to make sure that the evidence assembled
against him was in perfect condition for use by the federal
prosecutors committed to convicting him (these were the same
tapes they had had access to and which they had edited). Bakker
served prosecutors his every spoken word so politely on a silver
platter, with each tape labeled and boxed. But that's not the
point here. These videotapes had been hermetically sealed on
Funk and Wagnall's porch since 1987 and when Ron Heacock
lit them up, it was opening night—PTL was back on the air.

And what a different PTL it was from what the criminal jury
had seen.

Heacock told me that he looked for three things as he went
through those 200 hours of tapes: 1) What did Jim Bakker tell
his viewers about the lifetime partnerships? 2) What did he tell
them about where their lifetime partnership money was going?
3) What did the tapes show about how the money was actually
used at Heritage USA?

I asked Heacock for his conclusions after viewing all those

tapes. He said emphatically "I truly don't believe there was any fraudulent intent involved. Had the videotapes I found been presented as evidence in Bakker's criminal trial, they probably would have given the jury reasonable doubt about his guilt. Had the jury seen these tapes, I doubt they could ever have concluded that there was any type of racketeering or con here."

What makes Heacock's observations and analysis even more compelling is the fact that he approached his work as an independent investigator without any preconceived opinion about whether Bakker had perpetrated a fraud. In fact, Heacock told me that he questioned Bakker pointedly about the allegations of fraud. Heacock really did want to put the pieces together for himself and make an independent judgment about Bakker and the crime for which he was convicted. So, he asked Bakker tough questions just as he would have had he been investigating the case as the detective assigned to it at the time.

Heacock told me "So, he [Bakker] had to explain to me everything about the lifetime partnerships and all that was said and done." In the end, Heacock was satisfied that Bakker was no con man and that Bakker had not committed criminal fraud. "I know frauds, I know how a fraud thinks, and I know how a fraud works. I don't believe that Bakker ever had criminal intent in promoting those lifetime partnerships," Heacock concluded.

The most that could be said, in Heacock's view, was that some PTL funds may well have been improperly diverted to the Jessica Hahn payoff or Bakker vacation homes and luxuries to which Bakker had admitted. But, Heacock says today, "that is not the same as charging that Bakker committed a $160 million fraud selling those hotel partnerships and that he diverted that amount to his personal use."

The Civil Trial Jury Sees the Tapes

The amazing irony of all the evidence that Heacock uncovered was that it came too late to save Jim Bakker from doing five years in prison. What Heacock was able to accomplish, however, was to dispel the plaintiffs' contention in the 1996 civil trial that Bakker had committed securities fraud.

Heacock was the last Bakker witness to testify and he confined his testimony to the question of whether the PTL lifetime partnerships were securities. He played for the jury those excerpts from the *PTL Club* videotapes where Bakker had promoted the lifetime partnerships and explained them to his viewers. Repeatedly, on those television programs, Bakker told his audience that the partnerships in the hotels were not time shares and that people were not buying a specific room. He emphasized that they would not necessarily have the same room each year that they visited, and that they would have to come only when rooms were available during the year and only after they had made reservations. Obviously, Bakker wasn't selling securities or time shares.

After seeing some of Heacock's taped highlights of those 200 hours of *PTL Club* programs and hearing his testimony about what he found in that vault on the Heritage grounds, and as well after hearing all the other witnesses and evidence in the case, the civil trial jury after a one-week trial and just a few hours of deliberations, found that the PTL lifetime partnerships were not securities and that Bakker therefore had not committed securities fraud.

Predictably, the plaintiffs again appealed the latest verdict. That appeal is still pending before the Fourth Circuit Court of Appeals in Richmond.

It would be inaccurate to say that, after seeing Ron Heacock's *PTL Club* tapes, the civil trial jury found that Jim Bakker was innocent of fraud. It was much more complicated than that. They found him innocent of securities fraud, and there is a difference. One could be found guilty, for instance, of criminal television fraud and at the same time be found innocent of securities fraud if a jury found that the item that was promoted was not a security.

However, the 1996 civil trial verdict is staggering in every respect. For starters, it marks the first time any jurors have been shown the exculpatory statements that Bakker had made on the air. And when they saw them, this jury bought Bakker's position. They agreed with Bakker's attorneys. Based on that and what he saw in the PTL vault, Heacock is convinced that if a jury had ever seen all that he found, there would have been reasonable doubt about Bakker's criminal fraud guilt.

Most reporters who covered the 1989 criminal trial contend to this day that Bakker was done in by his own telecasts that the government used against him. Those tapes were regarded as the most powerful evidence of the entire trial against Bakker. So, what is jarring about the 1996 developments is that there in fact are videotapes and excerpts from Bakker's programs which portray him in a much more positive light than that which was portrayed to the jury by the government in the 1989 trial. In those 1989 excerpts the government used, Bakker was always hawking lifetime partnerships, raising money and never talking about the other projects at Heritage for which partnership money could be used. In the tapes that Heacock found, just the opposite can be seen right there on television.

And, of course, beyond the parts of those programs that involved Bakker disclaiming that the partnerships were time shares, there were numerous and repeated statements by him that the partnership money raised would be spent on many other PTL projects and needs, and not only on the hotels. How in the world could any impartial observer argue today that evidence of that kind could not have turned the entire trial around for Bakker in 1989? It is the hard, visual evidence which powerfully refutes the government's claim that the heart of Bakker's fraud was diverting partnership funds to other purposes.

Questions that Demand Answers Today

Many questions scream out.

Why wasn't Bakker's vindication by the civil trial jury well reported in the national press? Had the jury come back with a verdict against Bakker, wouldn't the press have reported it as prominently as it reported the last guilty verdict in Bakker's life a few years before? What was it about the verdict in the civil trial that failed to capture the media's interest? Was it that the verdict failed to support the media's long-held opinions of Bakker as a con man? Did the verdict cast doubt on the guilt of Bakker which the media for years, and particularly the *Charlotte*

Observer, has professed since the zenith of PTL? The civil trial jury came back more than a year ago, but it's as if they had announced their verdict in a courtroom on Venus and due to the two years that it takes for sound to travel from there to Earth, no one has heard about it yet.

Of course the verdict in the civil trial calls into question Bakker's guilt in the criminal trial. It is the perfect reversal of the O.J. Simpson saga where Simpson was found not guilty in his criminal trial, but was found liable in the subsequent civil trial. As every Simpson case watcher in the country knows by heart, the burden of proof in a criminal trial is much higher than that in a civil trial. One reason many explain Simpson's defeat in the civil trial is that the plaintiffs' burden of proof was less than "beyond a reasonable doubt." They only had to prove he caused the murders by a "preponderance of the evidence."

What a delicious irony, then, that the plaintiffs in Bakker's civil trial, those few disgruntled PTL partners who sought to hold Bakker civilly liable for money damages for promoting those lifetime partnerships and defrauding them in the process, were unable to meet that lower burden of proof in their case. With Bakker's new-found videotaped evidence and energized legal team, he was able to prevail even though the plaintiffs had less of a burden than the government had when he was convicted of criminal fraud a few years before. It is just all amazing.

The most searing question standing today is whether the criminal fraud jury, if it had seen the videotapes that Ron Heacock found, would have concluded that Bakker defrauded his followers. That is a question that can never be answered and will haunt Jim Bakker the rest of his life. It should concern everyone else, too. Did an innocent man spend five years in prison?

Seeing the New PTL Videotapes from a Juror's Eyes

What follows are the excerpts of 200 hours of PTL videotapes reviewed by Ron Heacock in 1996. This verbatim transcription was prepared by Theresa G. Sapp, a registered professional reporter in North Carolina.

Knowing what you do about the evidence in Jim Bakker's criminal case after reading this book, place yourself in the jury box in that Charlotte courthouse as the Bakker trial is unfolding before you. And change just one thing: take a look at these pro-Bakker PTL videotapes. If you were a juror, would this change your vote?

EXCERPTS FROM 200 HOURS OF PTL VIDEOTAPES REVIEWED BY RON HEACOCK, JUNE 20, 1996

Transcribed Verbatim by Theresa G. Sapp, Registered Professional Reporter (North Carolina)

Date of Broadcast	*Verbatim Transcript*
February 20, 1984	**Jim Bakker:** When you give your $1,000 gift, you'll receive a special membership card that will allow you to stay here in the Heritage Grand for four days and three nights every year for the rest of your life. We don't guarantee any one particular room—one—you might have a suite, or you may have this room we just showed you on camera.
February 22, 1984	**Jim Bakker:** You can come any time that you can get reservations.
February 24, 1984	**Jim Bakker:** You must make reservations each year. ***and these are just for those who give a special gift to PTL right now to help us in our world-wide ministry.
February 28, 1984	**Jim Bakker:** You can make your reservations for any time you want to come, and it's—it's not a certain time of the year.
September 20, 1984	[On this program with Jim Bakker is Walter Richardson, the head of the PTL affiliate division who was responsible for keeping PTL on the hundreds of television stations around the country.] **Jim Bakker:** We still owe about $5 million, but we're believing God in the next few days, Walter, that we are going to see every bill paid. **Walter Richardson:** When somebody gives to the Towers, they can complete three things at once. **Jim Bakker:** That's right.

Walter Richardson: And I am excited that, you know, we can complete the Grand, give them three days and—four days and three nights and then pay all the affiliates current.
Tammy Faye Bakker: Amen.

April 16, 1985

[Efrem Zimbalist, Jr. is a guest]
Jim Bakker: This is not time-share, so you can come anytime of the year you can get your reservations.

August 5, 1986

Jim Bakker: For a $500 gift to the ministry, to help us stay on the air and to help us build and do all the things we are doing, we want to let you stay in a family bunk house every year for three days and two nights the rest of your life.

February 22, 1984

Jim Bakker: So, when you give this $1,000 gift, you don't just get world missions. You don't just help in the prayer ministry. You are not just receiving a lifetime membership of four days and three nights at the Heritage Grand and helping us build a conference center and a preaching center and a school and all the things that are going on here, reaching out into prisons, reaching out with the People That Love Centers and the People That Love Home, and, with the state willing, we'll open our Tender Loving Care Village too—to help the people that need bed care.

February 22, 1984

Henry Harrison: And, if you want to stay at the Inn one time and the Hotel one time . . . and the camp another time, you can do that.
Jim Bakker: Every year you can stay in a different place . . . you know, and we may even—as we build other areas here, we may be able to expand it to those other areas in the future as—as like value, and that's what we are going to be doing.

February 25, 1984

Jim Bakker: When you pledge that $1,000 lifetime membership, you help us go around the world with PTL. You help the English speaking PTL. We are reaching out to several hundred million people with the Jim Bakker Program, and then of course, the Spanish PTL, the Italian PTL, the African PTL, the Thailand PTL, the Japanese language PTL, and the French language PTL. And the PTL records and tapes, the music, the printing of Bibles and literature and the great production center at Heritage Village where we produce the gospel, one of the largest producers of religious programming now in the world.

March 1, 1984

Announcer: PTL is building Heritage USA to help evangelize the world and to let the world know that Jesus is Lord.

July 25, 1984

Jim Bakker: We've got to pay the bills, and so we're just believing God that this week the last of the lifetime partnerships will come in at $1,000 . . .

September 17, 1984

Jim Bakker: When you give this $1,000, you are not just building a hotel, you're giving to a ministry that's helping to preach the gospel to the whole world. We're going to be in 42 nations before the year is out—with our giant Chinese PTL Club now.

September 21, 1984

Jim Bakker: Your funds are used to help PTL in all different ways, but, when you give to this lifetime membership, you not only help us to build the Grand. You help keep PTL on the air.

September 25, 1984

Jim Bakker: And remember, they gave $1,000 to pay TV air time and to build this center and to build the Towers. And then to think that you are helping to preach the gospel in 41 nations, in prisons with 7,000 prison workers, helping with the Girls' Home, helping with all the total ministry, helping to pay our TV stations now, it—it is so tremendous.

May 26, 1986

Jim Bakker: What you are giving to, you are giving to Heritage. You are giving to Fort Hope for street people. You are giving to the Girls' Home. You are giving to all this. When you give to PTL, you don't just give to one thing. You're supporting the whole ministry, the world-wide ministry, the television ministry, 24 hours a day. I think people take the satellite for granted.

June 14, 1986

Jim Bakker: For a gift of $1,000 to help us finish Kevin's House, to finish Fort Hope, to be on television around the world, to pay our bills everywhere, to—to minister to people, to build our church buildings, to build all of it, you're donating $1,000 to this ministry.

September 20, 1984   **Jim Bakker:** We owe our—we're behind, and we've got places where if we don't pay the bills, we're off the air. And, so, in this time of telethon, we're not just building, but we are paying the TV stations. We are paying the cost of television in foreign lands, 42 nations now with PTL around the world in their own languages with their own hosts.

September 21, 1984   **Jim Bakker:** But, when you give to this lifetime membership, you not only help us to build the Grand. You help keep PTL on the air.

Jim Bakker: The 30,000 people that it will take to build the Towers and to finish the Grand and to actually take care of all the TV stations, that's all we need is 30,000 people.

September 28, 1984   **Jim Bakker:** 5,000 of those memberships will take care of paying all of our TV stations.

Index

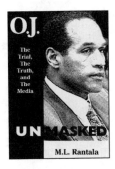